Praise for *Turncoats, Traitors and Heroes*

"An absorbing book, as fascinating as a whodunit."
—Christian Science Monitor

"Bakeless has made an engaging investigation of the spies and counterspies who infested both sides of the American Revolution. *Turncoats, Traitors and Heroes* is a spider's web of conspiracy, concealment, and confusion. Bakeless is to be commended for having brought these activities so adventurously into the clear."
—Atlantic Monthly

"[Told] with the narrative skill and occasional humor of an able biographer and thoroughly qualified historian . . . [this book] is recommended for all readers with a taste for history, true stories of detection, and realistic intrigue."
—Library Journal

"A vivid chronicle. . . . Based on previously unexplored manuscripts, these accounts . . . have appeal for both the general reader and the student of the American Revolution."
—Booklist

"This book on an unknown part of the Revolutionary War should appeal to addicts of spy stories and students of historical espionage."
—Kirkus

"Refreshing, rumbustious, and erudite. . . . [An] Aladdin's Cave of espionage. . . . As an exciting record of spying in wartime I warmly recommend Bakeless's book."
—Saturday Review

TURNCOATS, TRAITORS AND HEROES

★

John Bakeless

DA CAPO PRESS • NEW YORK

Library of Congress Cataloging-in-Publication Data

Bakeless, John Edwin, 1894–
   Turncoats, traitors, and heroes / John Bakeless.
     p.   cm.
   Originally published: New York: J. B. Lippincott, c1959.
   Includes index.
   ISBN 0-306-80843-9
   1. United States—History—Revolution, 1775–1783—Secret service. 2.
Spies—United States—History—18th century. 3. American loyalists. 4. Es-
pionage—United States—History—18th century. I. Title.
E279.B3   1998
973.3′85—dc21   97-31872
                                                 CIP

First Da Capo Press edition 1998

This Da Capo Press paperback edition of *Turncoats, Traitors and Heroes* is an
unabridged republication of the edition first published in New York in 1959.
It is reprinted by arrangement with the Estate of John Bakeless.

Published by Da Capo Press, Inc.
A Subsidiary of Plenum Publishing Corporation
233 Spring Street, New York, N.Y. 10013

★ ★ ★

★

Preface

After I had finished preliminary collection of material on the history of American military intelligence (in the Revolution and later) and just as I was about to begin the last four years of more intensive research, I was—somewhat to my surprise— warned by a solicitous friend that the attempt was bound to fail, since most documents relating to secret service in the Revolution must certainly have been destroyed. Having already collected materials for nearly two decades and having learned the voluminous abundance of the Clinton Papers, I knew this view was needlessly pessimistic. I had, indeed, even then, located enough manuscript material to make a fairly adequate study, without the additional four-year search that I actually undertook.

It was, nevertheless, a surprise to find, as the study progressed, how embarrassingly abundant the supposedly lost documents really were. Eventually, as new spies, new facts, and new manuscripts revealed themselves, it became necessary to reduce the scope of the work five times, eliminating first, the story of British and American espionage overseas; then, the story of frontier espionage; then, the plotting and intrigue in New Hampshire and Vermont; and also American espionage

3

in Canada—the last being no great loss, since the work of these secret agents, though skilled and daring, never led to important military results. As a fifth and final limitation, I have dealt as briefly as possible with such facts as are already known about the intelligence services of the Continental and the British armies. Thus, the Arnold-André affair, which could not possibly be omitted, has been briefly treated, with emphasis on its relation to other intelligence nets and the narrow margin by which American counter-intelligence failed to detect it.

The book as it now stands is a study—complete and thorough, I trust—of the espionage, counter-espionage, and other military intelligence services in the Continental and British armies in the main theatre of war, with only a few absolutely essential references to military intelligence elsewhere.

Though I have made an extensive search for new sources, with such good fortune that a large proportion of the material here discussed is wholly new, it is probable that further research will reveal many additional facts—a desirable result, to which I hope these pages may in some degree contribute. The numerous debts I have incurred are listed elsewhere. It is, to my regret, difficult to express adequately all I have learned from many able and devoted colleagues in the American and British services, from friends in other Allied services, and even —now that the war is over—from some of my erstwhile opponents.

JOHN BAKELESS

Elbowroom Farm,
Great Hill,
Seymour, Conn.

★ ★ ★

★

Contents

TURNCOATS, TRAITORS
AND HEROES

I

★ ★ ★

★

The Case of the Dangerous Doctor

THERE WAS a sudden stir and bustle in Brattle Street. Lieutenant General George Washington, commanding the Continental Army, then engaged in siege operations against the city of Boston, looked curiously through one of the windows at headquarters. They were the same windows through which Henry Wadsworth Longfellow would, in years to come, contemplate the River Charles; but, on a late September evening in 1775, the spectacle in Brattle Street was not poetic. General Washington stared. The stern countenance, more marble than any of his busts, relaxed. The general burst into one of his rare fits of laughter.

That chunky—nay, positively rotund—hero, Major General Israel Putnam, in full uniform, was clattering up to headquarters on horseback. The general was not really of the same dimension in all directions, but looked as if he might be, very soon. His was, in short, the kind of figure not at its best on horseback.

General Putnam had ridden up to the Vassall House, which General Washington now occupied, in tremendous haste, with a female—one cannot possibly say a lady—riding pillion behind him. No man's dignity, not even a major general's, is enhanced

9

when he appears, mounted, with a female on a pillion. The only way his passenger can keep her seat is to embrace the horseman in front of her—and embrace him closely. A major general, riding publicly down Brattle Street, clasped tightly at the waist by a buxom wench, was a spectacle—well, the troops must have enjoyed it!

Worse still, General Putnam's passenger was a hussy of dubious repute. That her sins were as scarlet did not worry anybody. The trouble was this hapless young creature had added to her transgressions the guilt of trying to communicate with certain gentlemen in Boston whose coats were just as scarlet as her sins—the officers of the enemy. She had carried an enciphered letter, addressed to one of General Gage's staff officers.

The reception Putnam's captive received was terrifying. From the head of the staircase, General Washington glared down. In his face there was no laughter now. Six feet tall, in blue and buff, he made an imposing figure. He did not wait to have the culprit formally brought before him. From his place high above the prisoner, he warned her grimly that "nothing but a full confession could save her from the halter." It was not the way this attractive young creature was usually received by the opposite sex.

The commander-in-chief, who had been an examining magistrate in Virginia, was on familiar ground. Were there tears, shrieks, feminine flutterings and protestations? Very likely.

But all that was no use at headquarters. It took time. It took pressure. It took threats. As General Washington put it, "For a long time she was proof against every threat and perswasion to discover the Author." Who wrote the letter? She wouldn't tell. What was in the letter? She hadn't read it. What was it about? She didn't know. Where was the cipher key? How could she guess it was ciphered? She hadn't opened it. So question and answer, thrust and parry, must have gone through a long and exhausting interrogation.

The girl was told she had been carrying information to the enemy. There would be a terrible penalty. Her only hope was to tell all. She stood silent. How many hours the terrified creature squirmed under the inquisition, there is no telling.

Probably it went on all night, until exhaustion began to tell at last and they broke her down. She gave a name. Dr. Benjamin Church, Jr., had given her the letter. The traitor was the rebel army's own director general of hospitals.

Send out a guard and bring the doctor in! You could hardly condemn one of the foremost medical men in New England on the accusation of one loose wench. Still, the girl ought to know. She was the doctor's mistress.

A reasonably alert counterintelligence would have been looking anxiously into the doctor's affairs long before this; for, though long undetected, he had been an appallingly careless secret agent. But the rebel army had no counterintelligence service. For many months, the doctor had been a paid British spy, reporting regularly to General Gage every move of the Massachusetts patriots, using his seat in the Provincial Congress to keep the British governor informed of its most secret plans. His espionage had begun months before the war broke out; but no one seriously suspected anything until after he gave his mistress the ciphered letter.

That part of the story, General Washington never learned. It is doubtful if the doctor's light lady knew it herself. Only Doctor Church, General Gage, and a close-mouthed British staff officer or two were in the secret, which they kept so successfully that most of the sordid facts never came to light until a century and a half had passed. Yet, though the story, as General Washington learned it, went back only a month or two, it was bad enough.

Doctor Church had given the girl a sealed letter. Though she probably did not know it, the letter was in cipher. It was not a very good cipher. A modern cryptanalyst would laugh at it—as several of them have. Exactly what the doctor told her, there is no way of knowing; but her actions show about what her instructions must have been.

Sometime in July or August, 1775, the girl arrived at the house of Godfrey Wenwood, who ran a bakery and bread shop on Bannister's Wharf, in Newport, Rhode Island. He was no ordinary baker, but a man with a reputation for "that celebrated article 'Wenwood's butter biscuits' the art of making which no man to this day knoweth."

The pair were well, far too well, acquainted, for the lady and the bachelor baker had once shared idyllic hours of dalliance. All this in prim colonial Boston, or Cambridge. Whether the dalliance was renewed on this occasion has never been discovered. It is not very likely, for Wenwood was about to marry and settle down. The professional lady can hardly be said to have reformed, but she had more or less recovered her amateur standing. She was Doctor Church's property now; she was in Newport on his errand; and the doctor was a good meal ticket. Still, the doctor was at the moment far away in Cambridge military hospitals, and she definitely did want Wenwood to do her a favor.

Would he arrange for her to see Captain Sir James Wallace, commanding H.M.S. *Rose,* then on station at or near Newport? Wenwood's bakery business gave him a convenient excuse for going aboard to arrange supplies. If he could not put her in touch with the naval officer, the girl wanted to see Charles Dudley, royal collector of customs. Or, if neither of these, then the Tory merchant and shipowner, George Rome, who was helping Captain Wallace supply the British garrison in Boston, and who had long since begun to send General Gage "intelligence of much importance," which came "from the Rebel camp itself."

Now, though Wenwood may not always have been a sterling exemplar of moral virtue, he was no Tory and no traitor. The girl can hardly have known how stanch a patriot he really was or she would not have gone to him in the first place; but their past relations had not been of a kind that involved political discussion.

Wenwood did not like the sound of anything he heard. Besides it was embarrassing to have this creature in Newport at all. Amorous dalliance far away in Boston was one thing. Having his trollop turn up in Newport, where Wenwood was a respectable tradesman, was another matter. His bakery was in his basement. "In the rooms above that he often had as guests the best society of the town, whom he entertained with a princely hospitality"—doubtless including "butter biscuits," made from the secret recipe. Wenwood definitely did not feel his present female visitor would fit very well in "the best society" of Newport.

Besides, his days of colonial flaming youth were over. He was about to marry "a young lady of great beauty and merit." He did marry her the following May. Newport was a small town. If someone saw him with this fancy lady! What if his two slaves gossiped?

Why was this trollop so eager to meet the naval officer and these two prominent citizens, anyhow? He questioned the girl till she admitted that she had been given the letter in Cambridge—she did not say by whom. She had been asked to give it to one of the three men she had named. It was to be sent on to the enemy in Boston; Wenwood could see that it was addressed to a British officer there.

What was likely to be in a letter addressed to a staff officer of the British Army, sent secretly through an officer of the Royal Navy or through a prominent Tory? Why this roundabout way of getting it to Boston? The amorous baker, his ardor for the lady long since cooled, liked the story less and less, the more he heard of it. It all smelled of "some Traitor in our Army." In the end, he got rid of the girl by persuading her to entrust the letter to him, for later delivery.

Left with the mysterious paper, the Newport baker puzzled over it for weeks, without opening it. After some time, he hunted up a friend of about his own age, the schoolmaster Adam Maxwell, who, the year before, had been keeping school in the front chamber of the Brick Market, not far from the bakery; and who was probably still there in 1775. Wenwood confided in the teacher, a stout patriot who had no compunctions. He broke the seal. He found three pages closely scrawled with mysterious characters.

At this stage, both men should have headed for the nearest American Army officer or any official known to them as completely loyal to the patriot cause. Instead, they put the mysterious paper away. The wonder is they did not complete their folly by burning it. In that case, the story of Doctor Church's treason might still be as completely lost as the recipe for Wenwood's butter biscuits; and Gage's best spy might have continued his treachery throughout the Revolution.

Perhaps it was Church himself who brought on the catastrophe. Late in September, Wenwood received a letter from the doctor's mistress. It looks very much as if Church had visited her—for business or pleasure—on her return to Cambridge; had discovered that the incriminating letter was not in safe hands; and, in his anxiety, had told his "miss" to make inquiries. Washington's papers show that Doctor Church tried to resign as medical director on September 20, though he was under no suspicion, as yet.

Now hopelessly involved in affairs too grave and dangerous for her rather feeble wits, the girl wrote her quondam lover:

> Dear Sir
> j now Sett Down to right afue Lines hoping thay will find
> [you] in good helth as thay Leave me jexpeted you would
> have arote to me be for this But now jexpet to Sea you
> hear every Day j much wonder you never Sent wot you
> promest to send jf you Did jnever reseve it so pray Lett
> me know By the first orpurtunty wen you expet to be hear
> & at the Same time whether you ever sent me that &
> wether you ever got a answer from my sister j am alitle
> unesey that you never rote thar js aserten person hear
> wants to Sea you verey much So pray com as Swon as
> posebell jf you righ [write] Direct your Lett^r to mr Ewerd
> Harton Living on M^r tapthorps farm in Littel Cambrig

That stirred Wenwood to action at last. His suspicions had been slow to kindle, but they were fully ablaze now. How did this girl know that her letter—"wot you promest to send"—had never reached Boston? If she knew that, she had some kind of contact with the British, from Cambridge itself. He had already known that she had been trying to get in touch with the Royal Navy and Tory officials at Newport. He knew now that she was in contact with the enemy in Boston.

What did she mean by saying that "aserten person hear wants to Sea you"? Was she hinting at a renewal of their old liaison? Was this a lure? Or was some sinister third person waiting for him? Wenwood knew he was out of his depth. He consulted his friend, the schoolmaster, again.

The two decided to do, at last, what they should have done in the beginning. They went to Henry Ward, patriot secretary of the Rhode Island colony. That experienced individual, who saw at once how the land lay, told them to hasten to Cambridge with the letter and a full report. To avoid alarming the British spy—whose identity they could not guess—Ward urged Wenwood not to ride straight into the town, but to wait in a neighboring village and send the papers on by other hands.

Disregarding Ward's advice in this respect, Wenwood went straight to Cambridge, whither, so far as records show, Maxwell did not accompany him. As evidence of good faith, the baker carried a letter from Ward to Brigadier General Nathanael Greene, commanding Rhode Island troops. In this, Ward summarized the story for Greene's benefit. Wenwood, who had the ciphered letter with him, could give the general further explanation.

After one look, Greene started with Wenwood and the mysterious document for headquarters, where he asked to see Washington privately, handed him the cipher, gave him Ward's letter, and introduced Wenwood to tell his own story. One glance showed General Washington that treason was afoot. He sent Wenwood hurrying off to find the girl and, "by using the confidence she had in him," to get her to reveal "the whole secret"; but, though he found the spy's messenger easily enough, Wenwood met with no success. The girl may have been, as James Warren, the army's paymaster general, said, "an infamous hussy," but she was also "a subtle, shrewd jade." Wenwood had to report failure.

Orders rapped out swiftly. Arrest the woman. Bring her in.

When interrogation at length elicited Doctor Church's name, everybody was astounded. That ardent patriot? The surgeon general? A member of long standing in the Massachusetts Provincial Congress? One of the men who had ridden to Springfield to greet General Washington on his way to assume command in Cambridge?

(Incidentally, one gets an idea of the efficiency of British in-

telligence in this, as in all wars. It had an agent riding with
the rebel general before he had time to reach his new command!)

It seemed incredible that such a man as Dr. Benjamin
Church could possibly be guilty. A graduate of Harvard, he
had studied medicine in England; had traveled in Europe;
had married an English girl; had returned to settle down in
Boston; had built an expensive summer house at which his
neighbors marveled; had written political verse in defense of
the Whigs; had seen the fight at Lexington—or said he had;
had been in frequent touch with the Continental Congress itself. It was only a few days since (September 24) General Washington had refused to consider his resignation because of
"unwillingness to part with a good Officer."

It was true that Paul Revere's American spy ring in Boston
had noticed some suspicious leaks, but no one ever thought of
connecting them with the doctor. It was true, too, that, for a
little while before the Revolution, some people had wondered
whether Doctor Church was really so wholeheartedly for the
colonial cause as he professed; but that unkind suspicion speedily died down as patriots beheld his care of the army's wounded.
Nobody ever accused him of neglecting them.

It was easy enough for General Washington to find the surgeon general. Doctor Church, though disturbed at his lady
friend's failure to deliver his letter, could comfort himself with
the belief that it was in an unbreakable cipher—all ciphers seem
unbreakable until somebody breaks them. The doctor was going quietly about his medical duties when the guard caught
up with him. That was the only thing he could possibly do,
unless he tried to slip away to the British.

Brought to headquarters, the doctor was bland, confident,
almost convincing. He answered questions easily enough. The
letter? Oh, yes, it was his. Why not? A good many letters were
being openly sent through the lines to Boston. In fact, Major
General Charles Lee, of the Continental Army, had been in
fairly steady correspondence with his old friend, Major General
John Burgoyne, of the British Army in Boston, openly, under
flag of truce, through the lines. General Lee was just trying to

persuade General Burgoyne that King George was pursuing the wrong policy. It is true that he failed to convince General Burgoyne, who replied in many pages of polished political prose. But that was all right. There was nothing surreptitious about it. General Washington had been fully informed of the correspondence by Lee himself.

Church's correspondence had been a little different. It had been kept secret. Why? It was in cipher. Why? Doctor Church had no answer and was not obliging enough to offer his cipher key. Why? An innocent man would have turned it over at once.

If Doctor Church had wanted to send a letter to Boston, General Washington pointed out icily, he could have done so under a flag of truce at any time. Why did he send his letter secretly via Newport? The doctor mumbled an admission that he had been indiscreet. (On that point, everybody agreed with him.) As for treason, he denied the whole idea. (On that point, nobody agreed.)

Doctor Church was kept under guard.

The next step was to find some way of reading the letter. The use of cipher was not in itself so suspicious then as it appears today. Since a letter in that day was merely folded over and sealed with a wax wafer, without a protecting envelope, it was not unusual to encipher personal messages to insure safety against prying eyes. Thomas Jefferson used more cipher in his personal than in his official correspondence. Since cipher was so common, it did not take long to find that the Continental Army had three men who knew how to break it. One was a Massachusetts chaplain, the Reverend Samuel West, of Dartmouth, Massachusetts. Then Elbridge Gerry, of the Committee of Safety, who was "somewhat acquainted with decyphering" himself, suggested Colonel Elisha Porter, of the Massachusetts Militia.

The fact that the letter was written in English made the task fairly easy. It is a characteristic of the English language that letter frequencies run in about the order used on the modern typesetting keyboard, that is, ETAOIN SHRDLU. Modern cryptographers use two orders of frequency, ETOANIRSHDL or ETOANRISHDL. West, Gerry, and Porter evidently knew this simple principle. All they had to do was count the number of times each symbol occurred and arrange the symbols in order of frequency, perhaps also noting certain combinations of letters common in English—ee, ng, th, etc.—which gave further clues.

Two independent analyses were made, one by the Reverend Mr. West working alone, the other by Porter and Gerry together.

On October 3, General Washington received two separate deciphers. The versions agreed perfectly—there was no more doubt.

In his letter, Church had told the enemy all about his recent visit to Congress in Philadelphia. He had also reported fully on American strength, artillery, ammunition supply, rations, recruiting, currency, and the proposed attack on Canada. He gave exact figures on the artillery at Kingsbridge, New York, which he had been able to observe and count. He reported troop strength in Philadelphia and the mood of the Continental Congress—"united, determined in opposition."

His letter also revealed that he had unquestionably made three previous attempts at surreptitious correspondence, and probably a good many more. Once his messenger had been caught with a message sewed into the waistband of his breeches. Obvious though the hiding place was, the man was released after a few days, with his message still undiscovered. Bribery helped. Church wrote: "A little art and a little cash settled the matter." It was now evident that he had dispatched his mistress to try the roundabout route through Newport only when all else had failed.

The day he received the deciphered text, General Washington called a council and laid the incriminating message before his generals.

When they interrogated Church, the wretched man admitted that, in general, his letter had been correctly deciphered. To make matters worse, headquarters had, in some unexplained way, secured another ciphered letter, of which only a deciphered version now survives. Church tried to explain this away. He had not written it.

In his own defense, Church asserted that his motives had always been entirely patriotic. The letter Wenwood had revealed might seem suspicious. But Doctor Church protested he was entirely loyal. He had written only to frighten the British with an exaggerated account of American strength and so prevent them from attacking.

The listening generals knew well enough that part of this was true. Church really had magnified American numbers. They may, however, have reflected that a simple agreement with Gage to reduce reported figures by another agreed figure would have provided the spy with this argument in his own defense without preventing the enemy from getting accurate information.

It is more probable that Church simply overestimated the numbers of the troops he was observing, as secret agents are very likely to do. As medical director, he had no access to General Washington's strength reports, and it is extremely difficult to reach a correct estimate simply by watching soldiers in an occupied town.

His defense made no impression on the alarmed American generals who heard it. The doctor, still loudly proclaiming his loyalty, was marched off to confinement.

The indignant generals turned to the army regulations that Congress had adopted in the previous June. There it was! Congress had foreseen such cases. Article XXVIII provided that anyone communicating with the enemy should suffer such punishment as a court-martial might direct. That seemed to fit the situation. Try the man and string him up!

At this point, someone searched a little further and made an embarrassing discovery. Article LI limited the punishment a court-martial could inflict. It could give penalties of thirty-nine lashes or a fine of two months' pay and it could cashier the offender—and that was all! No one had been thinking about British spies when that article had been adopted. It had simply never occurred to patriotic members of the Continental Congress that such an offense as Church's was possible. Congress hastily authorized the death penalty for espionage, November 7, 1775 (there was no difficulty in hanging André, later), but this change could not be applied to Church.

General Washington could, however, hold the doctor in custody; and the man's papers must be seized at once.

Too late!

Somewhere, in or about Cambridge, lurked another British spy. That quick and clever agent, whose identity has, to this day, never been discovered, had already searched Church's records. When the Americans seized them, they were pure as driven snow. Eagerly Joseph Reed, of the staff, examined the remaining papers. They were perfectly ordinary records, such as any medical man might keep. Not a single document showed Doctor Church's guilt, though his cipher key must have been in those innocent files only a few weeks before.

Though none of the investigators ever knew it, Doctor Church had become alarmed some time earlier. A document discovered in recent years shows he had learned that the rebels had a spy of their own, deep in the councils of the Ministry in London. This unknown American agent was learning the names of "the friends of Gov.ᵗ in all the Colonies." Shivering at the thought that he, too, might be discovered, the doctor begged General Gage: "Therefore conceal my name." He need not have worried. Apparently the American agent in London simply missed him.

The Massachusetts Provincial Congress dealt with its treacherous member as best it could; but it had no power to punish spies, either. Church, after a vigorous defense, saved everyone a great deal of trouble by resigning; but the legislators were not satisfied till they had "utterly expelled" him, even after his resignation.

Eventually, the Continental Congress ordered him kept in a Connecticut prison, under the severest restrictions. Though this was probably illegal, Governor Trumbull saw to it that the dangerous doctor stayed where he could do no more harm to the patriot cause. No one yet imagined how much harm he had already done or how long he had been doing it. James Warren, paymaster general, had some shrewd suspicions, but no proof. He guessed quite correctly why Church had been able to enter Boston and leave again, even after Lexington:

"I have now no difficulty to account for the knowledge Gage had of all our Congress Secrets, and how some later plans have been rendered abortive; or for the Indulgence shewn him [Church] when he went into Boston after the Lexington Battle. do I discover a want of charity that the Evidences won't warrant?"

The evidence warranted a far worse judgment, but it took one hundred and fifty years for Americans to find it, and the doctor was, by that time, safe at the bottom of the sea. The fact was, he had been Gage's secret agent long before the Revolution began.

Governor Trumbull put Church in confinement of the severest sort. Gilbert Saltonstall describes it in a letter to Nathan Hale, November 27, 1775: "Doct: Church is in close Custody in Norwich Gaol, the Windows boarded up, and he deny'd the use of Pen, Ink, and Paper, to have no converse with any Person but in presence of the Gaoler, and then to Converse in no Language but English. Good God what a fall—."

In January, 1776, Trumbull relaxed sufficiently to grant the use of pen, ink and paper, long enough for Church to write an appeal to the Continental Congress. In this, the prisoner complained that the severity of his jailers had brought on asthma, which threatened his life—or so the physician diagnosed his own case.

Congress, after receiving the spy's request for "clear, elastic air," relented sufficiently to order him moved to another jail and allowed him to ride out under guard. As nothing was done about this order, Church again petitioned—this time with a certificate from three physicians. Congress then authorized his liberation, if he would give sureties for £1,000 and swear not to correspond further with the British and not to leave Massachusetts.

Though allowed to visit Waltham in June, he still was not set free, since it was soon clear that indignant patriots would lynch the man unless he was kept confined. When his Waltham jail was raided, Church saved his life only by jumping out of the window. If this was an attempt to escape, it failed, for he was soon back in durance.

A year later it looked as if he again had a chance of freedom. The tolerant, indolent and kindly Sir William Howe, who had now replaced Gage, sympathizing with Church's troubles, offered to exchange a captured American surgeon. The Massachusetts government agreed; but a patriotic mob caused such a commotion that Church had to be sent back to jail after he had actually gone on board the cartel vessel, sent for him. A newspaper of the time shows that this vessel came in during July, 1777.

Church went back to a Boston jail. But, according to Mrs. Church, the mob "broke open his house pillaged and destroyed every thing it contain'd." The agitated wife, whom Church had abandoned for his mistress even before his arrest, was not left "a change of cloaths, nor even a bed for her and her children to lie on." Somehow, the poor woman found enough money to pay her passage to England.

General William Heath vigorously protested against letting the doctor go. His release, said the general, would allow him to give information "greatly Detrimental to the United States at this Juncture of our Publick Affairs"; for by this time Burgoyne's army was moving menacingly southward from Canada, and no one dreamed, as yet, that it would surrender in a few months. Though two years had passed since his arrest, it was no time to release a spy; and General Howe's well-meant effort to secure Church's freedom merely convinced Americans that he was too dangerous to let go.

By 1780, the situation had somewhat changed. Though the war was not over, Congress at length relented, knowing that the doctor would now do little harm, since any military intelligence he might once have had was long since out of date. He was "exiled to some Island in the West Indies, and threatened with death in case he shõd ever return."

He sailed in a small schooner, commanded by a certain Captain Smithwick, and nothing was ever heard again of Doctor Church, Captain Smithwick or their schooner. They were presumed to have been lost at sea. Mrs. Smithwick was so sure of it that, by May, 1782, she "married another husband." Mrs. Church had seen quite enough of matrimony.

At home in Boston, Church's father alone retained his faith in "my Lost son the Doct^r," whose expenses he had paid during eighteen months of his imprisonment. To the end, he stoutly maintained the doctor was no traitor, "but alas! for him, & me! He was improvident—and thereby expos'd himself to ye resentment of his Country." Pathetically clinging to the belief his son might still be somewhere safe in hiding, the old man left the fugitive five pounds and his library, in a will dated 1780. But even the father was not quite sure. He made the bequest to his son, if alive, "for alas; he is now absent—being cruelly banish'd his Country—and whether living or dead God only knows."

II

★ ★ ★

★

The Secret Story Behind Lexington and Concord

GENERAL WASHINGTON, horrified as he was when he discovered how closely the far-seeing eye of British intelligence had been watching him, would have been a great deal more disturbed, had he ever guessed how long Doctor Church had been spying for the enemy; how much he had reported; and how many other secret agents General Gage had had actively at work, watching all the patriots' early preparations for the Revolutionary struggle. Though Doctor Church was not caught until long after Lexington and Concord, he had been spying for many months before those battles. Probably he had been betraying the patriots' secret plans for about two years, since by 1775 he had become a trusted British secret agent—which cannot have been a quick or easy process. The real story was never revealed till General Gage's secret papers came to light in the present century.

So far as can now be ascertained, Doctor Church's espionage may have begun sometime in 1774, when General Gage reached Boston, to succeed Thomas Hutchinson as royal governor of Massachusetts. That none of Church's espionage reports is dated earlier than 1775 proves nothing; for he was in medical practice in Boston, where he could report orally instead of in writing.

From the beginning, casual suspicions of the doctor had occasionally crossed the minds of various patriots, but they were soon forgotten. Doctor Church had always been—at any rate, he had always seemed—a furious patriot. He had delivered one of the anti-British orations on the anniversary of the Boston Massacre. He had displayed a neat gift for anti-British political doggerel, in smoothly rhyming couplets. But skeptical patriots had noted that adroit parodies of these same verses, turning their meaning quite around, invariably and promptly appeared in pro-British colonial papers. In their new forms, the verses supported the king's cause. Unkind persons suspected Doctor Church might be writing both. Nobody could prove anything, then; nobody can prove anything, now; but people wondered who else had a style so exactly like the literary doctor's—a little closer than ordinary parody.

By November, 1774, Paul Revere knew there was a leak somewhere in the patriot spy ring he was helping to operate. "A gentleman who had connections with the Tory party, but was a Whig at heart" warned him that the group "were discovered." To prove it, the nameless gentleman repeated correctly what had been said—supposedly under the protection of an oath of secrecy—at a meeting the night before.

Despite all this, there was still very little suspicion of Church, though Revere and his friends knew that he was privy to their leaking secrets. But so was John Hancock; so was one of the Adamses. How could anyone suspect stanch patriots like these? In the end, the Revere group reluctantly concluded that the traitor was one of their own number, though they could find no clue to his identity. Rather naïvely, they changed their meeting place. It was the only precaution they could think of.

Presently the anonymous gentleman spoke to Revere again. Everything the Revere group did was still being reported to Gage. How did the gentleman know that? He had it from no less a personage than Thomas Flucker, secretary of the province.

Distressed patriots noted with alarm that Church spent a

good deal of time with a half-pay British captain named Price, and a British commissioner named Robinson. While this caused some comment, no one suspected treason. Doctor Church just seemed a little careless about his company. When, at last, an anxious friend remonstrated, Church laughed the whole thing off: Associate with Tories? Of course he did. "He kept Company with them on purpose to find out their plans."

Still another queer thing about the doctor was observed, then ignored. A medical associate was mildly surprised to note a sudden improvement in his finances, during 1775. Popular physician though he was, Church spent so lavishly that he often seemed hard up. He had built an elaborate house. He had a wife and family to support. He also had a mistress—and that kind of sin costs money. Suddenly, he had plenty of bright gold guineas. His friend wondered, but no real question crossed his mind—until it was too late.

Paul Revere's own vague doubts were set permanently at rest when he met the doctor in Cambridge, the day after Lexington (April 20, 1775), and found him proudly displaying a bloodstain on his stocking, "which he said Spirted on him from a man who was kill'd near him, as he was urging the Militia on." It never occurred to Revere that the doctor had had a whole day to get a clean pair of stockings. Untroubled by skepticism and completely won over, he put away all uncharitable thoughts: "I well remember, that I argued with my self, if a Man will risque his life in a Cause, he must be a Friend to that cause; & I never suspected him after, till He was charged with being a Traytor." Church had never been near the firing line at Lexington.

By this time, the physician had grown dangerously bold. He went in person to see Gage, at headquarters. Another caller, waiting to see the general, was amazed when Gage and Church emerged from Gage's private office, with every mark of friendship; but he felt no need to do anything about it. After all, he, too, had reason to call upon the general.

The full extent of Church's treason would be a secret, still, were it not for a casual remark in a single letter, which definitely proves that he is the author of a long series of intelligence reports which now survive in the Gage papers, in the Clements Library at the University of Michigan. Gage received this secret letter sometime in May, 1775, and his headquarters noted on it the date May 24. It was full of military information about the new American fortifications outside Cambridge. It also reported the resolute mood of the colonists: "They will not lay down their arms."

Then come the words which, after a century and a half, convict Church: "I am appointed to my vexation to carry the dispatches to Philadelphia." Church received such an appointment in the middle of the month. No one else received any similar appointment. On May 16, 1775, the Massachusetts Provincial Congress had "Resolved, that Doct. Church be ordered to go immediately to Philadelphia," to consult with the Continental Congress. Gage's secret agent was now in close association with both provincial and national governing bodies. It was a master stroke of espionage. Not till Benedict Arnold, did any British spy come closer to American secrets.

There is no doubt that Church is the author of several other reports of the same kind and in the same handwriting. One letter carries the identification a little further, for it contains a reference to "Mrs. Fleming." Church's sister-in-law, in Boston, was Mrs. John Fleming. Though this letter is in parts illegible, some passages refer to the destruction of papers and a "Cypher." Two sentences, though obscure, give further proof that Church had been a British spy for a long time: "instant death w^d be my portion should a discovery be made." Another still-legible passage reads: "Secrecy respecting me on the part of the Genl is indispensable to my rendering him any services and be the event what it may is necessary to the preservation of my life." Either passage is plain evidence of espionage.

Another letter in this series and in this same hand ends: "The 25th of this month finishes a quarter." This is a plain request for cash, since the Americans of that day still followed the British practice of settling accounts quarterly, instead of monthly.

Though Doctor Church was General Gage's most valuable and most strategically placed secret agent, he was only one of a numerous group operating in a highly efficient intelligence system which had been keeping up a steady flow of accurate information about nearly everything the patriots were doing, long before the fight at Lexington. By January, 1775, the need for military intelligence was becoming so great that Gage ordered all officers and men familiar with the Massachusetts countryside to report to his adjutant general, who, as usual in British staff organization of that period, doubled as chief intelligence officer. It was helpful that Gage's adjutant general, though a regular, was American-born—Lieutenant Colonel Stephen Kemble, son of a New Jersey Tory, who continued to hold his dual staff post under Howe and Clinton, until Major John André took over in 1780.

Both sides in the American Revolution were about equally well served by their intelligence services—and quite as badly served by their counterintelligence. Except for Church, not one of Gage's agents was ever captured; only a few were suspected; and most of them have never been identified. On the other hand, the patriots in Cambridge and Boston spied upon the British with equal impunity; and, though Church knew who many of the spies were, only two—Paul Revere and James Lovell—were ever caught; and both were soon free again.

Next to Doctor Church, the most deadly of Gage's secret agents was a mysterious individual in or near Concord, who was always intimately acquainted with everything the patriots were doing there. He may have been a local Tory, with an ardent but carefully concealed loyalty to the crown; but comparison of handwritings suggests that he may have been a certain John Hall, of whom little is known, save that he had seen service in Canada. From this Concord agent, whoever he was, General Gage received during March and April, 1775—in other words, during the last weeks before the fighting started at Lexington—a series of detailed reports on American supplies of arms, ammunition and food.

For some reason, this active spy wrote his reports in French. Why he did so is hard to explain; for, while it is true that Gage understood the language perfectly and used it in preference to English in his official correspondence with the French-Swiss soldier of fortune, General Sir Frederick Haldimand, there seems to be no special reason for an English spy to use a foreign language in writing to an English general—especially since the excruciating badness of grammar, accents, genders, idioms and spelling shows that, whatever the man was, he was neither French nor French Canadian. Perhaps this points to John Hall, who may have learned French in Canada, and may have learned it rather badly.

It seems likely that the spy used a foreign language because he hoped for temporary security in case one of his reports should fall accidentally into the wrong hands. Some such precaution was desirable, for, strange to say, in early 1775 the British commander-in-chief had no code, no cipher, and no officer who knew how to make one. He had to appeal for help to the commanding general in Canada, from whom he probably obtained the clumsy substitution cipher that Doctor Church was found using, later in the year.

Though the unknown Concord spy sometimes came to Boston, he was careful to avoid being seen at headquarters. Some of his letters, though actually written in the city, seem to have been stealthily conveyed to Gage by a go-between. One of these messages describes the roads *"d'ici"* to Concord. *"Ici"* can only mean Boston.

Whatever this agent's linguistic shortcomings, this report, like others that he wrote, is a model of its kind. It conveys full information of artillery, small arms, powder and bullets stored in Concord, and locates exactly the supplies of lard, dried peas and flour on which American soldiers would have to depend for sustenance. It also discusses roads, guides and the manufacture of arms and tents in Charlestown. It is noteworthy that when the time came for the British to march to Lexington and Concord, several competent guides were instantly available.

The report closes with a warning about desertion:

> Spies and messengers are continually in the city to lure away the soldiers and there is a boat which, as an ordinary thing, carries them from behind the city to the other side of Cambridge Bay [i.e., the mouth of the Charles River]— landing at Phipps's Point. This information is confirmed

by a deserter, who recently gave information to the priest
at Concord (named Emerson, a very bad subject), to whom
he stated that he escaped by the route.

The boat may have been one of the Boston ferries or a small
craft that Paul Revere kept concealed for emergency use. The
"prêtre de Concord" named Emerson, who was *"un mauvais
sujet,"* was the Reverend William Emerson, father of the philos-
opher. Apparently the secret agent was trying to say that he
was a bad subject of the king, rather than that this blameless
man was a bad character. (It was, to be sure, bad French, but
that was the kind of French the spy wrote.) The surprising fact
is that the writer knew all about the deserter's highly confidential talk with the loyal and patriotic clergyman. Whoever
he was, this spy was deep in patriotic councils and completely
trusted.

It was a report of special interest to General Gage, for desertion was becoming a serious problem. Any regular who wanted
to leave the army knew that the patriots would welcome him
for the intelligence he brought, and would give him employment as drill master for their numerous awkward squads. Only
two days after this report, Gage received another, saying that
the royal militia were also deserting. General Nathanael
Greene had a British deserter training American troops in
Providence. A deserter from a Boston artillery company was
training patriot artillerymen in Worcester, where the "French"
spy had seen him—and also thirteen field guns, lined up in front
of the church. Furthermore, fifteen tons of gunpowder were
now hidden in Worcester. It is no wonder Gage at once sent
more secret agents to Worcester.

By April 6, 1775, the Concord spy had located four brass
cannon, stolen from Boston, together with some mortars, at the
home of "B——" (in other words, Colonel James Barrett). Redcoats rushed off to look for them as soon as they reached the
town, leaving a guard to secure the bridgehead, and thereby
bringing on the fight with the minutemen.

Other secret reports to General Gage, in three different handwritings, deal mainly with political secrets, giving detailed ac-

counts of what the Provincial and Continental Congresses were doing. One of these, which may be by Church, comments on the probable reaction of Massachusetts people to an "excursion"—probably an ordinary route march to harden the troops—on March 30, 1775. When the soldiers destroyed property, there were the usual complaints, not to the general, but to the Provincial Congress. That body kept its decision secret.

But General Gage knew all about it in a few days. His spy reported on April 3 that the provincial legislators had made up their minds "that should any body of troops wth Artillery, and Baggage, march out of Boston, the Country should be instantly alarmed, and called together to oppose their March, to the last extremity."

Gage acted on this intelligence two weeks later. The spy's warning explains why Lieutenant Colonel Francis Smith's infantry column set off for Lexington on the night of April 18, unsupported by artillery and without baggage. Only when, on the nineteenth, Lord Percy had to bring out a reserve force to rescue Smith, did artillery appear.

Another report, on April 9, discusses the alarm of the patriots over the arming of Tories; the colony's probable refusal to provide barracks for more troops; flight of Whigs from Boston; the actual movements of prominent patriots like John Sullivan. Two days later, another describes "great Consternation in Congress" over Parliament's support of the king and over the reinforcement sent to Gage. The spy urges Gage to strike at once: "A sudden blow struck now or immediately on the arrival of the reinforcements from England should they come within a fortnight would oversett all their plans." It is hardly an accident that Gage moved against Lexington and Concord a week later. The general had already shown that he could act promptly on intelligence received. He had learned, on February 21 and 24, that the rebels had stored cannon at Salem, and that "the Seizure of them would greatly disconcert their schemes." Two days later, his troops struck, though they accomplished little.

Other secret agents appear to have been volunteers. One of these men reports Gage's soldiers selling uniforms and arms.

The price of muskets was four dollars, and there was no doubt who was buying them. An unsigned letter warns that the patriots are trying to cut off supplies of straw and oats for British cavalry and to keep Boston's food supply at a low level. John Lovell, father of the patriot spy, James Lovell, was busy with what he called "private services" for Gage. When the general wanted papers of the rebel committee, he called upon Lovell. That stout Tory soon "did procure them & deliver'd them to the Gen¹ himself."

Unwilling to rely wholly on civilians, General Gage had also secured strictly military intelligence about the situation in Concord from Major John Pitcairn, of the Marines. The major, more or less disguised in civilian clothes, had been a frequent visitor at the Jones Tavern, some time before the battle.

But it was a civilian spy's report that finally touched off the Revolutionary War. When, on April 15, General Gage learned that the New England colonies proposed to raise 180,000 men —an absurd figure—he lost no more time. That very day he withdrew his grenadier and light infantry companies from garrison duty, allegedly for special training. That night Admiral Graves began to get his boats ready.

The suspicious Americans immediately commenced moving matériel out of Concord—as a British spy reported, April 18, one day before the battle. Provisions had not yet been removed, the agent said, but military stores were hidden, and only four field guns remained in the village, because the Americans feared "a sudden march of the troops might dispossess them of the Stores."

That was enough for Gage. A sudden march was just what he would make. Lieutenant Colonel Smith, with all the grenadier and light infantry companies, started that night.

The spy concluded this report with an analysis of the rebellious popular mood in the Connecticut and Rhode Island assemblies: "There is no doubt entertained among us but that they will readily embark in the common cause & chearfully furnish proportionable supplies." Rhode Island had just received four hundred barrels of gunpowder, three hundred muskets and several tons of lead. The colonies might soon be expected to "declare a direct denial of Parliamentary supremacy." Information that the Massachusetts rebels would soon have this support encouraged Gage in his fateful decision.

When General Gage sat down to write Lieutenant Colonel Smith's orders for the march to Concord, he had before him a summary, which still exists, of this intelligence; but his march order of April 18 omits it. Instead, he gave Lieutenant Colonel Smith a specially prepared map, with locations of the patriots' arms and supplies marked on it. After listing what was to be destroyed, the order says: "You have a Draught of Concord, on which is marked, the Houses, Barns, &c., which contain the above Military Stores." General Gage knew the rebels had not yet had time to find new hiding places for all the supplies they had collected.

At Woburn, about ten miles from Concord, another British agent was living, quite openly. This was Major Benjamin Thompson (later Count Rumford), of the New Hampshire Militia. Because Thompson had already made his New Hampshire home too hot to hold him by sending British deserters back to General Gage in Boston, he had settled down in Woburn, his boyhood home, where he came instantly under patriot suspicion. Documents discovered in our own century show that the suspicion was only too completely justified; but nobody ever saw those documents in Revolutionary times, except General Gage and a few trusted staff officers; and the future Count Rumford protested his devotion to the "true interests" of the colonies so loudly that few people thought to ask just what he meant by "true interests." It is said that General Washington—who, as a Virginian, knew little of New England's local scandals—was prevented only by his officers' protests from giving the British spy a commission in the Continental Army.

It is doubtful that any of the reports on munitions supplies in Concord came from Major Thompson; for he was already under suspicion, and any curiosity about patriot stores in the vicinity would have led to instant trouble. There is, however, plain evidence of his espionage. In the Gage papers is a "sympathetic-ink" letter from him, which is a spy's report and nothing else, though masked by an innocent message in ordinary ink. The name of the addressee and one signature have been completely erased, the second signature being cut out—there must have been some cautious staff officer in Gage's headquarters. The cover letter, May 6, 1775, is merely a short and formal note of thanks. A more experienced secret agent would have written a longer letter, leaving less blank paper, and would then have used invisible ink between the lines.

The unknown Bostonian who received it, knew enough about his friend Thompson's activities to take the apparently innocent letter to General Gage. As it now appears, in the Clements Library, the paper shows plain traces of a chemical wash; and the two separate messages are now in inks of quite different colors. One is the faded yellowish brown of most eighteenth-century ink. The other is paler; and some trouble with the developer has caused the loss of two words—a not unusual occurrence.

Thompson ignores the Lexington and Concord battles, then two weeks past, remarking that Gage has "already better intelligence of them affairs than I am able to give." He has, however, been conversing with an unknown but far too talkative "Field officer in the Rebel Army (if that mass of confusion may be called an Army)."

There is a fair chance that this was Colonel Loammi Baldwin, who in July had taken over intelligence at Chelsea and Malden, Massachusetts, for General Washington. It is impossible to doubt Baldwin's loyalty, but he may easily have trusted a brilliant and plausible rogue like Thompson, too far. They had been lifelong friends; they had worked together in saving the Harvard College Library from wartime damage; and Baldwin had observation posts close to Thompson's refuge at Woburn.

In addition to what he learned from the chatty American officer, Thompson assured General Gage that he had further information from "a member of the Provincial Congress that is now sitting at Watertown." This may mean either that he had been working with Doctor Church or that he had found a second traitor within the Provincial Congress. More probably, the British spy had found one of those not unusual legislators who let things slip out, from sheer self-importance.

Thompson reported that "an Army consisting of 30,000 effective men is speedily to be raised in the four New England Governments, & that the quota for this Province is 13600." (It is true that the New England colonies never raised such a force; but it is also true that they at one time planned to raise an even larger force.) Thompson thought the Americans were planning a feint against Boston, but would really attack Castle William, in the harbor. Congress was already considering independence and would seek European aid. Admitting that he had no accurate logistical information, he believed the rebels' supplies were scanty.

Though both signatures are gone, there is no doubt this letter comes from Thompson, since it is dated from Woburn, where he was then living, is in one of his two known handwritings, and describes his peculiar situation exactly. It is just possible, since he was living so near Concord, that he was serving the unknown "French" spy as a "cut-out"—that is, an intermediary, receiving intelligence reports and sending them on, so as to protect the reporting agent's anonymity. Or both men may have been in touch with the Concord Tory, Daniel Bliss or with another Tory, named Gove, of whom nothing is now known, except that he lived near Concord, and that on one occasion he not only sheltered a known British spy but got him, with the most expert ease, safely to Boston.

In October, 1775—just as Doctor Church's misdeeds were being discovered—Thompson went back to his New Hampshire home to say farewell to his wife. Either because suspicions of his Toryism had died down or because the local patriots had too many other things to think about, Thompson was not disturbed. Even so, he did not attempt to go straight on to Boston. Instead, he journeyed overland to Rhode Island. The British, who knew in advance that he was coming, had him met by a boat from H.M.S. *Scarborough,* and the frigate took him safely to Boston.

By November 4, 1775, he was writing out a detailed report on conditions in the American camp for Sir William Howe, who had by that time replaced Gage. When Sir William evacuated Boston the following March, Thompson sailed off to London to assist Lord George Germain, who was running the Colonial Office and the American Revolution.

He did not trouble to notify his wife, left in Concord, New Hampshire, with their little daughter. In despair, the poor woman (who never saw him again) finally wrote the American Army to ask what it could tell her. A stanch friend always, Colonel Loammi Baldwin replied from New York: "I have had no opportunity to find out whether Major Thompson is with the enemy or not."

It is the only case in history where a spy's deserted wife has applied to the enemy's intelligence service to learn where her spying spouse has gone!

III

★　★　★

★

Captain Brown and Ensign De Bernière

LONG BEFORE musket fire flashed across the bridge at Concord, General Gage had learned about other patriot stores in the Massachusetts towns of Charlestown, Watertown, Worcester, Salem, Marblehead, Mystic and Menotomy; and in Connecticut. On February 21, 1775, his secret service reported that, within five days, twenty wagonloads of flour had passed from Marblehead and Salem, through Mystic, in the direction of Worcester. Gun carriages were being made at Charlestown, Watertown and Marblehead. Twelve brass cannon at Salem were "lodged near the North River, on the back of the Town." Connecticut towns were laying in supplies of food and munitions, the largest store being at Hartford. Tools were being made at Menotomy, pickaxes at Mystic.

It looked as if the largest of these supply dumps was at Worcester; but, before he could send redcoats to seize them, General Gage needed professional observation by trained soldiers, both in Worcester itself and along the roads his troops would have to travel. On February 22, one day after receiving his intelligence reports, Gage started his first pair of disguised regulars toward Worcester, to be followed in April—after further alarming intelligence had come in—by a second pair.

Both got themselves—and the Tories who tried to help them—into a great deal of trouble.

It would be too much to say that both pairs of spies nearly got themselves hanged; for the dispute had not come to an open clash of arms; the laws of war did not apply; and no one was, as yet, in a hanging mood. But, even in early 1775, indignant patriots could make things extremely unpleasant for king's men, especially those detected in espionage, without actually executing them. One band of patriots near Worcester had already laid in an adequate supply of tar and feathers for the Tory host of one of Gage's spies, which they intended to use the moment they could prove he was harboring a British agent; and there would assuredly have been enough left over to adorn the spy.

Both pairs of agents were detected, but neither pair was captured; and both missions returned to Boston with full reports, while one brought back a map and other military drawings, together with a full road and terrain report.

As his first pair of spies, General Gage chose Captain William Brown, of the 52nd Regiment of Foot, and Ensign Henry De Bernière, of the 10th. Though the British commander knew there were supplies at Worcester, he had to find out in exactly what part of the town they were stored; and he needed information on roads and terrain, if he was to move troops into Worcester to destroy them. Guessing this would happen, he had in January, 1775, sent out a call for officers "capable of taking Sketches of a Country," and in De Bernière he had found a good one, whose work is still a valuable historical source. As the disguised officers were likely to be seen making road maps and terrain sketches, they were ordered to pose as ordinary surveyors. The general's instructions were in writing:

> You will go through the counties of Suffolk and Worcester, taking a sketch of the country as you pass; it is not expected you should make out regular plans and surveys, but mark out the roads and distances from town to town, as also the situation and nature of the country; all passes must be particularly laid down, noticing the length and

breadth of them, the entrance in and going out of town, and whether to be avoided by taking other routes.

General Gage also wanted information regarding streams, woods, hills, defensible places in towns, the possibility of constructing additional roads parallel to main roads, camp sites, and local supplies of food, forage, straw, and extra horses.

Someone, probably Ensign De Bernière himself, kept a copy of these orders and also a written "narrative" of the spies' experiences. This was probably the ensign's personal file copy, identical with the report turned in to Gage, though no official copy now remains in the Gage papers. When Boston was evacuated a year later, the owner of the surviving copy forgot it. It was found by the Americans and promptly "printed for the information and amusement of the curious."

The narrative begins by stating quite specifically Gage's reason for this secret mission: "he expected to have occasion to march troops through that country the ensuing Spring." The spies had hardly started when the general found he was going to have even more occasion. An unsigned report of February 24, 1775, warned him that if his troops attempted "to penetrate into the Country," Worcester, Leicester, Plymouth, and Marblehead would turn out fifteen thousand minutemen. The rebels already had thirty-eight field guns, most of them at Worcester, others at Salem and Concord; and additional military stores were being sent to Worcester and Concord.

The two officers took with them Captain Brown's soldier servant, who would in the modern British Army be described as a "batman." All three disguised themselves "like countrymen, in brown cloaths and reddish handkerchiefs round our necks." Leaving Boston by way of Charlestown, they passed Cambridge, "a pretty town, with a college built of brick," and reached Watertown without being suspected. They paused for dinner at Jonathan Brewer's tavern, just over the Watertown-Waltham boundary. They could hardly have selected a worse place, for not only was the landlord an ardent Whig but he would, a year later, be commanding troops at Bunker Hill.

The two officers dined together, while Captain Brown's man

went to the kitchen with the servants. Brown and De Bernière were served by a young Negro woman, who was "very civil," but who, as the uneasy secret agents presently noted, "began to eye us very attentively." In their effort to appear wholly at ease, they tried to strike up a conversation with her. This, they remarked, was "a very fine country."

"So it is," replied the girl, "and we have got brave fellows to defend it, and if you go up any higher you will find it so."

Since Gage had told them to try to pass for surveyors, the two officers had, with an apparently casual indifference, let some rough notes for a map be seen. The Negro girl, far too bright to be thus deceived, went straight back to the kitchen, where she announced her suspicions. Captain Brown's servant, John, hearing her, warned his officers at once.

"This disconcerted us a good deal," says De Bernière, "and we imagined she knew us from our papers which we took out before her." Hastily the two resolved not to spend the night at the inn as they had intended. They paid their bill and went on, interrogating John as soon as they were at a safe distance. Had he been with the servants? How much had that Negro girl guessed?

"He told us," says the ensign, "that she knew Capt. Brown very well, that she had seen him five years before at Boston, and she knew him to be an officer, and that she was sure I was one also, and told John that he was a regular—he denied it; but she said she knew our errant was to make a plan of the country; that she had seen the river and road through Charles-town on the paper; she also advised him to tell us not to go any higher, for if we did we should meet with very bad usage."

Disturbed by this inauspicious beginning, the three spies held a council of war. Temporarily, the rigid caste lines of eight-eenth-century military Britons were beginning to break down. "John" would soon be eating at the same board with the two officers. It was agreed "that if we went back we should appear very foolish, as we had a great number of enemies in town, be-cause the General had chose to employ us in preference to them; it was absolutely necessary to push on to Worcester, and run all risks rather than go back until we were forced."

It is hardly necessary to comment on Gage's folly in letting this secret mission be known to a "great number," in a town where Paul Revere, William Dawes and other patriot agents had long been watching every British move. To make matters worse, Brown, in leaving Boston, had been incautious enough to walk past a sentry from his own regiment. The soldier could hardly fail to draw conclusions (and gossip about them), when he saw a captain of the 52nd pass his post in the rough clothes of a laborer.

Soon after leaving the tavern—was it really an accident?—they encountered a "country fellow" and another man who looked like a deserter from Gage's army. These men seemed unnaturally eager to "join company." Going to Worcester? By a strange coincidence, the dubious pair "were going our way." This would never do. The importunate fellow travelers may have been nothing but what they seemed to be, for American colonists had long since lost any British reserve their ancestors may once have possessed; and, since strangers were none too common, colonists liked to talk with them. But, however unsuspicious these obtrusively friendly individuals may really have been—at least to begin with—they would not long have remained so if the British agents had begun to draw military maps. The spies shook off their undesired acquaintances by stopping at the Golden Ball Tavern, in Weston, kept by the notorious Tory, Captain Isaac Jones.

Gage does not seem to have briefed his agents properly before starting. They should have had some idea where to look for sympathizers along the way and some means of identifying themselves. In sending out later agents, Gage went to the opposite extreme, providing so much identification for his spies to use in Tory houses, that there would have been no possible question of their guilt had the patriots caught them.

Recognizing with relief that Jones was not inquisitive, the two officers resolved to stay the night, asked for a fire, and ordered coffee. This was the period of eighteenth-century British coffeehouses, and it is just possible they really did want coffee. They knew well enough, however, that with the Boston Tea Party (December 16, 1773) only fourteen months in the past, no patriotic American was drinking tea. To ask for it openly would have been courting trouble in many a Yankee inn, but not in this one. Very quietly the landlord volunteered information: "We might have what we pleased, either tea or coffee." It was a not uncommon recognition signal, quite unofficial, but not to be mistaken. Tories had to be careful to whom they made such an offer; but Jones probably had no doubt at all that he was speaking to British officers.

"We immediately found out with whom we were, and were not a little pleased to find, on some conversation, that he was friendly to government." Having got into trouble at one inn and out of it at another, and realizing that they needed to know more of what lay ahead, they asked their host "for the inns that were on the road between his house and Worcester." Jones told them to go to Buckminster's Tavern in Framingham, on the old Boston-Worcester road, and to the house of another Jones, in Worcester. The gentlemen would be safe enough under their Tory roofs.

The next day was "very rainy and a kind of frost"—in other words, a Massachusetts February. Consequently the road was so nearly deserted that the spies could take their time about sketching a defile, after which they went on to Buckminster's. There seemed no danger of detection and, says Ensign De Bernière, "we felt very happy, and Brown, I, and our man John, made a very hearty supper; for we always treated him as our companion, since our adventure with the black woman." It had dawned on them at last that genuine colonials, traveling afoot, would not be accompanied by a batman.

They reached Worcester, with no cause for uneasiness except a chance meeting with two men who looked like British deserters. There was danger that, if they really were deserters, they might recognize the officers; but nothing happened; and the spies, pausing only to sketch a "pass" about four miles from the city, came safely into Worcester, where they put up at the inn of the other Jones.

No one in Worcester paid any attention to them, but it was evident that the worried innkeeper was not exactly glad to see them, knowing very well the risks he was running in receiving such guests in such a center of rebellion. "He seemed a little sour, but it wore off by degrees."

With breakfast came the usual code. Their host had made no request for identification; but when the visitors asked what there was for breakfast, the Tory reply was at once given: "Tea or anything else." It was "an open confession what he was." But his guests were careful to involve the innkeeper as little as possible. They were sure he knew what they were; and, if so, he could have no doubt what they were doing; but the prudent Tory asked no questions, and his equally prudent guests vouchsafed no information.

As it was Sunday, they dared not leave their lodging, fearing that anyone walking the streets during church services would be arrested and examined. Prudently, they kept out of sight till sunset, the end of the Puritan Sabbath, after which, secure in the early February dusk, they walked freely about the town, seeing what they could see, then out on the hills, sketching whatever they wished and returning safely to their lodgings. It was presumably either Brown or De Bernière who made the plans for a camp and fortifications on Chandler's Hill, outside Worcester, which were found after the British evacuated Boston.

Presently the landlord announced that two gentlemen wished to speak with the travelers. Who were the gentlemen? The landlord was noncommittal. But he was sure his guests "wou'd be safe in their company." The intelligence officers took a cautious attitude. Their callers might be genuine Tories. On the other hand, they might be *provocateurs*.

Hastily assuming a casual attitude, the spies replied that of course they were safe. They "did not doubt that." Why shouldn't they be safe? After all, they were just "two gentlemen who traveled merely to see the country." There is no evidence that anybody winked, and Jones seems to have maintained a perfectly straight face.

Though it is doubtful whether anybody was deceiving anybody in the remotest degree, the two spies declined to see their uninvited visitors, who, after about an hour, went away. In view of Jones's willingness to vouch for them, they were almost certainly local Tories, eager for a chat with the king's officers, perhaps ready to give some military intelligence. But if they had information, it would be easy for them to send it directly to General Gage, and it was too risky for the spies to consort with known Tories. It was dangerous enough for them to be lodging with Jones.

The landlord, not offended and not at all deceived, chatted, talked politics, helped drink a bottle of wine, and explained, with a knowing air, that "none but a few friends to government" knew of the officers' presence. Again the pair feigned a calm they were far from feeling: "We said it was very indifferent to us whether they did or not, tho' we thought very differently."

By the time they had secured their information and made their sketches, too many people were showing an interest in them. Clearly, they had "staid long enough in that town." At daybreak they started back for Framingham, where they wanted to make a few additional observations, since Gage was likely to move his troops that way. They took the precaution of carrying some roast beef and brandy ("very necessary on a long march"), so that there would be no need of stopping for meals at farmhouses, "where perhaps they might be too inquisitive."

Beyond Shrewsbury, just east of Worcester, something happened that ought to have put them on their guard. They had had no real trouble so far, and since leaving Worcester had been "unobserved by any one." Then, as De Bernière describes the incident: "We were overtaken by a horseman, who examined us very attentively, and especially me, whom he looked at from head to foot as if he wanted to know me again; after he had taken his observations he rode off pretty hard and took the Marlborough road, but by good luck we took the Framingham road again to be more perfect in it, as we thought it would be the one made use of." The British spies did not guess their danger, for they had not recognized the inquisitive horseman, who—though he ought to have been more subtle in examining them—was a formidable antagonist.

The patriot Committee of Correspondence, far more alert than either the officers or their host realized, already knew strangers had been at Jones's tavern, and had strong suspicions of their motive for this midwinter visit. The pretense of being surveyors was hardly convincing. Road surveys, at best infrequent in colonial Massachusetts, were not likely to be conducted at such a season.

Why did these two strangers, with no discoverable business, visit Worcester just as it was becoming a munitions center? The committee began to wish it knew a little more about them, and Captain Timothy Bigelow, commanding Worcester's minuteman company, went out to see. Though he was only the town blacksmith, Bigelow was a first-rate officer, the discipline of whose company later roused enthusiasm from the exacting General Washington himself. After seeing the spies a few miles from Marlboro and walking in that direction, he rode ahead to prepare a reception for them. It was pure luck that the two British officers turned off toward Framingham and thus evaded him. Though they had noticed him looking them over, they were not, as yet, fully alarmed.

Their next fright came when, reaching Colonel Joseph Buckminster's inn at Framingham about six o'clock, they found the local militia at drill. Presently the troops moved toward the inn and continued drilling under the window of the worried spies, who "did not feel very easy at seeing such a number so near"; but, in the end, this turned out to be mere chance.

Brown and De Bernière listened gravely to an address by the local commander to his men, after which the company, dismissed, came tumbling into the barroom and drank till nine o'clock, quite unaware that two regular army officers had been watching them all the time.

Next day, the spies were back in Weston, at the Golden Ball Tavern, where they "received several hints from the family not to attempt to go any more into the country." They were not satisfied, however, with their knowledge of the "Sudbury road" —the northern road between Boston and Worcester. After all, their general might wish to use that road, too. He might even move in two columns, using both roads. The captain and the ensign had been sent out to make a road report and they meant it to be both full and accurate.

Disregarding warnings, therefore, they started back toward Worcester along the upper road next morning, to reconnoiter as far as the point where they had turned off for Framingham, two days earlier. They either knew or soon found out that Bigelow had preceded them to Marlboro; and, aware there might be difficulty, they collected all their sketches and started the batman, John, off to Gage's headquarters with them. If the officers were caught and searched now, they would have nothing incriminating on them.

Meantime, though the hunt for them was up, the spies had no immediate trouble. Passing through Sudbury, they took time to note the condition of the causeway and the high ground commanding it, beyond Sudbury River. Since it was snowing hard, they were undisturbed until, about three miles east of Marlboro, another horseman caught up with them and paused to chat.

Where did they come from? Weston.

Did they live there? No.

Well, then, where did they live?

"At Boston." (Which was true.)

They now realized, in desperation, that there was no way of getting rid of the man until they satisfied him. Refusal to answer apparently innocent questions would merely add to suspicion. There was still just a chance that the questions were as innocently casual as they appeared. Rural New Englanders were an inquisitive breed.

Where were they going?

"To Marlborough, to see a friend." (This also had the merit of truth.)

Were they in the army?

They were in fact both old infantrymen, veterans of many a route march, and the swing of an old infantryman's shoulders on a long march is unmistakable. Had this betrayed them? "A good deal alarmed," they denied it.

After several more "rather impertinent questions," the stranger rode on to Marlboro. Though the two worried "surveyors" guessed that he must be going "to give them intelligence there of our coming," the only thing they could do was to walk straight ahead, looking as innocent as possible. To turn around in the middle of the countryside and start back would be a confession of guilt, and they could easily be overtaken. Probably the whole countryside between Weston and Marlboro had been alarmed by this time. Dismally they foot-slogged ahead through the driving snow, wondering what would happen when they reached Marlboro.

The town was all ready for them when they tramped in. Everyone seemed to be waiting. In a day of no telephones, it was a remarkable turnout. "The people came out of their houses (tho' it snowed and blew very hard) to look."

"Where are you going, master?" a baker asked Captain Brown.

"To see Mr. Barnes," replied the captain, briefly.

It did not help very much, since Barnes was a notorious king's man; but there was no use lying, since everyone could see where they turned in, and there was no place else to go. They were allowed to reach their destination undisturbed, for the Marlboro patriots meant to deal with them a little later. To Barnes, the Englishmen apologized "for taking the liberty to make use of his house," and at last admitted that they were "officers in disguise."

Barnes, in tones that must have been a trifle grim, "told us we need not be at the pains of telling him, that he knew our situation, that we were very well known (he was afraid) by the town's people." The popular mood was "very violent." Marlboro patriots had been hunting for the spies all through the cold night before.

Was there a tavern where they could be safe? Hardly. Where then? They "could be safe nowhere but in his house," and even that began to look like a rather thin hope.

Only now did Captain Brown and Ensign De Bernière realize what Timothy Bigelow had been doing. "We suspected, and indeed had every reason to believe, that the horseman that met us and took such particular notice of me, the morning we left Worcester," says the rueful ensign, "was the man who told them we should be at Marlborough the night before, but our taking the Framingham road when he had passed us, deceived

him." If Gage's intelligence in Worcester had been a little better organized, De Bernière would have known all about Bigelow—who was, in fact, described in the French-speaking
Concord spy's report, a few weeks later, as *"un grand chef"*
among the rebels. But that was too late to help the map-mak-
ing officers.

By this time, people were gathering in small groups throughout the town. Barnes asked anxiously who had spoken to them
as they entered Marlboro.

"A baker," said one officer.

Barnes was startled: "A very mischievous fellow." In fact,
at that very moment, "there was a British deserter at the baker's
house."

Captain Brown wanted to know the fellow's name. He could
use that, later.

"Swain," said Barnes. "He had been a drummer."

Captain Brown looked glum, for he "knew him too well."
Swain had deserted from Brown's own company a month before. He could not fail to recognize his captain and, as a deserter, could best protect himself by making trouble for Brown.

The officers asked Barnes anxiously, "if they did get us into
their hands, what would they do with us?" No one on a secret
mission can possibly keep that unpleasant subject from running through his mind every now and then. Barnes hesitated.
He did not really know, but he knew well enough it would be
something acutely unpleasant, and he also knew that whatever
happened to the spies was also likely to happen to the man who
harbored them. But he hesitated not an instant in protecting
the men who held his king's commission.

Just after this alarming conversation, Barnes was called out.
He came back more worried than ever. Dr. Samuel Curtis had
suddenly arrived for supper, entirely uninvited. Curtis was
selectman, town clerk, justice of the peace, and—this was the
sinister part—a member of the patriot Committee of Correspondence. He had not been inside Barnes's house for the last
two years. If he was forcing himself on the Tory at this particular moment, there could be only one reason. As the ensign put

it, he "came now for no other business than to see and betray us."

In a far from hospitable mood, Barnes went to talk with the intrusive physician. Barnes regretted: "He had company and could not have the pleasure of attending him that night." Curtis was strangely slow to take the hint. He did not go. First he "stared about the house." Was there anything revealing left lying about? A stranger's hat or cloak would prove nothing. Curtis knew that there was "company." He had been told so, without being invited to join them. He was probably hoping to find some article that could be identified as uniform. Failing in that, he chatted with Barnes's little daughter. (Children do, sometimes, unconsciously reveal military intelligence worth having.)

Who was with her father?

"She had asked her pappa," said the little girl, "but he told her it was not her business." The child's answer could not fail to add to the doctor's already aroused suspicions; but in the end he retired, discomfited. De Bernière gloomily assumed he went "to tell the rest of his crew." All this had happened within twenty minutes.

It was clear by this time that to remain would be dangerous both to themselves and to their host. The pair decided, however, to rest two or three hours before leaving, as they had walked sixteen miles that day through the worst kind of New England winter weather. First, they wanted food.

They were just sitting down to it when Barnes, who had disappeared, rejoined them. He had gone out to see what his servants could tell him and came back, very uneasy. The patriots were going "to attack us." There was no possible safety for the two officers anywhere in Marlboro that night.

The spies decided to set forth instantly, though, as De Bernière wrote later, "it snowed and blew as much as ever I see it in my life." Sneaking them out of the house by the stables, Barnes pointed out a "bye road," which would take them around Marlboro at a quarter mile distance. (A better-trained counterintelligence than the Marlboro patriots boasted would,

by this time, have had the house under surveillance, and all
roads, especially "bye roads," blocked.)

Deprived of their dinner, the Englishmen carried along some
bread, their beef and brandy being long since exhausted. As
soon as they got to the hills overlooking the causeway at Sudbury, they slipped into the woods (no use taking a chance of
discovery on the roads) and there "eat a bit of bread," instead
of the dinner they had missed. A little brandy would have
been opportune in the storm; but bread was all they had, and
the best they could do was to "eat a little snow to wash it
down."

When they started again, they had hardly gone more than a
hundred yards before a man emerged from a house.

"What do you think will become of you now?" he asked,
sepulchrally. The remark may have been a mere pleasantry, in
view of the weather, but it sounded menacing.

They now feared that a trap was waiting in Sudbury; and
their fear was heightened when, a quarter of a mile west of the
town, they met a group of horsemen, who opened out to right
and left of the road to let them through. It was nothing but
courtesy. No effort was made to stop them, but, says De Bernière, "our apprehensions made us interpret everything against
us." They reached the Golden Ball Tavern at Weston once
more, "after walking thirty-two miles between two o'clock and
half-after ten at night"—in other words, four miles an hour, the
very limit of a forced infantry march. They had done this,
"through a road that every step we sunk up to the ankles, and
it blowing and drifting snow all the way." Jones supplied a
bottle of mulled Madeira; and, thus fortified, they "slept as
sound as men could do, that were very much fatigued."

The moment they had breakfast next morning, they hurried
on to Boston. Jones had been careful to point out a road that
took them a quarter of a mile below Watertown, for, having
been recognized there on the way out, they wisely "did not
choose to go through that town."

As they came in sight of Boston, they met Generals Gage and
Haldimand, with their aides-de-camp, "walking out on the
neck." The generals did not recognize their own spies until

they revealed their identity—in public, which, of course, was all wrong. As they went on into the city, they noted with satisfaction that other officers did not recognize them either: "We besides met several officers of our acquaintance who did not know us." Their disguises had not deceived New Englanders. It was some comfort to fool their brothers in arms.

A few days later, when Barnes, their host at Marlboro, came to Boston, the spies learned how narrow their escape had been. They were fortunate to have lingered in his house no more than twenty minutes. The patriot Committee of Correspondence had quickly appeared to interview Barnes. Refusing to believe the mysterious travelers had gone, they had searched "from top to bottom, looked under the beds and in the cellars." Convinced at length that their prey had given them the slip, they had sent horsemen out on every road. De Bernière guessed that, "the weather being so very bad, they either did not overtake us, or missed us."

Barnes had tried to persuade the suspicious patriots that his visitors were not officers at all. They were relatives, just relatives of his wife's, on their way from Penobscot to Lancaster, Pennsylvania. If the patriots pursued toward Pennsylvania, they had a long, cold, snowy ride that profited nothing.

There is no formal record that Captain Brown's batman, John, got through with the maps and sketches safely. No maps that can be recognized as De Bernière's now remain among the Gage papers; but there are three good reasons for supposing that John "made it": (a) There is no American record of his capture; (b) De Bernière would hardly have failed to mention so great a disappointment; and (c) Isaac Thomas, the patriot printer of Boston and Worcester, himself saw, after the British evacuation, a military sketch of a Worcester hill which was probably made by these two officers.

Captain Brown and Ensign De Bernière had hardly returned to Boston when Gage decided they might be equally successful at Concord. Orders issued accordingly on March 20, 1775, less than a month before the fatal march to Lexington. Captain Brown and Ensign De Bernière were "to set out for Concord, and examine the road and situation of the town." They were also to get what information they could regarding the "quantity of artillery and provisions."

In disguise once more, probably about the same they had used on their Worcester journey, the two officers set off again, this time taking the precaution of going armed. Since army flintlocks would have been too conspicuous, they probably carried small pistols, which could be concealed in their garments. Since De Bernière remarks that "we were three and all well armed," they presumably took Brown's invaluable batman, John, with them again.

Perhaps with a view to avoiding suspicion, they did not follow the direct road, northwest to Lexington, but went in the opposite direction—to Roxbury, then through Brookline, and then to the village of Weston, which lies due south of Concord, avoiding Jonathan Brewer's tavern, between Waltham and Watertown, with its dangerously observant Negro waitress. Only then did they strike north to Concord, making the trip "without any kind of insult being offered us."

The village of Concord, they duly noted, "lies between hills that command it entirely." The river had two bridges. In summer it would be "pretty dry"—in other words, probably fordable, a matter of interest to infantry commanders. The houses were scattered in small groups. Houses in small groups can become formidable strong points; though when the war broke out, there was no house-to-house fighting in either Concord or Lexington, only some casual firing from windows and rather savage British retaliation.

There were already patriotic troops on duty in the village: "They fired their morning gun, and mounted a guard of ten men at night." Clearly, these men were guarding colonial stores.

The spies' local contact man was the Tory, Daniel Bliss, a Harvard graduate of the Class of 1760. Though it would have been easy to find out exactly where his house was before they left Boston, they had been careless enough to neglect doing so and now had to ask their way, forgetting that sharp patriot eyes were watching all strangers.

The two officers had hardly reached the Bliss home when the

woman who had directed them came in, weeping. She had been warned to leave Concord. Otherwise she would be tarred and feathered "for directing Tories on their road." Bliss gave them dinner. Presently a threat reached him, too. "They would not let him go out of town alive that morning."

It was disquietingly evident that the patriots were very much on the alert. The disguised officers had met with no difficulty, yet the town seemed to know all about them. It was time to get out.

Dangerous as their position now appeared, Brown and De Bernière paused long enough to get a fair idea of the supplies the Provincial Congress had stored in Concord. The Bliss home was a good place from which to do so, as flour for the rebel troops was being ground only two hundred yards away and a harness shop nearly as close was making artillery harness, cartridge boxes and accouterments. The two spies learned that the stores included flour, fish, salt and rice, and that there was "a magazine of powder and cartridges." Bliss assured them that the patriots would fight; and, as his patriot brother, Thomas Bliss, passed them, said: "There goes a man who will fight you in blood up to his knees." The patriots' Joint Committee of Safety and Supplies had, on February 13, ordered four brass field guns and two cohorns (mortars) sent to Concord. The British officers were able to ascertain that the guns had already arrived.

The report on the artillery is so detailed that one or both of the British officers must actually have seen it. The guns "were mounted but in so bad a manner that they could not elevate them more than they were, that is, they were fixed to one elevation." There were also ten iron cannon "kept in a house in town." The brass artillery, which would suffer less from the weather, was hidden "in some place behind the town, in a wood."

Since Bliss's life was threatened—he was later proscribed and had to leave New England forever—he decided to go back to Boston with the officers. Crossing the river, they went on to Lexington, observing the road that the redcoats would soon be following. "The road continued very open and good for six miles, the next five a little inclosed, (there is one very bad place in these five miles) the road good to Lexington. You then come to Menotomy [modern Arlington], the road still good; a pond or lake at Menotomy. You then leave Cambridge on your right, and fall into the main road a little below Cambridge, and so to Charlestown; the road is very good almost all the way."

On April 19, 1775, Ensign De Bernière was guiding Lieutenant Colonel Francis Smith's column along those very roads, on the march to Lexington and Concord. Bliss was safe in Boston, as commissary of the British forces.

IV

★　★　★

★

The Adventures of John Howe

CAPTAIN BROWN and Ensign De Bernière had scarcely finished
mapping the roads to Worcester when Doctor Church and other
British spies began to report that the patriots were still collecting large military stores. Toward the end of March, 1775, it became clear that, though Concord was thoroughly covered by
British agents, there would have to be more espionage in
Worcester; and, since the American munitions were being
transported through Watertown and Weston, spies would have
to visit those villages, too.

A fortnight before the fights at Lexington and Concord, on
April 5, 1775, General Gage started off Lieutenant Colonel
Francis Smith, 10th Foot, and an assistant named John Howe,
both in disguise, for a second investigation at Worcester. It is
characteristic of the fate of secret agents that John Howe, who
succeeded brilliantly, is totally forgotten; whereas Lieutenant
Colonel Smith, by getting himself soundly defeated at Concord
a few days later, became a general and earned a permanent
place in history. Who or what John Howe was, is not clear.
He may have been the "John" who accompanied Brown and
De Bernière; and he was attached to the British Army in Boston, though he was not an officer and is never referred to as

an ordinary enlisted man. Whoever he was, John Howe made such a reputation in the secret service that, nearly forty years later, as the War of 1812 approached, the British sent him back to the United States, on another secret mission.

Before leaving Boston, the two British spies dressed as a pair of wandering laborers, with leather breeches, gray coats, "blue mixed" stockings, and handkerchiefs knotted about their throats. Each carried his luggage in the customary bundle, tied up in a homemade handkerchief. Each also carried the usual foot traveler's stick, which could be thrust through the knots of the handkerchief, so that the wayfarer's bundle could be carried on his shoulder.

Starting before breakfast when no one was about—the colonel can hardly have wished the 10th Foot to behold him in these undignified habiliments—they trudged through Cambridge to Watertown, where Lieutenant Colonel Francis Smith's career as a secret agent came to a swift and humiliating close. After six miles on empty stomachs, the two spies paused for breakfast at a Watertown tavern, apparently the one where Captain Brown and Ensign De Bernière had been spotted. No one had warned them against the watchful Negro maid who had voiced her suspicion of the first spies.

Lieutenant Colonel Smith, in an effort to keep up his pose as a rural laborer, presently inquired where they could find employment. The girl's reply was so completely unexpected that, says Howe, it "about wound up our breakfast." The spirit of equality was abroad and the maid had no reverence for rank.

"Smith," said she bluntly, "you will find employment enough for you and all General Gage's men in a few months."

The girl must have enjoyed the impression she created. "Smith appeared thunderstruck," his companion records, "and my feelings were of the keenest kind."

The alarmed pair could hardly flee instantly; but, when their host came round to inquire how their breakfast "suited," one chagrined officer replied: "Very well, but you have got a saucy wench there."

The landlord, trying to smooth matters over, agreed that the girl was indeed a saucy creature, but "she had been living in

Boston, and had got acquainted with a great many British officers and soldiers." Was it accident or sly malice that made him add, eying their costume: "and might take you to be some of them"? Hastily paying their bill, Smith and Howe departed, followed by the landlord's suggestion that they might "find work up the road."

Up the road the crestfallen pair hurried, as fast as they could go, but not in quest of work. All they wanted was to put as much space as possible between themselves and that tavern. As soon as they were out of sight, the two climbed one of the ever-present New England stone walls and settled down behind it to discuss matters. Since they agreed it was useless for Smith to continue, he handed over to Howe their "journal book" (the kind of written record no secret agent should ever carry with him!), a pencil, ten guineas, and letters to various Tories (which, if discovered, would convict the bearer and all the addressees, of espionage). As he did so, Lieutenant Colonel Smith uncharitably remarked that, "if he came out with his regiment that road, he would kill that wench."

Then, after promising Howe a commission if he came back alive, Lieutenant Colonel Smith, who was very fat, made a regrettably undignified departure, "running through the barberry bushes to keep out of sight of the road."

Howe went on toward Waltham, alone, making a decorous pretense of asking for work, but taking good care not to get any. As he made inquiries, he was careful to remark that he was a gunsmith by trade, for the shrewd fellow knew there was no surer way of learning about the rebels' stores of small arms. At Waltham, just beyond Watertown, a farmer directed him to Springfield, where "they were in want of hands to work at that business." Howe had better hurry: "They were in want of guns, for they meant to be ready for them."

The espionage business was looking up. Here was information as to rebel armament; location of an arms factory; a note on its activity; evidence that the rebels expected the British to move far to the west against them (a good reason why General Gage should move elsewhere—northwest against Concord); and a definite statement, probably correct, of enemy intentions.

The rebels meant "to be ready," which meant that they would fight.

Howe showed his cleverness a moment later, when the talkative farmer asked if he didn't want a drink. Spirits, perhaps? No, no, said Howe, carefully keeping up his pose as a wandering New Englander. He would like a glass of "New England and molasses." This meant rum and molasses, a beverage much enjoyed by Yankees of heroic mold. "I well knew that to be a Yankee drink," says Howe, who was always careful not to give himself away on the small matters that get you hanged.

Going on, he presently came to a causeway, which he stopped to study, to see if it would carry artillery. A Negro, setting traps, asked what he was looking for. The question seemed to be mere friendliness, not suspicion. Howe, as usual, had an answer all ready—he was trying to find sweet flag, a swamp iris whose root was a specific for stomach-ache. Offering to take him where the plant grew, the trapper chanced to walk by a large buttonwood and, glancing at it, casually remarked that "the people were going to cut it down to stop the regulars from crossing with their cannon."

This was just the kind of thing Howe had been sent out to learn: (a) There would be resistance near Waltham; (b) passage of artillery and transport could be easily blocked; (c) British engineers would need plenty of axes to clear the way.

Since it is a mistake to ask too many questions, Howe ventured only one more: How would the people know when the regulars were coming?

"They had men all the time in Cambridge and Charleston looking out"—another bit of information General Gage would be glad to have.

The two parted amicably.

Phenomenal luck of this sort could not long continue—nor did it. The Negro had directed the thirsty spy to two taverns, one "by Weston meeting house," the other "half a mile above." The first, he said, "was kept by Mr. Joel Smith, a good tavern and a good liberty man; the other was kept by Capt. Isaac Jones, a wicked Tory, where a great many British officers go from Boston." (Innkeepers were often militia officers.) The

British officers were probably just in innocent search of dinners that would be a relief from an army mess, but people were already beginning to watch suspiciously everything they did.

Though Howe knew better than to say so, he already knew all about that loyal subject of King George, Captain Isaac Jones. He had in his pocket a letter to the "wicked Tory" from General Gage himself, for Jones had already helped Brown and De Bernière.

Howe knew, however, that the right place for him was not in this Tory household. Far safer to make straight to the tavern of a "good liberty man" like Joel Smith; and to the hospitable door of that irreproachable patriot the British spy ostentatiously proceeded. If he later wanted to drop in at the Tory captain's tavern—well, many a thirsty man, after walking half a mile from Smith's tavern, naturally stopped for a second drink at Jones's.

By what at first seemed extraordinarily bad luck, Howe walked up to the tavern of the hundred-per-cent patriot, Smith, just as two teamsters were "tackling" [harnessing] their teams. The teamsters, too, were hundred-per-centers. It is reasonably clear that they had driven their loads out from Boston that morning, had paused for a mid-day tavern meal, and were now ready to go on. They had heard stories, along the way, about two suspicious travelers at Watertown; and they had their doubts as soon as they set eyes on John Howe. They accused him only of being British, not of being a spy, though the two were, outside of Boston in early 1775, pretty nearly the same thing. Curiously enough, they did so not because of his accent, but because he "looked like them rascals they seen in Boston."

To disarm suspicion, Howe hastily called for more rum and molasses, a mixture which no Englishman, then or since, has ever been known to drink. One of the still suspicious teamsters followed him into the tavern, however, to warn the landlord that the stranger was a spy. To offset this, Howe prattled glibly about gunsmithing in Springfield, where all these rebels must know small arms were being made. If anyone challenged his claim to be a gunsmith, he could easily demonstrate his skill. He explained that he needed work, any kind of work, to get a little ready money.

This sounded better in Yankee ears. A British spy would assuredly be well supplied with British gold. (Howe was, but he knew better than to admit it.) Wayfarers looking for temporary jobs were common enough. To Howe's joy, the patriots themselves sent him straight to the tavern of Captain Isaac Jones, where, they said, he would be likely to find work—thereby providing the very excuse he needed for visiting this known Tory. It was a relief to see that he had apparently quieted the teamsters.

Little did the spy realize that the local patriots could play a few tricks, too. If this fellow really was a British agent, he would linger at the local Tory's house. That was why they sent him there. Meantime, the teamsters stopped telling the spy they suspected him (which had been the wrong thing from the start) and were getting ready to spread the news about Howe where it might do some good. If the suspicious stranger failed to guess that trouble was brewing, all the better!

Handing Jones his letter from General Gage, Howe told the Tory his mission and what had happened at the other tavern, down the road. Either because he was shrewder than Howe or because he knew the local situation better, Captain Jones took no chances and thereby, within a very short time, saved himself from a coat of tar and feathers. He sent his hired man to take this dangerous visitor away from the tavern instantly, to a remote house, belonging to a thoroughgoing loyalist named Wheaton, whom Jones knew he could trust. When the hired man told Wheaton frankly that Howe was a British agent, the hospitable Tory promptly provided a private room, candles, paper and brandy—no necessity now to pose as an enthusiast for "New England and molasses."

Howe settled quietly down to write some notes. He had unquestionably collected essential elements of information that would interest General Gage; but it was all the kind of information he could easily have carried in his head. To write it down was simple madness, which could easily have hanged him.

Meantime, news that the Negro waitress at Watertown had

recognized a British officer in disguise had spread. Since the teamsters had heard all about it on their way out, various patriotic secret committeemen had probably heard about it, too. No one knew that Lieutenant Colonel Smith had skulked through the barberry bushes back to Boston. People were mistakenly looking for two spies, but one spy would do.

Before long, thirty angry patriots were clamoring at Jones's tavern. He had British spies in his house, they told him. Somewhere in the background the teamsters and Joel Smith, patriot keeper of the first tavern, must have chuckled. Jones would really be caught with a spy this time, for they themselves had sent the spy.

Blandly, Captain Jones invited the inquirers to search his house. (Few experiences are more agreeable than watching the other side's counterintelligence frantically searching where there is positively nothing to find.) Taken aback by their failure, the patriots then interrogated Jones's Negro woman.

Were there strangers or Englishmen in the house?

The girl hardly thought so.

Had there been any?

One or two gentlemen had dined upstairs.

Where had they gone?

To Jericho Swamp, two miles away.

Suspicion began to die down. Captain Jones helped it die, with a free bottle of spirits.

Undisturbed by this excitement and safe at the Wheaton house, Howe spent a few quiet hours; added to his journal data, thoughtfully supplied by Captain Jones, about the local militia; dined; was introduced to the Wheaton daughters as "a British officer in disguise"; played cards with the Misses Wheaton; and with them drank "a dish of tea," a beverage against which this household had no prejudice.

Once more the patriots tried a trick. Though they had ostentatiously left the Tory tavern after searching it, they had been secretly keeping it under observation all the time, hoping to entrap Howe, should he venture to return. Of all this, Isaac Jones was well aware. While the patriots were lurking about, awaiting Howe's return, the hired man quietly guided him from Wheaton's, along a back road, to the main Worcester road. They forded the Sudbury River some miles from Framingham, and went on to Marlboro, traveling along back roads or perhaps even cross-country.

Waking Barnes, the Marlboro Tory, they gave him two letters, one that General Gage had given Howe, one that Jones had given his hired man. Convinced of their good faith, Barnes provided liquid and other refreshment. News of the spy scare at Watertown had, he said, preceded them, but was not believed by the local people. With this news the hired man departed, since it was dangerous for any member of a Tory household to be conspicuously absent. The sooner he was back at his usual duties, the better it would be. Howe got to bed about four o'clock in the morning.

Barnes waked him at nine with bad news. During their night journey, Howe and Captain Jones's hired man had been seen by a woman, "up with a sick child." Leaping—in that atmosphere of general suspicion—to the correct conclusion that these were spies, she had watched long enough to see that they went in the direction of Worcester. Barnes, himself unsuspected, had hung about the local tavern while his secret guest was sleeping, and had picked up this word of approaching danger. To the tavern he again promptly departed, to see if there was any real "stir about the spies," and what ought to be done if there was.

During daylight, Howe could do nothing but stay in the house and keep away from windows. About four in the afternoon, his host came back from the tavern to say that the spy scare had "turned out to be Negro stories," not generally believed. At eight o'clock Howe started for Worcester, now only about fifteen miles away, riding Barnes's horse and surveying roads and bridges as well as he could in the darkness. The fact that Gage wanted the road survey by Brown and De Bernière confirmed shows plainly that he still contemplated a raid on Worcester. Howe had specifically asked his host "what he thought of an army coming from Boston to Worcester."

At Worcester, an unnamed Tory, another link in Gage's chain, received him, after examining letters from Barnes and the general. Hidden in a private room all day, Howe was given further information as to local militia strength and local munition stores and, after dark, personally visited the unguarded American magazine. Without any trouble, his well-informed Tory host took him to "the place where I could break in" and showed him "two old wells hard by," into which British raiders could dump the flour and gunpowder. Similar plans had been made to destroy military supplies at Concord, though they were not fully carried out when the redcoats at last got their hands on the patriots' munitions there.

Howe also inquired into the morale of patriot forces in Worcester and near it. His host, exuberantly optimistic, averred "he did not think a man dare lift a gun to oppose the regulars." It was nearly the worst forecast on record!

No wishful thinking of this sort for John Howe. He had already seen enough to know better. Pledging his host to secrecy, Howe "told him if General Gage sent five thousand troops, with a train of artillery, from Boston to Worcester, they would never one of them get back." There was some exaggeration in this. Gage sent only eight hundred men to Lexington and Concord, and most of them got back to Boston alive— though very much the worse for wear and only after a reserve force with artillery had been sent to their rescue. The events of April 19, 1775, showed what would have happened on the longer, harder march to Worcester, which Gage was wise enough never to attempt. After Lexington and Concord, his regulars dared not leave Boston.

The Tory was greatly cast down at what his guest told him. If that was so, he said, "we His Majesty's friends, are in a bad situation"—which, in the end, proved true.

In the darkness, Howe "collected up" his papers and started back from Worcester to Squire Barnes at Marlboro. With too much time to think, he himself began to feel depressed as he rode along, like many another agent on a desperate mission: "I was now fifty miles from Boston, and in danger of being captured every moment. The night was long and dismal, I often wished this night that I had never undertaken the business of a spy." But luck rode with him: "Nothing particular took place during the night," except an unseasonably heavy April snow-fall.

Reaching Marlboro near dawn, he drew rein for the second time at Barnes's door, ate a warm breakfast, and drank some hot "sling" (toddy with grated nutmeg). He took the precaution of turning his papers over to Barnes (who presumably had a safe place to hide them) and went to bed. The cautious Tory went off again to the tavern to "see if he could make any discoveries" and came back about one o'clock with word "that all was safe; but it would not be best for me to tarry in his house over night."

After dinner, Howe took over his papers again. It was an egregious piece of folly. Long before this, they should have been on their way to Gage, in the hands of some safe courier, unsuspected, well known to everybody, able to travel openly, and with some good reason for visiting Boston. There, through a cut-out, they could have been passed on to Gage safely and easily. Instead of that, Howe foolishly added to his notes a dangerous and minute "account of the militia and ammunition from there to Weston, and from this place [Marlboro] to Worcester." Barnes had combed out all this information for Gage, while Howe had been visiting Worcester.

Unobtrusively, from an attic window (darkened, let us hope!) Barnes pointed out a safe route to Concord, "across the lots and the road." Then, retiring to a secluded room, they chatted about the chances that British troops could reach Worcester. It was a matter very much on both their minds and also on General Gage's. A few days later, it was the first question he asked his returning spy.

About eight o'clock that night, the hour when Howe had planned to start, there was a knocking at the front door. As Barnes rose to answer it, he told the spy to slip out the chamber window, climb down a shed roof, head for a neighboring swamp, and thence make his way to Concord, if he heard anything suspicious at the door.

A moment after his host had gone downstairs, Howe heard a strange voice saying: "Esq, we have come to search your house for spies."

Then he heard Barnes: "I am willing."

That was quite enough for the anxious man, listening above. Up went the chamber window. Out into six inches of snow he crawled, slipped, and fell from the roof to the ground, flat on his back. The amateur spy catchers, thundering on the front door, had never thought of the elementary precaution of surrounding the house first. Neither do any of them seem, later, to have noticed the trail Howe left in the snow; there is no mention of any pursuit, after the searchers had satisfied themselves there was no stranger in the house.

As he reached the swamp, Howe, looking back at Barnes's house, saw "lights dodging at every window" and heard "horses' feet in the road, as if great numbers were collecting at the Esq's house"—providentially obscuring the fugitive's footprints.

Knocking at a strange house, he found it occupied by a Negro and his wife, was invited to stay the night, explained that his business was urgent—as, indeed, it was—offered silver if they would put him on the road to Concord. The Negro not unnaturally inquired what business could possibly be urgent enough to force anyone through such a night afoot. Howe revived the good old lie that had served so well a few days earlier. He had to get to Concord. He was "going to make guns to kill the regulars" and ventured the opinion "they would be out of Boston in a few weeks." (They were out nine days later.)

The Negro hesitated. The spy story had now grown into a soldier story. The woman said she heard there had been a number of regulars around Squire Barnes's house a day or two earlier. Howe grasped the awkward situation at once. Was Squire Barnes a Tory? Indeed he was! Then, said Howe venomously, "I hoped they would catch him and hang him."

As this sounded suitably disloyal to George III, the Negro guide set out with him, borrowed a canoe from another Negro at the Concord River, paddled his passenger safely across, and offered to go a little farther for a little more money. Eventually —it must have been nearly midnight—they came to a tavern where the Negro said they could buy rum. They knocked, entered, had some brandy instead, and spent the night there. In the morning, Howe saw the village of Concord at a little distance. Somebody named Wetherly went to Concord with him and introduced him as a gunsmith. A Major Buttrick and other gentlemen greeted him as "the very man they wanted to see," found a shop for him, and brought him several gunlocks, which he "repaired with neatness and dispatch, considering the tools I had to work with." It was all very convincing.

After dinner, his confiding American friends took the British secret agent to the Concord magazine of military stores, thus enabling Howe for the second time to make a direct examination of a patriot munitions dump. Eager for his expert opinion, they took him inside to see the stores of small arms, ammunition and flour. General Gage must have found Howe's oral report, a few days later, a useful check on the reports he had already received from his regular Concord spies on these same munitions.

Finally getting away from the gullible Concord patriots, on the plea that he must go "down East" to fetch his own gunsmith's tools, Howe took shelter with a Tory named Gove, at Lincoln, only a few miles away, and wrote out the rest of his notes. He found that his new benefactor had been in the vicinity of Barnes's house during the patriots' raid and learned for the first time of the tar and feathers the patriots had prepared. Gove sheltered him in an outhouse that night, gave him a final report next morning on a prospective new armory in Concord and, after dark, personally drove him to Charlestown. By two o'clock he was across the Charles River and safe in his own quarters in Boston.

Putting on his British uniform and starting down the street next morning, the triumphant spy met Lieutenant Colonel Smith, who greeted him with, "How do you do, John? We heard you broke your neck jumping out of Barnes' chamber window." (The speed with which this news reached Boston points to another intelligence net, serving Gage in Worcester.) Going with Smith to report to Gage, Howe turned in his papers, was promised a bonus of fifty guineas, and was given one guinea immediately, with the injunction, "Take that, John, and go and get some liquor, you are not half drunk enough for officers' company."

By the time he got back to the commanding general's headquarters, as ordered, at eleven o'clock, a group of senior officers
had gathered to listen to him. Asked whether British troops
could reach Worcester, he told Gage ten thousand men could
not do it—which was, incidentally, pure nonsense, but the kind
of overestimate of enemy strength to which secret agents are
prone.

Upon this, Lieutenant Colonel Smith burst out: "Howe has
been scared by the old women."

It gave a splendid opening to Major John Pitcairn, of the
Royal Marines, who would soon be marching with Smith to
Lexington and who would die at Bunker Hill. He turned to
Howe.

"Not by a black wench, John," said Major Pitcairn.

There was a roar of laughter from the assembled officers.

V

* * *

*

The Paul Revere Gang

HOWEVER ACTIVE British espionage may have been, the patriots usually knew nearly as much about the British as Gage and his staff knew about the patriots. Ever since the autumn of 1774 (and probably earlier), there had been an organized and active American intelligence service in Boston, which continued its work until the British evacuation in March of 1776, though the personnel inevitably changed, as various members had to flee. The American espionage network began as one of those volunteer groups of amateur secret agents that spring up naturally in invaded countries, very like the resistance groups that proved so useful to the Allies in World War II.

This first known American intelligence net was set up by Paul Revere and about thirty others, chiefly "mechanics," whose purpose, as Revere himself reports, was "watching the movements of the British soldiers, and gaining every intelligence of the movements of the Tories." As the fateful spring of 1775 drew on, they "frequently took turns, two and two, to watch the soldiers, by patrolling the streets all night."

The patriotic plotters had the advantages such improvised local spy systems always have. They needed no elaborate cover to explain their presence in Boston, being all well-known citizens, established businessmen or tradesmen. Revere himself was a distinguished craftsman, whose exquisite silver was already in many of the better New England homes. They had friends, whose houses could give shelter and concealment in emergencies. They knew the byways of the city better than any red-coated patrols.

That so many of Revere's fellow "mechanics" took so many very long walks at night should have aroused suspicion; but such British counterintelligence service as existed failed to note what was happening; and, anyhow, all this quiet reconnoissance was divided among thirty-odd men, working in pairs. The same men were not likely to be out reconnoitering oftener than once a fortnight, so that their nocturnal rambles could be made to appear suitably casual.

Unfortunately, the group had the faults—as well as the advantages and enthusiasms—of amateur secret agents. The one fundamental rule in all such organizations is that the various agents must not know one another; but the eager Bostonian spy net, instead of guarding the anonymity of its agents, held regular meetings at the Green Dragon Tavern, which included the whole network. Though well aware of the need of secrecy, they had no idea how to get it. All they could think of was to take an oath at every meeting, swearing to reveal their work to no one except Hancock, Adams, Warren, one or two others—and Doctor Church!

Fortunately for the American cause, General Gage and the diabolical doctor let slip this perfect chance to wipe out the patriot intelligence service. The Gage papers, though filled with Church's reports, contained nothing to indicate he ever betrayed the patriot spies who trusted him or any of the information they collected. The reason is now forever beyond discovery. A series of swift arrests about April 17, 1775, might have kept America in the British Empire forever.

Though they knew a good deal about Revere's activity as a messenger for the patriots, the British seem to have had no idea how much espionage he and his associates were carrying on. When he carried messages to the Provincial Congress of New Hampshire in January, 1775, General Gage noted: "Paul

Revere went express thither," adding, "it protends a storm rather than peace." On April 14, a British spy in Concord reported: "Last Saturday the 7th of April P:——R:—— toward evening arrived at Concord carrying a letter that was said to be from Mr. W——n"—i.e., Dr. Joseph Warren. But there is not a word about patriot espionage.

Just how the intelligence collected by the Revere network reached the patriot leaders is by no means clear. The spy ring was in close touch with Doctor Warren, who may have been its leader; and Revere himself was in touch with Colonel William Conant, across the river in Charlestown, and with patriot leaders in Concord. Probably information was passed orally to Warren, Conant, the Adamses—and Doctor Church.

The Revere ring had its failures as well as its successes. It did not detect plans for the swift British raid on Charlestown, September 1, 1774, probably because at that time the patriot espionage system was just beginning. Before patriots in Charlestown could be warned, a force of two hundred and sixty British regulars crossed the Charles, went up the Mystic River, destroyed gunpowder and other stores and were safely away before any patriots even guessed they had left Boston. Thousands of indignant colonists swarmed into Charlestown, too late. Their fury, however, was so evident that Revere remarks in a letter to a friend that the British "troops have the horrors amazingly by reason of some late movements of our friends in the country." It is interesting to note that he understood the importance of enemy morale.

When, in early December, 1774, the Revere gang learned that Gage meant to send two regiments to Portsmouth, New Hampshire, where British munitions were stored, Revere carried prompt warning. A few men sailed down the river in a "gundalow" that night, waded ashore, overpowered the small garrison after a few shots, and carried off about a hundred barrels of gunpowder, some of which, according to tradition, was used at Bunker Hill. Next day, another raid carried off cannon.

The American spies were able to steal or damage a great deal of British artillery in and around Boston. In Charlestown, all the guns were stolen from the local coast-defense battery, hidden for a few days, then carried secretly into the country. On September 15, 1774, American secret agents "spiked up" all the guns in the North Battery in Boston itself. A local diarist has an entry for September 20, 1774: "Some cannon removed by the men-of-war's men from the mill-pond." It is hard to see why this ordnance happened to be reposing at the bottom of the pond, unless patriotic Bostonians had tossed it there. As the Mill Pond was near the North Battery, it looks as if the raiders flung the lighter guns into the water, after spiking those which were too heavy to move.

At about the same time, two brass field guns disappeared from Major Adino Paddock's Tory artillery "company." The major put his two remaining guns under guard, the result being that they, too, promptly disappeared. All this was the work of a well-organized gang of saboteurs with wagons. It takes a good many men to steal a whole battery of field guns, and a good organization to conceal them afterwards. A strong suspicion still lingers that Revere's friend, the patriotic tanner, William Dawes, was not very far away when some of these things happened.

He was certainly involved in a gun-running episode which may have been the one in which Major Paddock's guns were stolen or may have been still another raid. The schoolmaster, Abraham Holbrook, William Dawes, and four others pried planks from the rear of a house used as a gun shed in West Street, Boston, so quietly that the British sentry on guard over the house never noticed. They removed the barrels—fine brass tubes cast in England—and carried them to Holbrook's schoolhouse, near at hand, where they were concealed in a wooden box. British officers had inspected the gun shed half an hour before the guns vanished. Later, the barrels were taken to the American lines, where wooden mounts were easily improvised. A spy's report to Gage in May, 1775, notes that the colonists have moved all their guns from Concord to Cambridge, "Excepting the four that ware Paddocks." Yet, amid all this patriotic burglary, the Americans never found two old iron cannon that had been lying in a Boston warehouse, "Ever since Last War"—that is, since the French and Indian War.

The quiet sabotage constantly going on in Boston was probably largely the work of the Revere group. Loads of straw for the cavalry were always tipping over. Boatloads of brick for repairing the harbor forts mysteriously sank. So many laborers refused to work on the forts that Gage had to bring men from Nova Scotia to complete them.

The ease with which Gage's own secret service had been able to penetrate the patriots' secrets should have warned him that his own secrets might also leak. He and his officers, however, seem to have had no idea of the extent to which they were being spied upon; and they were shockingly careless in their failure to conceal preparations for the troop movement to Lexington and Concord. Both Admiral Graves and General Gage unconsciously gave the rebels full warning of what they meant to do.

On April 15, the admiral ordered all small boats lowered from the transports in the Charles River and left floating under their sterns. This was done at midnight, but the boats continued to float there, in broad daylight and in full view from both banks, for three days. Revere's spies soon found out that the boats were being specially repaired.

No one could fail to see that the British meant to cross the river, since that was the only possible use they could have for small boats; nor was it hard for observant patriots to guess where the troops were likely to go from there. The military stores were at Concord and Worcester. The City of Boston in those days—before the Back Bay had been filled in to produce the "made" land of the modern city—stood on the round end of a peninsula, shaped like a frying pan and connected with the mainland only by the long and narrow strip then known as Boston Neck. The troops would cross the Charles River at Boston only if they were marching northwest to Concord. If they had been marching west to Worcester, they would have taken the easier route down Boston Neck.

Gage made one feeble effort to conceal his intentions. Under the British Army's tables of organization of that period, every regiment had a company of light infantry (specially trained for skirmishing, flank protection and reconnoissance) and a company of grenadiers (large and powerful men for heavy fighting). The light infantry were meant for just such swift movements as the dash to Concord. The grenadiers would provide support. Since light infantry and grenadier companies were frequently withdrawn from their regiments for special duty, there would be no disorganization of the other troops, left in Boston. Bostonians would think this was normal military routine—or so General Gage hoped. He took care to spread the rumor that the troops were being detached for special training; but that story deceived no one.

By April sixteenth, the day after Admiral Graves slung out his small boats, the patriot intelligence net was convinced that the British would raid Concord. Revere himself rode to Lexington, to warn John Hancock and Samuel Adams, who had been attending the Massachusetts Provincial Congress there and were about to start to Philadelphia to attend the Second Continental Congress, of which they were also members. At the moment, both were guests in the Lexington parsonage of the Reverend Jonas Clark, whose wife was Hancock's cousin.

Concord was immediately warned. Ox teams began to move stores. Artillery was carted off to new hiding places. Bullets were put in sacks and hidden in the swamps. The time was too short to move everything; but the detailed reports which his secret agents had sent Gage were mostly out of date by the time the British troops arrived. Gage's Concord spy, whoever he was, must have seen the munitions being moved; but he could not possibly tell where everything went; and he does not seem to have been able to get a new report to Gage in time.

Revere rode quietly back to Boston, pausing at the Charlestown home of Colonel William Conant. From Charlestown the steeple of Christ Church—later known as the Old North Church—in Boston was plainly visible. Revere promised that his group would show one lantern in the steeple if the British went "by land"—that is, over Boston Neck. They would show two lanterns "if the British went out by water."

Of course, there was never any possibility that the British

would go, as Longfellow's poem has it, "by sea." There was no "sea" route to inland Lexington. Longfellow just needed to finish a stanza with a rhyme for the line "I on the opposite shore will be," but even that was wrong. Revere did not wait on the opposite shore; he was still in the city of Boston and very busy, when the lanterns flared in the Old North Church steeple. In fact, he helped hang them. Or, at least, he went as far as the church door with the man who did hang them. The lanterns were meant as a signal to Colonel Conant, not to Revere, who knew already exactly what was happening.

The light signals had been agreed on in advance, because, as Revere said after the war, "we were apprehensive it would be difficult to cross the Charles or get over Boston Neck." In other words, Gage might be expected to station guards and send out patrols to cut off communication along Boston Neck. Admiral Graves would probably keep guard boats moving, to stop any American boats that tried to slip across the Charles. If no patriot messenger could get out of Boston, the lanterns would still give the news.

Having made all arrangements, Revere went placidly home. He had for some months had a boat safely hidden away for use on just such missions as the one he would undertake that night.

General Gage still expected no trouble. He thought his men could reach Concord, destroy American munitions, and be safely back before the alarm could spread; but this time Doctor Church and the other spies had failed the British commander. Either Revere did not tell the doctor what he was doing or Church had failed to send Gage a report. Headquarters in Boston had no way of knowing that the minutemen had been alerted for two or three days, or that many of the stores at Concord had already been moved.

The patriots, on the other hand, at this critical moment, were very well informed indeed. Everyone in Boston knew, almost at once, where the redcoats were going. British officers in Boston, professional soldiers though they were, talked carelessly. Their laxity was especially dangerous because many were living in American private homes, where everything they did or said was observed and reported. Major John Pitcairn was living almost next door to Paul Revere. Less suitable quarters could hardly have been chosen for the marine officer who was to be second in command on the march to Lexington.

British enlisted personnel, even though not billeted in Boston homes, were in close touch with Boston people. Some soldiers' wives worked as servants. That was why one red-coated sergeant, when he could not find a soldier named Gibson, thought he knew what to do. The sergeant left word with the American woman who employed Mrs. Gibson as a housemaid. Gibson was to report "at the bottom of the Common" (modern Charles Street) at eight o'clock. The sergeant was foolish enough to add that Private Gibson was to be "equipped for an expedition." When the missing soldier appeared, the shrewd and loyal American housewife tried to get a few more facts out of him.

"Oh, Gibson, what are you going to do?"

Perhaps Gibson knew more about security than anybody else in Gage's army; perhaps he was just badly informed. Whatever the reason, he made a model reply: "Ah, madam, I know as little as you do."

The patriotic lady tried to inform the patriot organization; but her quick-thinking loyalty did very little good. She told her husband, who sent the news to Doctor Church at his house, near by.

Happily, British preparations for the march were equally apparent elsewhere. It is always practically impossible to conceal the fact that troops are about to move. It *is*, however, possible to isolate the area in which they are preparing. D Day in 1944 was a complete surprise to the German Army, because all communications from Great Britain, even diplomatic dispatches, were suddenly and completely cut off.

Just as Paul Revere had expected, the British command tried to cut off Boston in the same way, but not very adequately. H.M.S. *Somerset* was anchored in the mouth of the Charles River, to block the patriots' water communications, and failed. Officer patrols were sent out to intercept American couriers, but caught only one, Revere himself. The Neck, connecting

Boston with the mainland, was blocked unsuccessfully, though it was only sixty yards wide.

Worse still, the loose talk in Boston continued. Officers, making sure their horses were ready for the coming night march, foolishly chattered about "hell to pay tomorrow." A groom at the Province House is said to have heard them and talked to a hostler, who rushed to Revere.

"You are the third person who has brought me the same information," said he, then warned the boy to remain silent. Dr. Joseph Warren also had the news.

Lord Percy (who next day would command the relief column sent out to rescue Lieutenant Colonel Francis Smith at Lexington), after leaving Gage at the Province House that evening, walked down through the dusk of the Common to see the troops embark. He was not recognized—a scarlet uniform covered by a cloak looked at night very much like civilian clothing.

Suddenly, he heard a voice from the darkness:

"The British troops have marched, but will miss their aim."

"What aim?" asked the startled nobleman.

"Why, the cannon at Concord," said the voice.

Percy hurried back to his commander to report. The secret had leaked in Boston. It might not yet be known at the objective in Concord. No matter what had happened, it was too late now to halt the raid.

One early history of the Revolution says that the first warning of the march to Lexington came from "a daughter of liberty unequally yoked in point of politics." This was at once taken for a reference to Mrs. Gage, who was of American birth. It is true that she felt keenly her anomalous position and, horrified by the slaughter at Bunker Hill, is said to have quoted sadly the words of Blanch, in Shakespeare's *King John:*

> Which is the side that I must go withal?
> I am with both; each army hath a hand;
> And in their rage, I having hold of both,
> They whirl asunder and dismember me.
> Husband, I cannot pray that thou mayst win. . . .

But there is not a scrap of evidence that she ever betrayed a military secret—or knew one.

When Dr. Joseph Warren was sure that the troops were actually falling in on the Common, he started William Dawes, on horse, down Boston Neck. Though the road was cut off, the sentry at the roadblock happened to be a friend, who let Dawes through. About ten o'clock, Doctor Warren sent for Revere. He knew that, though Hancock and Samuel Adams had been warned two days earlier, they were still lingering at Parson Clark's in Lexington. As Dawes might not get through, Revere would have to carry a second warning.

First, however, those lanterns in the Old North Church. For though Paul Revere on the opposite shore would *not* be, Colonel Conant certainly would be somewhere near the river bank or in sight of the steeple, and wide awake. Revere hunted up his friend Robert Newman, sexton of the church, who was expecting him. Newman lived with his mother, in whose house British officers were quartered. He tactfully went to bed early, slipped out through a window, crossed a roof, and dropped into the darkened street, where he waited in the shadows till Paul Revere stealthily arrived. Together, they collected John Pulling, a vestryman of the church; and probably also Revere's neighbor, Thomas Barnard. Lanterns were stored at the church. One of the group—probably Newman, though a case has been made out for Pulling—slipped up the stairs, past the eight bells of the church, and on to the top of the belfry.

How long the two lanterns were displayed, no one knows. It cannot have been very long, for Pulling was "afraid that some old woman would see the light and scream fire " and the lookout on H.M.S. *Somerset,* in the river below, might raise an alarm at any moment. Indeed, there must have been some kind of disturbance in front of the church very soon, since Newman, instead of leaving by the church door, through which he had come, left through a back window. Slipping quietly home, he returned by the roof-and-window route to his bedroom, where he lay awake, too excited to sleep, listening to the British officers, laughing over their card game in the room downstairs.

As soon as the British learned of the signals, Newman was

arrested. Under interrogation, he was elaborately innocent. What had *he* done? Pulling had asked him for the keys. Yes, it was late at night. But Pulling was a vestryman, Newman only the sexton. What could a mere sexton do, after a vestryman had given orders? He had turned over the keys and gone to bed. He really had gone to bed. The officers living in the house could testify to that, if anybody asked them—and somebody probably did. Newman, it is true, hadn't stayed in bed; but none of his interrogators knew that; and in the end they believed him—at least, they released him.

Newman could say what he pleased without endangering his companion, Pulling. A neighbor's wife had long since brought the vestryman warning that "he had better leave town as soon as possible with his family." Pulling was already where the British could not get their hands on him.

After returning safely to his own house in North Square, Revere had difficulty leaving again on his next errand. Troops had fallen in near it and were allowing no one to leave. Somehow, Revere got away in spite of them; but he went without spurs—which might have been hard to explain if he had been stopped. His dog followed him out of the house.

Meantime, the boat builder, Joshua Bentley, and one Thomas Richardson were waiting to row him across the Charles. Obviously these men, as well as Newman and Pulling, were all part of Revere's group of patriotic "mechanics" and spies.

Suddenly the trio remembered they would need cloth to muffle the oars. One of Revere's companions knew a girl. She lived at the corner of North and North Centre streets. At a very special whistle, the young lady's window went up quietly. There were some whispers. Then a flannel petticoat fluttered down from the window. Revere used to tell his children, appreciatively, that it was still warm.

So far the story is credible enough, but Revere also used to tell his children that he sent the dog home with a note to his wife and the sagacious animal presently returned with his spurs.

Silently the oars, muffled with the flannel petticoat of the self-sacrificing patriot maiden, took the little craft past the looming bulk of *Somerset,* with her sixty-four guns. The lookout and the officer of the deck failed to see it. Admiral Graves's sailors were ferrying the regulars across the Charles, or getting ready to do so. They, too, saw nothing.

A group of patriot leaders were already waiting at Colonel Conant's home in Charlestown when Revere arrived from Boston. They had seen the two lights in the Old North steeple, though the signals had really been needless. Even before they shone out, Richard Devens, of the committee, knew "that the enemy were all in motion and were certainly preparing to come out into the country." It was now apparent that they would move against Concord. The lights, according to Devens, confirmed this "soon afterward," since they showed the enemy meant to cross the Charles.

Richard Devens had had an adventurous night. The American Committees of Safety and Supplies had been meeting on the eighteenth at Wetherby's Tavern—and perhaps also at Newell's Tavern—in Menotomy, now West Cambridge, or Arlington. Elbridge Gerry and some others lodged there; but Devens, with a friend, had started for Charlestown in a chaise.

A suspiciously large number of British officers had dined in Cambridge that night; and as Devens and his friend had come down the road, they had passed "a great number" of them, far too many to be natural. More suspicious still, the officers had stopped the chaise to ask about "Clark's tavern." There was no Clark's tavern, but Hancock and Adams were still at Clark's parsonage. These redcoats seemed to know a great deal too much.

Devens drove on a little distance, just for the look of the thing, then turned his horse around and drove back the way he had come, passing straight through the group of mounted officers for a second time, without hindrance. He reached the tavern in time to watch the officers ride by. Gerry then sent a messenger to Hancock with word that "eight or nine officers were out suspected of some evil design." Even then, Hancock did not leave Lexington, but calmly sent back word that the officers had already ridden harmlessly through Lexington on their way to Concord and that he would warn the village.

Turning back once more, Devens proceeded placidly to Colonel Conant's and was there before Revere arrived. (Probably Dawes had warned either Conant at Charlestown or Gerry at Menotomy.) The group of officers Devens had seen were probably the patrol, led by Major Mitchell, who caught Revere later that night and nearly caught Dawes and Dr. Samuel Prescott.

There was a hasty consultation at Conant's house. Though Gerry had already sent a warning to Hancock, he could not be sure the messenger would reach him. Revere would have to make another ride and he would need a good horse. John Larkin, a wealthy citizen, turned over the best nag he owned.

Everyone knows the rest of that story: how Revere, almost caught near Cambridge, escaped cross-country; how he "alarumed almost every house"; how Hancock wanted to stay in Lexington and fight; how William Dawes rode up to the Reverend Mr. Clark's, half an hour after Revere; how Revere and Dawes rode toward Concord together with that gay young spark, Dr. Samuel Prescott, who had been courting a girl in Lexington; how Revere was caught and Dawes driven off, while Doctor Prescott jumped a fence and got through to Concord with a warning; how Dawes lost his watch in the excitement, thriftily retrieving it a few days later.

Eventually the officers took Larkin's horse and left Revere on foot, to get back to Lexington as best he might. He arrived at the parsonage, for the second time, to find Hancock still full of fight. It was dawn before they got the pugnacious statesman started toward Woburn, and on to Congress in Philadelphia. Revere helped hide Hancock's papers. The British officer who had captured and released him, Major Mitchell, rode back from Lexington, met the advancing British troops, and reported to Lieutenant Colonel Francis Smith, commanding the column, that he "had taken Paul Revierre but was obliged to lett him go." (There was really no charge on which to hold the man.)

Somewhere ahead of the British, young John Howe, Gage's favorite secret agent, had again donned "Yankee dress" and was already out rousing the Tories, as Revere had been rousing the patriots.

Around them, in the night, the advancing British troops

could hear alarm guns, church bells and drums. Their effort at surprise had plainly failed. There was sure to be a fight now, and more troops would be needed. After listening to Major Mitchell's story, Colonel Smith sent a courier back to General Gage, asking for Lord Percy and the reserve—eight hundred more redcoats, this time with artillery. The patrolling officers turned around again and rode back to Lexington, guiding Major Pitcairn and six companies of light infantry, who were pushed ahead of the main body.

Unknown to them, as they approached the Lexington Common, Paul Revere looked down from a window in Buckman's tavern. Somewhere in Lexington, two spies of Louis XVI, King of France, were quietly watching, too.

VI

★ ★ ★

★

Spies at the Siege of Boston

WHILE THE BRITISH, after the defeat at Lexington and Concord, were besieged in Boston, General Gage's secret service continued business as usual. American espionage was equally active, though handicapped by the loss of Paul Revere, who no longer dared enter the city, and of Dr. Joseph Warren, who had fled in time to escape arrest, only to be killed at Bunker Hill.

Lieutenant Colonel Kemble, Gage's adjutant general and chief intelligence officer, had to make a few changes in his organization. With the rebels blocking all approaches to Boston, it became too dangerous for officers to venture forth, out of uniform, as they had been doing. Local civilian agents had to take over, though months afterward General Washington still feared the enemy might send "trusty soldiers, sergeants, and even commissioned officers in disguise," to spy upon the Continental Army.

Doctor Church, still unsuspected, continued his usual espionage. Within two weeks after the battle, on April thirtieth, he sent General Gage a report on American strength—ten thousand men, already in arms—with a warning that eventually the four New England colonies would enlist thirty thousand, a figure which grossly exaggerated the rebels' real prospects. The paperwork of the hastily organized patriot army was so confused that it is impossible now to tell its exact strength; but it is doubtful whether all the American forces in Cambridge ever much exceeded fifteen thousand or sixteen thousand. Church was much more accurate when, in May, he warned Gage that the rebels would seize Bunker Hill (which they did occupy, together with Breed's Hill, in June); and would build fortifications on Dorchester Heights (which eventually forced Gage's successor to evacuate Boston).

Church and other British spies carefully noted that the Americans had begun to build boats and were getting together a small fleet of the whaleboats common in New England coastal towns. Throughout the war, intelligence agents on both sides were greatly interested in the number of small boats the enemy possessed, especially those that hostile columns carried with them on wheels. When Americans built or assembled boats outside Boston and, later, outside New York, the British command immediately expected attack.

During the siege of Boston, British spies wandered about the patriot camps at will. An undated report, probably made in April or May of 1775, shows that a secret agent from Boston "got into Roxbury" without trouble; observed the rebel troops there; watched rebel artillery at drill; then rode on to Cambridge, observing the troops that marched past him on the road; counted the tents (not over twenty) in one small camp; and examined artillery and artillery trains in Cambridge itself. When the troops in Cambridge barracks piously fell in for prayers, the spy seized this edifying occasion to estimate their number at three thousand—a figure not meant to include troops on duty on the lines. After this, he hurried back to Roxbury to observe more patriot troops in formation for prayers—not over four hundred, there, he thought. Pausing only to note ten four-pounder field guns near Roxbury meeting house, he sat down to prepare his report for the British command.

When, toward the end of May, the Americans planned to raid Hog Island and Noddle's Island (then in Boston Harbor, now part of the East Boston mainland), General Gage was fully informed, from some mysterious source, a day ahead of time.

The ferryboat which continued to ply from Winnisimet (Chelsea) to Cambridge during the summer of 1775, was a godsend to Gage's spies. One agent, recorded only as "the deponent" or "———," managed to get aboard this craft and make contact with a secretly pro-British Boston butcher serving in the American artillery. This man, he reported in early August, did "not much like" the American cause and was corresponding with a sergeant of the royal artillery in Boston. From the treacherous butcher and from his own observation, this British spy was able to report the personal movements of Generals Washington, Lee and Putnam; artillery emplacements; strength and exact location of guard detachments; movements of ammunition; oxen put out by the rebels to decoy the redcoats into ambush; floating batteries; whaleboats; fortifications; the strength of riflemen; and total American strength. The British spy had one pleasant chat with the unsuspicious General Israel Putnam; and, as he sometimes dined with the captain of the American guard, he was able to get General Washington's orders and a good deal of other information, though he was wise enough not to dine with the careless captain when General Washington was present. A blacksmith in Mystic served as one of his subagents.

There was a certain irony in British spies' penetration in Roxbury and at the ferry. In March, 1776—much too late—General Washington was urging special precautions against enemy agents in Roxbury and "the different landing-places nearest the shipping." But this was only after the British had evacuated the city, and this danger was over. General Washington was worrying about spies the enemy might leave behind them; he never guessed how many secret agents had already bored into his army.

While he was penned up in Boston, General Gage contrived to receive a good deal of information from other colonies, his communications being greatly assisted by command of the sea. Immediately after hostilities began, devoted loyalists outside Massachusetts began to pour information in to him. Most of these spies seem to have been volunteers, eager to aid the king's cause, but not part of the regular intelligence system. One eager Tory, living near New York, went to Greenwich, Connecticut, to make sure hostilities had really begun. As soon as he had verified the news from Lexington and Concord, he realized that intelligence of troop movements outside Massachusetts would be valuable to Gage, and went on to Newport, where he tried to get Captain Wallace, of H.M.S. *Rose,* to take him to Boston. Failing in this, he started overland, found he could not get beyond Dedham, Massachusetts, and went all the way back to Newport, where Captain Wallace finally took him aboard. When he reached Boston in May, he brought news of troop movements through Connecticut and notes on the stubborn mood of the rebels.

Another volunteer secret agent of the same sort, known only by the initials "W.C.," after watching the march of American troops through Goshen, Orange County, New York, managed to send word to Gage, before he was caught by indignant patriots and forced to drink a toast to the damnation of Lord North, the Prime Minister, under threats of flogging, tar and feathers.

Beginning in May and running through July, the British commander received a series of very early secret reports about a new American device, "that would effectually distroy the Royal Navy." This was "Bushnell's Turtle," a primitive submarine invented by David Bushnell, of Saybrook, Connecticut, an engineer officer, which was later tried out against British men-of-war. British tars were greatly surprised when the strange, turnip-shaped object bobbed up out of the water, but it did no damage. The same unknown spy who reported it was also able to give a great deal of information about General Charles Lee's proposed troop movements at Philadelphia.

In early September, intelligence "from no bad quarter" enabled Gage to warn William Tryon, royal governor of New York, of patriot plans to kidnap Tryon himself, "and every Governor and Officer of Government on the Continent." This was the first of an interminable series of kidnaping plots, in which both sides engaged for the next five years, a few of which were successful.

Three British spies had already been working for Gage in

Pennsylvania for some time. Joseph Galloway, supposedly a patriot leader there, had been spying on the Continental Congress in Philadelphia, just as Church had been spying on the Provincial Congress in Massachusetts. How early this began, there is no telling; but on May 12, 1775, Galloway was able to smuggle to Gage, through the lines of the American besiegers outside Boston, a report that Benjamin Franklin, just back from England, was already advocating independence and had warned the Continental Congress that the royal government was embarking four thousand troops to reinforce the Boston garrison. Galloway, or someone else, had been making earlier reports on Franklin, for, only a few days after Lexington, General Gage—as yet unaware of Franklin's return—ordered the captain of a vessel leaving Boston with mail to wait till he was far out at sea; then to examine all letters addressed to Franklin and a few other Americans abroad; and to send the letters back to Boston. Other suspicious letters were to be turned over to the government in London, as "they might contain some intelligence of the Rebels here."

Dr. John Kearsley—a violent Tory, manufacturer of "Kearsley's pills," horse trader, physician, and proprietor of a vinegar factory—was collecting intelligence in Philadelphia for the government in London, perhaps sending his dispatches through Gage's hands. Co-operating with him in some way was John Brooks, of Skenesborough, New Hampshire, eminently respectable, "accustomed to dress very genteelly," who was engaged in espionage between Albany and Philadelphia for both Gage and Howe.

The Americans arrested both these men and imprisoned them at Lancaster, Pennsylvania, October 5, 1775, though Brooks had probably been under quiet American surveillance since May. Brooks escaped in 1777. Kearsley suffered so much in prison at Carlisle, Pennsylvania, that he died the day after his release. Just what Mrs. Kearsley was doing in 1775-1778 no one is ever likely to find out now; but, whatever it was, to the British Army it was worth $214.16 from secret service funds, and a permanent pension of £100.

Not all the intelligence Gage received was accurate. The

most successful hoax of the Revolution was perpetrated by Georgia patriots, who planted false information on the British commander in Boston. James Wright, the royal governor in Georgia, had written both General Gage and Admiral Graves asking for a warship to overawe the rebels. The Georgia Secret Committee stole his letters, opened them, and inserted forgeries of their own composition. These new documents assured both the general and the admiral all was so quiet in Georgia that no British naval support would be needed against the rebels. Since the British had also been alarmed about gunpowder in Georgia, the letters were reassuring on that point, too. The powder would be used merely to give Indians their usual supply for hunting, the forged letters declared.

Governor Wright had really reported that there was "no probability of quietude" in Georgia, and had asked Admiral Graves for "immediate assistance," at the very least "a sloop of war of some sort." He also expressed alarm lest the patriots seize his gunpowder. In the secret committee's forgeries, Gage was told, "No danger is to be apprehended," after which the patriot committeemen added that the apparent rebellion was "by no means real," and that there was "nothing formidable in the proceedings or designs of our neighbors of South Carolina." To send British troops or ships would "totally destroy the present favorable appearances." Governor Wright's real letter to Admiral Graves, asking for naval support at once, was revised to read: "I now have not any occasion for any vessel of war."

Not content to forge Wright's signature, the wily rebels made an impression of the governor's seal in moist clay and forged that, too. An unverifiable legend has it that when they met in London some time later, Wright complained to Gage of the failure to send warships. Only then did the British general guess what had happened. Whether that is true or not, the fraud had been discovered by January 3, 1776, when Governor Wright ruefully told the story to the Earl of Dartmouth. Rarely has espionage had such clear and far-reaching consequences. Wright was sure Georgia could have been held for the crown with four or five hundred men.

American espionage, penetrating into Boston, achieved quite as many successes as British espionage upon the rebels in and around Cambridge, though General Washington at first had no agents except the remnants of Paul Revere's group. Revere's friend William Dawes is said to have been able to go in and out of beleaguered Boston almost weekly; and there are tales of a patriotic barber who used to swim the Charles, bearing military intelligence. John Carnes, a Boston grocer, spied for Colonel Loammi Baldwin, while protected by two cut-outs. Baldwin's queries were handed to a man named Dewksbury, who lived about four miles from the colonel's station in Chelsea. From Dewksbury they went to an unknown "waterman," whose boat took him to Carnes in Boston; and the secret intelligence came back the same way.

These men, or others like them, smuggled Paul Revere's engraving equipment out of Boston, so that he could begin making Continental and Massachusetts currency at Watertown. Mrs. Revere, who remained in Boston, made the mistake of trusting Doctor Church (whom everyone still regarded as a sterling patriot) with a letter and £125 for her husband. Nothing more was ever heard of Rachel Revere's letter until it turned up among General Gage's papers a few years ago—and nothing has *ever* been heard of the £125.

Since he was turning in his espionage reports to Dr. Joseph Warren, the American schoolmaster-spy, James Lovell (whose father, John Lovell, spied for the British) must also be regarded as part of the original Revere spy ring, which worked closely with the doctor. Lovell remained busy with espionage in Boston until the British, searching Doctor Warren's body after he had been killed at Bunker Hill, found some of the spy's "billets." They arrested young Lovell on June 29, 1775, but, instead of hanging him, sent him as a prisoner to Halifax. Exchanged later, he sat in the Continental Congress and became its leading specialist in codes and ciphers.

Admiral Graves's willingness to let fishing boats operate, to increase Boston's food supply, made it easy to smuggle Yankee spies into the city. The Tory proprietor of a Boston dram-shop reported to General Gage that, when the boats went out with British passes for four men, they really carried three genuine fishermen and one patriot spy. "As soon as they get below," said the Tory (evidently meaning some point on the coast below Boston Harbor) the crew landed the spy and took aboard another in his place. The agents, thus smuggled into the British lines, picked up information, then returned to the Americans. This had begun as early as May or June, 1775. Active in the work were two American agents named Goodwin and Hopkins—"as bad Rebels as any"—who were helping smuggle men in and out of Boston, sometimes in disguise. When they themselves visited the city, they always spent their time "up in Town," gathering intelligence. Once, they were incautious enough to let the owner of the dramshop hear them talking "as high as any man in the Province against Government"; but, though this fact was immediately reported to Gage, there is no record of their arrest.

One of these fishermen, George Robert Twelves Hewes, after evading suspicion by supplying fish to the British fleet for nine weeks, quietly landed at Lynn, Massachusetts, and was taken overland to General Washington. The intelligence he brought delighted the general. "He didn't *laugh* to be sure, but *looked amazing good natured*," and invited Hewes and his small crew to dinner. Martha Washington "waited upon them at table all dinner-time and was remarkably social." Unhappily, Hewes telling the story to his biographer in his old age, forgot to tell what intelligence he supplied.

Soon after Lovell's arrest, General Washington took steps to get a paid secret agent of his own into Boston. On July 15, 1775, less than two weeks after the general had taken command, his accounts show the entry:

> To 333 1/3 Dollars given to ————* to enduce him to go into the Town of Boston; to establish a secret corrispondence for the purpose of movements and designs.

At the bottom of the page is a note:

> * The names of Persons who are employed within the

Enemys lines, or who may fall within their power cannot
be inserted—

an excellent rule, though the general did not observe it con-
sistently. There was also a mysterious man named Hichborne,
whom the general paid for espionage, but of whom nothing
else is known.

In addition to intelligence, one daring patriot contrived
to smuggle munitions, which the rebels badly needed, out of
Boston, even after the siege began. Desperate for provisions,
Gage allowed some farmers to bring produce into the city.
Among them was George Minot, of Dorchester, who, after
entering the British lines with vegetables, managed to smuggle
gunpowder out to Washington on the return journey. When
he was allowed to make two more trips into Boston with an
ox team, he brought back a four-pounder field gun each time,
with the assistance of a Negro servant, and the connivance of
patriotic Boston selectmen.

Before long, General Washington had a spy system that
extended as far as Nova Scotia, while Benedict Arnold was
sending spies of his own into Canada. This espionage was
at first meant to facilitate the invasion of Canada in 1776,
but it was kept up throughout the war. Washington's papers
show that he continued to receive various reports from the north
and at one time had a plan of Halifax Harbor; but the work of
these spies led to no further military action, after the invasion
of Canada had failed.

The two French intelligence agents who had watched the
fight at Lexington, entering the American camp in Cambridge
some time before General Washington's arrival to take command, carefully studied the improvised American forces—somewhat scandalized by the lax, unmilitary methods that they
found. These French spies were Achard de Bonvouloir and
the Chevalier d'Amboise, who had come up from the West
Indies and had for some time been touring the colonies, collecting information useful to the government of Louis XVI.
Bonvouloir was—then or later—working for the French embassy
in London; and D'Amboise was almost certainly engaged in

the same service, though both men may have begun their anti-British espionage in the American colonies as volunteers, without official orders. They stayed with the American forces only a little while, to watch the first stages of the siege of Boston and form an estimate of the rebel army, then hurried off—not to Paris, but to London, to report to the French ambassador.

Obviously pleased with the intelligence they brought, the ambassador was soon suggesting to Bonvouloir that he had better cross the Atlantic again, to find out *"ce qui se passera en Amérique parmi les Américaines."*

Though the pair had passed undetected through the colonies, British counterintelligence in London spotted them at once, and one of its agents was turning in a full report on both men by August 6, 1775. The British agent thought he had plied Bonvouloir with enough champagne to loosen the Frenchman's tongue—but he underestimated the strength of Bonvouloir's head. The British spy never noticed that, while the French spy made the usual criticisms of the raw American troops, he let slip not a word of anything he knew about the British forces. Bonvouloir went back to America in September, 1775, and, posing as an Antwerp merchant, was soon deep in consultation with the Committee of Secret Correspondence, with regard to the possibility of French aid to the patriots.

All this was part of the survey of British armaments that the French had begun during the French and Indian War and had continued vigorously ever since. Already they had full information on British arsenals, naval strength, number and location of regiments, the military geography of the southern English counties, where invaders might land, and the defensive capabilities of the East and West Indies. Sad to say, when naval war began in America, it was discovered too late that no French naval intelligence agent had learned that the larger French men-of-war could not enter New York harbor.

Nevertheless, the French intelligence service had long paid special attention to the material resources of North America and the mood of the colonists; and a British historian has said that French naval intelligence reports on the British Navy were more accurate than the speeches of the First Lord of the Admiralty.

The French government, though smarting from its defeat in the French and Indian War, was still perfectly neutral and was maintaining a correct diplomatic attitude. Still, if the rebellion showed signs of strength; if the British proved unable to crush it promptly; if a supply of uniforms, arms and ammunition might help the rebels—well, who knew what might happen later? At any rate, it could do no harm to have a French secret agent find out what the American rebels really needed.

Bonvouloir's was really one of the most important secret missions of the war. It seemed of small importance at the time—just one more task for one more spy; but it was the first, hesitating step toward French intervention, which led to Yorktown and victory.

VII

★ ★ ★

★

Kidnaping George Washington

ON MARCH 17, 1776, the British evacuated Boston, and the American troops entered, a little hesitantly, since they could still see British sentries at their posts—though these turned out to be nothing but dummies in scarlet coats. That afternoon, a triumphant army chaplain preached from a long text, beginning: "The Egyptians said, Let us flee from the face of Israel."

The trouble was, the Egyptians didn't flee far enough. Their fleet lingered for several days at anchor, just off Boston, though the winds were fair. Why didn't they go?

General Washington, doubtful, moved only a few troops. One day after the evacuation, he started his riflemen and five regiments of ordinary infantry for New York, the obvious point of the next attack. Three days later, General William Heath led out an infantry brigade. But was it safe to send more? General Washington wondered if the redcoats might try to "give us a Stroke, at a moment when they conceive us to be off guard." The lingering of the fleet seemed suspicious: "The enemy have the best knack at puzzling people I ever met with in my life," wrote General Washington. There was, besides, a further danger: "There is one evil that I dread, and that is, their spies." To deal with them, he ordered "a dozen or more of honest, sensible, and diligent men to haunt the communication between Roxbury and the different land-ing-places nearest the shipping, in order to question, cross-question, &c., all such persons as are unknown."

At last a signal fluttered from the flagship. The white sails spread. The fleet moved out to sea . . . turned . . . turned north. They were going to Halifax! At leisure now, the Continental Army proceeded to New York and began to strengthen its defenses.

Not least of these defenses, though a quite unconscious one, was Henry Dawkins, a far from edifying character. Henry Daw-kins got out of jail in New York City, sometime in January or February, 1776, before the siege of Boston ended. Nobody now can tell why Henry Dawkins had been sent to jail, to begin with. Neither does anybody know how long Henry Dawkins had been there. But the events that immediately followed Henry Dawkins's jail deliverance convinced every-body—except, perhaps, Henry—that jail was the best possible place for that expert, but too enterprising, artist and engraver. Sound reasons for putting Henry Dawkins back in jail de-veloped almost as soon as Henry got out. Indeed, there seems never, at any time, to have been any lack of good, sound reasons for putting Henry Dawkins in jail. Such, at any rate, was the very general impression in New York City in the memorable year 1776. The Provincial Congress of New York felt this so strongly that, not content with incarcerating Henry again, they took the added precaution of putting him in irons.

There was no real reason why Henry Dawkins should take to crime, for during the twenty years since he had come to America he had become a fairly prosperous engraver, making bookplates, caricatures, maps, coats of arms, seals and rings for the gentry of Philadelphia, and an elaborate astronomical plate to illustrate an article on the 1769 transit of Venus. There might, however, be more money in counterfeiting than in other forms of engraving; and there is no way of telling how long he may have been engraving counterfeit currency in

Pennsylvania before the New York patriots laid him low at last.

Stirring matters were afoot, as Henry Dawkins made his way from jail in New York City to Long Island, in the early weeks of 1776. Already hard-pressed in Boston, the British were about to withdraw to Halifax, before beginning their attack on New York. Overseas, a mighty fleet of men-o'-war was preparing to sail with transports bearing a new army— British and German—to strengthen at New York the army that had failed at Boston. Just off the New York coast, aboard H.M.S. *Duchess of Gordon,* William Tryon, royal governor of New York, feverishly plotted with Tories in the city, on Long Island, and far up the Hudson Valley, while his spies and secret messengers went back and forth on sinister errands. H.M.S. *Asia* and *Savage* also lay off the coast, ready to assist.

Untroubled by such thoughts, unaware that the destiny of a continent rode with him, Henry Dawkins, enjoying his new-found freedom, proceeded at leisure through Long Island lanes to Huntington. The thoughts of Henry Dawkins were not upon the fate of nations, the movement of armies or the progress of history. Henry was cheerfully thinking out a scheme whereby he could easily turn a dishonest shilling and a dishonest dollar at the same time. He had no conception of the inconceivable rumpus his little get-rich-quick scheme was about to unloose. Henry Dawkins was merely contemplating a little profitable crime; but he was, in fact—though he never knew it—about to save the United States of America.

With the peaceful calm of a man who feels reasonably sure he is on to a good thing, Henry Dawkins arrived at the home of the brothers Israel and Isaac Youngs in Huntington, Long Island, quite ordinary provincial subjects of the king, except that they were men of most remarkable and upright virtue— according to the enthusiastic description of their own blameless lives that the brothers Youngs gave when arrested.

Comfortably ensconced in the Youngs home, Dawkins presently made a perfectly honest proposal. He suggested that Israel Youngs should help him buy a printing press. He was very insistent that it should be what was then called a "rolling press," for he felt sure he could work up a profitable little printing business. Something was said about producing labels for the local hat industry to paste inside its products.

Israel Youngs was a singularly unsuspicious individual. It didn't occur to him—or so he later averred with much emphasis—that a rolling press was used to print engravings; or that currency issued by Congress and the new State governments was so printed. To a suspicious man, this might have seemed a remarkable coincidence. No such thought of evil occurred to Israel Youngs. He said so! Youngs did admit, later, under considerable pressure, that at one time the thought just crossed his mind that something might be wrong with Dawkins. He thought it a little bit odd when he learned that his friend had signed his order for the new press with an assumed name. But Israel Youngs was like all three Japanese monkeys at once. He neither saw, heard nor spoke evil— not when there was a prospect of easy money in being blind, deaf and dumb.

Skilled in the fine art of asking no questions, Youngs did not ask any when, a little later, Dawkins installed his press in an attic, where, since it had no floor, boards had to be laid on the beams. Though it all seemed strange, the guileless Youngs brothers were still unsuspicious when the door leading to the attic was carefully concealed.

After the press arrived, the engraver remarked to Israel Youngs that "he could make as good money as ever was, undiscovered"; but when Israel repeated this remark to his brother, the virtuous Isaac replied primly that "if he could it would be a sin." Or so he later told the irate American officials who interrogated him. Dawkins himself blamed the whole thing on "the Instigation of Israel Youngs"; but, by this time, all the conspirators were in a great deal of trouble and lying hard.

Counterfeiting in those days was not really very difficult. Lacking the innumerable protective devices of modern bank notes, the crude currency of the new American states was easily imitated. State and Continental "shinplasters" were produced from ordinary engraved copper plates—perhaps at times from ordinary type; and counterfeiters' only trouble was getting the right paper. Even the unsuspicious provincial treasuries of those days knew enough about currency to use a special kind —but, alas for them—any printer could buy the same paper on the open market. To get some, the Dawkins counterfeiting ring turned to one Isaac Ketcham.

Bills of that period were printed from several plates at a time, in large sheets, several notes to a sheet, after which the individual notes were cut apart. It was always possible to get a sample of the paper by taking it from the space between the notes. Carrying such a specimen, Ketcham visited Philadelphia, an early center of the American paper industry, examined paper, and asked for prices. No harm in that. It was ostensibly an innocent inquiry in the usual course of business. In ordinary times, Ketcham's effort to buy a little paper would have interested no one save some willing salesman. The times, however, were far from ordinary. Someone suspected a plot to counterfeit; and, about May of 1776, Ketcham was arrested. To make matters worse, Dawkins got drunk about this time, made several rash remarks, and was likewise arrested.

Dawkins, Ketcham and the brothers Youngs, who presently joined them in jail, were themselves guilty of nothing worse than attempted counterfeiting, a crime long common in the American colonies, scarcely more than a profitable pastime. So far as they were concerned, the American Revolution meant only that new governments were issuing new currency, of which to make new counterfeits. But in the jail were others, still less innocent than the counterfeiting ring, engaged in dark affairs of state. They talked incautiously of other plots. Isaac Ketcham, hearing of graver matters, saw a chance to save himself. He did save himself and—without in the least intending it—his country.

This fantastic sequel to their counterfeiting scheme is one of the ironies of American history: Dawkins involved the Youngs brothers and Ketcham in counterfeiting. Their scheme sent all four to jail. There, among other unholy things, they learned of Tory plots which, if successful, would have destroyed the Continental Army. With no motive higher than the preservation of his own skin, Ketcham betrayed them and then began service as a stool pigeon in the jail, so that the Tory plots were quashed in time. Without these sorry rogues, George Washington would never have been the father of anybody's country. A new world power would never have arisen. No starry flag would fly from coast to coast. No one is likely to build a monument to Henry Dawkins or the brothers Youngs or Isaac Ketcham. Still, unintentionally and from the worst possible motives, they saved America.

Ketcham had, so far, been engaged in nothing worse than crime; but all this time, unknown to the counterfeiters, a powerful Tory group had been plotting, too. Not all that they plotted can ever be discovered now; but enough of their secrets leaked out to show that there were at least two sinister schemes. Was there still a third? The answer depends on how far one is now prepared to believe what everybody in New York believed, by June of 1776.

The Tories meant, in the first place, to kidnap General Washington from his New York headquarters, together with as many men of his guard as they could capture. Though the Americans hushed this up, the existence of such a conspiracy is made perfectly clear by what the ringleader, David Matthews, Tory mayor of New York, told a royal commission in London, when the Revolution was over. He had, said Mayor Matthews, being upon his oath, "formed a Plan for the taking Mr Washington & his Guard Prisoners but which was not effected."

It is equally clear that there was another plot for a sudden rising of secret Tory armed forces, in rear of the American Army, in New York City, on Long Island, and along the Hudson as far north as the Highlands, while General Howe and the British Army, supported by Admiral Lord Howe and the Royal Navy, were attacking the American front. The Tory partisans meant, at the same time, to blow up American magazines, seize all American artillery, and shell the Continental Army from behind, with their own guns. King's Bridge was to be cut, so that the rebels would have no chance of escaping into Westchester County.

Whether there was still a third plot, to stab or poison General Washington—as was firmly believed in New York at the time—is less certain. What *is* certain is that any attempt to capture the commander-in-chief, together with his guard, in his own headquarters, would have led to some very lively scenes, in which someone would have been killed, perhaps the general himself. There was no reason to stab or poison him if he could be kidnaped, for the British government very much wanted the archrebel alive, for trial and execution. But the vengeful Tories, once they had reached his headquarters secretly, would never have let George Washington live if they saw the plan to capture him alive had failed, though they would hardly have used poison.

Fantastic though these schemes may sound today, they had a fair chance of success, for strong Tory forces were already secretly organized and prepared to go into action. One band of seven hundred king's men was ready to rise on Long Island. There was another, almost as large, at Goshen, New York. Tories at Cornwall were ready to seize the new American fortifications in the Highlands long enough to spike their cannon. The number of such guerrilla bands was steadily increasing, for recruiting agents were by this time moving through the American lines into New York City, upstate New York, New Jersey and Connecticut, very much as they pleased, organizing more and more secret companies of king's militia. They continued to do so for the next two or three years. When the agents were caught, American courts-martial enthusiastically hanged them; but they were hard to catch.

The king's men had the further advantage of a wide-ranging system of spies and secret couriers, which had been established in and around New York almost as soon as hostilities began. The Tory governor of New York, William Tryon, aboard H.M.S. *Duchess of Gordon;* Captain Vandeput, aboard *Asia;* and Captain Wallace, aboard *Rose,* could move about the coast as they pleased. There was no American Navy to chase them off. Boats could put off from the shore at any time, bringing aboard recruits, spies, news, arms or supplies. The governor could land couriers or secret agents anywhere along Long Island or the Jersey coast. Thence they could make their way into New York with practically no trouble at all. Indeed, a shoemaker in New York City had been repairing shoes for British sailors aboard H.M.S. *Asia,* quite undetected.

Secret communication was so perfect that not only could the enemy deliver and call for shoes; they could also deliver secret mail from H.M.S. *Duchess of Gordon,* directly to a British prisoner in New York City. On one occasion the British Captain Savage, one of the prisoners, had the audacity to keep the Royal Navy's secret courier hanging around the jail till he could get all his answers composed in satisfactory prose. Placidly, the enemy's agent waited in the American prison. Nobody disturbed him.

When not engaged with his private British mail service in and out of his American confinement, Captain Savage spent his time persuading his American guards—and even members of General Washington's own bodyguard—to sign up for service with the British Army.

Under such conditions the plots to kidnap Washington and to attack the American rear with secret forces, seemed almost certain of success. British agents had corrupted several soldiers of Washington's guard. The Tory bands were armed, organized and ready. The arrival of the British forces was timed for late June and early July. The plotters were installed in two New York taverns—the Sergeant's Arms, kept by Alexander Sinclair; and Corbie's Tavern, near Spring and Wooster streets, not very far southeast of General Washington's headquarters. "A Mullotto Coloured Negro dressed in blue Cloaths" went back and forth with messages to Governor Tryon, hovering offshore.

Then suddenly three things went wrong. According to Mayor David Matthews, the plot to kidnap Washington failed because of "an unfortunate Discovery that was made of a Letter." Since he himself was at once arrested, Matthew never learned—or never admitted—that some of his conspirators, chatting about their plans indiscreetly, were overheard by a patriotic waiter, William Corbie, who informed Joseph Smith, a prominent citizen of the day.

While there is no reason to doubt that a plotter's letter may have gone astray or that William Corbie eavesdropped, official records clearly show that it was the Dawkins counterfeiting scheme that really wrecked the plot against General Washington. In the court-martial that followed, the incriminating letter —if it ever existed—was not put in evidence at all; the eavesdropping waiter did not appear as a witness; nor was there any mention of plans to poison or stab the general.

Dawkins and the Youngs brothers may never have learned anything about the Tory plots; but Ketcham, soon after he had been confined, got wind of the conspiracies, probably from gossip among the prisoners, perhaps from eavesdropping, perhaps in some other way. The Dawkins counterfeiting plot had gotten him into jail. But his imprisonment for counterfeiting had enabled him to stumble on something far more dangerous. Could he escape punishment for one plot by revealing the other, atone for crime by revealing treason?

Pondering his problems in the illimitable leisure of confinement, Ketcham thought he saw a way out and, in early June of 1776, sent a petition to the Provincial Congress. It was suitably humble. Ketcham was now "deeply imprest with shame and Confuseon for his past Misconduct." He told a sad tale of "six poor Children." He wanted to be let out on bail to take care of them.

The plight of Ketcham's children did not interest the rebel government very much. What did interest New York officials was a note to the speaker of the Provincial Congress, which Ketcham had slyly appended, as if a mere afterthought: "Sir I the subscriber hath something to obsearve to the honourable house if I cold be admitted Its nothing concearning my one afair But intirely on another subgyt."

The speaker was quick to take the hint. His reason is made clear in a further note somebody added later, at the bottom of Ketcham's petition: "The application of Isaac Ketcham And the memorandum which finally ended in the execution of Thos Hickey for High Treason." It is infuriating that the memorandum itself, which told the whole story, has vanished; but this annotation is enough to show that it was Ketcham who first revealed the plots.

This penitent prisoner emerged from confinement long enough for an interview with the speaker, who made him a "purposual." Upon his acceptance, Ketcham was told, "Liberty was depending." The speaker meant the liberty of America; but what mainly worried Isaac Ketcham was the liberty of Isaac Ketcham. Accepting the offer made him, he returned to prison and went to work as an American spy.

He soon had definite information, for two new prisoners arrived, charged, at the moment, only with passing counterfeit money, but also (though Ketcham and his patriot employers did not know it yet) deeply involved in both the Tory conspiracies. These new arrivals in the jail were Sergeant Thomas Hickey and Private Michael Lynch, of General Washington's guard, both of whom had been arrested on June fifteenth. There would never have been any more serious charge against either of them had not Hickey foolishly boasted of being in the Tory plots. Two days later, after he had had a chance to pump both Hickey and Lynch for information, Ketcham sent word to the Provincial Congress he believed both men were involved in the treason he had already discovered.

At this moment, the New York authorities received further alarming news, which confirmed what Ketcham had learned. A patriotic businessman, William Leary, of Orange County, New York, had met a former employee, James Mason, who confided that he and some others were already in British pay. Leary informed the authorities, who arrested Mason. Mason, under pressure, implicated Thomas Hickey and others—Gilbert Forbes, a Broadway gunsmith; William Green, a drummer in the guard; James Johnson, a fifer; a soldier in the guard named Barnes; and one William Forbes. Both Leary and Mason implicated the Tory mayor, David Matthews, who had long been under suspicion and who, Mason testified, had contributed £100 for the expenses of the plot.

Arrests were swift and sudden. Hickey was already in jail when Ketcham and Mason implicated him in treason, in addition to the counterfeiting, for which he had originally been arrested. General Greene's troops seized Mayor David Matthews at his Flatbush home, at one o'clock in the morning of June 22, but could find no papers. Gilbert Forbes was arrested at nearly the same hour and immediately interrogated. Green, Johnson and Barnes, of the bodyguard, were arrested on the twenty-second or twenty-third. Some Tories took to the woods, but twenty or more were seized before they could escape.

As usual in wartime, the wildest rumors spread. It was reported that Hickey had instructions to stab General Washington. The story went around that he had poisoned a dish of green peas (of which Washington was specially fond); but that the general's housekeeper warned him in time to send the peas away untasted. Someone, so the story ran, threw the peas into a chicken pen and all the chickens died.

Sergeant Hickey went before a general court-martial, convened by warrant from General Washington himself. The official record describes it as the court-martial of Thomas Hickey "and others"; but there is no indication that any of the prisoner's equally guilty accomplices ever stood trial. Neither is there any hint why Hickey alone was singled out for the hangman. Washington says merely, "the others are not tried." The three conspirators who testified against the sergeant were probably granted their lives as a reward.

Presiding over Hickey's court-martial was Colonel Samuel H. Parsons—whom, in a few years, the British would be trying to persuade to change sides, too. Hickey was formally charged with "exciting and joining in a mutiny and sedition, and of treacherously corresponding with, inlisting among, and receiving pay from the enemies of the United *American* Colonies." Since such charges, which the judge advocate could easily prove, were enough to hang any soldier, nothing was said about kidnaping or assassinating the commander-in-chief, capturing American artillery or attacking the Continental Army from the rear. There was no use putting bad ideas into people's heads or causing uneasiness in the ranks. The British would be disembarking at Staten Island in a day or two and would soon attack. The high command didn't want Continental soldiers looking uneasily over their shoulders when that attack came.

Though Hickey pleaded not guilty, there was never any hope for him. Appearing against him were four witnesses: William Green; Gilbert Forbes; Isaac Ketcham, who had tricked Hickey into his fatal confession; and William Welch, an American soldier, not a conspirator, who had been court-martialed on different charges and acquitted, in May. The judge advocate was so sure of his case that he did not call Lynch, Barnes, Johnson and Mason as witnesses, though the authorities by this time knew all about them. Dawkins and the Youngs brothers were not involved at all in treason; but their counterfeiting scheme had brought together in jail Hickey, who was involved in both counterfeiting and treason, and Ketcham, who, though accused of counterfeiting only, first revealed the Tory plot.

Green swore that, about three weeks earlier, he had sounded out Gilbert Forbes. He found that *"Forbes's* pulse beat high in the Tory scheme." Eventually, when Forbes tried to get Green to enlist in the British service, while still in General Washington's guard, Green agreed. But—or so he tried to persuade a rather unsympathetic court-martial—he did this with the best and most completely patriotic intentions. He did it only "with a view to cheat the Tories, and detect their scheme." Green said he had broached the plan to Hickey and "told him the principle I went upon, and that we had a good opportunity of duping the Tories."

How much of this Green thought anyone would believe there is no way of telling. He was trying to clear himself and, at the same time, do the best he could for his friend Hickey. The silence in which the court-martial officers listened must have been rather stony.

What had happened then?

"I proposed to him to reveal the plot to the General, but *Hickey* said we had better let it alone till we had made further discoveries."

This was fairly obvious nonsense. An enlisted man, if he is approached by the enemy's agents, should lay the matter before his officers. Secret negotiations with the enemy, no matter what their purpose, are not matters for the rank and file.

The court-martial, which must have listened with growing skepticism from the beginning, soon heard evidence that confirmed its worst suspicions. Though Gilbert Forbes had at first refused to talk, a visit from a very gloomy clergyman, within an hour or two of his arrest, quickly changed his mind. When the parson, perhaps sincerely, told the prisoner "that his time was very short, not having above three days to live, and advised him to prepare himself," Forbes's resistance broke down, and he revealed a good deal. Green had sworn it was Forbes who led him into the plot. Not at all, said Forbes, on his oath. Quite the contrary: it was Green who had tempted *him.*

> A night or two after General *Washington* arrived in *New-York* from *Boston, Green* fell into company where I was. We were drinking, and *Green* toasted the King's health, and I did so too. A day or two afterwards *Green* called upon me, and said, that as I had drank his Majesty's health, he supposed I was his friend, and immediately proposed to in-list some men into the King's service, and told me he could procure considerable numbers to join him. I put him off, and declined having any hand in the business. But in repeated applications from him, I at last fell into the scheme. *Green* was to inlist the men, in which I was not to be concerned, nor have my name mentioned. In a day or two *Green* gave me a list of men who had engaged, among whom was the prisoner, *Hickey.* Soon after which, *Hickey* asked me to give him half a dollar, which I did, and this was all the money *Hickey* ever received from me. *Green* received eighteen dollars, and was to pay the men who inlisted one dollar apiece, and we were to allow them ten shillings per week subsistence money. I received upwards of a hundred pounds from Mr. *Matthews,* the [Tory] Mayor, to pay those who should inlist into the King's service, who, after inlisting, were to go on board the King's ships, but if they could not get there, were to play their proper parts when the King's forces arrived."

Welch testified that he had let Hickey swear him to secrecy in a grogshop, but insisted secrecy was all he swore. Hickey "then said that this country was sold, that the enemy would soon arrive, and that it was best for us Old Countrymen to make our peace before they came, or they would kill us all. That we Old Countrymen should join together, and we would be known by a particular mark, and if I would agree to be one among them, he would carry me to a man who would let me have a dollar by way of encouragement."

Welch did not like the sound of it or, as he put it: "I did not relish the project, and we parted."

Though Isaac Ketcham had been perfectly willing to escape counterfeiting charges by spying on his fellow prisoners, even if it got them hanged, he had no desire to stand up in open court and tell about it. As Ketcham himself put it: "With the help of Define Providence I suckseeded in the undertaking, thow not Expecting to B called as a Publick Evidence and theare to Declare what I gathered from one parson one month by Laying sceams and useing arguments to get it from him, which was a considerable shok of conscience."

Testify, nevertheless, he did. Hickey had asked Ketcham why he was in jail.

"I told him, because I was a Tory. On this a conversation ensued upon politicks. In different conversations he informed me that the Army was become damnably corrupted; that the [British] fleet was soon expected; and that he and a number of others were in a band to turn against the *American* Army when the King's troops should arrive, and asked me to be one of them. The plan, he told me, was, some were to be sick, and others were to hire men in their room. That eight of the General's Guard were concerned."

Hickey's efforts to conduct his own defense were pitiably weak: "He engaged in the scheme at first for the sake of cheating the Tories, and getting some money from them, and afterwards consented to have his name sent on board the man-of-war, in order that if the enemy should arrive and defeat the army here, and he should be taken prisoner, he might be safe."

A good many people in New York were wondering, just then, what would happen to them if they came again into the royal power. It was natural that a native-born Irishman, in arms against his king, should worry over that aspect of the matter.

But the desire to save his own skin—no matter how natural—is no defense for a soldier caught communicating illicitly with the enemy.

That is what the court-martial thought. Its verdict was unanimous: "That the prisoner *Thomas Hickey,* suffer death for said crimes by being hanged by the neck till he is dead." The court adjourned, and Hickey went back to his cell in a surly mood. Asked whether he wanted a chaplain, he snarled that "they wear all Cut throats."

Somebody started to put up a gallows, near the Bowery. Next day a council of seven general officers, with the commander-in-chief presiding, confirmed the sentence and fixed the execution for eleven o'clock in the morning, the following day, June 28.

The military justice of Revolutionary days moved swiftly. The man was guilty. Give him a day and a half for repentance. Then hang him. Four brigades were ordered to witness the execution and draw from the pinioned, dangling, twitching form of Sergeant Thomas Hickey such moral lessons as they might. Others, too, might profit. There were certainly more British agents in New York than anyone had yet discovered. Better give them something to worry about.

Orders came out on the morning of June 28. The brigades of Generals Heath, Scott, Spencer and Lord Stirling were ordered to parade at ten o'clock and march to the place of execution. Eighty men—twenty from each brigade—"with good Arms and Bayonets" were ordered out as a guard for the unfortunate Hickey on his last mile. There had been so much plotting already that there might be an attempt at rescue; but a guard of eighty men, with four brigades in reserve, could deal with anything the Tories or British might attempt. In all, about twenty thousand people are supposed to have watched Hickey die. Eighteenth-century Englishmen found executions rather interesting spectacles, and their American congeners had the same tastes.

Hickey was sullen as he stood at the gallows. In spite of his low opinion of the clergy, a chaplain went with him to the end. Hickey "appeared unaffected and obstinate to the last, except that when the Chaplain took him by the hand under the Gallows and bad[e] him adieu, a torrent of tears flowed over his face." Hickey, however, quickly recovered from his outburst of tears. "With an indignant scornful air he wiped 'em with his hand from his face and assumed the *confident look.*"

In his last few moments of life, Hickey breathed threats against someone named Green. Unless Green "was very cautious, the Design would *as yet* be executed against him." One medical officer understood this to refer to General Nathanael Greene. It is true that General Greene had been active against Tories, and his troops had made some of the arrests. But Hickey's bitterest resentment would naturally have turned against William Green, who had been a fellow conspirator, who had testified against him—and who was not going to be hanged in the next few minutes, who was not going to be hanged ever.

On went the noose and blindfold. Hickey swung off into air, writhed for a few dreadful minutes, hung limp. The twenty thousand spectators gazed. "Kip, the moon-curser, suddenly sank down and expired instantly." ("Moon-curser" was current slang for a smuggler—who preferred dark nights.)

Remorselessly, General Washington drove home the moral of the ghastly spectacle his court-martial had provided. Orders for the day said:

> The unhappy fate of *Thomas Hickey*, executed this day for mutiny, sedition, and treachery, the General hopes will be a warning to every soldier in the Army to avoid those crimes, and all others, so disgraceful to the character of a soldier, and pernicious to his country, whose pay he receives and bread he eats. And in order to avoid those crimes, the most certain method is to keep out of the temptation of them, and particularly to avoid lewd women, who, by the dying confession of this poor criminal, first led him into practices which ended in an untimely and ignominious death.

Just what "lewd women" may have had to do with it all is far from clear. There is no hint of a "sex angle" in any document save this one. Soldiers, however, are single men in barracks, who have never grown into plaster saints. Neither British nor Continental Army consisted entirely of Galahads. New York, during both American and British occupations, had a notorious vice district, ironically known as the "Holy Ground." But there is nothing save this one allusion in orders to connect the frail ladies who plied their ancient trade in the "Holy Ground" with the great plot that failed.

To Congress, General Washington reported: "I am hopeful this example will produce many salutary consequences and deter others from entering into like traitorous practices." It did. True, Tory conspiracies continued. True, too, some of the sorely tried troops mutinied once or twice. But the enemy never again attempted anything like the Hickey plot.

The conspiracies had been detected just in time. General Howe's personal transport had been lying in New York harbor for three days when Sergeant Thomas Hickey swung from the gallows. American alarm flags were flying on Staten Island. A forest of British masts was now appearing in the bay. Howe's attack was coming; but the Americans need no longer fear a second attack from the rear.

In a sense, Lieutenant General Washington and the Continental Army owed all this to Henry Dawkins. But they were not very grateful. Ketcham, as a reward for his espionage, was released. But where was Henry Dawkins? It is very probable that he was sitting in the damp, dark mine which served for a prison at Simsbury, Connecticut. Henry Dawkins was back in jail—again!

VIII

★ ★ ★

★

Nathan Hale—A Wasted Hero

TWO DAYS after Hickey swung from his gallows, the enemy's forces began to arrive. On June 30, 1776, General William Howe landed his army on Staten Island. On July 12, Admiral Lord Howe, his brother, arrived with a powerful fleet and more troops. On August 1, Sir Henry Clinton returned from Charleston. He had been defeated, but he brought back with him additional redcoats for the attack on New York, which now could not be far off.

Though it was clearly impossible to defend Manhattan and Long Island very long against a hostile army, supported by a hostile navy, Congress insisted the attempt be made; and General Washington, ever the well-disciplined soldier, obediently undertook his hopeless task. Now was the time to set up an intelligence net like Revere's in Boston—first on Staten Island, which could not possibly be held, for lack of troops; later on Long Island and Manhattan, ready to begin espionage when the Americans were forced to withdraw, as they assuredly would be. Such a network could have kept General Washington fully informed, as successful networks on those very islands did, later in the war; but no one thought of that in time. One or two patriot spies, probably volunteers, did remain on Staten Island, but they had no means of transmitting intelligence when they got it.

After Howe's landing there, the need for intelligence became pressing. On July 14, 1776, General Hugh Mercer could find no one to enter the British camp, which was being observed by at least one resident agent, who still had no means of communication. On August 20, however, Brigadier General William Livingston, later governor of New Jersey, sent out a courier, who reached his Staten Island colleague about midnight and was back next day with full details. The courier was probably Lawrence Mascoll, since Washington's warrant books show a payment to him on August 23, 1776, for going into the enemy's lines for information.

The secret agent on Staten Island whom he met—almost certainly one of the devoted Mersereau family, who spied for Washington throughout the war—had been keeping his ears open, had "heard the orders read, and heard the Generals talking." He reported enemy strength as thirty-five thousand and predicted that twenty thousand men would be landed on Long Island—information that turned out to be surprisingly correct, for Howe had about thirty-four thousand men, of whom he landed some twenty thousand on Long Island. The resident agent was also sure that the British wagon train was prepared to move and that all but two of Howe's field guns were already aboard the transports. All this was confirmed within two days, when the British tents on Staten Island began to disappear and ships could be seen moving to the east end of Long Island.

This information was out of date in a few days, however, for on August 27 the British won the Battle of Long Island and, two days later, General Washington withdrew his forces from Brooklyn to Manhattan.

Again American headquarters found itself unable to find out what the enemy was doing. On September 1, General Washington was urging General Heath and General George Clinton to establish some "Channel of information," as it was by this time "of great consequence to gain intelligence of the enemy's designs, and of their intended operations." The general hoped Clinton, as a New Yorker, might be able to find volunteer spies, "in whom a confidence may be reposed." If no patriots could be found, perhaps some Tory might be bribed to spy "for a reasonable reward."

Within a few days, the worried commander needed information so badly he did not care whether the reward was "reasonable" or not. By September 5, 1776, he was writing: "Do not stick at expense to bring this to pass, as I was never more uneasy than on account of my want of knowledge."

Just as getting military intelligence of any kind began to seem hopeless, on September 8, Colonel Isaac Nicoll, of the New York Militia, commanding at Fort Constitution, up the Hudson, sent the first real information of the enemy since the loss of Long Island. This made General Washington hope for "regular Intelligence of the Enemy's Movement," but Nicoll could send no more. Governor George Clinton managed to get two agents, George Treadwell and Benjamin Ludlum, from New Rochelle to Long Island, where they remained until September 12, bringing back a grossly exaggerated estimate of British strength; but, though this was sent to General Washington at once, intelligence remained inadequate.

There was only one thing left for General Washington to do. He would have to send a spy into the British lines on Long Island. A more experienced intelligence service than the Americans yet possessed would have sent in several agents, in case one was caught. Instead, General Washington ordered Lieutenant Colonel Thomas Knowlton to find a solitary volunteer. Knowlton asked Lieutenant James Sprague, veteran of the French and Indian War, to undertake the dangerous task. Since no soldier is ever ordered on such a mission, Sprague had a perfect right to refuse, and did so. "I am willing to go & fight them, but as far as going among them & being taken & hung up like a dog, I will not do it."

Either before or after Sprague's refusal, the lieutenant colonel called a meeting of all the officers of Knowlton's Rangers, none of whom liked the idea, either. Just as it became apparent that no one would volunteer, there was a sudden stir at the door, Nathan Hale, still pallid from a recent illness, joined the group.

"I will undertake it," he said.

The volunteer was a young Yale athlete of the Class of 1773, a schoolmaster at Haddam, Connecticut, tall, sturdy, handsome, an ardent patriot, impelled solely by a sense of duty to undertake a mission in which there was a prospect of disgrace, no chance of glory, and imminent risk of ignominious death.

Though the story that the commander-in-chief personally gave Hale his orders is not improbable, there is no clear evidence, since exact instructions were too secret to be written down. Whoever may have been responsible, American intelligence planned this dangerous mission as badly as it could be planned. Anyone who had ever seen Nathan Hale was sure to recognize him, for the spy was literally a marked man; exploding powder had scarred his face. Worse still, his cousin Samuel Hale was the British Army's deputy commissary of prisoners. Though wholly inexperienced in intelligence, Hale was given no training, no planned cover, no contact with patriotic American civilians within the British lines. There is no record that he was given the money he was certain to need. No line of communication was arranged. He was given no "sympathetic" ink, though the British had been using it for a year or more, and Sir James Jay, brother of John Jay, had invented a formula of his own three years earlier. The kind of memorized code a man can carry in his head was not even thought of. Having run the hideous risk of collecting intelligence, Hale would have to carry about with him the written notes that would, if he were caught, instantly prove him a spy.

Efforts to maintain secrecy were very clumsy. No false orders were issued to explain the captain's disappearance. Asher Wright, the captain's "waiter," was sure to wonder what had become of him. So were the men in his company. Every officer in the Rangers knew Captain Hale was going out as a spy. No breath of suspicion has ever touched the loyalty of these officers or men; but loyalty is not the same as silence. Any chance British spy might hear the gossip by the campfires.

Worst of all, Hale was not cautioned to maintain silence himself. Before starting, the daring young captain talked over the whole plan with Captain William Hull, a Yale classmate, who had been a brother officer in Webb's Regiment, before Hale transferred to the Rangers. Hull was perfectly loyal, too; but a spy has no business discussing his mission with anyone.

Hull, being still assigned to Webb's Regiment, knew nothing about the meeting of Ranger officers. Horrified to learn what his friend meant to do, he tried hard to dissuade him; but Hale was determined: "He owed to his country the accomplishment of an object so important, and so much desired by the Commander of her armies, and he knew of no other mode of obtaining the information, than by assuming a disguise and passing into the enemy's camp."

Hull continued to expostulate. He told Hale that, "though *he* viewed the business of a spy as a *duty*, yet, he could not officially be required to perform it. That such a service was not claimed of the meanest soldier." Besides, "his nature was too frank and open for deceit and disguise." There was also the disgraceful nature of espionage: "Who respects the character of a spy?"

"For a year I have been attached to the army," replied Hale, as Hull reports him, "and have not rendered any material service." As for the supposed disgrace of espionage, "every kind of service, necessary to the public good, becomes honorable by being necessary."

When Hull again begged him to give up the scheme, his friend said only: "I will reflect, and do nothing but what duty demands."

After that, Hale simply disappeared, and Hull knew nothing more, though he "feared he had gone to the British lines, to execute his fatal purpose."

The gallant spy's next movements can be accurately traced because he took with him Sergeant Stephen Hempstead, who, long after the war, published the story in Missouri. Hale had been provided with "a general order to all armed vessels, to take him to any place he should designate." He called in Sergeant Hempstead, who records that the captain "said I must go with him as far as I could, with safety, and wait for his return."

They left Harlem Heights about September 12, 1776, looking for a safe place to cross Long Island Sound "the first opportunity." This proved impossible near New York City, because the coast was guarded by British naval vessels, whose tenders could row close inshore to reconnoiter and block any passage. The captain and the sergeant could find no way to reach Long Island until, at Norwalk, they came upon the armed American sloop *Schuyler,* commanded by Captain Charles Pond. This vessel took Hale across and dropped him at Huntington, Long Island, where American secret missions continued to slip in during the rest of the war.

Thus far, Hale had remained in uniform—though not the colonial buff and blue with epaulets, which only a few senior officers owned. Asher Wright remembered in old age that the captain's uniform was a "frock" and that it was "made of white linen, & fringed, such as officers used to wear," the kind of thing—"frock and kerchief"—much worn by American officers for field service. It was something like a frontier hunting shirt, which Washington once proposed as a uniform for the entire army.

Hale had with him, however, "a plain suit of citizen's brown clothes," very likely the "Linen Cloth Similar to brown Holland for Summer ware," which his sister Rose had planned to make into clothing for him in June of 1776.

Since he had had two years' experience in teaching, he naturally assumed "the character of a Dutch schoolmaster." Besides, it was September, when any unemployed pedagogue would naturally be looking for a school. He had his Yale diploma with him. Why he had taken this with him on active duty is hard to understand; but Yale diplomas of that period were small enough to carry about, and he had good reason to take it with him, behind the enemy's lines, as "an introduction to his assumed calling." He was shrewd enough to leave his silver shoebuckles with Sergeant Hempstead, "saying they would not comport with his character of schoolmaster."

From the moment Captain Pond put him ashore at Huntington until his capture, Hale's movements are veiled in mystery; which is not remarkable, since he was on a secret mission, his papers disappeared, and his captors hanged him without trial. In the absence of a court-martial record, all that is really known is what Captain John Montresor, chief engineer of the British Army, told the American officers who received him under a flag of truce the evening after Hale had been hanged. Montresor, who had seen Hale just before the execution, said "that Captain Hale had passed through their army, both on Long Island and New York [i.e., Manhattan]. That he had procured sketches of the fortifications, and made memoranda of their number and different positions."

Hale was on familiar ground when he reached Long Island, where his regiment had been stationed in the early part of 1776, before moving to Manhattan. Benson J. Lossing—perhaps quoting a local legend—says that he went on after landing and, "at a farm-house a mile distant he was kindly furnished with breakfast and a bed for repose after his night's toil." This may be true, especially if Washington's headquarters were well enough informed to know in advance where their agent would be safe. The farmhouse may be identical with the tavern of the Widow Chichester, better known as "Mother Chich," where some accounts say he paused.

The spy had hardly reached Long Island when the military situation changed entirely, for on September 15 the British seized Manhattan. Since British positions on Long Island were no longer of any interest to Washington, a less devoted secret agent might simply have returned; but the conscientious Hale went boldly on to Manhattan, to observe the new positions. There is no way of knowing how he managed to cross the East River; but it has been conjectured that he found work on one of the market boats, carrying produce into the city from Long Island. This would take him to Whitestone Landing, Flushing and Hellgate, with a chance to see what the enemy were doing at each stop. Plausible though the idea is, it remains unconfirmed. If Hale did try such a scheme, the boat would eventually take him into New York, along with its load of vegetables, inconspicuously.

By the time he reached New York City, the Americans had been pushed back to where 127th Street now runs. The British held the 106th Street line, with advanced posts as far north as 110th Street or beyond; and there was some vigorous bickering between the lines, in which for the first time American troops, in the open field and without entrenchments, put the regulars to flight.

By September twenty-first, probably several days earlier, the disguised captain found himself back on Manhattan, from which he had started. He had by this time been in enemy-held territory more than a week, in danger of being recognized at every instant. It has been said—probably correctly, though without adequate evidence—that he pushed resolutely northward till he reached the British front, where the most valuable information was to be had. If so, he passed through (and observed) Lord Percy's troops (in reserve somewhere near the eastern part of Eightieth Street); Sir Henry Clinton's troops (in support, along a line not far from Ninety-third Street); and Lord Cornwallis's troops (disposed in depth with a main line of resistance near 106th Street). This gave him the exact military intelligence General Washington wanted.

From the British front, the secret agent could look across to American outposts—and safety—on the high ground not far north of 127th Street. Though the prospect of crossing the front was remote, Hale may have hoped to row a boat around the flanks of both armies and safely into the American rear. Or he may, as has been reported, have hoped to slip through the no man's land around what is now Columbia University and back to the Continental Army.

Since Sergeant Hempstead had been ordered to wait at Norwalk, the original plan had evidently been to send a small craft of some kind to pick his captain up on the north shore of Long Island. However, the military situation having completely changed, to return to Long Island and use the escape route there was now extremely dangerous.

Hale, having secured detailed intelligence of British troop dispositions and field fortifications, was mainly concerned to get back to his own lines when, sometime during the night of September 21, he was arrested. There are three discrepant accounts of this episode. According to one version, probably the true one, Hale was captured because he mistook a boat from a British man-of-war for an American craft sent to take him off. It is incredible that this could happen by daylight, since the oarsmen would be in uniform, but it could easily happen in darkness. The incident is sometimes placed in Manhattan, along the East River; sometimes on the north shore of Long Island.

Hale is also said to have been betrayed by a Tory who recognized him at "Mother Chich's" tavern. A third version makes the Tory betrayer his cousin, Samuel Hale, though there is no reason whatever to suppose that this is true.

According to the first and most probable version, Washington's spy was captured by sailors from H.M.S. *Halifax,* lying off Whitestone Point. Lieutenant William Quarme—captain by courtesy, since he commanded the ship—went ashore in a small boat, near the foot of 111th Street, either between the lines or at a point where the British lines had been pushed forward toward 110th Street or a little farther.

Hale certainly had no reason to suppose that a boat from the American forces would put in here to take him off, but he may have supposed that the little craft contained Americans from Long Island, who would take him across the East River. When he saw his mistake, he is said to have betrayed agitation. Even without this, Captain Quarme would naturally have been suspicious. There was something very queer about a civilian schoolmaster at the front. If Hale was beyond the British front between the two armies, suspicion was inevitable.

He was immediately seized and turned over to the army. The time of the capture is clearly fixed by British Army orders:

> Head Q^rs New york Island, Sep^t 1776 . . . A Spy f^m the Enemy (by his own full Confession) Apprehended Last night, was this day Executed at 11 oClock in front of the Atilery Park—

The main outline of the final tragedy is clear. In addition to Montresor's account and the official note on the execution, several British officers' diaries mention the incident. Howe had set up his headquarters in the house of James Beekman, near the East River, now the corner of First Avenue and Fifty-first Street. Since Hale was under serious suspicion, he must have been searched before being taken to the commanding general, and the incriminating papers he carried must have been found at once.

Satisfied that the prisoner was an American officer in disguise —as Hale himself admitted—Howe simply ordered him hanged, without trial. It is extraordinary that, in all the subsequent outcry over Hale's fate and the harshness with which he was treated, this hasty condemnation has been passed over. André, who also admitted his identity, was nevertheless tried by a board of generals. Even the ruthless Germans gave individuals accused of espionage a court-martial; and the German spies who landed on Long Island in World War II were allowed to carry their appeal to the Supreme Court.

A British officer who was present when the prisoner was condemned says the good-natured Howe was regretful. Hale's "manly bearing and the evident disinterested patriotism of the handsome young prisoner, sensibly touched a chord of General Howe's nature; but the stern rules of war concerning such offenses would not allow him to exercise even pity."

Once Howe had ordered the execution, his prisoner passed into the custody of William Cunningham, provost marshal of the British forces. According to tradition Hale was confined for the night in the Beekman greenhouse, adjoining the mansion. As he was to be hanged next morning, it was hardly worth while taking the prisoner four miles down Manhattan Island to the city jail, which stood near the present Hall of Records.

Reports of British cruelty at Nathan Hale's execution have been much exaggerated. Cunningham was undoubtedly a brute; but the story that he tore Hale's letter to his mother to pieces before his eyes is plainly false, since she had been dead for some years. Hale wrote only two letters, which remained in the provost marshal's hands for some time after his victim's death.

Montresor told the story of the hanging to Captain Alexander Hamilton, of the artillery, and Captain William Hull, of

Webb's Regiment, in which Hale had begun his army career. Hull says specifically: "I learned the melancholy particulars from this officer, who was present at his execution, and seemed touched by the circumstances attending it." Hamilton must have recorded the incident at some time or other; but there is now no trace of what he wrote.

Even Montresor, Howe's chief engineer, described Cunningham as "hardened to human suffering and every softening sentiment of the heart," and there is irony in the fact that Cunningham himself was hanged for forgery in London in 1791. Montresor also admitted that Hale "asked for a clergyman to attend him. It was refused. He then requested a Bible; that too was refused by his inhuman jailer." Montresor was fully acquainted with the facts. He had been alone with Hale just before the hanging. He had no reason to blacken the character of his own army's provost, in talking with enemy officers; and he seems to have reached the American camp in a state of shock and indignation at what he had witnessed that morning.

For some reason, there was a delay after Hale reached the gallows at the artillery park, where Captain Montresor had his tent. The humane Montresor, pitying the condemned man, "requested the Provost Marshal to permit the prisoner to sit in my marquee, while he was making the necessary preparations. Captain Hale entered; he was calm, and bore himself with gentle dignity, in the consciousness of rectitude and high intentions. He asked for writing materials, which I furnished him: he wrote two letters, one to his mother and one to a brother officer."

Without quoting Montresor further, Hull hurries over the rest of the ghastly story in his own words: "He was shortly after summoned to the gallows. But a few persons were around him, yet his characteristic dying words were remembered. He said, 'I only regret, that I have but one life to lose for my country.' "

The famous dying words are thus fully authenticated. Montresor had heard them only a few hours earlier, when he repeated them to Hull and Hamilton. They were, in fact, derived from a line in Joseph Addison's *Cato:*

> What pity is it
> That we can die but once to serve our country!

The play was much read by educated Americans and was often in the mind of Washington, whose writings frequently quoted or paraphrased passages from it. Hale's eager reading and his activity in the Linonian Society as a Yale undergraduate, all indicate a knowledge of the English classics. In fact, a letter still extant, written to him by a girl with whom he corresponded, quotes from *Cato,* though it does not quote this passage.

He had gone to war, quoting a tag from Horace;

> *Dulce et decorum est pro patria mori.*

His career as an American soldier began and ended in the same mood, each time with a quotation from the classics, as befitted a scholar in arms.

Hale must have handed the farewell letters to Montresor, who must have passed them over, however reluctantly, to Cunningham, instead of bringing them across the lines later in the day.

The executioner was probably Richmond, the mulatto who usually served as British hangman. Hangings in that day were offhand affairs. A noose was thrown over the limb of a tree or a simple timber frame. The victim, bound, was forced to stumble up a ladder. He was then forced to jump, was pushed off or had the ladder pulled from under him. André stood on a cart, which was drawn away to let him drop. Hale's body was probably left hanging, as a warning to others, as was the custom of the day. British soldiers, with grisly humor, found "in a rebel Gentleman's garden, a painted soldier on a board,"— perhaps an old inn sign. This they hung up beside the swinging corpse, labeling it General Washington.

Sometime between December 26, 1776, and January 25, 1777 (not very long after Hale's death), Major John Palsgrave Wyllys, who had been captured September 15, during the American retreat from New York, was exchanged. The Reverend Enoch Hale rode to Wethersfield, Connecticut, to see him and inquire about his brother's death. Being himself in confinement, Wyllys had not seen Nathan Hale, but he had spoken with Cunningham soon after the hanging. As Enoch Hale records it in his diary: "He saw my Brother's Diploma which the Provost Marshall showed him who also had two letters of his— one to me, the other to his commanding officer written after he was sentenced."

Probably Captain William Hull was right when he noted that "The Provost Martial, in the diabolical spirit of cruelty, destroyed the letters of the prisoner, and assigned as a reason 'that the rebels should never know they had a man who could die with so much firmness.' "

Undeterred by Hale's fate, a spy named Joshua Davis—who would later assist the successful Culper ring of American spies on Manhattan and Long Island—entered the British lines almost immediately, returned safely, and was paid September 29, 1776.

IX

★   ★   ★

★

Spy Catching on the Hudson

THE SECRET SERVICES of both sides became more active along
the Hudson as soon as Howe's army had occupied New York.
A hastily improvised American espionage soon began to penetrate the city, while the Tories in the already existing British
net continued their espionage, together with active, though
surreptitious, recruiting. Howe's officers had great confidence
in the accuracy of the military intelligence which their spy
rings supplied. An American secret agent heard a British intelligence officer declare, late in 1776 or early in 1777, "that by
means of their Emisaries they were informed of every thing
that passed among us and that Women were the most proper
persons for that purpose"—the first suggestion that female
agents were being used.

Though there was still no adequate American espionage,
some secret agents began to get into New York, secure a certain amount of information, and get safely out again; and the
system swiftly improved. In 1776, the Mersereau family had
begun the espionage (first on Staten Island, later in New York)
which they were to continue to the end of the war.

At first, both sides gained a good deal of information from
ordinary travelers, since each army allowed people on private

business to go back and forth with dangerous freedom. British intelligence officers, well aware how much information refugees and temporary visitors brought with them, picked them up for interrogation as soon as they reached New York. But, since they allowed many to go home again, nearly as much information as the British themselves secured, leaked back to the Americans.

Thus, one Alexander Cruikshank, entering New York on March 10, 1777, was met at the ferry and sent to General James Robertson to give information on the American militia. William Cunningham, the provost marshal who had hanged Nathan Hale, soon appeared with questions about American fortifications. Though General Washington was later remarkably successful in feeding false information to the enemy, efforts by such casual visitors to deceive British interrogators were not likely to succeed. One patriot, otherwise unknown, named Cummings, when questioned by General Robertson about this time, tried to make him believe that the Americans had forty or fifty thousand men. Robertson cut him off with the curt remark "that they knew better." Yet both Cruikshank and Cummings brought back military intelligence of value to the Americans.

With people going back and forth so freely, many British military secrets leaked out. The most important was the general plan of Burgoyne's intended march via Ticonderoga down the Hudson, which was reported to the New York State Committee on Conspiracies on February 15, 1777, thirteen days before Burgoyne submitted his written plan to the king—in London! The American spy who brought the information from Manhattan predicted that Burgoyne would march south; that Howe, after capturing Philadelphia, would attack the rebel forts blocking the Hudson, and would then co-operate with Burgoyne; that Howe and Burgoyne would jointly attack New England. All of this intelligence was confirmed by another agent a month later (March 17, 1777). Both men had probably heard officers discussing plans made before Burgoyne sailed for England.

The information was remarkably accurate. Everything happened exactly as predicted, with two exceptions: it was Clinton, not Howe, who attacked the American forts; and, after Burgoyne had surrendered, there could be no British attack on New England.

Both these American spies knew all about British efforts to hire Russian troops for the American campaign—a scheme much favored by Sir Henry Clinton, who had observed the Russian Army. It came to nothing only because Catherine the Great scornfully refused to sell her subjects.

Not only were the rebels in 1776 able to get secret agents in and out of New York; they were also able to catch some of the British agents sent against them. Four days after he reached New York (April 13, 1776) and long before the enemy arrived, General Washington took steps to close their "regular Channel of intelligence" from the city. He knew the British had such a system, "by which they are, from time to time, made acquainted with the number and extent of our Works, our Strength, and all our movements." Before he arrived, New Yorkers had been selling supplies and even arms to the enemy's warships. This, too, was stopped, at least in part, especially after the New York Provincial Congress set up Committees for Conspiracies; but the patriots' counterintelligence measures were not always effective.

Nevertheless, the Americans soon began to lay a good many of the enemy's agents by the heels. In July, 1776, they found a man "Dressed in Women Close trying to go above the ferry" —perhaps at Hoboken. When stripped, searched, and found to have two letters, he was at once confined; but there the record ends. It is by no means certain he was hanged, for American jails could not always hold the enemy's resourceful agents. One Samuel MacFarlane, for example, arrested at the house of a certain John McDale, escaped at once, with his host's aid; and, though McDale himself was ordered to appear in court, the suspected spy had disappeared for good.

In September, 1776, a certain William Wallace, "taken up upon susption," also escaped. A scouting party picked him up again on April 1, 1777, at "Cutlensman" (Courtland Manor), but Wallace, a persevering fellow, escaped a second time.

When he was caught again, it was discovered that he had carried secrecy so far as to disguise his horse! He owned a brown mare with a white blaze. He had colored the white hairs black. The committee asked a natural "question why he altered the mark in the face of the mare." Wallace was perfectly frank about it: "the mare was well None and he did it that he should Not Be discovered"—practically a confession of guilt.

It was difficult to detect the secret Tory militia companies, which the British established with great speed. Howe disembarked on Staten Island June 30, 1776. By July his secret army extended, behind the American lines, as far up the Hudson as Albany, where there was a company of fifty men and three officers. As a reward for its services, the regiment to which this company belonged was to be given a tract of land six miles square. The fact that land grants were allotted by regiments, shows how large a secret army the Tories meant to raise.

It was not long before the Hudson Valley buzzed with mystery. Furtive messengers passed down isolated country lanes at night. Wakeful women by midnight windows watched groups of armed men, stealthily passing. Lonely farmhouses opened noiseless doors to silently arriving travelers. Companies of Tory guerrillas, behind their neighbors' backs, secretly prepared to fight for their king, then slipped away to join the redcoats. Reports from innumerable spies sped down the river to Howe's headquarters; and straight through this web of intrigues passed unobtrusive couriers, mysterious travelers on the king's business, between Canada and the "lower party," on Manhattan.

The organization was very skillful. Howe's recruiting agents knew where to find sympathizers' houses and secret hideouts. One Tory recruiting agent explained "ther was not much dainger of Being Ketch^d for the Torys had prepared private Cellars a long the way."

By 1777, however, the Committee on Conspiracies was actively ferreting out both the Tory militia and the Tory spies, and was hanging a good many men who badly needed it. One of the first victims was Daniel Strang, who, when brought before a court-martial in January, admitted he was recruiting for the enemy, but denied he was a spy. The evidence, however, showed that he had both recruited and supplied information. He was sentenced to be "Hanged by the Neck Untill he be Dead Dead Dead."

When, in April, 1777, American militia surrounded and searched the house of John Hunt, at White Plains, they found, first, "some Oranges, Tea & some Buckles," then a man hiding between a straw mattress and a feather bed. Tea and oranges were British importations. Besides, why was the stranger hiding? A man doesn't sequestrate himself between a straw mattress and a feather bed merely out of a desire for privacy. Searching further, the Americans found, in a back room, one Simon Mabie (or Mabee), with a warrant issued by General William Howe, authorizing him to enlist Tory recruits. This was dated March 30, 1777, only a few days earlier. There was also a certificate of Mabie's loyalty to the king, dated March 29.

A court-martial at Peekskill heard testimony that Mabie had already enlisted some soldiers for the royal forces and sentenced him to hang. Presently one of his recruits was also captured, court-martialed, and likewise sentenced to hang. Mabie—perhaps a relative of another Tory, Peter Maybe, of Saratoga, who survived to guide Burgoyne—had been caught within two weeks of his arrival.

In May, 1777, General Washington was alarmed to learn that a British captain, a British lieutenant and two British sergeants were among his troops, disguised as countrymen; but no one was ever able to find these spies and others like them, though their presence and sometimes even their physical appearance was known. There was, for instance, a British agent with a "withered" hand, who ought to have been easily identified, and "a middle sized Indian of about 50 years of age," who carried messages to Clinton in New York. Neither was ever caught.

In May, another court-martial at Fort Montgomery, on the Hudson, passed a death sentence on two men named Alexander Campbell and Arthur McKenny, for giving aid, comfort and intelligence to the British. Campbell was further charged with corresponding with the enemy and concealing British secret agents. Another conspirator, Arnout Viele, was also sentenced to the noose, May 23. Jacobus Rose and Jacob Midagh were

ordered hanged for British recruiting, and their petition for re-
prieve was rejected on the very day of the execution.

Not all the sentences were so severe. Courts-martial, in more
lenient moods, passed sentences of imprisonment for a year, six
months or only three months, or fines as low as fifteen dollars,
or sentenced Tories to be branded with a hot iron in the form
of the letter "T." In some cases the patriots' leniency was truly
surprising. A suspected clergyman, ordered to leave New York
state, was eventually allowed to remain on parole. When the
mother of a Tory prisoner complained that she needed her
son's support, the Committee for Conspiracies obligingly let
him out on bail. The wife of a Tory on active duty with the
enemy was gallantly sent to join him under flag of truce. Other
wives whose husbands were in the enemy's ranks were allowed
to remain in their homes for years, until, in 1781, a state law
at last compelled their departure.

Various methods were used to detect the British spies and
secret recruiting agents. American *agents provocateurs* were
not uncommon—convinced patriots, who pretended to be Tories till their victims were entrapped. One such *provocateur*,
a Bostonian named Edward Davis, went about Albany posing
as a British officer and in British uniform—which should have
been enough to warn any genuine Tory that he was not what
he seemed. Nevertheless, one of his dupes was foolish enough
to offer him a list of volunteers to send to General Howe, concealed in a hollow staff.

Occasionally, some outraged patriot took a hand as a volunteer detective. Such a man was Simon Newall, or Newell, who
lived near Peekskill. Chance has preserved a remarkably full
account of his success in exposing several active members of the
Tory underground. His special quarry was a man named John
Likely.

Newall went to work entirely on his own initiative, though,
unlike most amateur spy catchers, he took the laudable precaution of first getting official approval. He went to General
Oliver Wolcott, a Connecticut brigadier in Israel Putnam's division, and explained what he wanted to do. Since John Likely
was already under suspicion—he had been a tenant of the Tory,

Colonel Beverly Robinson, later involved in the Arnold treason --any prospect of trapping him roused official interest. Newall proposed to take "a Proper Person" with him and call at Likely's house for shelter, which would seem entirely natural in those days, when almost any farmhouse would take in a traveler for the night. Once in the Tory's home, Newall proposed "to Personate one Dissafected to his Count^ry and on my way to join Genl How and ingage in his service as Many as posible." It was too bad to abuse Likely's hospitality to get him hanged; but war is war, and the counterintelligence service has never been a place for squeamish people. Nothing whatever indicates that either Newall or General Wolcott had any compunctions. Having heard Newall's scheme, the general gave it his blessing.

As the "Proper Person" to go with him, Newall chose a friend named Eleazar Curtis, and the pair went off one rainy night to Likely's house, asked for a night's shelter, and were warmly received. They told their prospective victim that they came from the Upper Nine Partners Mine—a plausible tale, since there was such a mine not very far away, and it was then working—and were trying to "spy out a way" to send recruits to General Howe. There was no exchange of sign and countersign, no recognition conversations, no display of agreed tokens. The trusting Likely, who was clearly not cut out for a life of intrigue, took the two strangers for exactly what they said they were, and also took them straight to his heart.

Newall and Curtis may have been extraordinarily good actors or Likely may have been an overconfiding innocent. Whichever was the case, when Newall and Curtis revealed their supposedly mysterious errand as British agents, Likely fell instantly into the pitfall. Or, as the exultant Newall later put it, "John Likely after we had divulg^d our Business Rejoiced at it and gladly receive[d] us as true subjects of King gorge. many things were said by him & us Relative to the Rebel Army and Genl Hows, in all of which he evidently manifested a firm attachment to and friendship for the latter but an avow^d dissafection to the former calling them *the Whigs, The Rebels, the Hot Heads,* &c."

Still foolish enough to accept these wandering and unidentified strangers as being exactly what they said they were, Likely rushed into eager explanations. He told them just how the British Army's local volunteer spies were watching the American forces in Worcester. They knew, he said, "all the movements of the Provential Army and of their march towards Danbury, and further said the friends of government had Persons Redy when ever gen¹ McDougal marched to carry the intelligence to the Regulars."

With his fish well hooked, Newall proceeded to feed him a little more bait. He asked how to find "True subjects to the King that I kneed not fear to tell my Business." With incredible naïveté Likely rose to the lure.

"I have repeatedly," he said, "in the course of the last winter and this spring Harb^oured, assisted and Pioleted King Gorge subjects on their way to N. York and ever will when in my power assist and help the side of Government."

Probably, at this stage, Likely heard a few admiring murmurs, meant to encourage him to further indiscreet disclosures. Utterly gulled, the poor fellow plunged recklessly ahead, as if determined to incriminate himself.

"I have Intelligence from N. York every week," he boasted, "and soon expect to see the Regulars in possession of this Place and then 'twill be better times."

Newall now led him on until he disclosed the names of fellow Tories, also engaged in intrigues against the American cause. Likely rattled off the names of Anthony Umaman (or Uman), "a good man & true subject," Peter Drake, Benjamin Field, one Valentine Lounsbury (or Lomaree) and a man named Fretenborough, living near the Croton Bridge. Fretenborough would be a great help to them, the besotted Likely told the supposed Tories, for he could get them across the Croton River—always an obstacle to secret travelers, heading for New York City.

The two counterintelligence men listened eagerly. All these revelations had a certain interest. Some of the news they heard was startling. Umaman had always appeared to be on the American side, was a member of the patriot Committee of Safety, and had served in the American militia.

Likely passed the two American agents on to his neighbor,

the supposed patriot, Umaman, who, after a few inquiries, was convinced of the strangers' good faith and began to talk as recklessly as their first victim. He had assisted many people on their way to the British, Umaman said, and "was glad of the oppertunity." True, he admitted, he was posing as a patriot. "He was a Committee man but he could not help it that he seldom sat with them had been Drafted as a soldier and once went a short Campaign but twas to still Peoples talk and save him self from Trouble." He warned against the local American commander, Brigadier General Alexander McDougall: "Old McDougal was D—d sharp."

Umaman went on to explain that Reuben Drake, chairman of the patriot Committee of Safety, was also helping the British. If Newall and Curtis wanted to get through the American lines, Drake, because of his high position among the local patriots, was the man to help them. He "had given Passes to people on the same Design, to secure them from the Rebels."

This was news indeed. Newall and Curtis hastily made mental notes, but kept their faces straight.

As if determined to get himself into as many difficulties as possible, Umaman stepped through the door to show them the quickest way to reach the houses of the men he had just named. The Americans went to the Drake homestead, but found too many people there and, fearing discovery if they went farther, started back to report to the patriot authorities. To their dismay, they met Likely on the road, but they still had not roused his suspicions.

Likely pointed out a supposedly safer route "acrost that lot," and the two got out of sight as quickly as possible. Only when they felt secure from observation once more, did they turn toward General Alexander McDougall's headquarters. That officer was delighted.

"Go on by all means," he told them.

As Curtis was now coming down with "Fever and ague" (in other words, malaria), Newall left him behind and, with one S. Hoskiss as his new companion, hurried to the home of Peter (not Reuben) Drake, whom the agents soon found to be a genuine Tory. From his house, they went on to find Daniel

Strang, who was not at home. His Tory family urged these loyal friends to wait for him, and Strang soon arrived.

Strang was as full of royalist sentiment and good advice as the two others; but he warned the counterintelligence men to "be exceeding carefull for the Army Hanged a good many"— as he had good reason to know, since the Daniel Strang hanged earlier in the year was certainly a relative and perhaps his father. Quite as incautious as Umaman, he repeated a list of local Tory names and gladly agreed to shelter an entirely imaginary detachment of Tory troops that the two American spies said would soon be following them.

Strang sent his son out to see whether the way was clear, while the patriot spies hid in the barn. Strang, Junior, soon came back, with word that Benjamin Fields would be glad to lodge them for the night.

Fields turned out to be a Quaker, loyal to constituted authority, as Quakers were likely to be, but opposed to war. He told his visitors they had better go home: "said he never ment to fight on either side. he chose to stay at home and would be glad the liberty People would let him alone. he would hurt nobody if they would not molest him." He added some advice: "Thee had better go home again and let everybody alone. . . . it is a Dreadfull thing to fight and kill folks."

"I could not live at Home in Peace but should be Drafted for the Continental Army," Newall told him, "and if I must fight I would fight on the Right side and stand for my King."

"Ay, friend," said the Quaker, "thee art Right again, but thee must be exceeding carefull for if thee is taken and caried into Peeks Kill twill go very Hard with thee."

In the morning this pacific monarchist passed them on to Valentine Lounsbury, who gave them four more Tory names and sent them on. Each Tory they met was as innocently confiding as his predecessor. When to one Thomas Levinus they told "the old story that we told them all," this simple soul replied:

"God bless you then you are not the first and I hope not the last who will go over to the Kings side."

When they inquired about a man named Huson, whom Lounsbury had foolishly mentioned, Levinus volunteered further damaging information: "huson had a number of men and ment to go into New York that very night and he was a Dam'd good fellow and had another Dam'd good fellow with him." The second damned good fellow was a certain Lent Far —"who I afterwards took," says Newall grimly.

The American spies dined with Levinus, Huson, Far, and one or two other prospective victims, at the home of a Tory named Tompkins. Levinus seized the occasion to incriminate himself further. He "God Bless^d the good luck that so many had gone and were going to How. hoped the Dam-nd Rebels would get Defeated and more to the same import."

Lent Far, chiming in, proceeded to convict himself of treason. Chatting gaily with the patriot agents, he told them "he came from the great nine partners [that is, the mine]. had been with Huson some time. had two mates Came with him but they were taken by the Dam'd Rebels which he swore he never would for he would fight till he Died before he would be Taken. said his Design was to go into York. said Huson and himself could go when they Pleas^d for they knew all about the Damd Rebel Guards and they had good Guns and amonition enough. said he ment to set out with Huson that very night but was glad to wait till the next Monday night for our Recruits which was the Time we agreed to meet at Tomkins House. Lent Far manifested every expression of joy at so many Coming to join their Party. Far said he had been in the Rebel service but he never would again. said huson and his business was to plunder the whiggs and they had as good will to kill them as a Dogg. Far said he had known many to go into N. York and many more would. said he would go and join How himself and fight his way through the Reble guards to get there or Die. we all Dined Heartily, Drank King George Health and Hows, confusion to Congress and Washington &c."

With enough evidence to convict the whole Tory group, the counterintelligence men made once more for their own headquarters. Newall himself arrested Far a little later.

If Newall and his superiors had known a little more about the game they were playing, they would have let this little knot of Tory conspirators alone and worked one or two of their own men into the ring; or they would, in some other way, have maintained a friendly and co-operative contact with them. They would thus have known all about future recruits going to New York, who could easily be gathered up at the American outpost line, if outpost commanders were forewarned. American headquarters would thus have gained useful insight into the British intelligence system and it would have been possible to feed General Howe some thoroughly unreliable information—a trick which General Washington soon began to employ.

The Americans, however, were too inexperienced to realize this possibility. The men were traitors. Arrest them! Somebody with stars on his shoulder probably pounded a desk.

Within about a month, Likely and Umaman were facing a court-martial, convened by General McDougall at Peekskill.

The charges against Likely were sweeping enough to satisfy any judge advocate: "Treason against the State of New York in adhering to the King of Great Britain, at open War with the United American States aiding and abeting the unnatural War against them, declaring they had & would do it, comforting the Enemies of these States and acting as Spies & Agents for the Enemy."

Newall, Curtis and Hodgkiss (so the name is now given) appeared as witnesses against him. Newall's evidence mostly repeated what he had already said in his report, adding only the fact that Likely had boasted: "a Night or two before Thirteen had passed on their way to New York." Curtis confirmed Newall's story.

The judge advocate now introduced another witness. On April 29, Newall's friend Hodgkiss, accompanied by Amsey Hart, had also visited Likely. According to Hodgkiss, "they told the Prisoner they were going to New York to join the Enemy. he seemed much pleased with their intentions. gave them directions at what Houses to stop on their way down. told them Twenty or Thirty had gone down a few days before chiefly Armed. he said he had afforded such sort of People meaning those were going to the Enemy, all the assistance in his Power. that he should have gone to the Enemy himself, but for his Family—when they left him he wished them success &

directed them which way to go." Amsey Hart added a few details.

Though denied counsel, Likely did fairly well in his own defense. From the beginning, he said, he had distrusted Newall and Curtis. Finding they were Tories, he had "sent them to Anthony Umans [Umaman's] one of the Committee in order that they might be apprehended." What better evidence could there be of his devotion to the patriot cause? The trouble was that, by this time, everyone realized that the patriotism of Umaman, too, was only skin deep.

When Umaman was also brought before the same court-martial, Newall and Curtis again appeared as witnesses, but their testimony brought out little against him that was not already in evidence.

The court-martial found both Likely and Umaman guilty. But the army officers sitting as its members began to feel doubts about "the propriety of this Court trying State Prisoners," even though the New York State Convention had authorized it to do so. The officers had further qualms about the failure to provide the defendants with counsel. They also thought them entitled to a jury trial. And, furthermore, said the court-martial, "we fear whilst we are Strugling for the Sacred Name of Liberty we are establishing the fatal Tendency to Despotism."

It may be that the defendants Likely and Umaman (who were unquestionably guilty) owed their lives to these scruples. The court-martial's hesitation did not, however, prevent it from sentencing each to a hundred lashes and imprisonment throughout the war.

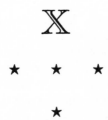

X

Spy Catchers Extraordinary

IN THE LATTER half of 1776, the rather hit-or-miss methods by which the New York state civilian authorities had been running down spies improved; and a regular group of counterintelligence men was set up, mainly under the direction of John Jay, the future Chief Justice, and Nathaniel Sackett, another leading figure of the day. At least ten agents worked under their orders. Four—Enoch Crosby, Martin Cornwill (or Cornell), Nicholas Brower and John Haines—seem to have been continuously at work. The others—Benjamin Pitcher, William Denney, Henry Wooden, Joseph Bennett, Elijah Frost and Samuel Hopkins—were probably called on irregularly, when needed. Various other local patriots co-operated, including one of the local physicians; and militia forces were always ready for raids and arrests.

The most successful of all these counterintelligence agents, and the only one about whom anything is now known, was the shoemaker, Enoch Crosby, from whom James Fenimore Cooper —no matter what he himself said about it—took many of the traits of Harvey Birch, hero of his novel, *The Spy*. A whole book (two whole books, if you count *The Spy* as well as Crosby's own volume) deals with his adventures; and his story is now confirmed by his own detailed manuscript narrative (supported by numerous affidavits from his associates), a document which has lain, unknown, in the archives, ever since the aging secret agent signed it.

Born in Harwich, Massachusetts, Crosby had been brought up in the town of Southeast (near Carmel, New York) and had learned the trade of cordwainer (shoemaker) in Phillipstown (now Kent), Connecticut. He was living in Danbury when the news of Lexington came.

Crosby, the first man to respond to the call for recruits for a Danbury company, saw service in the invasion of Canada, after which he returned to civil life, his health having suffered from the hardships of the campaign. Late in August, 1776, he enlisted again, at Carmel, New York, and set out for the American camp, at Kingsbridge.

Mistaken by a Westchester Tory named Bunker for a royalist sympathizer, he wormed his way into the man's confidence so deftly that he was soon being introduced to various pro-British plotters, and learning all about a Tory company which was getting ready to "go down" to the British in New York, within a few days. He learned even the names of the officers, which might be helpful in making arrests.

Once he had secured this intelligence, Crosby explained to the confiding Tories that he himself must start for the British lines at once. Changing direction as soon as he was out of sight, he made for the house of "Esquire" Young, whom he knew to be a member of the Committee of Safety. Young took him to John Jay and the committee at White Plains, who asked him to help capture the newly recruited Tory company, and promised to explain to his regimental commander why he had not reported for duty, after which they sent him, as a "prisoner," to the company of rangers stationed in the town.

The ostensible captive soon "made an excuse to go out" under guard—the excuse probably being the lack of sanitary facilities. Whatever his pretext was, it led him over a fence, into a patch of tall corn, and out of sight of the soldier guarding him. There was much banging of muskets, and the spy, after a most convincing "escape," returned to join the Tories.

When the new Tory company was ready to march, Crosby

made a stealthy trip from Bunker's house to Young's, four or five miles away, where he met the American ranger captain from whom he had "escaped." After giving full details of Tory plans, he rejoined the enemy safely, in time to be impressively arrested with the others. He was allowed to remain a prisoner for about a week in various places, ending in a hatter's shack in Fishkill, from which he was bailed out.

Jay now retained him as a permanent secret agent, again promising to set matters right with his regimental commander. Gathering some tools in a peddler's pack and posing as an itinerant shoemaker, Crosby wormed his way into a Tory household, where he soon learned of another new company of Tory recruits and, by scraping acquaintance with its captain, was himself invited to enlist. Hoping to learn the identity of the recruits, Crosby protested that he did not want to join unless some of his friends were among them, and thus managed to see the muster roll. When the American agent professed to find no one there he knew, the Tory captain showed him special, confidential rolls, hidden under a flat stone, then completed his folly by displaying a place to hide recruits in a hollow haystack.

Before midnight, Crosby was reporting everything to the patriot committee in White Plains; before dawn he was safely in bed in the home of his Tory host. Next morning, he joined the company, though declining to sign the muster roll till he was within the British lines.

When the entire Tory force met at its commander's house that night, American mounted rangers closed in. Crosby was hauled out of the closet in which he had hidden, and dragged off in irons with the others, first to White Plains and Peekskill, later to Fort Montgomery, a hint being passed to him to continue his Tory pose till another escape could be arranged.

At Fort Montgomery, Crosby had an embarrassing encounter with a former teacher, who was also a friend of his father's. Horrified "on beholding his favorite pupil, the son of his dearest friend, manacled like a felon, and dragged to prison, with a gang of unprincipled wretches," the pedagogue promptly passed the bad news on to the Crosby family. Since there was nothing else to do, the American spy went right on posing as a Tory and presently found himself once more a prisoner. A fellow American soldier remarked later that he was surprised to see Enoch Crosby arrested so often and escaping so easily!

Meeting with the committee again, secretly, the pseudo-Tory agreed to sign future reports "John Smith" (later he also used the names of Levi Foster and John or Jacob Brown) and was returned to prison with orders to manage his own escape. Forcing a window during the night, Crosby got out; but he had gone only fifty yards when he encountered a sentry and ran for his life, dodging a fusillade of American bullets.

Still posing as a shoemaker, Crosby made his way to Marlboro, New York, on the west bank of the Hudson, above Newburgh. This was at the end of October, since he mentions hearing the firing at the Battle of White Plains, October 28, 1776. As "John Smith, a faithful friend to his majesty," he was introduced to another British officer and was again welcomed as a promising recruit.

In about a week this new Tory company was ready for a rendezvous at Butter Hill, near Cornwall, New York; and Crosby was again ready to report. On November 4, 1776, the spy sent a trusted courier to the Committee of Safety:

> I hasten this express to request you to order Captain Townsend's company of Rangers, to repair immediately to the barn, situated on the west side of Butter-Hill, and there to secrete themselves until we arrive, which will be to-morrow evening, probably about eleven o'clock; where, with about thirty tories, they may find,
>
> Your obedient servant,
> JOHN SMITH

An answer came back before Crosby set out for the rendezvous.

He joined the Tory band, who were resting in a haymow, knowing they had a night's march ahead of them. Presently the waiting secret agent heard someone cough, outside. It was Colonel William Duer, of the Committee of Safety. Crosby coughed, too. Duer and Townsend, with a party of rangers, burst in. For the benefit of his audience, Crosby hid in the hay; but, when "fifty bayonets were instantly plunged into as many different sections of the haymow," he hastily reappeared.

Though Duer knew perfectly well what Crosby was doing, he dared not tell Townsend, who, recognizing the "Tory" prisoner that had escaped from the church at Fishkill, at once had him securely bound. In view of his record and former escapes, the American agent was now jailed in a specially secure room—in the house of John Jay, who employed him! Jay was not at home, or at any rate did not appear; but a quick-thinking maid opened some of his best French brandy, drugged it, put both Townsend and his sentry to sleep with it, stole a key from the pocket of the slumbering officer, and released Crosby.

When the fugitive expressed fears for her safety, the girl told him only, "Dr. Millers opiates are wonderfully powerful when mixed with brandy," and sent him off with the assurance: "I shall be at Hopewell by the time the alarm is given." Though the name Miller is used in the printed account of this exploit, Crosby's manuscript statement gives the name as something that looks like "Oisboden."

Still hampered by his irons, Crosby paused in a thicket to get rid of them. That he was twice able to free himself of handcuffs would seem incredible were there not evidence that other British prisoners found American irons equally insecure. The Tory spy, James Moody, in General Washington's own guardhouse, and the British lieutenant governor of Detroit, Henry Hamilton, in Thomas Jefferson's jail, both freed themselves of fetters with no great difficulty.

Hiding the rest of the night and all next day on West Mountain, Crosby pushed south the following night, and, being familiar with the terrain, was able to keep away from farmhouses, till he reached a house he knew was a Tory's. Soon afterward, in another farmhouse, he was trapped by two armed patriots, was recognized as a Tory spy, and was dragged off with the warning—meant to be grim, though unintentionally comic—that "Jay and Duer are determined to make an example of you." Fearing he might be killed before reaching either of his employers, Crosby produced a secret paper, hidden in the lining of his vest, and identified himself.

The harassed spy had hardly been released when he was accused by a suspicious Tory, two miles farther on, of being exactly what he was. Crosby bluffed or fought his way to safety and, after making sure that Townsend's rangers had left Peekskill, managed to reach Duer's home unobserved. Since Crosby, now under suspicion by both sides, was temporarily useless, Duer let him take cover in a German household on Wappinger Creek, in Dutchess County, where another American agent, John Haines, was already reporting Tory activity.

Two days later, Crosby was recalled to Fishkill, whence, because the village was already dangerous for him, he was sent on to Hopewell. Here Doctor Miller (or Oisboden), the physician who had supplied the opiates used on the guards at John Jay's house, was to find a safe place for Crosby to confer with a member of the committee that afternoon. Like many medical men of the time, the doctor also ran a drugstore. The doctor was not at home, but Crosby was received by a girl whose face seemed vaguely familiar.

Seeing his puzzled look, the maiden murmured demurely: "Dr. Miller's opiates, you recollect, are very powerful when mixed with brandy."

She was the maid at Jay's house, whom Crosby had seen only in the dark. This resourceful damsel gave "Mr. Brown" (manuscript sources show that Crosby used this name, as one of his pseudonyms) a seat by the fire, to await the doctor's return. Crosby spent the evening listening to a lively discussion, by the doctor's waiting patients, of his own exploits as a British spy. It was both useful and gratifying to learn that he had such a bad reputation.

Presently John Jay himself came in, ostensibly to buy medicine. While Crosby politely held his stirrup, Jay whispered an order to return to the German farmer, to avoid discovery. Crosby obediently remained on the farm, as the peaceful cobbler, "Jacob Brown," making shoes for the family, until well on in December, 1776. He was then ordered, by way of Bennington, Vermont, to Sharon, Connecticut, to report on Tories there. To make his pose as a loyal subject of George III more convincing, the committee supplied him with a bundle of British proclamations, offering pardon to rebels, which Admiral Lord Howe, and his brother, General William Howe, had been spreading about the countryside. This made it easy to approach genuine Tories, but might have cost his life if he had been detected by his own side.

Returning to Fishkill, he was sent off to Pawling, New York, in the general vicinity of Wappinger Creek. The patriot spy, John Haines, had reported on December 23, 1776, that a Tory militia company would soon rendezvous at the home of a certain Captain Chapman, near Mount Ephraim. A few days later Nicholas Brower, another patriot agent, warned Nathaniel Sackett that there would be a Tory rendezvous—probably the same one—between Fishkill and Wappinger Creek.

As soon as Haines's report came in, December 23, the committee decided to have Crosby "use his utmost Art to discover the designs, Places of Resort, and Route of certain disaffected Persons in that Quarter, who have form'd a Design of Joining the Enemy." He was given all the information the committee had, a double set of passes—one American, the other British, enabling him to pass both lines—also thirty dollars, a horse, new clothing and a new name. This time, he was "Levi Foster." Sackett, instead of Jay, took charge of his mission. One Martin Cornwill, or Cornell, was also deep in the American plot.

On December 30, 1776, John Jay authorized Sackett to alert Captain Peter Van Gaasbeek's militia company to apprehend "certain persons." By January 4, 1777, Sackett had preliminary reports from both his spies. On January 10, he suddenly remembered something must be done to protect Crosby and wrote the captain:

> I had almost forgot to give you directions to Give our friend an opertunity of making his Escape Upon our plan you will Take him prisoner with this party you are now wateing for his name is Enoch Crosby Alias John Brown I could wish that he may escape before you bring him Two miles on your way to Committee. . . . By no means neglect this friend of ours.

Meantime Crosby had once again joined a company of Tory

recruits and had also made the acquaintance of a Tory physician, Doctor Proesser, or Prosser, who at the moment had as a patient the lieutenant of the company. Doctor Proesser rashly told the patriot spy all about Tory plans, leaders and houses, meantime giving him a fine chance to make the lieutenant's acquaintance.

On February 9, 1777, Doctor Proesser brought Crosby word from Silvester Handy, a Tory agent. All was ready for the recruits to assemble. Crosby was to go to the house of one Enoch Hoag, another Tory. Here he tarried four or five days, undiscovered, taking notes of his host's disloyal talk, picking up information identifying the men who were guiding Tories to New York City, learning all about a force under Captain Zebulon Ross, Jr., which included Connecticut Tory recruits. He passed from one Tory "safe house" to another, identifying more and more British agents, and, on the night appointed, was back at Enoch Hoag's to join the Tory recruits assembled there.

Seeing that there was no chance of notifying the committee, which was holding Van Gaasbeek's company in readiness for a raid, Crosby passed the word to Colonel Andrew Morehouse, who lived only three miles from Hoag. Grimly, Morehouse promised "they should be attended to."

Some of the Tories gathering at Hoag's had noticed "a gathering under arms at old Morehouses," but, before anything could be done about it, there were American shouts of "Stand, stand!" The house had been surrounded. Tories who fled were at once met by militia "coming from a different direction," and presently the whole band were lashed together in pairs.

Crosby tried to beg off, explaining to his captor that he was too lame to walk. Morehouse, who knew perfectly well who Crosby was and what he was doing, was very stern about it.

"You shall go dead or alive," said he, "& if in no other way you shall be carried on the horse with me." Crosby was released on reaching the colonel's home. Morehouse marched his other prisoners off to the committee, reporting only that he had acted on information from "the Immissary"—the committee knew well enough who "the Immissary" was.

In spite of all efforts to conceal his identity and make things look natural, Crosby's series of successes had, by this time, destroyed his usefulness as a secret agent. He had joined one Tory company after another; each company he had joined had been seized; but Crosby always escaped.

Since, by this time, there had been too many such coincidences, and he was a marked man among Westchester Tories, it was decided to send him to Albany, where he was still unknown; and, as smallpox had broken out there, he was sent to Doctor Miller (or Oisboden) for inoculation. After he had spent some time at Albany and Claverack, on the east side of the Hudson, acting openly in the transfer of Tory property, he was allowed to withdraw from the secret service entirely. John Jay had turned to other duties and Nathaniel Sackett would soon be managing an espionage ring on Manhattan Island, where Crosby lacked the necessary contacts.

At last the spy's parents were allowed to know the truth about their son, and he returned to live openly with a brother in the Highlands, until Tory efforts to get revenge became dangerous. Once a bullet, fired through a window, grazed Crosby's neck. A militia officer who had assisted him was almost shot through a window in his home, in the same way. This man escaped because he happened to be at table and a hesitant Tory exclaimed at the last minute: "Oh, it is too bad to shoot him while he is eating."

A few nights after the first attempt on Enoch Crosby, armed Tories burst into the house. There was an exchange of shots. Then the leader yelled, "Let us pound him to death!" By the time they were through, Crosby lay unconscious, and the gang probably thought him dead. After a period of several months to recover from this assault, Crosby went back to the army, joined the 4th and later the 2nd New York Continental Line, and served to the end of the war. Compared to his earlier adventures, active duty at the front must have seemed a little dull.

While the army caught fewer spies in the Hudson Valley than the Committee for Conspiracies, some of its cases were more sensational. Two of its most famous captures were Edmund Palmer and Daniel Taylor, the spy with the silver bullet.

Edmund Palmer was a Tory from Yorktown, Westchester County, who had joined a Tory regiment as lieutenant in 1775, leaving his wife and children on his farm. Early in the spring of 1777, the British sent him back to his native Westchester. Whatever else Palmer's mission may have been, it included both recruiting and espionage and may have involved a plot to kill or capture Israel Putnam, then in command in Westchester. There is no way of knowing how many trips Palmer had made within the American lines, before he was caught.

He undertook the final mission, which led to his capture and execution, in late June or early July of 1777. One afternoon between July 8 and 15, with a single companion, he entered a blacksmith shop, where—perhaps by chance, more probably by Tory treachery—he found Captain Henry Strang, of the 3rd Westchester Militia. The two spies overpowered the American captain, pricked him with a bayonet when he tried to resist, and tied him up, after which, in broad daylight, they marched their prisoner about a quarter of a mile, across the the Croton River and into the woods.

When the forlorn little procession was seen from a farmhouse and a woman called to ask "what they had got there," Palmer boldly answered, "One of the Rebel Committee." His rashness can be explained only by supposing that he felt safe in a district where there were so many Tories.

When Strang asked a man named Griffen to let his family know what had become of him, Palmer threatened him: "If he said anything more about it he would Run him through, and pricked him again with his Bayonet." While he held Strang captive, Palmer had used his bayonet on the helpless man ten or twelve times "and Occasioned him to bleed in many spots." He seized Strang's pocketbook, probably looking for papers, then returned it.

That night Strang in some way regained his freedom, though how he did it has never been explained. One story says he escaped; another that his captors set him free about eleven o'clock, first exacting a promise that he would not molest the owner of the blacksmith shop. This strongly suggests that Strang had been betrayed into Palmer's merciless hands, and that Tories at the blacksmith shop were guilty. Otherwise, Palmer would have been indifferent to the smith's fate.

It was not long before the hunt for the British agent was up; and it is sometimes said that Strang himself had the pleasure of catching his own late captor. All that is really known is that, about July 18, three militiamen brought Palmer to General Israel Putnam's headquarters. After search had revealed "enlisting papers" from Governor Tryon, the prisoner went to the provost guard on charges of "Robing the Inhabitence & Leving war Against his Country."

On July 22, 1777, he went before a court-martial at Peekskill. By this time the charges had been expanded, and he was tried for "Plundering, Robbing, and carrying off the Cattle, Goods, &c. from the well-effected Inhabitants and for being a Spy from the Enemy." The court found him guilty and ordered him hanged August first, between 9 and 11 A.M. The execution was later postponed for several days.

Efforts to save Palmer began at once, a bit of luck few spies ever enjoy. The British command soon learned the story, as was inevitable with all Westchester County still swarming with undetected agents, continually reporting to New York. H.M.S. *Mercury* put in at Verplanck's Point on the east bank of the Hudson, with a flag of truce, sending an officer forward to General Putnam's camp at Peekskill, to warn him that, if Palmer was executed, the British would take reprisals.

There are several versions of "Old Put's" reply. The spiciest and earliest printed text is given in General David Humphreys's life of Putnam:

SIR,
    Nathan Palmer, a lieutenant in your King's service, was taken in my camp as a Spy—he was tried as a Spy—he was condemned as a Spy—and you may rest assured, Sir, he shall be hanged as a Spy.

                    I have the honour to be, & C.
                              ISRAEL PUTNAM

His Excellency Governor Tryon
    P.S. Afternoon. He is hanged.

The fact that this letter is addressed to Governor Tryon, while the only known protest is said to have come from General Mumford Brown, suggests that there may have been several protests and several replies. (Though the spy's name is here and elsewhere given as Nathan, he was certainly named Edmund. Several early accounts make the same error.)

The only existing manuscript dealing with the Palmer case and signed by Putnam is now in the Clements Library. It reads:

> Head Quarters   August 4th 1777
> This Certifies all whom it may Concern that Edmund Palmer an Officer from the Enemy was taken up as a Spy within our lines has been Tried & Condemned & will be Executed as Such and [words illegible].
> The Flagg is hereby ordered to depart immediately
> ISRAEL PUTNAM

As this manuscript is now in the Clinton papers, it must have been sent back to New York with the returning flag of truce. It remains possible, however, that Putnam also wrote the letter to Tryon which Humphreys quotes, or one of its variants, since the British may have made several efforts to save their agent.

There was a tragic interview between General Putnam and the condemned man's wife, who was still living in Yorktown, only a short distance away. The agonized woman came to headquarters with a child in her arms, pleaded for her husband's life, was refused, and had to be carried out in a faint.

While he waited for execution, the doomed spy, trying to provide for his family's future, carefully set down an account of his property. The rebels, he knew, would seize everything he owned; but someday his king would do justice to his son. (In the end the British government allowed the boy £200 for his lost inheritance, cutting the claim down from £600.) Then, with his mind scarcely free from his careful inventory of cattle, horses, cheese, tallow, a saddle and a bridle, Palmer faced his end on a log gallows at Peekskill.

Putnam may have specially wished to make an example of

him, because a number of other British spies had lately been caught near Peekskill, one of whom, Daniel Curwen, "confessed he was sent out from N York by Col Robertson to make Discoveries of our Condition and Carry him Intelligence." Lord Stirling, the American general who claimed a Scottish earldom, ordered the man "immediately hung up before his Door." Such execution without trial shocked Putnam, who immediately wrote General Washington to explain that he knew nothing about it till the poor devil was dead and buried.

As Burgoyne's army moved southward from Canada in the summer of 1777, a continuous stream of secret messengers began to pass up and down the Hudson Valley, between his field headquarters and headquarters in New York. The British could communicate with Canada either by sea (in perfect safety) or by courier (at considerable risk); but after Burgoyne had started south, the only way to reach him was to send daring couriers, out of uniform and technically spies, straight through American territory. Sometimes, instead of making the whole journey, they met midway and exchanged dispatches. Livingston's Manor (between Rhinebeck and Kinderhook, New York) was one such rendezvous.

It was dangerous and difficult for these couriers to get through. One of them did not even try. Henry Williams, of Peekskill, who had been paid to carry a letter to Burgoyne, in July, 1777, simply stopped en route and turned his message over to the patriots. Francis Hogel, alias Hope, and his guide, William Showers, were caught the same month, a week after leaving Burgoyne. Just before capture, Hogel was heard to remark that several of Burgoyne's messengers had never returned.

When it was discovered that "a mulatto wench" had passed through Poughkeepsie in August, bringing intelligence to local Tories, the Americans felt sure she had gone on to Burgoyne, as they could not catch her. "A Scotchman" got through from Clinton in early July, and, in September, Captain Scott, of the 24th Regiment, reached Clinton with word that Burgoyne would hold on till September 16, if communication with Clinton could be kept open. Otherwise, he wanted to get back to

Canada before cold weather. This explains Clinton's offensive from New York up the Hudson three weeks later.

The British took every precaution to conceal the messages they carried. At times, the hollow quills of large feathers were used. Some messages, still extant in the Clinton papers, have been cut into a series of long, narrow strips, evidently to make insertion in the quills easier. The idea seems to have been that, if in danger, a courier could get rid of such papers more easily than if folded.

A far better means of preserving secrecy was the use of code "masks." These were sheets of paper, with openings cut into them. The real message was written in these openings, after which the lines were filled in to make the document read as if it were something quite different. The officer receiving the letter merely laid his mask over it, so that the original message reappeared.

One such letter from Clinton to Burgoyne, August 10, 1777, reads like an ordinary message until it is covered with a paper mask, which has a large opening in the shape of a dumb-bell cut out of it. Laid upon Sir Henry's apparently harmless communication, the mask at once reveals the secret. Without the mask, the whole letter reads:

> You will have heard, Dr Sir I doubt not long before this
> can have reached you that Sir W. Howe is gone from hence. The
> Rebels imagine that he is gone to the Southward. By this time
> however he has filled Cheasapeak bay with surprize and terror.
> Washington marched the greatest part of the Rebels to Philadelphia
> in order to oppose Sir W^{ms} army. I hear he is now returned upon
> finding none of our troops landed but am not sure of this. great part
> of his troops are returned for certain I am sure this [illegible]
> must be vain to them. I am left to command here, half my force may
> I am sure defend every thing here with as much safety I shall therefore
> send Sir W. 4 or 5 bat^n I have too small a force to invade the New England
> provinces, they are too weak to make any effectual efforts against me and
> you do not want any diversion in your favour I can therefore very well
> spare him 1500 men I shall try something certainly towards the close
> of the year not till then at any rate. It may be of use to inform you that
> report says all yields to you. I own to you that the busine∫s will
> quickly be over now. Sr W.'s move just at this time has been Capital
> Washingtons have been the worst he could take in every respect I

sincerely give you much joy on your succe/s and am with
great /incerity. . . .

Seen through the mask, everything is different. The letter
now reads:

> Sir
> W. Howe
> is gone to the
> Cheasapeak bay with
> the greatest part of the
> army. I hear he is now
> landed but am not
> certain. I am
> left to command
> here with a
> too small a force
> to make any effectual
> diversion in your favour
> I shall try something cer
> At any rate. It may be of use
> to you. I own to you I think
> S͟r W.'s move just at this time
> the worst he could take
> much joy on your succ

Clinton was clever enough to include a little military information (mostly false) in the part of the letter that the enemy
would understand, in case it was captured. Another such mask,
with oblong holes to reveal the concealed message, is also
among the Clinton manuscripts.

In the desperate week just before Burgoyne's surrender at
Saratoga, Clinton tried one more expedient. It was important
that Burgoyne should know that the British forces in New
York were at last advancing up the Hudson. They were too
little and too late—and too far off—to do much good; but, at
least, they were moving in the right direction. At Verplanck's
Point a certain Captain Campbell, from Burgoyne's army, reported to Sir Henry. Campbell had made his way through,
or around, Gates's army facing Burgoyne at Saratoga, and had
come secretly through American territory in about a week.
He bore a letter from Burgoyne, dated August 28, telling of

his predicament and asking whether he ought to advance or retreat.

Sir Henry replied in a dispatch dated from the American Fort Montgomery, a little farther up the Hudson, which he had just captured. His letter, written on thin silk instead of paper, is dated October 8, 1777:

> *Nous y voila* and nothing now between us but Gates, I sincerely hope this little success of ours may facilitate your operations. In answer to your letter of the 28th Sepr. by C. C—— I shall only say, I can not presume to order or even advice for reasons obvious. I heartily wish you success, & that &c.

After this had been concealed in an oval silver ball, about the size of a rifle bullet, it was handed to Daniel Taylor, a young officer who had been promised promotion if he got through alive. The bullet was made of silver, so that the spy could swallow it without injury from corrosion. He concealed it in his hair, which was easy enough in a day when gentlemen wore long hair with large queues. (Both the silver ball and the letter are now in the museum at Fort Ticonderoga.)

Taylor had already made the perilous journey through the American lines once at least, leaving Burgoyne above Fort Edward in late July, 1777, with a message stating the northern army was delayed by bad roads. On his return journey, he was foolish enough to carry personal letters from British officers, which were in themselves enough to convict him, even if he had been able to get rid of the silver bullet.

Captain Campbell started back to Burgoyne on October seventh, traveling separately from Taylor, but with the same message. He may have been the courier who is known to have reached Burgoyne after negotiations had begun; but, if he got through at all, he came too late to prevent the surrender.

Taylor followed on the evening of the eighth, unaware that the Americans were already on the lookout for him. When Henry Williams of Peekskill had turned over to the patriots the secret British messages he was carrying in July, just about the time of Taylor's earlier journey, he had warned of "a person who constantly plyes between NYork & Canada his Name Taylor, his dress a blue Camblet Coat with white facings & silver Epaulets."

Almost as soon as he started, Taylor was captured at New Windsor, just below Newburgh, apparently in company with a man named Isaac Vanvleek, whom Taylor's captors brought in as a spy at the same time. After losing his way, the carrier had fallen in with an outpost or patrol from Webb's Connecticut Regiment, who happened to be wearing scarlet uniforms taken from a captured transport. Since this had been Nathan Hale's regiment, the patrol were not inclined to deal gently with the enemy's spies.

Like André, Taylor, when he saw the uniform of his own army, assumed he was in friendly hands and made remarks which his captors thought suspicious. A quick-witted sergeant, guessing what his prisoner really was, took him to "General Clinton," as the prisoner himself demanded. As Taylor had gone only a little way beyond his own lines and knew that Sir Henry Clinton was then at Fort Montgomery, ten miles down the river, he was not yet alarmed and did not get rid of his silver bullet and the letters, while he had a chance.

Not till he was led before General George Clinton in New Windsor, and saw a strange officer in American uniform, did the wretched man apprehend his situation. Realizing his peril too late, the spy fell into a paroxysm of terror and, crying, "I am lost!" swallowed the silver bullet.

Recovery was easy. Dr. Moses Higby, who had an office near headquarters, provided "a very strong emetic, calculated to operate either way." Taylor, overpowered and forced to swallow it, vomited the bullet, instantly snatched it up, swallowed it again, and tried to escape; but, when General Clinton threatened to hang him and cut it out of his stomach, he consented to a second dose. When the hollow silver was opened, Sir Henry Clinton's message was revealed. General Clinton ordered both men hanged within an hour, then relented when—tricked by a false story that Captain Campbell had also been captured—Taylor seemed willing to give information. This, however, did not permanently save him. He was court-martialed and sentenced to death, October 14, 1777, and his execution was ordered two days later. Vanvleek may have revealed enough to save his life. Taylor was allowed to write farewell letters to his family, which, after being carefully read to make sure they contained no military information, were sent to Sir Henry Clinton. A rather heartless American joke went round that Taylor had been condemned "out of his own mouth."

As the Americans moved on up the Hudson, a horseman came galloping down, bearing news of Burgoyne's surrender. With the troops in hollow square around him, the adjutant read out the news—and also Sir Henry's now futile letter, taken from the silver bullet.

XI

★   ★   ★

★

General Howe's Spies

UNLIKE THEIR American opponents, the British found the groundwork of a good intelligence system ready and waiting when the troops began to disembark on Staten Island, at the end of June, 1776. Better still, the ideal man for extending the British intelligence net in New Jersey, the prominent Tory, Cortlandt Skinner, had fled to H.M.S. *Duchess of Gordon* only a little while before; and Beverly Robinson, an equally prominent New York Tory—whose house across the Hudson from West Point would one day be occupied by Benedict Arnold —would soon arrive, to assist with intelligence in New York state.

Cortlandt Skinner had long been secretly supplying intelligence to the British before, detected at last, he had to flee for his life. In January, 1776, the patriots captured papers that William Franklin—Tory governor of New Jersey, Benjamin Franklin's illegitimate son—was sending to London. These included secret records of the Continental Congress, some of which were in Skinner's easily recognized handwriting; for the New Jersey governor, distrusting his own secretary, had asked Skinner to help copy the documents. To make matters worse, the captured papers included a confidential letter from Skinner to his brother in London, which did not mince words about the rebel Congress.

After one look at these papers, the patriots ordered Skinner's arrest; but the Tory's personal intelligence system was already so good that he was on his way to safety aboard *Duchess of Gordon,* the day after the incriminating papers had been intercepted. Skinner probably received several warnings; but one of them certainly came from the Tory, Samuel Hake, a Manhattan importer who, while visiting New Jersey, "heard of some Dispatches being stopped," and hastily informed Franklin, who swiftly passed word to Skinner. It has been suspected that Skinner also had rebel friends who, patriots though they were, strained their consciences a little to save him. Hake himself, rashly going on to Newark, was arrested for aiding the Tory's escape, was tried, and was miraculously (and quite wrongly) acquitted.

General Howe promptly made the fugitive Skinner a colonel and then a brigadier general, with headquarters on Staten Island, conveniently close to the Jersey coast, "in order that he might keep up the Correspondence he had formerly established in Jersey, and furnish the Command^r in Chief from time to time with Intelligence."

When Cornwallis was advancing through the Jerseys, as he himself later testified, Skinner was with the troops and "he had from him once a week a perfect Acc^t of the real State of Washington's Army." Skinner himself remarked that "there was scarcely any Material Information of the Encampment of the Rebel Army which he did not obtain the first Intelligence of." Though this far from modest claim was not strictly accurate—since British intelligence went badly awry at Trenton and at Princeton—General Washington more or less agreed with it. "General Howe has every Species of Intelligence he can wish for," he wrote, only a few weeks later.

It is a curious fact that neither Colonel Elias Dayton's American spies (passing military intelligence about the British from Staten Island to New Jersey) nor Skinner's British spies (passing military intelligence about the Americans from New Jersey to Staten Island) ever discovered each other.

Though Skinner's family were arrested, they soon cleared themselves, after which Mrs. Skinner began secret correspondence with her husband, through two of his as yet undiscovered secret agents, George Derbage, the king's deputy Surveyor for North America, and his American wife—for the Derbages also made espionage a family business. Mrs. Derbage was "a very confidential person & used to carry Letters from M[rs] Skinner to Gen[l] Skinner," being looked upon, says an appreciative Tory, as "an active woman," who, since she had an equally active spouse, caused much difficulty for New Jersey patriots.

The Derbages were not caught until May, 1776, when Colonel Benjamin Tupper, aboard the American sloop *Hester,* laid hands on the husband and presently collected Mrs. Derbage as well. Tupper, who soon found he had caught something a great deal worse than a Tartar, was completely baffled by the spirited Tory matron, against whom he could prove nothing whatever, no matter how much he suspected. Mrs. Derbage refused to answer his questions; she refused to answer questions by the local committee; and she defiantly added that she would not answer questions by General Washington, either. "It is my opinion," sputtered Colonel Tupper, indignantly, "a little smell of the black-hole will set her tongue at liberty. It is the opinion of our friends in this town that she is able to bring out a number of rascals and villains in sundry towns nigh here."

Since the American Army often went hungry, Colonel Tupper may have resented the fact that the defiant lady had accompanied John Hartwick, a suspected Tory of Brunswick, aboard a British man-o'-war with a supply of hams and fresh meat. Worse still, the colonel could get no information against another Tory, one Thomas Stevens, "unless the lady's tongue should be set at liberty." Stevens was "a late collector," and the chance to hang a tax collector was something no sterling patriot cared to miss. Colonel Tupper appears to have come off a bad second best. There is nothing to suggest that he ever got any information at all from the spirited Tory lady he had captured.

When it finally appeared that nothing could be proved against Mrs. Derbage, she and Mrs. Skinner were ordered "into the country at a Distance from the Enemy," and her husband, too, was presently freed.

By that time, Howe's intelligence service had its tentacles throughout New Jersey. William Luce, a British spy in Bergen, probably one of Skinner's men, was able on July 27, 1777, to give warning of the American Army's intended march to Philadelphia, though General Washington did not issue the order until four days later.

When, in November, 1777, General Philemon Dickinson, of the New Jersey Militia, attempted an attack on Staten Island, Skinner's intelligence was so swift and accurate that the attack was blocked before it had well started. To preserve absolute secrecy, Dickinson had concealed his intentions from his own officers, until the night the troops were to move. Nevertheless, by three o'clock next morning, Skinner knew all about it, and his men were manning their fortifications. Dickinson gave up.

Nearly three years later, General William Irvine and Lord Stirling found Skinner as well informed as ever. Their reconnoissance in force had been ordered by General Washington on January 10, 1780. The troops began to move January 14. On January 15, Stirling found Skinner fully prepared and waiting for him. The British had known of the attack so far in advance that they had had time to cut the ice in New York harbor—which had frozen during that exceptionally severe winter—and had commenced sending boatloads of reinforcements to Staten Island.

Early in 1777, the most redoubtable of Cortlandt Skinner's secret agents joined Howe's forces. This was James Moody, an ardent king's man, who had begun to find his farm in Sussex County, New Jersey, a dangerous place to live. In April, taking more than seventy Tory recruits along, Moody fought his way to Bergen, New Jersey, where, with most of his men, he joined Barton's Battalion of Skinner's Brigade. Service under Skinner naturally led to secret recruiting in New Jersey and so to espionage. By June, 1777, Moody had recruited and organized a secret force of five hundred Jersey Tories, ready to rise whenever the British Army moved forward toward Philadelphia—

a scheme that failed only because, in the end, Howe decided
to go by sea.

Moody's first specific mission in military intelligence, as
distinguished from illegal recruiting, was assigned him in May,
1778, just as General Howe was giving up the command to
Sir Henry Clinton, for whom Moody, in the next few years,
was to carry out one daring feat in espionage after another.
This first of many missions was a journey to "interior parts
of the rebel country," to get information from Colonel John
Butler, the frontier Tory leader commanding Butler's Rangers,
whom Clinton supposed to be at Fort Niagara. Moody left
New York May 18, 1778, with four companions and, after a
secret visit of one day to his own home, spent the summer
lurking in rebel territory, sending back information from time
to time and returning only in mid-September.

He managed to establish direct contact with Butler, by sending a "trusty loyalist," who met the rangers and Indians "between Niagara and Wyoming," on their way to the Wyoming
Massacre; stayed with them until the capture of Forty Fort,
near modern Wilkes-Barre; then returned with the news. It
was clearly this subagent of Moody's who sent in a long report
on the Wyoming Massacre still extant in the Clinton papers.
The British agent had seen it all (July 3/4, 1778)—yet was able
to get the information from the wild and distant Pennsylvania
frontier to New York City by July 28. On September 13, when
Moody at last returned, there also arrived—probably in his
party—one Thomas Anderson, who had left Butler four days
after the Massacre, and who, of course, brought more news.

British intelligence, active in Philadelphia from the beginning of the war, was expanded greatly after General Howe
occupied the city. The Pennsylvania Tory, Joseph Galloway,
while still a supposedly patriotic member of the Continental
Congress, had, like Skinner, begun supplying the British with
intelligence, which passed through William Franklin, to London. The two spies who independently provided the British
with plans of the *chevaux de frise* defending Philadelphia, one
in March, the other probably in May, 1776, may have been
Galloway and Samuel Wallis—the latter a Quaker businessman,

described as a "Gentleman of Credit in Philadelphia," soon to be more deeply involved in the intrigues of the intelligence service.

When some suspicious patriot at length sent Galloway a hangman's noose as an anonymous gift, the traitor took the hint and fled to British headquarters, where he advised Howe on "the Strength and Nature of the Country." He secured military maps of Pennsylvania and, before the Brandywine, collected intelligence to which he himself attributed the victory.

When the British entered Philadelphia, Galloway became "Superintendent General of Police" and a very active spy master. After the Revolution he boasted that he had "sent out upwards of 80 Spies," had planned a mass kidnaping of the whole Continental Congress (Sir William Howe thought it a madcap scheme), and had tried to capture Governor William Livingston and all New Jersey magistrates. Though these ambitious projects failed, Galloway was able to get inside information of what the Continental Congress was doing in 1777 and 1778, besides reporting to General Howe on American recruiting, strength, troop positions and hospitals.

Well acquainted with Philadelphia and its vicinity, Galloway advised Admiral Lord Howe on the navigation of the Delaware and secured for Sir William Howe detailed information on Valley Forge. He may have had something to do with the map of Washington's camp there, which is attributed to a mysterious "Mr. Parker."

It was no fault of Galloway's that two spies—one probably, the other certainly, part of his net—were caught and hanged in June, 1778, just before the enemy evacuated Philadelphia, when they needed intelligence most. Both were Pennsylvanians, who knew the country—Thomas Church, former ensign in the 2nd Pennsylvania; Thomas Shanks, formerly an officer in the 10th Pennsylvania. Church was hanged on the grand parade June 4. Thomas Shanks was caught at about the same time, with Galloway's pass in his possession. Shanks had had the misfortune to be passed through a British guardhouse, as a spy, on the very night when Sergeant William Sutherland, of the 45th Foot, was deserting from it. When he reached the

Americans, Sutherland at once warned them that Shanks was on his way to Valley Forge. Washington paid Sutherland £60 on June 3, "for his discovering Shanks a spy send by the Enemy."

Before Sutherland received his blood money, Shanks went before a board of general officers, who promptly sentenced him to "Death by the Cord." Shanks was no model of the self-sacrificing and heroic secret agent, for he had lost his American commission on charge of stealing shoes; but it was ironic that Major General Benedict Arnold sat on the board that sent him to the gallows.

Galloway tended to exaggerate the importance of his intelligence service. When the war was over and the Tory wanted compensation for his losses, Sir William Howe testified that, though the man had indeed procured information, it was "not very material." He pooh-poohed Galloway's claim that his intelligence had made possible the British victory at the Brandywine; and further, said Sir William, after he had tested Galloway as an intelligence agent, he decided the man was not very competent; and, "soon after altering his Opinion of him he removed him."

Another Philadelphia spy, perhaps part of the same system, was Judge John Potts, who fled when the Americans occupied the city, but returned when the British drove them out. A British intelligence officer described him as "one of the most confidential Men Sir Wm Howe employ'd," giving information so important that "several Movements of the Army were made in Consequence thereof," though there is no indication which movements these were. The judge was given a single payment of $948.98 in secret service money, much more than spies usually received.

When the British withdrew, Potts went along to New York to continue espionage from there, being specially successful in secret communication with his native Philadelphia. Other recipients of secret service money in Philadelphia were Thomas Robinson, a Delaware refugee ($628.32); and Peter Dubois, a New York refugee ($428.18).

There was also the turncoat, Thomas Badge, "Soap boiler & Tallow Chandler" in Philadelphia, who, after serving in the American Army, went to New York in 1777, to give intelligence of its movements. He was able to enter American territory to buy tallow and, on these journeys, "took great pains to acquire information for the British Army," thus becoming "a person to be employ'd on any confidential Service." He was one of Howe's guides on the march from Head of Elk toward the Brandywine and later to Philadelphia.

The one great success of British intelligence in Connecticut during this period was the espionage that cleared the way for Governor Tryon's raid on Danbury. Early in 1777, Colonel Guy Johnson, Tory leader in upper New York, sent out an agent to "ascertain the state of the rebel garrisons." Moving about "under an assumed character," this spy examined all posts between Ticonderoga and Albany, then swung far enough south for a secret visit to Danbury, where he found "a large magazine of military stores and provisions"—news of which Johnson promptly sent on to Howe. This information led to Tryon's raid, April 26, 1777, though there was probably Danbury espionage as well, since four young Tories were waiting to assist the local guide the British brought with them.

It is possible the Danbury raid was also assisted by Zechariah Hawkins, innkeeper of Derby, Connecticut, who had been planning other raids on American stores at Derby and New Haven. These were to be carried out by troops in green uniforms—who were to pass for Russians! This was doubtless an effort to confuse the Americans. Some Tory troops wore green uniforms, and the Americans knew that the British had been trying to hire Russian as well as German mercenaries. Hawkins was forced to confess six days after the Danbury raid.

Otherwise, Howe's espionage in Connecticut was a chapter of disasters. One of the victims was Moses Dunbar, a Connecticut Tory, who, after accepting a captain's commission in British loyalist forces, returned to his native state to recruit. Having apparently begun espionage late in 1776, he was caught, was tried at Hartford in January, 1777, and sentenced to be hanged March 19. By opening his irons with a knife, secretly supplied by a friend, and knocking down his guard, Dunbar escaped; but he was recaptured and duly hanged on the scheduled date, on what is now the campus of Trinity College.

The local minister was indignant because the condemned man declined to attend a special sermon upon his own execution; but Dunbar could not escape another sermon, on the same dismal subject, delivered in the jail, where he could not choose but hear. Legend says that his bride went with him to the gallows; and that, just after the trap had been sprung, a white deer leaped out of the woods and ran beneath his swinging body.

Another of Howe's spies, Robert Thomson, of Newtown, Connecticut, was caught after he had visited New York and returned to recruit Tories for the British. A court-martial in Danbury convicted him April 21, 1777, and he was sent back to his home for execution, doubtless to discourage any remaining Tories there, who might try the same thing. He was hanged June 9, with his own family among the spectators, ready to claim the body after it had dangled the required hour.

There must have been other and luckier British spies, who did their work, undiscovered, and survived; but the records now available show only one such man in Connecticut. This was John Lyon, who enlisted in Rogers's Rangers in May, 1776, and managed to find twenty-two recruits in Fairfield County, Connecticut, under the very noses of the Yankee patriots.

After Howe set off for Philadelphia, British intelligence work in New York was in Sir Henry Clinton's hands and the records survive among his papers.

No amount of American counterintelligence could catch all the British agents, especially when Burgoyne's advance made it absolutely necessary to have both spies and secret couriers along the Hudson. When Burgoyne entered Vermont, he had the help of a local spy named Blackman Browning, who lived somewhere near Cambridge, New York, close to the Vermont border. Major Philip Skene sent him to spy on the forces General John Stark was raising to the eastward, on Burgoyne's left flank. Browning risked his neck for only $20; but the risk may not have been very great, for not until September 22, 1779, did the

Americans find out what he had done; and, even then, there is nothing to show they ever caught him.

There were probably a good many others who, like William Rose, Sr., of Saratoga, continued espionage in perfect safety for years. Rose had been captured with Burgoyne's troops, but was, in some way, able to settle down in New York state. From that time until 1780, he later remarked, he "keep'd up Correspond:ce with Scouts from Canada and furnished them with provisions and all the intelligence in my power." In 1780 he fled to join the British openly and, when the war ended, settled in Canada with other Tories.

Daring couriers were always able to keep up secret communication between Clinton, in New York, and Burgoyne, advancing from Canada; and there was some highly efficient espionage. In August, 1777, a British corporal, after a week's examination of the American Forts Montgomery and Constitution, below West Point, brought back a full report, without being discovered.

When the British attacked these forts in October, 1777, to assist Burgoyne, they knew exactly what they would find and had a meticulously detailed geographical report, giving full information on roads, distances, terrain and streams near Spuyten Duyvil, Teller's Point and Verplanck's Point, where they meant to operate. This was almost certainly the handiwork of the Tory, Beverly Robinson, later involved in the Arnold treason, who had known this country all his life. In the last few hours before surrender, Burgoyne managed to dispatch Joseph Bettys, courier and spy, to carry the news to Clinton.

British espionage in Portsmouth, New Hampshire, collected a list of American naval vessels there in May, 1777, including the armament and captain of each. It also sent a list of arriving French volunteer officers, together with the names, armament, captains and ports of departure of the French ships that brought them. Some of this information probably came from France, where Lord Stormont had an active spy system.

So complete was the intelligence these agents supplied that British headquarters knew the exact cargo of the French ship, *Amphitrite,* which brought the Continental Army twelve thousand pounds of artillery powder, twenty or twenty-six field guns, six thousand muskets, and other military supplies, in May, 1777. The British spies even knew that the captain had "blacked & disguised" his ship, as soon as she left harbor. British spies in France had been watching *Amphitrite* from January until the day she sailed.

Under General Howe, British intelligence had swiftly expanded from the modest beginnings made by Gage. It was to become vastly more extensive when Sir Henry Clinton took over the supreme command, with Major John André, able, industrious, ambitious, and much better educated than his brother officers, as an active spy master.

XII

★ ★ ★

★

The First Real Intelligence Nets

As the American Army—driven out of New York City, then out of the state, then forced to fall back with dwindling forces across New Jersey—finally approached safety beyond the Delaware River in Pennsylvania, General Washington at last began to establish a series of intelligence nets that would assure him a steady flow of information, no matter how far he had to retreat. By November, 1776, General Mercer, who had failed to get an agent to Staten Island in July, was able to send into New York City itself a skilled but unknown observer, who came back with a full report of British intentions, troop movements, losses and reinforcements. When the Americans were forced beyond New Brunswick, in the first day or two of December, one more daring agent quietly dropped off, in preparation for eighteen months of undetected espionage; and others soon began work. The new intelligence system was first set up in New Jersey, where the immediate need was greatest; then around New York and Philadelphia, where there was certain to be fighting sooner or later; and last of all, after many months, in the Iroquois country, in wild western New York, though this final step was not taken until 1779.

When the beaten American Army was at last temporarily safe in Pennsylvania, in December, 1776, a screen of secret agents at once spread out in New Jersey, far beyond its front. Two of these men, Joshua and John Mersereau, always believed they saved the weakened Continental Army from complete destruction by finding and removing boats sunk in the Delaware, which local Tories meant to raise, so that the British could cross in pursuit. One spy—and probably more—had been dropped off before the Continental Army reached Pennsylvania. Soon General Washington had agents wandering through the Jersey camps of the British Generals Leslie and Howard, and the German Colonels von Donop and Rall. Patriot horsemen, disguised as ordinary country folk, rode through New Jersey as they pleased. They "talked Tory," loudly. Some of them peddled tobacco, for which the German troops were always eager. Unlike Hale, they carried no incriminating documents. Probably most of them were not soldiers at all, but exactly what they seemed to be—ordinary farm people who had volunteered for the emergency. Their missions were so perfectly concealed that the identities of most are unknown to this day. Of them all, the British detected only one—Abraham Patten, caught and hanged in New York, probably in June, 1777.

The first clear demonstration of how much American intelligence was improving was the capture of Trenton. Twelve days before the victory, Washington ordered all generals to look for "some Person who can be engaged to cross the River as a spy." Fearing the British meant to cross the Delaware themselves, he wanted to know whether they were building boats, collecting horses or bringing up more troops. "Expense must not be spared in procuring such Intelligence."

General Washington wanted to "get some person in to Trenton"; but the town was particularly dangerous, being filled with Tories who would be quick to recognize, and eager to betray, American agents. There was, for instance, the Tory, Jesse Wall, who had a courier "conveying Letters &c for the use of the Regular Army," from Trenton. It is said that some secret agents flatly refused to enter the town at all, though on December 10,

1776, the general had been able to send one man in to see whether the enemy was beginning to build boats.

Nevertheless, no matter what the danger, another agent would have to go in and observe; and General Washington soon found the right man. It is a British historian who declares that one conversation between the American commander and the courageous New Jersey weaver and butcher, John Honeyman, of Griggstown, New Jersey, made possible the victory.

Accepting the ignominious position of a pretended Tory—probably about the middle of December—the devoted Honeyman "fled" from his home in Griggstown and was appropriately denounced as a traitor. Orders went out for his arrest on sight. Only—on this point General Washington was very definite—the general wanted the rogue brought in alive. This particular traitor—so people were allowed to understand—was one whom the general especially wanted the pleasure of hanging.

Soon Honeyman was moving in and out of Trenton and through the whole countryside, ostensibly with no thought except business, but in fact quietly watching Colonel Rall's Hessian troops—watching them almost up to the moment when the first columns of the Continental Army emerged from the gray dawn of the day after Christmas, 1776.

General Washington's deception, meant to protect Honeyman, was a little too complete. A mob of superpatriots, taking his carefully spread rumors at their face value, soon raided Honeyman's home in Griggstown, where the supposed traitor had left his family. The mob was led by a hot-headed youth of eighteen, named Abraham Baird, from whom a later writer heard the story. When the raiders had searched the house for Honeyman in vain, and it was apparent that she had to do something, Mrs. Honeyman brought out a paper, signed by the commander-in-chief:

> It is hereby ordered that the wife and children of John Honeyman, of Griggstown, the notorious Tory, now within the British lines, and probably acting the part of a spy [General Washington must have chuckled as he wrote that!], shall be and hereby are protected from all harm and annoyance from any quarter until further orders.

But the general had added one more line:

This furnishes no protection to Honeyman himself.

Since it takes a soldier's eye to observe a military installation, John Honeyman was an almost ideal man for his mission. He had served in the French and Indian War, had been in Wolfe's bodyguard at Quebec, had seen him fall, and had been one of the men who carried him off the field—"walking most of the way in blood," the old soldier liked to say. As a British veteran with a fine record, his interest in the Trenton garrison would seem natural, and he would be above suspicion.

The spy and General Washington had been casual acquaintances for some time, having probably first met in Philadelphia, about the time the future commander-in-chief was attending the Continental Congress. They had met again as the Continental Army was beginning its retreat across New Jersey.

When he agreed to serve as a spy, Honeyman was told to leave his family and go over to the British, posing as a butcher and horse trader. In such a rôle, it would be natural for him to wander about the countryside from farm to farm, looking for cattle to slaughter and horses to trade. The Hessians in Trenton would be buying beef, and any officer, British or German, liked to talk with a horse trader.

The general would offer a reward for his capture and (this was important to both of them) the reward was to be for his capture *alive*. There were further orders that this dangerous man, if captured, was to be brought at once to the commander-in-chief in person. Perhaps the two overdid it, just a little; but Honeyman, unsuspected by the enemy, placidly continued the joint trades of cattle dealing, horse trading, butchering and espionage, until he could no longer be useful to the Continental Army.

When the time was ripe, Honeyman was to venture a little too far into the country in search of cattle, make certain the Americans captured him—and leave the rest to the general. Honeyman was able to study the British camps at both New Brunswick and Trenton, noting the lax discipline and inadequate defenses at Trenton, a small country village, where it was easy enough for the old soldier to learn all about Rall's troop dispositions, artillery positions and outguards. As late as December 22, 1776, he was still accompanying the enemy in pursuit of wandering detachments of American troops. Apparently he knew all about Washington's planned attack on Trenton; for he set off toward the Delaware River to report at exactly the right time.

Presently, as he wandered along through the chill New Jersey countryside, looking for a chance to be captured, he noted two American scouts, not very well concealed by bushes. To keep up his pose as a butcher, he appropriated a cow from the nearest pasture and drove her noisily toward the ambush, with a mighty cracking of his whip and a good deal of shouting. The scouts emerged. The "Tory" left his cow and fled, slipped craftily on some convenient ice, fought vigorously for freedom, yielded only with pistols at his head.

The scouts marched their prisoner in triumph to their general. Washington looked grave. He ordered the room cleared, while he, alone, interviewed this sinister character. The man was to be shot on sight if he attempted to escape. The general and the spy were alone together for half an hour. Then, about sunset, the prisoner was put into a log hut, to await court-martial in the morning.

Strange to say, a fire broke out nearby, almost at once. The half-trained sentries quitted their posts to help put it out. When they came back, their prisoner was gone—no one understood how he got away, but Honeyman was known to be a desperate and crafty fellow. American outposts saw the scoundrel pass the lines and fired, but he escaped. General Washington had been outwitted again!

Within a few hours, Honeyman was eagerly telling the enemy commander in Trenton all about his adventures. He had been in the American camp and could assure Colonel Rall that "no danger was to be apprehended from that quarter for some time to come." Having planted all this false information on behalf of that gay deceiver, General George Washington, Honeyman set off to New Brunswick. As he well knew, the American troops would soon be falling in for the Trenton attack, if not already on the march. Honeyman wanted to put as much distance between himself and Colonel Rall as possible before the German officer learned how badly he had been fooled.

When the march to Trenton began, General Washington took further, special precautions. Three volunteers in farmer's clothing—which made them, technically, spies—preceded the American column. They knew the country perfectly, since two came from Hopewell, New Jersey, and one was a resident of Trenton itself. They were to reconnoiter Hessian outposts and prevent Tories from carrying warning. There were not enough of them—General Washington had wanted twelve such men, but could not find them—so that, in spite of all precautions, one Tory did reach the threatened town with warning of the raid. But Rall, deep in Christmas festivities, refused to see him, and failed to read the note this devoted subject of the king insisted on sending in to him by a servant. The paper was still in the colonel's pocket, as he lay dying, after the attack.

The Americans had hardly returned from their victory at Trenton, when the new intelligence service again proved its value. A few weeks earlier, Washington had written to Colonel John Cadwalader to "spare no pains or expence to get Intelligence of the Enemy's motions and intentions." The general was well aware that spies cost money; and even then, at nearly the lowest ebb of the Revolution, he was always able to find cash for them. "Any promises made or Sums advanced, shall be fully complied with and discharged," he promised Cadwalader. By December 30, he was eagerly asking Robert Morris for "hard money," silver if possible, urgently needed "to pay a certain set of People who are of particular use to us." Morris sent two canvas bags filled with such coin as he could scrape together—"410 Spanish dollars, two English crowns, 10 shillings sixpence, and a French half crown." Seven years later, Washington still remembered this money, "the time and circumstances of it being too remarkable ever to be forgotten by me."

Cadwalader went to work so hard that within a few days after Trenton he could send the Continental commander a sketch map on which, from some unknown spies' reports, he had been able to plot all the approaches to Princeton, British artillery locations, British defenses, and the exact spots where the redcoats were quartered, as of December 30. He forwarded it December 31. When General Washington slipped away from the startled Cornwallis and bore down on Princeton, January 3, 1777, he knew exactly what he would find there.

As soon as the British had been pushed back in New Jersey and the Continental Army was safely settled in Morristown, after the Battle of Princeton, a whole new set of intelligence snares was laid. The extent of the secret service activity that now began is shown by the money spent on it, as recorded in General Washington's accounts. Lieutenant Colonel Joseph Reed received $238 in January, 1777; the Westchester spy catcher, Nathaniel Sackett, $500 to do some spying of his own, in February; Major General Adam Stephen, $200 in April; Major General Benjamin Lincoln, $450 in May. Other officers gathered intelligence without special funds. General Heath, ordered to send spies to New York in mid-January, 1777, had a regular network established there by April.

Espionage in New Jersey was in several hands. General Israel Putnam was told on January 5, 1777, to keep his spies—"Horsemen, in the dress of the Country"—watching for a British advance from New York City. Colonel Elias Boudinot, at Basking Ridge, New Jersey, began, during the spring, to combine military intelligence with the care of prisoners—a combination of duties which General Washington thought very effective.

Not content with this, however, General Washington at about the same time got in touch with Nathaniel Sackett, who, with Colonel William Duer, had long been active in counterespionage in Westchester County and who had employed the redoubtable Enoch Crosby in ferreting out Tory agents. On February 3, 1777, Sackett visited Continental headquarters, in Morristown. Next day Washington formally instructed him to secure "the earliest and best Intelligence of the designs of the Enemy," promising to pay him $50 a month and to allow him $500 to pay his spies and their expenses.

The new intelligence director soon found his first agent, a well-educated surveyor "every way calculated for the Business," who, on March 7, 1777, was passed through the American lines to the "English Neighborhood," with orders to "hire a room in the City and get a license to carry on a secret trade for poltry to enable him to convey our intelligence once or twice a week." Black-marketing poultry would give an excuse for going back and forth between city and country; and, since food was so badly needed in New York, the British were not likely to interfere with anyone who could bring it in. Nothing had been heard from him a month later—indeed, nothing more has been heard from him since, so far as the records go, though there is no reason to suppose he was ever captured; and the missing reports may be among those Washington destroyed.

Undiscouraged, Sackett soon found two more volunteers—"honest, sensible and intriguing"—who were willing "to go into the Enemy and seat themselves down in their camps." One of these was to be a resident agent at New Brunswick, the other at Perth Amboy, both towns being held by the British. One man was the father of a colonel in the British service, which gave an appearance of Tory sympathies—just what the American intelligence service wanted—and he carried letters of recommendation to two other British officers. At the last moment, it was discovered the spy had never had smallpox, and his mission had to be delayed till he could be "Enoculated."

To make this agent's cover still more plausible, he was authorized to take eight or ten men to the British with him—perhaps only posing as refugees or deserters, but quite possibly the real thing. When the spy, now proof against smallpox, was ready for his mission, he went to some "Principal Torys near the enemies Lines—in order to get Letters of Recommendation to some Principle Gentlemen in the enemies service."

Although nothing is known of what this man accomplished, the care taken with his cover shows how much the American intelligence service had learned since Nathan Hale had been sent, unprepared, to a useless death.

Presently the spy master found a genuine Hessian, who had lived in America "near 40 years." This thoroughly Americanized German immigrant—who may have been Christopher Ludwick, the Philadelphia baker—was instructed either to enter New York City himself or to send "one of that nation that may be relied on." Once safely established, he was to secure military information, encourage desertion, and "make use of the Deserters as pipes to convey Intelligence."

Still the indefatigable head of the new network was unsatisfied; but at the end of March, 1777, he found exactly the agent he wanted, "a woman—the wife of a man gone over to the enemy." Better still, she really had suffered at the hands of the Americans, who had seized her grain. If suspicious British officers investigated, they would soon find this part of her story was absolutely true. She was told to go into New York and complain to General Howe, meantime making such observations of his army as she could. Whatever she may have suffered at American hands, this woman made an effective patriot spy. She left New York on March twenty-eighth and was soon reporting to Sackett: The British were building a large number of flat-bottomed boats, which they meant to use in an expedition against Philadelphia "to subdue that city."

Rarely has a single spy's report had such far-reaching results, as can be seen from a significant series of dates. She must have reported to Sackett in the first few days of April. On April 7, Sackett sent her intelligence on to Washington. On April 10, Washington hurried General Thomas Mifflin, a former Quaker, off to Philadelphia to set up a spy system. On July 23, Howe sailed from New York. When, on September 26, he occupied Philadelphia at last the American secret service was all ready and waiting for him. A few days later, the spies' reports began to pour in on Major John Clark, who had by this time taken over Mifflin's Philadelphia network; and they kept coming steadily—at critical moments, several times a day—until Sir Henry Clinton evacuated the city. It all went back to what one courageous woman had learned in a single swift visit to New York, several months before.

At this point, strange to say, Sackett's espionage network disappears from the records completely. Though this may mean only that the documents have been destroyed, more probably it means that Sackett's group was merged in one of the other New York networks which were being swiftly created.

American secret agents were never very successful in New

Brunswick. About the middle of January, 1777, General Washington himself sent an agent there, who was soon followed by Sackett's man. One of these spies is probably identical with the supposed "Pennsylvania provision merchant," who was caught by the enemy in early June, 1777. The Hessians—who had already hanged one American spy before leaving England—have left the only record of this incident. The supposed provision merchant made a practice of persuading soldiers to desert and sending his messages back to Washington in their hands. His method worked successfully until he offered a grenadier £50 to desert and carry a letter, giving the "whole position" of the camp at New Brunswick, locating pickets and sentries, and offering to set fire to the enemy's magazine, if the Americans attacked. The grenadier reported everything to General Leslie, who arrested the American spy at once, only to find that he had already "sent off several deserters in this manner." There is no record of the spy's execution.

New Brunswick was, nevertheless, the place where two of the most impudent and successful of American exploits in espionage originated, one by Lieutenant Lewis J. Costigin, who in civil life was a New Brunswick merchant, the other by the younger John Mersereau, with the help of various relatives.

Costigin was originally sent out for intelligence by Washington himself, when, just after the Battle of Trenton, the Americans realized that Cornwallis was approaching from New Brunswick. Cornwallis could, perhaps, be dealt with; but what forces were behind him? Colonel Matthias Ogden, commanding the 1st New Jersey, was told to select a "suitable person" to enter the town, ascertain the strength of the British, and see how big their baggage train was (which might be a clue to either enemy strength or enemy intentions). Ogden asked Costigin, one of his own officers, to volunteer, because he came from New Brunswick and his family was still living there.

Instructed by General Washington in person, the lieutenant went straight into New Brunswick, or near enough to procure "all the information in his power respecting the strenth of the enemy." Unfortunately, British cavalry captured him on the way back, January 1, 1777. Though Costigin may have entered

New Brunswick in disguise, he was certainly in uniform again when the British caught him, for they treated him as an ordinary prisoner of war and sent him back to New York, where he was set free on a parole that lasted for nearly two years.

Parole released an officer from confinement and allowed him to move about freely, within limits set by his captors, after he had given his word of honor (parole) not to escape. Usually he was also pledged not to communicate intelligence; but either the British forgot this formality or Costigin stretched the terms of his parole illicitly or (more probably) he began spying after he had been exchanged and was released from parole.

In some way First Lieutenant Costigin had, by August 21, 1778, made Lieutenant General Washington extremely anxious to have him exchanged. On that date, orders went out to get the lieutenant back by "the speediest means," though not to seem so "over anxious" as "to alarm the enemy or induce them to detain him." Immediately on release, First Lieutenant Costigin was to report to the lieutenant general at headquarters.

So much interest in a subaltern on the part of the commander-in-chief is just not normal. It is clear that Lieutenant Costigin had already managed to get into secret communication with American intelligence; that he already possessed secret information; and that he had perhaps already sent some in. Costigin was exchanged September 18, 1778, and thereby freed from the obligations of parole; but he did not return to his own army, as an exchanged prisoner is supposed to do. Instead, acting on orders from General Stirling and Colonel Matthias Ogden (the colonel who had selected Costigin for his original espionage mission), the lieutenant simply stayed in New York. Either he pretended to have Tory leanings and to be unwilling to rejoin the Continental Army or else people in New York were so used to seeing him around, as a paroled prisoner, that it never occurred to the British staff that Lieutenant Costigin ought to be back with his own army.

Technically, he was hardly a spy. He was in uniform. Everyone knew he was an American officer. He was not violating his parole, since he had been exchanged. In this ideal situation, Lieutenant Costigin went happily to work. So many papers have been lost that it is impossible to tell all the lieutenant did; but four of his reports, under the signature "Z," remain, the first dated November 16, 1777, and the others December 7, 16 and 19.

With the eye of an experienced soldier, Lieutenant Costigin was able to find out all about the personal movements of Sir Henry Clinton, Major General James Grant, Governor William Tryon, Lord Cathcart and other leading figures; troop movements; shipping; the dispatch of an army to Pensacola (which Oliver Pollock, commercial and intelligence agent in New Orleans, was soon confirming); bread shortage, and supply of British rations from Shrewsbury, New Jersey—all valuable information which he could get by putting a little cash where it would do the most good, walking about Manhattan streets, and chatting with British officers who, during his long captivity, had learned to know him.

The most diverting aspect of this paradoxical situation is that the enemy could not legally have hanged him, even if they had found out what he was doing, since he was in New York perfectly openly, in uniform, and no longer on parole. If he was a little slow about going home—well, neither the British nor the American command had ordered him to hurry back.

Costigin himself says that he stayed where he was, "as long as he thought it safe," and the records show he rejoined the Continental Army on January 17, 1779.

It looks very much as if nobody told the scrupulous Washington just how sharp a game his intelligence men were playing. On October 5, 1778, almost three weeks after Costigin had been formally exchanged, the general still knew nothing about it, in spite of the special interest he had already expressed, and was explaining that the lieutenant's "being on parole would make it improper to take any steps in the affair, in which he is suspected to be concerned"—plainly intelligence of some kind. In fact, General Washington was puzzled because there had been "some mistake in executing" his orders to have the lieutenant exchanged at once.

The lieutenant was not on parole. The lieutenant had already been exchanged. But nobody told General Washington that. Plainly, again, some senior officer thought it would be better if the commander-in-chief did not know quite everything his intelligence service was doing.

Nobody told General Washington, either, that Lieutenant Costigin was identical with that fine spy, "Z." The "Z" reports were sent on by Colonel Ogden, through General Stirling, to Washington, who thought them very valuable and acknowledged receipt of one as late as January 2, 1779. Probably Ogden and Stirling never did tell their general who "Z" really was, for on March 15, 1779, two months after Costigin's return, Washington was asking what had become of "Z" and whether a new spy was needed to replace him.

Poor Costigin, meantime, had spent, in gathering intelligence, £113 of his own money, which he was still trying to collect three years later—a not unusual situation in the intelligence service. Washington at last learned the truth, when he received Lieutenant Costigin's petition for payment of his expenses; but that was not until 1782.

Quite as daring as Costigin was the younger John Mersereau—later called John LaGrange Mersereau, to distinguish him from his uncle—who was planted in New Brunswick to begin the work of the Mersereau spy ring, which was eventually headed by Colonel Elias Dayton, commanding the 1st (Essex County) New Jersey Militia. As the British approached New Brunswick, Washington asked Joshua Mersereau, a patriotic businessman who had fled from Staten Island, to procure intelligence—probably because the Mersereaus had already been giving some help in securing information before they had to quit their home.

It was agreed that Joshua Mersereau's son, the younger John, should remain behind in New Brunswick after the American forces were gone, then work his way to Staten Island and Manhattan. The result was eighteen months of highly successful espionage by young Mersereau himself and the later development of a large intelligence network by his father, brother, uncle, and numerous intrepid assistants.

At first, young Mersereau remained constantly within the British lines on Staten Island, using as a courier another young man, John Parker, who had been Joshua Mersereau's apprentice in shipbuilding. After three or more secret trips into American territory, Parker was caught at Amboy and thrown into a British prison, where he soon died—probably of hardships, though Parker himself thought he was being poisoned. Mersereau boldly visited his courier in prison, hoping to supply food and clothing; but the dying man refused help: "It was of no use, for he should not live long." When Mersereau came back next morning, he found Parker had died during the night.

After this, Mersereau, forced to assume the risks of a courier as well as a spy, began to cross the river on a raft, carrying his secret papers in a bottle tied to a "thread." In his own manuscript story, he does not explain what the thread was for, but it seems evident that he towed the bottle in the river, so that, if challenged, he could drop the thread and let the incriminating evidence sink. At Shooter's Island, between Staten Island and New Jersey, he deposited his papers under a large stone and sometimes picked up instructions. Light signals on either side of the river showed when papers had been hidden.

At times, young Mersereau crossed to the New Jersey shore, and once, hearing that his father was in Elizabeth, he boldly joined him there—a piece of rashness that was nearly his undoing. Finding an old skiff on the grass in an unguarded part of Staten Island, he used it to reach New Jersey, went on to Elizabeth, and found dawn breaking before he was ready to start back. Lying concealed in an old barn on the New Jersey side of the Hudson all day, he started for Staten Island the next night.

Meantime, however, someone had noticed the disappearance of the skiff, and a sentry was watching the spot. When the American spy heard his challenge, he says, "I fled on my hands & feet to a ditch, along which I could run without being much exposed to his fire." But when a bullet whacked into a post just over his head, Mersereau jumped out of the ditch, ran for his lodgings, pursued by several men, reached the house, and scrambled into his room. His pursuers, bursting in after him, met an irate and very drunk British major, also lodging there, who threw them out, swearing "there were no rebels in the house where he lodged." In the darkness, no one had recognized the fugitive.

After a few such exploits, Mersereau eventually came under suspicion, and, realizing this, escaped, rejoined the Americans, and assisted in caring for Burgoyne's captured army. He was never able to serve with troops in the field, because a defective right arm made it impossible for him to hold a musket; but for cold courage he was probably unsurpassed in the Revolution.

It was probably after the younger John Mersereau had been forced to give up espionage that his sixteen-year-old brother for a time replaced him, going back and forth to Staten Island in a skiff (normally kept hidden in the cellar of a relative's house), and bringing back files of the *Register,* desired by General Washington. These were collected for him by still another Mersereau—Paul—who had contrived to remain unsuspected on Staten Island.

Colonel Dayton now built up his group of agents rapidly, though he had to combine intelligence work with the ordinary duties of a line officer. By July 5, 1777, General Washington was able to tell Congress, "I keep people constantly on Staten Island, who give me daily information of the operations of the enemy." Five days later, Dayton was reporting to Continental headquarters that one of his men had just returned from New York, "after spending four days observing the enemy."

The network grew so rapidly that on July 26, Washington told the colonel to send twenty spies to Staten Island, to observe the enemy's troops, positions, guards and strength.

Colonel Dayton seems to have been the intelligence officer who, during the spring or summer of 1777, sent out the brothers Captain Baker Hendricks and John Hendricks, together with John Meeker, one of his own soldiers. At least, it was to Dayton they appealed when they got into trouble a few months later. These men had General Washington's authority to carry "market truck" to the British and bring back "a few Goods," illicitly, "to give the colour of going upon Business of that kind only."

To assist this illicit communication with the enemy, General Washington issued passes for the group and was soon receiving some extremely accurate intelligence. This network remained active for the next three years and probably all through the Revolution. For some reason, their only surviving reports are all dated 1780, though John Vanderhovan, one of the ablest of these spies, specifically says he began intelligence in 1777, like the Hendricks brothers. As payments to several others begin in that year, most members of the Dayton-Mersereau-Hendricks system probably entered the secret service at about the same time.

Though he must have transmitted a great deal more intelligence, the elder John Mersereau's surviving reports run only from May to September, 1780. No actual reports by the Hendricks brothers are extant, though they are frequently mentioned in the transmission of information. Their activity, however, is proved by an entry in General Washington's accounts, which shows him, on October 16, 1780, paying Baker Hendricks five guineas, "for Exp$ & Rewards of himself & others (whom he was obliged to employ) to open, & carry on a Corrispondence with persons within the Enemys line by the way of Staten Island."

John Vanderhovan eventually directed a group of subagents who sent their messages in through Captain Baker Hendricks or John Mersereau. He may have been the husband of Mrs. Elizabeth Vanderhovan, of Bridgetown (Mount Holly, New Jersey, not the modern Bridgeton), at whose home Hendricks said he picked up many of Vanderhovan's reports—though there is a strong suspicion that "Mrs. Vanderhovan" was a mere pseudonym for one of the male spies. Some of John Vanderhovan's messages were transmitted through Cornelius Vanderhovan, of Metuchen.

John Vanderhovan had four known assistants—Abraham Banker, Banker's brother, and two men referred to as "Bond" or "Jesse." Like the Hendricks brothers, Banker at one time came under suspicion of working with the British. When reporting to Washington himself, Vanderhovan usually signed his own name. When reporting through "Mrs. Vanderhovan" (if she existed) or Hendricks, he signed as "D. Littel." In the autumn of 1780, after three years of perilous service, Vanderhovan refused to send more information until paid. He was, he said, in urgent need of money, having spent heavily, "keeping the company necessary to obtain the information."

This spy also had contact with "A Stranger" and, eventually, with Caleb Brewster, whose whaleboats carried reports from the Culpers and other spies across Long Island Sound.

Six agents operated through John Mersereau, the elder: an unknown "J.C.," who may have been Tallmadge's spy, John Cork, and who is recorded only as having received six guineas; Paul Latourette, now only a name; "Amicus Reipublicae" (perhaps Abraham Banker); "A Stranger," still unidentified; "J. M.," who may have been John Meeker or any one of three Mersereaus who had the same initials; and "A. R.," believed to have been Asher Fitz Randolph, who on one occasion received four guineas. Randolph was a militia captain from Woodbridge, New Jersey, who saw a good deal of active duty with troops but doubled as a secret agent.

It is probable that the tentacles of one or another of Colonel Elias Dayton's intelligence organizations eventually reached into the ranks of the British Army itself. A suspicious British spy in Elizabeth, New Jersey, about the time of the mutiny of the Pennsylvania and New Jersey line, in 1781, noted with anxiety that a certain Sergeant Lloyd, coming from the British with a flag of truce, was on alarmingly cordial terms with the rebels. He brought presents of clothing and other articles from New York, was seen in conversation with Colonel Dayton (of whose activities the British were probably well aware), and was strongly suspected of giving intelligence of the British forces. But, though all this was reported to Sir Henry Clinton, nothing seems to have happened to the sergeant.

By midsummer of 1777, General David Forman, of the New Jersey Militia, had set up an intelligence service of his own, mainly to watch the British fleet. A great deal of his information came through a coast-watching service on the New Jersey side, which observed naval movements. But, not content with watching from the shore, the general had a group of secret agents on Staten Island and probably in New York City, who were active throughout the war, though there is no clue to the identity of any of these spies.

From the abundant intelligence provided by his New York and New Jersey spies, General Washington believed, early in 1777, that the British would eventually strike at Philadelphia, though he was never absolutely certain of it till they landed in Maryland, August 25. An unlucky British spy, whom the Americans caught in Philadelphia and "exalted upon a Gallows," as Washington grimly remarked, provided unintentional confirmation. He had been trying to secure Delaware River pilots. That could only mean General Howe was thinking of Philadelphia, especially as other British agents were found "measuring" the river. When Howe sailed on July 23, 1777, a bold American agent boarded H.M.S. *Centurion* and watched the fleet depart. A report went to Washington next day.

The American commander had, by this time, fully mastered the intricacies of military intelligence. He now intended to be fully informed about all the enemy's capabilities, without trying to make sure of his exact intentions. Though the main intelligence target was still New York, the commander-in-chief now realized that he must have his spy rings ready, no matter what city the British might occupy. "Where-ever their Army lies, it will be of the greatest advantage to us, to have spies among them." On April 10, 1777, Major General Thomas Mifflin was told to "look out for proper persons for this purpose, who are to remain among them under the mask of Friendship." They would be needed if the enemy moved to Pennsylvania. These agents were to be spotted in Philadelphia itself and in the country around it. No more untrained amateurs were to be used. "Give the persons you pitch upon, proper lessons," the commander told Mifflin.

General Washington thought "Some in the Quaker line, who have never taken an active part, would be least liable to suspicion." It was a good idea, except that the British had it, too. The schoolmaster, Thomas Long—inelegantly known in Rahway, New Jersey, as "Bunk Eye," from his too prominent eyes —was sent to Philadelphia toward the end of April, 1777, as an American spy, because he habitually associated with Quakers.

Two days later it turned out the man had Tory sympathies and might already be spying for the British. General Washington had to send hasty orders for his arrest.

Just what General Mifflin did to honeycomb southeastern Pennsylvania with spies, no one knows. By June, 1777, the brilliant Major John Clark was active in intelligence duties, almost certainly assisting Mifflin to prepare the network which Clark himself would soon take over, as the shining star of the Continental Army's intelligence service. Only one thing is wholly clear: when General Howe and his redcoats arrived in Philadelphia, a large, well-trained, active and perfectly concealed group of secret agents, headed by Major Clark, was waiting for them.

XIII

★ ★ ★

★

The Cherry Tree Hero Tells Some Whoppers

DURING THIS PERIOD, when at last he had an organized military intelligence service with a widespread espionage network, George Washington, who proverbially "could not tell a lie," began to reveal an unexpected talent for ingenious and elaborate deceit. The commander-in-chief seems suddenly to have realized that, if his secret agents could get accurate information from the British, they could also feed the enemy some remarkably inaccurate information cooked up by various far-from-truthful American officers, among whom the most ingenious in the art of prevarication was the general himself. George Washington began to lie—oh, how he lied!—but only for his country's sake.

Opportunity for the first in a long series of spectacular exploits in misinforming the enemy came not long after the Battle of Princeton, when the victorious but sadly depleted American Army went into winter quarters at Morristown. Though the episode cannot be exactly dated, it is certain that it took place at Morristown, early in 1777, at a time when American strength had sunk to one of its lowest points. Washington himself thought his army "only about Four Thousand strong," on February 20; and his first successful deception must have been planned about this time, when it was vital that the enemy should not guess how weak the Americans really were, especially as Howe had, at Amboy, thirty miles away, a British detachment larger than the whole Continental Army.

Colonel Elias Boudinot, who stage-managed the elaborate trick that followed, says the army had sunk to three thousand men; and that, to make a show of strength, Washington had been forced to distribute his scanty force "by 2 and 3 in a House, all along the main Road around Morris Town for Miles." This convinced the country people that the Americans were at least forty thousand strong, a most desirable impression, since many were Tories, certain to be in touch with the enemy. "We are deceiving our Enemies with false Opinions of our Numbers," General Washington wrote exultantly to Congress.

Presently there appeared in Morristown a New York merchant, posing as a refugee, with a dismal tale of British maltreatment. The man was, in fact, a British agent, sent to get an accurate estimate of American strength, as the Americans at once suspected. Though his adjutant general wanted to arrest the fellow, General Washington saw in the British secret agent a heaven-sent opportunity to plant false information—an opportunity which he seized forthwith. The British spy was left entirely undisturbed. Meantime, every brigadier at Morristown was ordered to prepare a false "return," immensely exaggerating the strength of his brigade. The various figures were carefully arranged to show a total American strength of twelve thousand. If Howe's agent tried to confirm this by chatting with civilians or observing the wide distribution of the troops, he was certain to get an idea of the strength of the American forces as high as this exaggerated figure, or even higher. The British general would hardly accept the supposed strength of forty thousand assigned the Continental Army by popular rumor; but that fantastically wrong estimate would help make the figure of twelve thousand seem nearly credible.

All the false reports collected from the mendacious brigadiers were carefully placed in pigeonholes in the desk of the adjutant general himself, who meantime scraped acquaintance with the "merchant," lent a sympathetic ear to his anti-British talk, and finally found room for the man to lodge in the same house.

Washington arranged that, while the two were at supper together, the American should be hastily called away, carelessly leaving the "official" papers unguarded. At nine o'clock an orderly sergeant burst in, with orders to report to General Washington at once; and the adjutant general rushed off, giving the spy half an hour—a longer period might have aroused suspicion—alone with the strength returns. To the great gratification of the American staff, the merchant disappeared next morning.

Making his way to New York with the planted information, the spy was cordially received by the British commander. The information that he brought, says Colonel Elias Boudinot, "convinced Genl Howe that we were too strong to be attacked & saved us thro' the Winter." Worse still, the beguiled British general got the idea of American strength so fixed in his mind that he would not believe the actual facts when an escaping British officer prisoner presently brought them to him.

A British prisoner whom Boudinot describes as "Colonel" Luce, captured at Elizabeth, had been brought to Morristown and allowed to lodge with a Tory family, moving about freely on parole. This was undoubtedly the British intelligence officer, William Luce, of Elizabeth, New Jersey, who sometimes operated in Bergen, though he was certainly not a colonel and probably never achieved a rank higher than captain. Since the Americans treated him as an ordinary officer prisoner, even going so far as to accept his parole, it is obvious that he had been in proper British uniform when captured and was not a spy, at least not to begin with.

Luce improved the opportunity his parole gave him to study the situation of the American Army and soon was able to make an accurate estimate of its real weakness, since he had "obtained full accts of the Army, Artillery, &c., with our Poverty, Sickness &c. &c. according to the Truth." When he had secured all this vital information, he fled, breaking his parole, to New York, where he reported to Howe in person.

To his horror, the fugitive was received with complete incredulity. With a flourish, Howe produced General Washington's fraudulent returns, "obtained in such a Manner that there could be no Doubt." Poor Luce, having already committed a grave offense in breaking his parole, found himself accused of joining the rebels and trying to deceive the British with false information. At first threatening to "hang him up at the first Tree," Howe was in the end content to treat the man who had brought him the true report, "with contempt & Severity." Boudinot avers that the poor wretch "took to drink & killed himself by it in The End," but that is only a rhetorical flourish. Luce lived to claim compensation from the British Government, when the war was over; but it is comprehensible that, in his description of his military service, he does not mention this ignominious failure.

Another opportunity to deceive the enemy presented itself almost at once. Colonel Boudinot had a double agent who—with General Washington's full approval—was already supplying military intelligence to both sides and would tell the British whatever Washington might desire. The commander-in-chief thought up a few choice fibs to be carried as genuine information to British intelligence officers and sent them on to Colonel Boudinot, in "a sketch of such matters as it will be proper for your Spy to report to deceive the Enemy." At the same time he suggested that, if Boudinot himself could think up some more completely false information for the spy to carry to New York, it would be all the better.

"If he can do us no harm by reporting what is intrusted to him—you may add what you please, only taking care to keep a Copy and send it to me, that if any other person should go in upon the same Errand, he may carry the same Tale." It was the first time General Washington is known to have deliberately planned to use what became his favorite scheme—making sure his false information should seem to confirm itself by reaching the enemy several times from different sources.

This double—sometimes triple—deception became characteristic of General Washington's methods. If possible, he always planted the same false story several times, arranging to have it reach the enemy through widely separated sources, apparently independent of each other and so apparently confirming each other. (Once he tried to have the same story reach Howe's staff four times!)

There were no more efforts to deceive the British—or, at least, no further efforts are recorded—until autumn. By that time, both sides had divided their forces. Howe had occupied Philadelphia, September 26, 1777, while Washington's forces, beaten at the Brandywine on September 11, beaten again at Germantown, October 4, hovered some distance outside the city. Meantime, Burgoyne's army from Canada was coming resolutely down the Hudson. No one could know, in September, 1777, that Burgoyne would be forced to surrender to General Horatio Gates in the middle of the next month. Sir Henry Clinton held New York, whence he might at any moment advance into Gates's rear. Sir William Howe might reinforce Clinton with troops from the British garrison of Philadelphia. In that case, Burgoyne and Clinton might crush Gates's army between them.

Burgoyne's surrender itself was due to an American intelligence coup by Alexander Bryan, a daring amateur secret agent, whose name has been totally unknown from that day to this. On September 12, 1777, Gates went into position on Bemis Heights; on the thirteenth, Burgoyne's British troops crossed the Hudson; on the fifteenth, his Germans followed. About this time, Gates asked Bryan, whose home was somewhere near the American position, to "go into Burgoyne's Army" and learn the "heft" of the artillery, the number of guns and troops, and Burgoyne's intentions. When Bryan explained that he had a pregnant wife and sick child at home, Gates promised to send an army doctor, and Bryan went out on his dangerous mission.

Going over to the British, Bryan bought a piece of cloth and then "went stumbling about to find a tailor." Just how this was possible is not explained in the story, as Alexander Bryan later told it to his son, Daniel. The spy was evidently looking for an excuse to move about among the enemy's troops. He might have found a better one; and it all sounds very queer today; but then, espionage is often a very queer business.

Bryan did manage to learn the enemy's strength and also

learned that Burgoyne would attack Bemis Heights, which Gates's army held. He managed to break away, was suspected and pursued, spent an hour concealed in the chill waters of a neighboring creek, but reached Gates with the news. According to the legend that came down in the Bryan family, Gates acted mainly on this information. Troops swarmed out at daybreak and the position on Bemis Heights was ready to repulse Burgoyne by ten o'clock.

Only then did Bryan discover that Gates had not kept his promise to send a physician. Hurrying home, he found that his invalid son had died, while his wife had suffered a premature confinement, from which she, too, nearly died. Suspicious neighbors had added to the poor woman's troubles, because they thought her husband had gone over to the enemy. Gates explained his failure by saying that his own army needed twice as many medical officers as he possessed.

If Bryan's story can be taken literally, he was the most successful spy in history, whose one mission led directly to a vital military decision. That is, it can be said that Bryan's warning made possible the victory at Bemis Heights. There is no doubt that Bemis Heights led to Burgoyne's surrender; that Burgoyne's surrender led to the French government's decision to intervene with troops; that the French troops made possible the winning of the war. It is true that Gates already knew, through ordinary reconnoissance, what Burgoyne was doing. It is also true that his fortifications were not so hasty as Bryan's story implies. But still, it is possible—it is just barely possible—that Alexander Bryan was the man who really won the American Revolution. That even General Washington ever knew his name is most improbable.

However that may be, Burgoyne's surrender confronted General Washington, far to the south, outside Philadelphia, with two problems: He had to frighten Clinton into thinking that Gates's troops, released by Burgoyne's surrender at Saratoga, would immediately attack New York. At the same time, he had to persuade Howe that those same troops would concentrate against him in Philadelphia. The sad truth was that General Gates was now foolishly keeping the army that had beaten Burgoyne idle along the Hudson, doing practically nothing, so that neither Howe nor Clinton was in any real danger.

The truth, however, was something in which General George Washington, at the moment, was not interested. If the right kind of false information could be used to delude both Clinton and Howe, the situation could be saved. Clinton would stay in New York; Howe would stay in Philadelphia; the Continental Army would be safe.

To the complicated series of elaborately arranged falsehoods required to keep the two British armies from combining forces, General Washington addressed himself with gusto, assisted by a competent group of talented and enthusiastic military liars. It was another splendid chance for the truthful general to show his skill in forging fraudulent intelligence; and, with magnificent mendacity, he rose to the occasion. To frighten Clinton, the Continental commander-in-chief ordered not one, but three, American generals to make ostentatious preparations for just such an attack on New York as Clinton feared—General Philemon Dickinson in New Jersey, General Horatio Gates on the west bank of the Hudson, General Israel Putnam on the east bank in Westchester County. It was all made to look like one of those converging maneuvers in which eighteenth-century generals delighted. There was not really going to be any attack on Clinton—but Sir Henry had no way of knowing that.

By this time, American counterintelligence had identified some local Tories who were leaking intelligence to the British in New York; but it had cannily refrained from arresting them and had let them go on sending their reports. They were useful now. Dickinson was ordered to make his preparations for an attack on Staten Island as noticeable as possible, at the same time making sure to assemble a great many small boats, the appearance of which always alarmed British intelligence officers. Gates was instructed to make similar preparations, as if to threaten Manhattan; Putnam, to threaten Long Island. After the three generals had done enough to make the supposed attack seem convincingly imminent, they were to let the secret become known to "persons who you are sure will divulge and disseminate it in New York."

At the same time, General Washington and Major John Clark—who had already gained experience in intelligence work in the New Jersey campaign—began to bamboozle Sir William Howe with the same untruthful tales, in as neat a series of prepared falsehoods as were ever perpetrated. These were carefully planned to make equally plausible, in Philadelphia, the alarming but totally false intelligence that Clinton, in New York, would receive from New Jersey, New York state and Connecticut. Howe would certainly send all such information on to New York; that would worry Clinton. Clinton would certainly send all his information on to Philadelphia; that would worry Howe.

Major Clark's well-organized ring of American spies, who were now sending so many accurate reports *out* of Philadelphia, could also be used to send the artistically inaccurate reports to Howe's headquarters in the city. Groundwork for these completely fraudulent documents was carefully laid. About the end of October, 1777, Major Clark sent one of his secret agents—traveling with an official pass from Howe himself—directly to the British commander, with a generous offer from the American major "to risque my all in procuring him intelligence." The offer was perfectly genuine, though Clark failed to add that the most important intelligence, including vital "stolen" documents, would be specially prepared for Sir William Howe by General Washington himself, together with a few ingenious contributions by Major Clark. To make the whole thing seem plausible, Clark made a mystery of his own identity, posing as a Quaker and informing Howe only that "the bearer would give him my name." When the bearer did so, it was the name of "a noted Quaker who I knew assisted him." Much amused, the American agent who carried this message to the enemy's headquarters reported that General Howe smiled approvingly, when he saw that "the letter was concealed curiously."

Rising to the bait, Sir William indicated that he would like first-hand, original American documents, stolen from the files of the Continental Army. Eager to please the commander of the British forces, Clark immediately wrote, asking if General Washington would be willing "to make out a state of the army and your intended movements, according to Sir William's desire."

General Washington would, indeed! He went obligingly to work at once. The truth was seriously fractured in the process; but after all, if the British commander was asking for documents, the least the American commander could do was to supply them.

General Washington's own correspondence shows that the commander-in-chief personally prepared the completely fraudulent returns, giving entirely erroneous strength figures for the Continental Army. He also wrote (one can hardly say forged, since the papers were genuine Washingtoniana) a few brief memoranda, showing his own "intentions"—of doing things he had not the remotest idea of doing. On November 22, 1777, Major Clark was able to report that his secret agent had placed the documents in the hands of Sir William Howe himself.

To help the scheme along, Major Clark had, at the same time, indulged in a few imaginative flights of his own. On November 4, 1777, when the orders went out to Generals Gates, Dickinson and Putnam, he was instructed to inform the enemy that Gates was sending "a very Handsome Reinforcement" to the American Army outside Philadelphia, but would still be able to attack New York City, "now having nothing to do to the Northward," after Burgoyne's capitulation. Clark was to repeat the story that Dickinson would attack Staten Island, adding that Washington himself, with large militia reinforcements, would attack Philadelphia, "to put an end to the War this winter." Major Clark's "friend" took all these fairy tales into the city, for the benefit of the enemy's credulous commander.

Two days later, the major was reporting to Washington—one can almost hear the deceitful pair chuckling—that the British now believed the Continental Army outside Philadelphia had received a reinforcement of eight thousand men from General Gates. Obviously, some unknown American spy of Clark's was so close to British headquarters that he knew what the staff officers were thinking, as well as what they were doing.

All of this false information was planted with such dexterity that the whole mass of fraud seemed to hang together. Each successive false report was confirmed by others just as false, which appeared to come from independent sources in three or four different states—though all of them had been guilefully concocted or ordered by the truthful hero of the legendary cherry tree. Clinton really was made to believe—as General Washington and Major Clark had hoped—that strong forces (which didn't exist) might attack him in New York at any moment. Howe was made to believe that other strong forces (which didn't exist, either) threatened Philadelphia. If the two distracted British generals compared notes, they found that all these military intelligence reports, from four "independent" sources, confirmed one another perfectly. Who could doubt the truthfulness of documents prepared by General George Washington himself?

Sir Henry Clinton, it need hardly be said, kept his troops in New York and manfully prepared for the worst. Sir William Howe, in Philadelphia, made ready for eight thousand new enemies (who were not there).

It is likely that one seemingly great success in espionage, upon which Howe's staff plumed themselves, was really part of Major Clark's elaborate deception. On December 6, 1777, an American spy, lounging about Howe's headquarters, saw a "plain Dreſsed Man" hand a note to a staff major, who took it at once to the general's private office, returning with the remark: "This is a damn'd clever fellow, his intelligence from time to time has been of great use to us." When another officer asked where the spy got his information, the major answered triumphantly: "From Washington's HeadQuarters." He was unquestionably right; for this was at the very time when General Washington and Major Clark had been fabricating information.

The two seem to have entered into their machinations with the mischievous delight of two naughty schoolboys. Clark knew well enough that a sense of humor, usually concealed, lurked beneath his general's statuesque and marble mien. In one report, the major writes that a recent exploit in espionage "will afford you a laugh." Under a flag of truce, Major Clark had himself openly entered the British lines, where he had been allowed to see a great deal he ought not to have seen, before a polite Hessian officer apologetically decided he would have to be blindfolded. But the cloth was so carelessly adjusted that the quick-witted Pennsylvanian could see almost all he needed to see.

General Washington kept up this sort of thing all through the war. In 1779 he was thinking out a good lie—plus some harmless truth—for his spy, Elijah Hunter, and supplying General William Maxwell with "Fictitious questions and answers respecting the American Army for the use of a spy," which Maxwell was requested to have copied "in an indifferent hand, preserving the bad spelling." In March, 1780, the commander-in-chief had a chance to supply false information, through the American General Robert Howe, to a man whose name is given as Beekwith and who may have been a spy, or perhaps Captain George Beckwith, aide to General von Knyphausen. "Beekwith" had written to someone whose name is indicated only by a dash, evidently a double spy who was also reporting to the Americans. General Washington, after writing out what he himself wished transmitted to the enemy, instructed his general "to fill up what I have left open, in such a manner, as will answer our purposes and at the same time suit the character which the writer bears with the enemy."

He was to pass on false intelligence which would "magnify the present force on the North river." Not too much exaggeration, either. A good, plausible prevarication. General Washington wanted everything to sound credible: "Keep it within the bounds of what may be thought reasonable or probable." In June, he gave orders to send a supposedly double agent to persuade the British that the Americans were specially interested in information about the magazines at Fort Washington and other places accessible by water, thus hinting at an impending attack on New York.

In July, he sent the spy, John Mersereau, an elaborate mass of naval misinformation regarding the French fleet and twelve thousand imaginary French or Spanish soldiers, which was to be passed to Brigadier Cortlandt Skinner. In September, Mersereau wrote, asking for false information from the south, which he proposed to transmit to the enemy.

There is a certain relish in his tone, which suggests that General Washington thoroughly enjoyed the tricks he was playing, just as Major Clark enjoyed the elaborate series of mystifications he and his general cooked up together. It is diverting to reflect that both Sir William and Sir Henry went to their graves believing the tremendous lies George Washington had told them. All that was missing was a little hatchet.

XIV

★ ★ ★

★

The Miracles of Major Clark

THE FAIRY TALES he helped General Washington compose for General Howe's benefit were but a small part of Major John Clark's achievements, during the anxious period before the Continental Army withdrew, in early December, 1777, to its bleak winter quarters at Valley Forge. The intelligence service that had been organized earlier in the year—before the theater of operations moved from New Jersey to Pennsylvania—was now supplying General Washington with a steady flow of accurate information, a large part of which can have come only from the patriot spies who had been carefully posted in Philadelphia and its vicinity before the enemy arrived.

The swiftness with which Major Clark, Captain Charles Craig and their agents collected and transmitted intelligence never flagged. In mysterious ways of their own, the American spies were able to get intelligence out of the enemy's territory with extraordinary speed and in perfect safety, no matter what the enemy (who knew very well what was going on) did to block them. Again and again, dates and hours of surviving messages show that information was on its way from Clark or Craig to General Washington only a few hours after spies had picked it up in Philadelphia. All these secret agents remained unsuspected except for two or three, who either escaped or talked their way out of their difficulties; and one of these may not have been a spy for either Clark or Craig—may not, indeed, have been a spy at all.

At least three times during this period, the alertness of the intelligence service—and nothing else—saved American forces from surprise and probable annihilation. It warned of attacks on Fort Mifflin and Fort Mercer, on the Delaware below Philadelphia, in time for the entire garrisons to get safely away. It warned General Washington repeatedly, over a period of several days, of Sir William Howe's intention of surprising him at Whitemarsh—so accurately and so far in advance that the British were completely baffled. It warned Lafayette of the British columns advancing to surprise and surround him at Barren Hill, when his own reconnoissance had totally failed. It warned of Howe's advance to Darby, Pennsylvania. Only once did the Pennsylvania spies fail. They did not warn Anthony Wayne before the Paoli Massacre, when the British were allowed to approach through the night completely undiscovered either by the intelligence service or by Wayne's own patrols.

How greatly the American secret service had improved, became apparent as soon as the Continental Army was driven out of Philadelphia. All winter long, the British were under continual observation. Near the British outpost lines, American reconnoissance detachments were always hovering. Individual officers at advanced posts were in direct touch with individual secret agents, permanently stationed in or near Philadelphia—unobtrusive private citizens, natives of the area, familiar figures for years, whose presence needed no explanation. Among so many ordinary and apparently harmless people, it was impossible for the British to guess which were spies. But the fact that numerous patriot secret agents were actively at work the moment the British came, shows how effectively the Americans had built up their system in advance.

The contrast with the situation in New York in 1776, only a year before, when Washington had been totally in the dark as to enemy intentions and capabilities, was positively startling. By 1777, the Continental commander always knew what Howe *could* do. He sometimes knew several days in advance exactly what Howe was going to do. And the commander-in-chief himself evaluated the intelligence, as it came in, with unerring skill.

Though General Mifflin had made the preliminary arrangements for organized espionage in Philadelphia and its vicinity some months earlier, he soon turned to other duties, leaving American intelligence in this theater of operations mainly in the hands of Major John Clark, who did nothing else; Colonel Elias Boudinot, who also served as commissary of prisoners; Captain Charles Craig, at Frankford, north of Philadelphia; and Major Allan McLane, chiefly engaged in cavalry reconnoissance, but ready to assist intelligence agents, when needed, and operating a small network of volunteer spies, all his own.

Major Clark, a line officer at the beginning of the war, had been gaining experience in military intelligence in New Jersey, probably in 1776, certainly during the early part of 1777. About this time, he thought of a plan—he never told what it was—"to gain immediate intelligence of the enemy." He was allowed to test his scheme, "at great personal hazard," after which he reported results directly to General Washington. So complete was his success—the exact nature of which still remains unrevealed—that the gratified commander-in-chief, as Major Clark wrote after the war, "gave me unlimited command and power to do as I pleased," in the intelligence service in southeastern Pennsylvania—an area with which he was perfectly familiar, since he had grown up there. By December 11, 1776, and probably long before that, he was on special duty in Bristol, Pennsylvania, midway between Philadelphia and Trenton.

The major soon had an almost perfect spy net operating out of Philadelphia. One of his agents was an old woman. Others were disguised as farmers or hucksters, carrying special passes that freed them from interference by American guards and patrols. Some were Philadelphia gentry. One agent was aboard the British fleet, while another had special orders to mingle as much as possible with British officers, with many of whom he was "Very intimately acquainted."

Most members of this ring have never been identified and

probably never can be; but, whoever they were, they revealed an uncanny ability to ferret out military secrets. A few days after the British occupied Philadelphia (September 26, 1777), an intelligence report from Clark's network was on its way to General Washington. Though fighting at Germantown did not cease till ten o'clock in the morning of October 4, 1777, Clark was reporting British losses, from intelligence sources within the British lines, by five o'clock in the morning of October 6. By ten o'clock, the major had a second report, this time from a secret agent whose name he dared not reveal, even to General Washington. The American spy had been chatting with General Howe at Germantown during the battle. The reports he gave Clark showed that the enemy had "suffered prodigiously." Several senior officers were reported killed. General von Knyphausen was wounded in the hand. "Many officers say that you had completely surprised them." The same message reported a movement of troops and wagons southward toward Chester.

After this brilliant coup, Clark was ordered to "tarry in this country" and hovered about the city, just out of British reach, for nearly three months, riding twenty to sixty miles a day in all weathers, keeping rendezvous with secret agents who came and went from Philadelphia almost at will, wearing out his own horses and then the army's, till he had to beg his commander for mounts.

"My horses are almost ruined; the only one I had left is foundered," he wrote within a few weeks." . . . I have ruined two or three of my own." He suffered severely from cold, because he had reached Pennsylvania in light clothing and could get nothing warmer. Once he tells Washington: "My hands are so cold I can scarce write you." This reference to summer uniform indicates how early in the year he had begun his share of organizing the Philadelphia network; and the number of his spies shows the same thing—for it takes time to set up so large a network.

Even after occupying Philadelphia, the British had still to reduce the American Forts Mifflin and Mercer, which blocked the Delaware River below the city, interfering with British transports trying to bring in supplies the redcoats had to have. Knowing that the British would eventually attempt to clear the lower Delaware, the Americans watched the two forts anxiously.

The combined land and naval attack on both of them began on October 22, 1777, after some days of operations against Fort Mifflin alone. Clark sent General Washington, that very day, a report for which an aide thanked him profusely, asking for more intelligence and sending a hundred dollars for expenses. The commanding general thought his intelligence officer too sanguine in predicting the British would soon give up this first attack; but Major Clark was right. After a little fighting, the enemy's land forces withdrew, though only for a brief period. Five days later, two of Clark's agents sent word that thirty-three boatloads of wounded had been brought in, the day after the fight. Always careful about accuracy, Clark took the precaution of riding through the night to verify these facts by another source, before reporting at 9:00 A.M.

By this time the enemy's counterintelligence had stationed local Tories, who knew patriots of the vicinity by sight, at all entrances to Philadelphia, to head off Clark's spies; and the high sheriff of the county was a particular danger. "However, we now and then get by him," observed Clark cheerfully, though admitting that he was not getting intelligence so easily as he once had hoped. Disaffected people of the countryside began to develop strong suspicions of the young major, whose mysterious comings and goings at all hours could not be wholly concealed. The Tories were now watching him, Major Clark noted, as "a hawk would a chicken"; and, since there was always danger that he might be betrayed to the British and captured in a swift raid, he was careful to change his quarters frequently.

It is startling to see how much the Americans by this time knew about what the British were doing in Philadelphia and how often they knew in advance what the enemy meant to do. General Washington had strength returns of British and German troops less than two months after the enemy entered the city, and had probably had others much earlier. Two American officers warned of the first attack on Fort Mifflin on October 17, 1777. On November 3, nearly three weeks before the second land attack on the fort, Clark's spy in Philadelphia, "an exceedingly intelligent fellow," was reporting British preparations to send troops against both of the river forts. Boldly mingling with enemy forces, the spy had been "treated with great politeness by the officers," had chatted with wagoners about ammunition for the attack, and had personally examined the enemy's troops, camps, artillery and trains, before reporting his conclusions. Major Clark received the commander-in-chief's "approbation" next day. By November 8, Washington himself had received a personal warning, through "a very intelligent person from Philadelphia," that Fort Mifflin would soon be attacked. Washington's agent had assiduously collected careless remarks by senior British officers to supposedly trustworthy people. Meantime, another of Clark's agents kept constant watch at Marcus Hook and Chester, in the lower Delaware, past which an attacking fleet would have to sail.

Forts Mifflin and Mercer were soon under another vigorous naval bombardment, but the troops Clark's spy had observed did not at first move against them. When at last the British decided to renew the land attack on both forts, General Washington had abundant information, well ahead of time. The first news that the British would move down the west bank of the Delaware, against Fort Mifflin, came from Captain Charles Craig, at Frankford, just above Philadelphia, on November 15, before Cornwallis had even started. Thus forewarned and fearing to be overpowered, the American garrison slipped quietly away on the night of the 15th/16th. Cornwallis did not march until about midnight of the 16th/17th.

An unknown American agent in Philadelphia at once reported to Washington the effect of the evacuation, the general British situation in Philadelphia, new batteries, and the probable next move, getting the report into his hands by November 17.

Finding Fort Mifflin abandoned, Cornwallis crossed the Delaware into New Jersey, exactly as predicted, to attack Fort Mercer, while American spies hung doggedly on his trail. "If the enemy are going to cross the Delaware," wrote Major Clark to General Washington at 10:00 A.M., November 17, "you will have information instantly," a promise which his spy system abundantly fulfilled. At nine o'clock next morning, November 18, Clark reported that "a young fellow of character" was at that moment in Philadelphia finding out "the enemy's designs," with special orders "to mingle with the British officers; as he is acquainted with several of them, and very intimately."

The first "hard" news of Cornwallis's intention to cross the Delaware into New Jersey and assail Fort Mercer also came from Captain Craig, who reported early the same day, "the enemy intend some Grand Menouver in Jersey." At eleven-thirty, Craig followed this up with news that Cornwallis had crossed the river with four thousand men. After that, spies' reports came pouring swiftly in, all day long. At noon, Clark reported five thousand men moving out of Philadelphia with artillery and about to cross the Delaware, obviously to attack Fort Mercer. At half-past two, that afternoon, Craig's assistant, Lieutenant John Heard, at Frankford, confirmed reports of Cornwallis's movements and added that the British had so stripped the Philadelphia defenses that they could not man the lines. Heard had this information "direct from the City," and it was independently confirmed by another agent, who had been chatting with a friendly British sergeant who thought the American spy was "well affected to the Royal Army." At three-thirty, Craig corrected his eleven-thirty report on British strength. Cornwallis had only two thousand men, would move to Wilmington, would cross the Delaware there, and would then attack Fort Mercer. At four o'clock Clark confirmed earlier reports of the enemy's intention to cross the Delaware and reported troops embarking.

There were two more confirmatory reports during the evening. At eight o'clock, General Potter reported the whole British force had crossed and that Fort Mercer could not be held. At nine-thirty Joseph Reed sent word that the British at Chester had crossed to New Jersey and might attack Fort Mercer that night. At ten o'clock, Washington suggested that Brigadier General Varnum try to find "some countrymen" to go visit the British under the usual pretense of selling provisions and see exactly what they were now doing.

On November 19, Craig reported in the morning, again at one o'clock, and again at two. The British had *not* all crossed the Delaware; Cornwallis was still on the Pennsylvania bank; but there would certainly be an attack on Fort Mercer—also called Redbank.

At 8:30 P.M., Brigadier General Potter confirmed the British crossing of the Delaware, adding "Redbank must now fall." At nine-thirty, Joseph Reed reported that Cornwallis had crossed, that the British "made no Secret of their Intentions to attack Red Bank," that they said they would storm the fort that night, but that the attack would probably not be made till later.

Sometime during the evening, an unknown spy managed to get out of Philadelphia with the news that General Howe was sending still further reinforcements to Cornwallis for the attack on Fort Mercer. Thus warned, the American garrison removed most of their stores to safety, burned some of their shipping, and themselves slipped away on the night of November 20/21. The safe evacuation of two forts was hardly a military triumph; but no troops had been lost; and it was the new intelligence service that had saved them. The last spy's report reached General Greene, instead of Washington—perhaps because Clark had been one of Greene's staff officers—on November 23, "by a Woman who came thro' the Enemy encampments this day." This plucky and skeptical lady reported the enemy's numbers: "They give out that they have 10,000 Men, but she thought they had not half the number." There were eighty to one hundred light infantry. Lord Cornwallis was living at "Mʳ Coopers." She had located the line of outguards and troop dispositions and thought there was a chance for an American attack on Philadelphia. Such definite intelligence proved that most of the enemy's troops were elsewhere; but General Washington decided not to try it.

Clark continued his intelligence work through December, taking an active part in the espionage that saved Washington from Howe's attempt to surprise him at Whitemarsh, early in December. His spies, sometimes posing as illicit dealers in provisions, went back and forth from Philadelphia, undisturbed by British precautions, and kept Washington constantly informed of the movements of foragers, work on entrenchments, British strength and British supplies.

A spy gave timely warning December 21, 1777, that the enemy would be out in strength to forage in Darby, Marple and Springfield townships. General Howe, with seven thousand men duly arrived in Darby next day, exactly as predicted. Major Clark reported his movements twice that day.

The success of Clark's spies was largely due to their boldness and to perfect concealment of their identity. One, caught by Howe's advanced guard and taken to headquarters, seems to have come to no harm. Two days after Howe's arrival at Darby, another penetrated almost to the British generals' headquarters, unsuspected. Washington gave up his idea of attacking Howe there, but only after consulting Major Clark and Light Horse Harry Lee, both of whom advised against it.

So well were Clark's secret agents covered that, though one or two others may have been arrested,—even these arrests are not quite certain,—none of them seems to have been executed. This is the more remarkable because some of the spies passed through the hands of the treacherous Colonel William Rankin, who, though a Pennsylvania Militia officer, was later in correspondence with Clinton and André, planning a Tory rising to restore British power. Perhaps Rankin thought the spies were genuine dealers in illicit provisions and had no wish to keep the British from getting food. At least once, however, Rankin seized one of Clark's agents, "Mr. Trumbull," and the provisions he was smuggling to the British, with Washington's approval, "as a cover to procure intelligence"; and the commander-in-chief had to intervene personally, to save Trumbull.

Once, too, Clark feared that a spy had met with disaster in Philadelphia, but as he says nothing further, the endangered agent must have escaped, after all. The Philadelphia merchant, Robert Ritchie, jailed by the British for "giving intelligence to Gen'l Washington's army," may have been one of Clark's men, though Mrs. Ritchie seems more likely to have been the real spy.

Once a Tory seized a startled American agent by the coat, snarling "damn'd Rebel" in the hearing of British sentries, but the man spurred his horse to safety. Presently he had the odd experience of seeing his accuser brought in as a prisoner by American troops, and hearing the Tory appeal to the man whose life he had endangered, as a witness to his patriotism! (It is, of course, just possible the Tory was really another American spy.)

Clark had far more trouble with zealous Americans who interfered with the black-market cover he arranged for his agents, and who once ruined a plan to secure vital intelligence by arresting an American spy before he could reach the British.

Major Clark's escapades went on till early January, 1778, when both armies were in winter quarters. Then—in failing health, partly from hardship and partly from an old wound— he retired to his home in York, Pennsylvania, to visit his wife, having first made sure that his spy nets would continue to operate. Washington secured for him a staff appointment as "auditor," which Clark held as long as he had the strength, though he was eventually compelled to leave the army entirely.

XV

Spies in the Quaker City

MANY OTHER SPIES added to the intelligence sent in through
Major Clark; but there is no way of telling whether they
belonged to his organization or to several different American
networks, operating independently. A surviving letter here, a
local legend there, an old soldier's casual statement in a pension
claim, occasional references in military documents and accounts,
and one complete story, which the gallant Quakeress, Friend
Lydia Darragh, told her daughter, are the only indications that
remain. It is clear, however, that by this time Colonel Elias
Boudinot was recognized as a staff intelligence officer; that Colonel Elias Dayton was still operating an independent system;
that the "Green Boys" along the Wissahickon were busy with
espionage of some kind—perhaps as part of Major Clark's organization; that at least three volunteer women spies were in
touch with headquarters; that various generals were operating
small spy rings of their own; and that Allan McLane, whose
cavalry hovered constantly just beyond the British outposts
covering Philadelphia, frequently employed spies as well as
scouts. Captain Stephen Chambers was also operating some
kind of intelligence service between Valley Forge and Philadelphia in March, 1778.

General Washington himself dealt with a few secret agents directly. One of these was probably the German baker—and specialist in fancy gingerbread—Christopher Ludwick, who, as "Baker General" of the Continental Army, supplied such bread as he could to the troops at Valley Forge. German born, long in business in Philadelphia, he was the ideal agent to encourage German troops to desert and could hardly help mingling espionage with these duties.

Another of General Washington's personal spies was the ex-marine captain, Jacob Bankson, whose first offer to enter Philadelphia as a secret agent led to strong suspicion that he was really a British spy. The ex-marine had always been able to go in and out of British-occupied Philadelphia in some mysterious way of his own. This uncanny ability or something else made General Washington so suspicious that, in the spring of 1778, he asked Governor William Livingston, of New Jersey, to have the captain watched. Four days later, Livingston put a counter-intelligence agent on the suspect's trail, which on that very day led—straight to General Washington's headquarters! Still unconvinced, the general had Alexander Hamilton check the man's background in Princeton. Fully cleared of all suspicion in a few more days, Bankson was twice paid $100 for secret service, April 11 and May 1, 1778, though what he did remains unknown.

There were still other spies in the Quaker City, with well protected channels for sending intelligence swiftly and secretly out of the city, to Whitemarsh and Valley Forge. Between Philadelphia and Continental headquarters, operated a highly irregular group of patriot guerrillas, "the Green Boys," among whom were the Levering brothers, covering the country between Manayunk, Pennsylvania, and Philadelphia, along the Wissahickon Creek. Jacob Levering frequently entered the British lines by canoeing openly down the Schuylkill to Philadelphia, posing as a Quaker farmer, and selling market produce from door to door.

The two other brothers were equally active, though only John Levering was known to Tories as a spy. Jacob, though still unsuspected, was captured and almost hanged by mistake, before his neighbors convinced the British that he was not the suspected John Levering. He was at once released; and no one felt obliged to add the information that Jacob was, if anything, a more active American secret agent than his brother. Jacob Levering habitually carried a pass from General Washington, which would at once have convicted him, had it been discovered. Either he was not carrying it the day of his capture or else his person was not adequately searched.

Some of the intelligence from Philadelphia was smuggled to "Old Mom" Rinker, whose family had long kept the Buck Tavern, in Germantown. "Mom Rinker's Rock" is still pointed out in Fairmount Park. Mom's flax was said to be the best bleached in the whole neighborhood, because she laid it out on a rock of her own, high on its cliff above the Wissahickon Valley, where sunlight lingered longer than anywhere else—a rock which also stood where everybody could see it.

Flax and sunlight were not the only things that lingered on Mom Rinker's rock. When intelligence of the British forces reached her, Mom Rinker—who was at that time still fairly young—would presently be seen, seated on the sun-warm stone, knitting. There was nothing suspicious about that. If by chance a British patrol passed that way, all it could see was a woman placidly engaged in the most peaceful of domestic tasks.

How could the British guess that that quiet figure was under observation by Green Boys, watching from the hillside opposite? Eventually, at the right moment, Mom would carelessly drop her ball of yarn, in such a way that it rolled over the cliff. Here, in due time, it was picked up by the Green Boys, and the papers around which it was rolled were sent on to Washington. It was dramatic in the most literal sense. Using her rock as a stage, Mom Rinker deliberately acted out in public an assumed rôle before two audiences at once—the Green Boys and any Tories who might be wandering that way. She was, it is true, often suspected of doing exactly what she was doing, but she acted her rôle so well, suspicion did no harm. She was also suspected of witchcraft; but nothing was ever proved against her; and, after all, the Articles of War do not forbid witchcraft.

When, on November 2, 1777, General Washington put the

beaten Continental Army in position at Whitemarsh, an easy night's march from the British in Philadelphia, he was in constant danger of attack. Well aware of this, the general was careful to place his troops in a strong position on thickly wooded hills, with a morass and a stream covering its front, a breastwork barring the only good ford. There was always a chance that the British might push in on either flank. General Washington was well aware of that, too.

After the Americans had been at Whitemarsh for about a month, Howe decided on a night march, a dawn attack, and a surprise that would smash the rebellion once for all. Orders went out to get the troops ready. Instantly, the American spy system began to pour information in upon the grave Virginian at Whitemarsh, each of the independent reports confirming the others.

On November 29, almost a week before Howe was ready to move out of Philadelphia, the Americans already knew that he was coming. On that date, General John Armstrong wrote President Wharton, of Pennsylvania: "Every intelligence agrees that General Howe now, no doubt with his whole force, is immediately to take the field in quest of this army." Since the Americans expected attack at any moment, Armstrong had already called in the Pennsylvania Brigade, which had been pushed forward to the west bank of the Schuylkill.

Armstrong's message is interesting because it refers to "every intelligence." Already, then, more than one report had come in; and it goes without saying that, if a mere division commander had all these facts, the commander-in-chief had fuller information.

On December 1, 1777, General Washington heard from Major John Clark, still "on spy service," who reported: "Orders were given to the troops to hold themselves in readiness to march." Enemy capability? "They either mean to surprise your army or to prevent your making an attack on them."

On December 2, Captain Charles Craig, at Frankford, warned of British preparations: "The enemy Intend to make a push out—and indeavour to drive your Excellency from the present encampment." Five hundred redcoats had crossed the Schuyl-

kill. On the same day, Robert Smith reported from Germantown that "Hardly anything has come out to Day"—which
sounds as if normally a good deal of intelligence reached him
there, in spite of the British occupation. Some ladies, who had
managed to leave Philadelphia "by special Favor," reported to
Smith gossip among British officers that there would be a movement early on the morning of the third. Destination and route
were doubtful, but the troops were being paid and issued new
uniforms. Smith's date was about a day and a half wrong, but
he was correct in predicting that the British would bring boats,
mounted on wheels, with them.

On December 3, Craig reported again. Three thousand
troops with six guns and boats had crossed the Schuylkill and
meant to strike the American rear. They seemed eager to know
where American stores and baggage were.

At one o'clock that afternoon, Clark sent the same intelligence: "The enemy are in motion, have a number of flat-
bottomed boats and carriages and scantlings, and are busy
pressing horses and wagons. No persons permitted to come out,
except those upon whom they can depend." "In motion" did
not necessarily mean that British troops were already marching,
but only that they were actively getting ready for a military
operation of some kind.

At six o'clock, Clark sent the report of an American spy who
had left Philadelphia at noon: "This morning a Sergeant, a
countryman of my spy's, assured him that the Troops had received orders to hold themselves in readiness when called for,
and to draw two days provisions. Biscuit was served out to them
when he came away, and 'twas the current language in the city
among the Troops and citizens, that they were going to make a
move." On December 4, an agent signing only "W.D—" also
reported the coming attack.

At the very last moment a final warning came in from Captain Allan McLane, reconnoitering with his cavalry: "An attempt to surprise the American camp at White Marsh was
about to be made."

But meantime, a quiet housewife was surpassing the whole
elaborate secret service that had been so long prepared and re-

vealing the enemy's exact plan, from within the enemy's most secret councils. In Philadelphia, a respectable Quaker matron had for some time been running an espionage agency all her own—from a vantage point few spies enjoy; for her house stood directly opposite an enemy headquarters, where she could see the daily comings and goings of the enemy's staff. At least once she walked boldly in, to talk with an officer there.

This daring volunteer spy was Lydia Darragh, whose family occupied the Loxley House, then No. 177 on the east side of Second Street, below Spruce Street, at the southeast corner of Little Dock Street. Almost opposite stood the Cadwalader House, for a time the headquarters of Sir William Howe himself, later taken over by the German Lieutenant General von Knyphausen. It has been conjectured that a Captain Barrington, then serving with the British, may have been Lydia Darragh's kinsman, for her maiden name was Barrington, and her schoolmaster husband, William Darragh, had been private tutor in the Barrington family in Ireland. If Captain Barrington really was Lydia's relative, it did American intelligence no harm, though the captain had no idea how he was being used; and no one ever suspected the clever Quakeress till the war was over and she told her own story.

Lydia Darragh's espionage was a strictly family affair. She herself collected the information. William Darragh then wrote his wife's reports in shorthand on bits of paper, small enough to be hidden in the large "mould buttons" of the period. Since these were covered with cloth of the same material as the coat they adorned, Friend Lydia could go on covering and recovering any number of buttons, whenever she had military intelligence to send to General Washington. Her fourteen-year-old son, John, then slipped off to the American camp, wearing the buttons, cut them off, and delivered them to his elder brother, Lieutenant Charles Darragh—a task to delight any adventurous teen-ager. The lieutenant, who, like his father, knew shorthand, transcribed his mother's notes for General Washington. Occasionally, Mrs. Darragh "sent little messages by other hands." She continued this as long as she had anything to send, without ever being suspected, though for one terrifying half hour she feared (quite needlessly) that the enemy had discovered her at last.

Exactly what military intelligence was in these messages is a secret now lost forever, except for one intelligence triumph of the first magnitude. Not long before their attempt to surprise General Washington at Whitemarsh, the British had unconsciously played directly into Lydia Darragh's hands. Needing more rooms, their billeting officers ordered William Darragh to turn over his house to the army "and find other quarters for his family." Lydia's personal protests at headquarters—presumably to Captain Barrington—led to a modification of British demands; and General Howe contented himself with one room for a "council chamber," allowing the Darraghs to keep the rest of their house.

Modern writers, who have never helped to occupy an enemy town, have sometimes doubted that officers of the occupation forces would use an American house for such a purpose. There are three answers to these skeptics. One is that an occupying army has to use such buildings as exist. A second is that the Darragh family were Quakers, who would supposedly take no part in the war. A third is that British billeting officers could not be expected to know that the Quaker son of this particular Quaker household was an officer in the American Army. (Eventually the Friends' meeting to which the Darraghs belonged cast out Lieutenant Charles Darragh for "engaging in matters of a warlike nature," and his mother for "neglecting to attend our religious meetings"; but that was some years later.)

Lydia gave the British one room at the back of the house and sent her younger children to the country. Officers in scarlet came and went. There was much conferring in the Darraghs' back room. On December 2, 1777, several days after the American intelligence service had already begun to warn the Continental Army, an officer instructed Lydia Darragh to send all her family to bed early, "as they wished to use the room that night free from interruption." The officers would arrive about seven.

It was as good as an invitation to eavesdrop—a temptation which the Quakeress at first heroically resisted. The Darraghs dutifully went to bed, as ordered, but Lydia could not sleep. "A presentiment of evil weighed down her spirits." This secret consultation boded ill for the Continental camp, where her son lay sleeping, within easy striking distance. From the conference room, she could hear the voices of the enemy's staff. At last she could stand it no longer. She slipped silently into a closet adjoining the conference room, where there was nothing between her and the conferring staff officers but a thin board partition, covered with wallpaper.

She had begun to eavesdrop far too late. The officers were about to leave; but she was in time to hear the final reading of the paper that summed up their decision. The British would march out of Philadelphia by night on December 4. They would "attack Washington's army, and with their superior force and the unprepared condition of the [American] enemy victory was certain."

Hurrying back to bed, the agitated mother feigned an unusually sound sleep. The conference broke up. Chairs scraped. There was a rattle of swords. Military boots clattered over the floor. Then a sharp tap at her bedroom door. An officer had come to tell her to lock the house after them and see to their fire and candles. Since the frightened woman at first made no reply, the gullible Briton noted with satisfaction that Mrs. Darragh seemed unusually sleepy.

It took her all next day (December 3, 1777) to decide on a course of action. It might not be easy to pass the British outguards. She would need a pretext and it would have to be a good one. According to one version of the story, she pretended to be going to see her children. According to another, she pretended to be on her way to a mill at Frankford, for flour. Either tale was perfectly plausible, and she probably told both.

But she told her husband nothing, merely announcing that she was going to use a British pass she already possessed, to go out into the country.

Lydia Darragh's unwillingness to confide in her husband is easily explained. The fewer people, however trustworthy, who are involved in such an affair, the better. This time, she would not need his shorthand. She was probably carrying the whole report in her head—and, if so, she was wiser than either Hale or André. Besides, her errand involved both risks and hardships. William Darragh might have tried to stop his dauntless Lydia, for he is said to have been mildly surprised that she did not wish to take her maid with her, when she announced her trip.

Once more, fortune favored the brave. Lydia Darragh had some hardships, but very little difficulty. She trudged along the road running northeast from Philadelphia to a mill on Frankford Creek. British outposts let her through. Why not? Her dress showed she was a Friend. She had General Howe's pass. A small and rather frail woman, no longer young, hardly seemed dangerous. Let her through! That she was trudging several miles afoot through Pennsylvania's December cold seemed less suspicious than it would today, for American women of the Revolution were sturdier than their great-great-granddaughters. Besides, her errand seemed quite natural. Philadelphians habitually did walk out of town to mills near the city; and, during the American occupation, General Washington had had to let them continue to do so, ordering the practice stopped only a few days before the British marched in. He may have realized what a fine excuse the journey was for spies wishing to pass the lines—something General Howe did not think about in time.

Lydia Darragh is said to have carried an empty flour bag, to make her story seem more plausible. If that is true, as it probably is, the Quakeress ended her arduous day by carrying a heavy bag of flour on her return journey, five miles back from Frankford Mill.

At Frankford, well outside British-held terrain, she could move freely and might encounter American scouts or patrols almost anywhere. Dropping her bag at the mill, to be filled, she turned westward along Nice Town Lane, toward the Rising Sun Tavern, kept by "Widow Nice," or Neuss.

She had taken the right direction. Somewhere in that general area were Captain Allan McLane's cavalry patrols, covering the American defense lines at Whitemarsh. Then, or a little later, Major Benjamin Tallmadge was also out on reconnoissance.

During the morning, Colonel Elias Boudinot had gone as far forward as the Rising Sun, where the Americans had "a small post," a few miles west of Frankford Mill. After dining at the tavern, the colonel had remained there, using it as an advanced post and message center. Somewhere near was Colonel Thomas Craig, of the 3rd Pennsylvania (or perhaps the spy master, Captain Charles Craig), mounted, well acquainted with the locality, probably in observation of Nice Town Lane.

It is perfectly clear what was happening. General Washington had already had three or four days' warning of Howe's contemplated surprise and was taking proper precautions. McLane had drawn a cavalry screen, as well as he could, with his few troopers. The Americans had a line of observers for several miles across all possible enemy approaches. With an attack imminent, the place for the G-2 of the Continental Army was well forward; and that is where Colonel Boudinot went. He would be just behind the cavalry. His task was to receive and evaluate information as soon as received, not to go scouting himself; and the event proved he was right.

Plodding wearily along, Mrs. Darragh presently met an American officer. In all probability this was Colonel Craig, though some later accounts say she met McLane, and she may have met them both. Any unexplained civilians wandering down Nice Town Lane from the east were certain to be stopped for interrogation that morning. Craig, a Pennsylvanian, who knew the Darragh family, was mildly surprised to find an eminently respectable Philadelphia matron trudging down the wintry lane, between two armies.

"Why, Mrs. Darragh," he is supposed to have asked, "what are you doing so far from home?"

Leading his horse, he walked along beside her, while she gave her news. If Colonel Craig knew his duty as a soldier—and evidence is abundant that he did—he either rode straight back to General Washington himself or hurried back a messenger, though it is said that he paused long enough to take the weary woman into a farmhouse and made sure she got some food. It is also said that she exacted a solemn promise not to reveal her identity.

Lydia Darragh may now have turned around, feeling somewhat better, picked up her flour at the mill—legend says it weighed twenty-five pounds—and trudged home with a sense of duty done. It is too bad that her daughter Ann did not add more such details when she later revealed her mother's exploit.

The Rising Sun Tavern seems to have been a kind of rendezvous for American women spies, operating in or near Philadelphia. Near it, about this time, Major Benjamin Tallmadge rescued another woman secret agent, a young girl, from pursuing British cavalry. This country girl had been sent into Philadelphia, ostensibly to sell eggs, actually to "obtain some information respecting the enemy." Tallmadge—who had ridden forward with a small cavalry force until, from the tavern, he could watch British outposts—saw the egg merchant emerge from the British lines and approach the tavern. While she was giving her information to the major, within the Rising Sun, there was an alarm, and, from the door, Tallmadge saw the British horsemen, "at full speed chasing in my patrols, one of whom they took."

With a leap, the major was in the saddle, then found the girl at his stirrup, begging for protection. Ever the gentleman, the gallant cavalryman "desired her to mount," she scrambled up, and they rode a brisk three miles, with "considerable firing of pistols, and not a little wheeling and charging." At Germantown, the girl dismounted and disappeared.

The end of Lydia Darragh's mission was much less like a moving picture. Colonel Boudinot's memoirs pick up her story at this point. Sometime during the afternoon—Boudinot says "after dinner," then a midday or afternoon meal—a woman came into the Rising Sun. She was, according to the colonel, "a little, poor-looking, insignificant old woman." This may have been Lydia Darragh herself. She knew that Craig might not get the information back in time. If she could inform another American field officer, all the better.

Boudinot's description is puzzling—if he really met Lydia Darragh. Mrs. Darragh, though perhaps not "little," was rather slight and, after several hours of walking along the road, she probably was "poor-looking." As for her being "insignificant," she was a Quakeress, and the Plain People have never been extravagant in dress. But even so, the description sounds like another woman. Lydia Darragh, according to her daughter, was "of a fair complexion, light hair, blue eyes, very delicate in appearance and extremely neat; conforming in her dress to the Society of Friends."

Whoever this woman may have been, she immediately began to talk to Colonel Boudinot about flour "and solicited leave to go into the country to buy some." It sounds as if the stranger wanted to make sure she was really talking to Americans. It was not always easy to be sure. The Continental Army was wearing various uniforms or no uniforms; and not all King George's troops were dressed in scarlet. Some of the Hessians were in blue.

Boudinot says "we" asked some questions. An advanced post occupied the Rising Sun, and several officers dining there may have joined in the interrogation of this mysterious female.

Presently, the stranger handed Boudinot "a dirty old needlebook, with various small pockets in it." Surprised, the colonel told her to go away and come back for an answer later. So far as is known, he never saw her again.

It strains credulity to suppose that two patriotic American ladies were wandering about wintry roads outside Philadelphia at the same time, both with the same important military intelligence and both babbling about flour, unless there was some connection between them. Since Lydia Darragh's time was getting short, it is possible that she put a written message in the needlebook and sent it on by some other woman, possibly from the house where Craig left her to get food. It was now the end of the morning. The sooner she was back in Philadelphia, the fewer questions would be asked. Besides, Friend Lydia had a reputation for neatness. "A dirty old needlebook" simply could not come from the Darragh household, but it might easily come from a wayside farm.

Eagerly, Boudinot examined it: "I could not find anything till I got to the last pocket, where I found a piece of paper rolled up into the form of a pipe shank. On unrolling it I found information that General Howe was coming out the next morning with 5000 men, 13 pieces of cannon, baggage wagons, and 11 boats on wheels"—the latter being pontoon bridge equipment. This agreed in the main with other information, though the strength estimate may have been wrong. The pontoons suggested a river crossing, and the Delaware and Schuylkill were the only rivers the enemy could possibly cross. There was no reason to cross the Schuylkill, though one spy reported they had done so. Crossing the Delaware would imply withdrawal to New York.

Hurrying back to headquarters, Boudinot gave a report of the kind General Washington had ordered: "the naked facts without comment or opinion." Washington listened thoughtfully. Boudinot went on to an interpretation of the enemy's intentions. He believed Howe would pretend he was retreating to New York; would actually cross the Delaware eastward into New Jersey; would cross westward into Pennsylvania once more, somewhere above Bristol, Pennsylvania; and would then crash into the American's unguarded rear "and cut off all our baggage, if not the whole army." This, of course, was about what Captain Charles Craig had reported.

The tall man in blue and buff, with the three silver stars upon his shoulder, had thus far had nothing to say. He had listened "without a single observation, being deep in thought." Boudinot gave his opinion all over again. Still his commander remained silent. Boudinot, thinking his ideas "unattended to," repeated them again, urging him to strengthen the rear, at once, as there was not much time.

Washington at last roused himself. In complete disagreement with his intelligence officer, he proceeded to estimate the situation with—as events proved—almost absolute correctness: "The Enemy have no Business in our Rear, the Boats are designed to deceive us." The British would attack a flank. "To morrow Morning by day light you will find them coming down such a bye road on our left." Calling an aide, he ordered the lines strengthened in front, not rear.

Boudinot departed, silently fuming, for he "thought the General under a manifest mistake." The colonel would not be the last G-2 to resent his commander's curt rejection of a carefully thought-out "appreciation." Glumly, he told the handful of officers quartered near him that the general was all wrong and the army was sure to lose its baggage train next morning.

Still, he was about to go to sleep a mile ahead of the American lines, on the very road down which General Washington said the enemy would come that night. Suppose the old man was right, after all! Conceding the chance that George Washington might know what he was talking about, Colonel Boudinot advanced a picket down the road, kept all horses saddled, and gave orders to have the officers' mounts at the door at the first alarm gun.

At three o'clock in the morning, there was a crash of many alarm guns. Along the route George Washington had predicted they would use, the British were coming! Boudinot and the others rode for their lives. By dawn, the redcoats occupied the quarters where the skeptical intelligence specialist had been sleeping. Boudinot was rueful: "I then said that I never would again set up my judgment against his."

The British had moved out of Philadelphia at eleven o'clock on the night of December 4, probably with a good many more men than the five thousand Lydia Darragh had reported. They kept wagons and field artillery rolling through Philadelphia all night, in the wrong direction, as if they were heading for the Schuylkill River; but Major Allan McLane was not deceived: "Every intelligence from the city agrees the enemy is in motion and intend a grand stroke." Before daybreak on the fifth, the advanced guard had halted on a ridge beyond Chestnut Hill, about three miles from the American right flank—not the left, as Washington had anticipated. This was his only error; and, after all, the British soon did shift to the left flank; and the only fighting took place there.

The Americans, forewarned, had been busy for some time, strengthening their positions. The enemy's main body came up about seven o'clock and deployed for action, with a reserve in position to the rear. It was evident that the surprise had failed. McLane's cavalry had found their column as it cleared Germantown and had harassed the last stage of the advance. The Continental Army was deployed, entrenched and waiting.

The two armies sat glaring at each other all day. The British lay on their arms that night. Most of the next day (December 6) was without event. Late in the afternoon, the redcoats disappeared in the direction of Germantown. It looked as if they were going back to Philadelphia. It was meant to look that way; but no one was deceived; and the Americans were still ready when, on December 7, the scarlet uniforms suddenly appeared on the American left, where Washington had originally expected them.

General Washington made the rounds of his brigades, extolling the virtues of the bayonet. The British reconnoitered, but could find no soft spots; and Howe, who had led his troops to slaughter at Bunker Hill, knew better now than to try a frontal assault on entrenched Americans. General "No Flint" Grey had a brush with Morgan's and Gist's riflemen, which cost a hundred British lives. Otherwise, the two forces merely looked at each other all day long. Again the British lay on their arms all night. Nothing whatever happened on the morning of the eighth. About noon, General Howe gave up. The British Army marched back to Philadelphia, "like a parcel of damned fools," said one of its disgusted officers. It was a magnificent example of what a few really good spies and some wideawake cavalry can accomplish.

The Whitemarsh fiasco greatly discouraged the enemy both in Philadelphia and in London. Cornwallis, who left Philadelphia for a brief leave in England, reported on Whitemarsh in London the next month, adding that the conquest of America was impossible—a bit of news which an American secret agent in London was reporting to Benjamin Franklin at Passy by January 20, 1778.

To British headquarters it was painfully apparent that there had been a leak somewhere. An impressive figure in scarlet and gold, topped with a serious face, summoned Lydia Darragh, demure in Quaker gray, to the conference room. It is probable the officer came as soon as the redcoats were safely back in barracks that night. The frightened Quakeress used to tell her family afterward that, but for the darkness, he would have guessed what she had done, because she was so pale.

The solemn-looking man in the brilliant uniform locked the door behind him. Had any of the Darragh family been awake on the night the officers had met?

"No, they were all in bed and asleep."

"I need not ask you," said this gullible sleuth, "for we had great difficulty in waking you to fasten the door after us. But one thing is certain; the enemy had notice of our coming."

Mrs. Darragh used to recall with a certain satisfaction that she "never told a lie about it. I could answer all his questions without that." The "inner light" of the Quakers is a wonderful guide in life.

XVI

★ ★ ★

★

General Washington's Manhattan Project

As the winter of 1777-1778 wore on toward spring, it became increasingly important for General Washington to learn what Sir Henry Clinton's army, in New York, and Sir William Howe's army, in Philadelphia, were going to do. Just as this problem was about to become crucial, came a minor disaster. Late in January, 1778, some suspicious patriot, with the very best intentions, very nearly destroyed Colonel Elias Dayton's intelligence system, working between Staten Island and New Jersey. Dayton's two star secret agents, John and Baker Hendricks, and one of his soldiers, John Meeker, were suddenly arrested on charges of "illegal Correspondence with the Enemy."

It was all very embarrassing. Of course, the three men arrested really had been doing exactly what they were charged with doing; but it would ruin everything to admit in public that it was on General Washington's orders. Like the stout fellows they were, the three spies stood heroically silent—for they knew that, at all costs, the secrecy of Dayton's intelligence network must be protected—while the country they served prepared to hang them.

To save his men, Colonel Dayton appealed directly to the general, who wrote privately to Governor William Livingston, of New Jersey. The three spies, Washington pointed out, would have to "bear the suspicion of being thought inimical, and it is not in their powers to assert their innocence, because that would get abroad and destroy the confidence which the Enemy puts in them." But realism could be carried too far. The Continental Army could not possibly be allowed to hang its own secret agents. Would the governor please do something?

Governor Livingston did do something, though whatever he did was—perhaps wisely—never recorded. Two weeks later, General Washington, in cautious language, was thanking him for "measures adopted." It looks very much as if the three spies just "escaped" and went right back to work; but, whatever happened, by February, 1778, the most important spy net General Washington as yet possessed in New York was again able to function. Three years later, the Hendricks brothers—and probably Meeker, as well—were still in Dayton's network, still unsuspected by the enemy, and still supplying important information.

The three spies were released none too soon, for things were happening in Philadelphia. General Sir William Howe had failed and knew it. In disgust, he had already resigned his command; resigned, too, his mistress, the golden-haired Mrs. Loring, and soon sailed back to England, where he was presently busy defending his conduct of the war before a critical Parliament. On May 11, 1778, General Howe had announced his return home. On May 13 (perhaps earlier), General Washington knew that Clinton was the enemy's new commander.

The American commander's main problem now was to find out what his new opponent meant to do. All reports indicated that Clinton would evacuate Philadelphia. If he did evacuate, the British would have three capabilities: (a) They might give up the thirteen colonies entirely, since France and Spain were hostile. In that case, they would try to save only their West Indian colonies. (b) They might go to New York by sea. (c) They might march across New Jersey.

By ostentatiously improving the Philadelphia fortifications, the enemy tried, for a little while, to trick General Washington into believing that they meant to stay there, after all. But the shrewd Virginian guessed at once that all this sudden construction was "merely calculated to deceive." He did not have to read the diary of the British chief engineer, which, a hundred and four years later, was published, proving that once again George Washington had been absolutely right and that all this ostentatious fortification was meant "to make appearance only."

For a little while, General Washington rather hoped the enemy really did intend "generally abandoning the Territories of the United States," until various essential elements of information all began to point to a withdrawal to New York. At the end of May, a huge fleet of a hundred sail started for that city. A spy in Chester, Pennsylvania, watched it go; and Allan McLane's cavalry rode near enough to see that the Philadelphia port was almost empty. Reports from New York began to show preparations for quartering more troops there. Spies and coast watchers reported that the fleet had actually arrived, but brought no army with it.

During the month of May, General Washington had told General Greene to send an "intelligent and confidential person" into New York, to see "what passes there." General Gates also received orders to send in "one or two Intelligent persons." If the enemy was preparing quarters for additional troops, Sir Henry Clinton really did mean to return to Manhattan.

Meantime a vigilant watch was kept on the redcoats still in Philadelphia. While spies carefully observed them within the city, Lafayette moved his troops forward to Barren Hill, eleven miles to the north, in the hope of discovering their "motions and designs." It was a risky move, and only the vigilance of one of Allan McLane's secret agents saved the young Frenchman from capture and his troops from slaughter. Sir William Howe, still in command, promptly sent overwhelming forces to surround "the boy"—feeling so sure of success that he invited friends to meet the Marquis de Lafayette, a prisoner, at dinner that night! Lafayette's militia and fifty pro-American Iroquois Indians failed to detect the enemy's approach; but, at the last moment, his spy in Philadelphia informed McLane, who warned Lafayette in time for him to get away.

Where Lafayette's reconnoissance had failed to get information, the Philadelphia spies succeeded. By May 25, they had supplied General Washington with correct intelligence; but, two days later, even though it was now clear that the enemy were "bound to New York," he wanted more detailed information. "The Grand fact of the enemy's design to evacuate the City being ascertained," he wanted to know when they would start and which route they would follow. The general still did not know whether they would go by land or sea, or what they might do before they started.

The enemy were capable of making an attack on the Continental Army before leaving Philadelphia; of making a mere rendezvous in New York and then moving elsewhere; of attacking along the Hudson, supported by redcoats issuing from Manhattan.

Three days later, General Washington felt certain there would be a move through New Jersey. He was right. The enemy's industry in collecting flat-bottomed boats, horses and wagons showed that they would cross the Delaware River and go by land. Within three weeks, Clinton was doing exactly what American intelligence had predicted.

Because it possessed all this advance intelligence, the Continental Army was ready to pursue the redcoats across New Jersey when the time came. A warning order, May 16, announced the probability that the Americans would soon be making a "sudden and rapid movement," and everyone could guess what that movement would be. Boats, arms and ammunition were ordered up. Supply dumps of forage were laid clear across New Jersey.

Though the Philadelphia spies were slow in reporting the first British march when it began, Major Allan McLane was entirely alert. A few British troops and all the horses crossed the Delaware June 14 and 15. The spies failed to note it, but McLane sent word on the fourteenth that the enemy was preparing to evacuate. When more British troops crossed on the seventeenth, it seemed clear McLane was right. But General Washington had no word that the enemy was actually marching away, until Philadelphia had been wholly evacuated—on the eighteenth.

On that day, last-minute news of the evacuation reached Valley Forge, twenty miles away, at exactly "½ after 11 A.M." The moment can be fixed because General Washington reported immediately to Congress, giving both day and hour: "I was this minute advised by Mr. Roberts, that the Enemy evacuated the City early this morning." George Roberts had been at the Middle Ferry, across the Delaware from the city, that morning. He could not get over the river because the bridge had been destroyed; but people on the other side yelled the news across—too late.

Clinton had marched his army out of Philadelphia on the night of June 17/18 and his entire force was across the river by ten o'clock on June 18. Sir Henry himself had spent the early morning hours sitting on a rock, ready to take personal command against an American attack that never came. Major Clark was gone. Lydia Darragh was silent. The Continental Army's intelligence service had blundered, and the spies' failure gave General Washington no chance to catch the enemy with his forces divided by the Delaware River. Clinton stood off the Americans at Monmouth on June 28, 1778, reached New York in safety, and settled down to hold it.

Espionage on Manhattan and Long Island now became more important for the Americans than ever. Colonel Elias Dayton's spies had long been operating in New York, and Nathaniel Sackett's network was probably still there, though no one really knows what became of it. Since, however, more intelligence was now needed, General Charles Scott about this time began setting up still another intelligence service, covering Long Island and New York City with a small group of resident secret agents who never left the islands, but sent out information through a regular system of secret couriers. At the same time, Major Alexander Clough, 3rd Continental Dragoons, had secret agents operating in New Jersey, perhaps under Scott's orders. In August, 1778, the general asked Clough to find "some intelligent person" to memorize a list of questions, go into New York without incriminating papers, and get this badly needed information, posing as an illicit trader. Almost at once, Captain Eli Leavenworth, 6th Connecticut, began espionage on Long Island for Scott; and after Washington sent the general twenty-five guineas, September 6, 1778, "to enable him to engage some of the Inhabitans betwⁿ him and the Enemy to watch their Movements & apprize him of them to prevent surprises," he soon had "two very good men" in New York City itself. Three disguised American officers went in as spies in October, and at the same time Major Benjamin Tallmadge, 2nd Connecticut Dragoons, began to take a hand in secret intelligence.

Toward the end of the year, Tallmadge, using the pseudonym, John Bolton replaced Scott, though Tallmadge himself says only, "This year [1778] I opened a private correspondence with some persons in New York which lasted through the war." To the end of his days, he never revealed their names; nor did he ever state the exact date when he began service in military intelligence. But a surviving letter shows him deep in the enemy's secrets by September 3, 1778.

As the major eventually organized it, the Manhattan project was a model of its kind, giving abundant information, accurate, detailed and valuable, in absolute secrecy and without detection. The Americans even kept a horse for the spies' use behind the British lines, for which General Washington paid the bills. Samuel Woodhull, of Setauket, Long Island, and Robert Townsend, of New York City, were the principal agents. Woodhull's code name was "Culper, Sr.," Townsend's was "Culper, Jr." Woodhull's main task was receiving and transmitting Townsend's intelligence; but he sometimes directly observed British headquarters, personnel, troops, supplies and fortifications on Long Island, besides reporting what he could see in New York City, on occasional visits—of which, for excellent reasons, he made as few as possible, never more frequent than would seem completely natural.

His colleague, Robert Townsend, had three advantages in espionage. He was a merchant, making frequent deliveries of goods on Long Island, so that communication with Woodhull was natural and easy. Then, too, his father lived at Oyster Bay, so that he could himself visit Long Island without rousing suspicion. Townsend was also an amateur dabbler in journalism, careful to write news with a violently Tory slant for the *New York Gazette,* published by the notorious Tory printer, James Rivington. Documents revealed in 1959 proved (what had long been suspected) that Rivington was another American secret agent. His greatest achievement was the theft of the British Navy's entire signal book, which American headquarters passed on to Admiral de Grasse.

As Rivington's reporter, it was natural for Townsend to frequent the coffeehouse that the Tory publisher operated, partly as a profitable side line, partly as a useful place to gather news. In the relaxing social life of the coffeehouse, in the unimpeachably royalist atmosphere that Rivington maintained, in conversation with the Tory's own newswriter, it was natural that the king's officers should talk freely.

If Woodhull happened to visit New York when intelligence was ready, Townsend gave it to him orally, to be written down later, in the relative safety of Setauket. Otherwise, Townsend turned his reports over to a courier, usually Austin Roe, who made the fifty-mile ride to Setauket ostensibly with merchandise. As a precaution, the courier did not visit Woodhull's house, but left the messages in a box, buried in an open field.

In due course, Lieutenant Caleb Brewster, a veteran of the whaling trade, crossed Long Island Sound with a specially picked crew of local men, received the reports from Woodhull, and returned to Connecticut, where Major Tallmadge had dragoons ready to ride with them to Washington's headquarters, though some reports went through Israel Putnam's hands.

These reports were dealt with by the commander-in-chief, personally. Captain Alexander Hamilton is the only staff officer known to have handled them; and it is doubtful that even he knew anything except the self-evident fact that they came from secret agents in direct contact with the enemy. Though Washington once expressed a desire to meet one of the Culpers, to give personal instructions, he withdrew the request at once, when he understood the danger this involved.

At first the Culper reports were submitted in ordinary ink,

uncoded and unciphered. The handwriting of Culper, Jr., betrayed him in the end (after 150 years), when the late Morton W. Pennypacker was able to show its identity with that of one set of intelligence reports—an identification confirmed by the distinguished specialist on questioned documents, Andrew S. Osborn. Culper, Jr., made one more mistake: He used the same paper for his secret reports that he used in ordinary correspondence—though his error did no harm, since the British never noticed it. (Neither, until a few years ago, did anybody else.)

Though at first the Culpers worked in perpetual dread lest captured messages reveal what they were doing, their problem was soon solved by John Jay's brother, Sir James Jay, who, as a practicing physician in England, had become interested in a writing fluid variously known as "white," "sympathetic," "invisible" and "secret" ink, and—to the Culpers—as "stain." As a physician, Sir James knew enough chemistry to make some for himself, after a good deal of experiment. "If one writes on the whitest paper," Sir James reported triumphantly, "the letters immediately become invisible"—to become legible once more only if brushed with his "sympathetic" developer.

This, Sir James realized, as the American Revolution drew nearer, might be more than "a matter of mere curiosity and entertainment." He knew his ink was good; but he and his brother, John Jay, had been using it privately for five or six years before they realized how valuable it would be to the army. General Washington mentions it first in a letter to Tallmadge, April 30, 1779. Three days later, though the general still had none of the magic fluid, he wrote Colonel Dayton: "It is in my power, I believe, to procure a liquid which nothing but a counter liquor (rubbed over the paper afterwards) can make legible. Fire which will bring lime juice, Milk and other things of this kind to light, has no effect on it. A letter upon trivial matters of business, written in common Ink, may be fitted with important intelligence which cannot be discovered without the counter part, or liquid here mention'd." The Culpers were using the secret ink by the end of May, but it was a one-way correspondence, for, as a precaution, the developer was never sent to any of the spies.

At first Culper, Jr., simply sent an apparently blank sheet of paper; but, if such a message was ever intercepted, the enemy would at once become suspicious, especially after a letter in ordinary ink, referring to the invisible ink, was captured, in June. It might not be difficult for the British to develop it, since Sir Henry Clinton had two secret inks of his own—one developed by heat, the other by "acid." To avoid this, General Washington suggested that Culper, Jr., "should occasionally write his information on the blank leaves of a pamphlet; on the first second &c. pages of a common pocket book; on the blank leaves at such [each?] end of registers almanacks or any new publication or book of small value. He should be determined in the choice of these books principally by the goodness of the blank paper, as the ink is not easily legible, unless it is on paper of a good quality. Having settled a plan of this kind with his friend, he may forward them without risque of search or scrutiny of the enemy as this is chiefly directed against paper made up in the form of letters."

When Culper, Jr., persisted in using blank paper during the next few months, the commander-in-chief made another suggestion. The blank paper, he said, "alone is sufficient to raise suspicion; a much better way is to write a letter a little in the Tory stile, with some mixture of family matters and between the lines and on the remaining part of the Sheet communicate with the stain the intended intelligence."

The Culpers themselves hit upon a third method of insuring secrecy. It was natural for Culper, Jr., as a merchant, to be sending packages of blank paper, amid other merchandise, to his Long Island customers. In some of these he wrote an invisible message on one blank sheet, which was then inserted among the other sheets. No matter to whom such parcels were ostensibly addressed, they went to Culper, Sr., who had previously been given a number, perhaps 25. He then counted through the sheets till he reached sheet 25, which he sent on to Tallmadge, still blank.

Eventually, Townsend hit upon the idea of writing short

business letters to notorious loyalists and filling the rest of the page with "stain." If these were intercepted, nothing would appear suspicious in a well-known businessman's business letter to an equally well-known Tory customer. The courier simply had to be careful that the letters never reached their ostensible addressees.

In 1779, Tallmadge added both cipher and code to the precautions already protecting his secret papers. The cipher was of the ordinary substitution type, such as Doctor Church had used. But secret ink and cipher were not Townsend's sole reliance. He also made a small dictionary in numbered code, though he was foolish enough to number the words in their alphabetical order, with very little variation: *they,* 629; *there,* 630; *thing,* 631; *though,* 632; *time,* 633; *to,* 634; *troops,* 635; and so forth. This meant that words in "a" had low numbers; "advice" was 15. Words toward the end of the alphabet had high numbers, "zeal" being 710. This might have made possible the breaking of the code, but fortunately that never happened. Important places and individuals had separate numbers. Washington was 711; Tallmadge was 721; Culper, Sr. (Woodhull) 722; Culper, Jr. (Townsend) 723; New York, 727; Long Island, 728; Setauket, 729.

Tallmadge made three code books—one for himself, one for Culper, Jr., and one for General Washington. There may have been a fourth for Culper, Sr.; but there were no other copies, for the books were dangerous objects, mere possession of which was enough to convict any spy caught with one.

The Culpers had several narrow escapes from discovery, one of which ended in pure comedy, though the others were serious enough. The British soon discovered that there was a leak somewhere—perhaps because their own counterespionage was active; perhaps because they so often found General Washington preternaturally well-informed. Once Culper, Sr., stopped and searched at the Brooklyn Ferry, was told, in so many words, that "some villain" was sending information to the rebels. Never guessing that they had one of the two leading "villains" in their hands at that very instant, the British control post searched Woodhull, failed to detect the reports of Culper, Jr., which he was carrying, and unconsciously passed both spy and intelligence on to General Washington.

Just after he had begun to use Jay's secret ink, a serio-comic incident gave Culper, Sr., his worst fright of the war. He was writing with it in his room, nervously aware that there were "several [British] Officers quarter'd in the next Chamber." Suddenly his door burst open and two people rushed in. Leaping to his feet in terror, Woodhull snatched at his papers, upset his table, spilled the priceless fluid, and whirled about, a man at bay—to be confronted by two playful women who meant to surprise him. They never guessed how much they did surprise him!

Once, Culper, Sr., riding from the city to his home in Setauket, was held up by four bandits and searched. As he had only a dollar in cash, they let him go without guessing that he had secret papers inside his saddle. The highwaymen may have been ordinary criminals, taking advantage of the disorder of the times; but, if they had found the papers, they could have taken them to Clinton, certain of reward for having exposed a spy. Twice British foragers near his home terrified the devoted agent. "Their coming was like death to me," he wrote in November of '79. But he added sturdily: "Have no fears about me and soon intend to visit N.Y." Once his home was raided, but the spy himself was away and the raid was not repeated.

More serious was a British raid on an outpost of the 2nd Light Dragoons, near Pound Ridge Church, New York, which was near the Connecticut border. Culper, Sr., had already sent warning of "the prospect of their making excursions into Connecticut very soon," adding: "You must keep a very good look out"; but the warning did not come in time, and the dragoons were completely surprised. There was a brisk clashing of cavalry sabers before the Americans were able to get away.

Tallmadge had been careless enough to keep, at this dangerously advanced post, some money General Washington had sent him for the Culpers and—worse still—secret papers, which included a letter from the general himself in which he had been careless enough to give the real name and address of one George Higday, in New York. Either Higday was already an American agent or the general, who had interviewed him, hoped he would soon become one. Lord Rawdon's troopers captured the money and the papers; but they did not get Tallmadge's code book or any specimens of Jay's invisible ink; and Higday, though arrested, apparently was not hanged.

The general rebuked the major in terms which, considering the magnitude of his blunder, were mild indeed: "The loss of your papers was certainly a most unlucky accident and shews how dangerous it is to keep papers of any consequence at an advanced post. I beg you will take care to guard against the like in future." But he offered to "replace the guineas."

Capture of the papers enabled the British intelligence service to learn some dangerous things. They now knew that the Americans had a secret ink, for Washington had written: "When I can procure more of the Liquid C——r writes for, it shall be sent." They knew that spies' reports might in future be forwarded "by Way of Bergen." They knew the name of one possible spy and the initials used for two more; but Higday's was the only name, and there was no clue to the identities of "S—— C——" or "C——r"; while, unless they could lay hands on some documents written in the secret ink, it was no great help to know the rebels were using it.

Communication remained a perpetual problem for the American spies on Manhattan. General Washington sometimes received the Culpers' intelligence too late for it to be useful. One effort to shorten the line, by reporting directly across the Hudson, failed so badly that the route was never used again. Culper, Jr., had persuaded his cousin, James Townsend, to carry a secret-ink message over the river, through British sentries and "guard boats" and no small peril from American sentries on the other side. On the evening of March 22, 1780, James made the mistake of pausing at a farm called Soldier's Fortune, owned by an ardently patriotic farmer whose nephew, John Deausonbury, was equally patriotic and much more suspicious. Both Townsend and his hosts mistook each other for Tories, and the courier thought it wise to give the impression that he was "something in Liquor." Convinced that the stranger was an "enimical person," the family retired, leaving the secret courier to the feminine wiles of the two young daughters of the house, "who undertook to examine Townsend, pretending they were Friends to Brittain." Meantime, John Deausonbury hid where he could hear Townsend's conversation with these amateur sirens.

Feeling sure that he was among Tories, Culper's messenger boasted to the artful maidens about his services to the crown, explaining that his present errand was to collect men to join the enemy, "when they came up the River." Encouraged by the two patriotic minxes—who were certainly shivering with delightful excitement as they entertained this peculiar caller— Townsend boasted how often he had crossed and recrossed to the enemy and how he had sent to the British ranks "many a good fellow." All this was pure fiction—Townsend had not been off Manhattan and Long Island for months. Outside the room, the eavesdropping Deausonbury swelled with indignation. "This and no more Deponent heard, for his Spirits rose." He rushed into the room "upon Townsend" and, as a patriotic American, made an important American secret courier his prisoner. What the two colonial Delilahs said, as their cousin captured their "date," has never been recorded.

Deausonbury, with the very best intentions, had amazingly complicated the American intelligence service.

The supposed Tory was searched. Since he might be a spy— he was!—everything found on him was sent to headquarters. The "find" was not very impressive, for Culper, Jr., had been using Sir James Jay's stain. Presently, General Washington was examining twenty lines of verse entitled The Lady's Dress. It was, from a poetic standpoint, pretty bad; but the commander-in-chief was not concerned with literary criticism. The twenty lines, very widely spaced, spread over two full pages. The paper had been folded up small—sixteen times. The thing looked queer and General Washington could guess why. He got out his bottle of the sympathetic developer, and the intelligence from Culper, Jr., at once appeared.

The general had a dreadful time getting James Townsend back to New York without exposing the Culpers. After that, they used the old transmission belt, no matter how slow it was.

Culper, Jr., had been living in terror till his cousin reappeared.

To analyze all the military intelligence these courageous men sent would occupy a volume—it has already occupied two; but some of their more important information deserves notice. On November 27, 1779, the net reported that the British had secured several reams of paper identical with that Congress was using to print American currency. The British were still counterfeiting. Presently the Culpers discovered that the counterfeit currency was being smuggled into Connecticut to help Tories pay their taxes, thus serving a double British purpose, by assisting the king's men financially and by further depressing the already collapsing American currency.

The Culpers' most important achievement was thwarting Clinton's movement to forestall the arriving French at Newport. The British commander knew Rochambeau was coming. The quick and accurate British espionage service in Paris had almost certainly warned him; but, whether it had or not, Benedict Arnold had been able to supply word of the French movements well in advance. When at last the French fleet did land, the British secret courier bringing the news rode into New York City just a little way behind the Culpers' courier, Austin Roe. Rochambeau had reached Newport on July 10, 1779. Like all troops on disembarkation, the French were in a state of temporary confusion. As yet there had been no chance to arrange a war plan with the American staff. Lafayette did not even leave American headquarters to begin consultation with Rochambeau until July 17.

Now was the time for the British to attack.

On Manhattan Island, on July 20, 1779, Austin Roe waited while Robert Townsend completed his report, showing Clinton was starting to move troops. Never had a warning to General Washington been more urgent. Never had Culper, Jr., so feared discovery. The British were now stopping everyone who might possibly carry intelligence of their movements. Roe must appear completely harmless.

The spy did not want to burden his courier with the usual letter, hidden in a ream of blank paper. If he carried one such package, he would have to carry others, since a single parcel would be suspicious. Many packages meant weight; weight meant delay; he dared not delay.

Instead of sending a package, Culper, Jr., wrote a letter to a well-known Long Island Tory, Colonel Floyd, who, having recently been robbed, would naturally be making purchases: ". . . the articles you want cannot be procured, as soon as they can will send them." That was a good safe message—so long as Floyd never heard about it. Roe covered the fifty miles to Setauket in time to send word across Long Island Sound, that very evening. Meantime, Sir Henry Clinton's troops were beginning to move.

Unluckily, General Washington was not at headquarters when this vital intelligence arrived. Captain Alexander Hamilton, who by this time knew all about the stain, developed the ink, and rushed a message after Lafayette, who could warn Rochambeau. Presently, back at Continental headquarters, General Washington considered matters. He knew the British were by this time embarking. His army was not strong enough for a successful attack on New York. But did he have to make a real attack? If Sir Henry could be made to think . . .

It is said that General Washington managed to have some "secret" papers captured. They showed plainly that the Americans meant to make an immediate offensive movement against Manhattan Island. The British troops hastily disembarked. In Newport, Rochambeau, entirely undisturbed, looked quietly after the French troops. When, a year later, Benedict Arnold fled to become a British brigadier, he expressed surprise at Clinton's "not having attacked the French upon their disembarking at Rhode Island." There is a fine irony in this: Culper, Jr., whose timely intelligence had prevented the attack, was at that very moment near Arnold in New York, shaking in his shoes for fear the traitor knew of his espionage. "Arnold's flight seems to have frightened all my intelligencers out of their senses," said General Washington.

By May, 1781, Rochambeau, whose own intelligence service had been "much imposed on, having been served with little more than common reports on Long Island," asked Tallmadge for help. Co-operation began at once, though Rochambeau's ability to pay spies in gold was not so advantageous as had been hoped. The American spies were afraid to be caught with French coins.

To the end of the war, the Culpers' flow of information proceeded—arrival and departure of British ships; British morale; British guesses about the peace; British losses in action; warnings against British agents in the American lines; maps and position sketches; exact location of individual units; quartermaster supplies; movements of British generals and other senior officers. Though less spectacular than some of the Culpers' other coups, it was this steady flow of accurate information that kept General Washington in touch at all times with what the enemy were doing.

It was made possible by the intrepid Caleb Brewster and his Connecticut and Long Island crews, who ran several whaleboats back and forth across Long Island Sound, based on Penfield's "tide mill," at Fairfield. The crews were mainly natives of Long Island or Connecticut, some of whom, like Joshua Davis, were withdrawn from the infantry for this special service. The name of one boatman besides Davis has been preserved—a certain Jonathan Pinner, or Kinner.

The romantic aspects of secret service were doubled for Joshua Davis, then in his early twenties, when he met eighteen-year-old Abigail Redfield in Fairfield and married her in the midst of his mysterious duties. The young wife, anxious and lonely during her husband's absences (which were probably no mystery to her), used to drop in at a neighbor's for comfort. The woman she visited explained, long after the war that "during this period s^d Davis was absent a considerable part of his time under Capt Brewster and that his, Davis, wife complained of being lonesome." Everyone in Fairfield seems to have known about Brewster and his "spy boat"; but, though the British also soon knew what he was doing, they had no way of stopping him.

XVII

★ ★ ★

★

More Manhattan Spies

THE CULPER, Sackett and Dayton nets were not the only employers of American secret agents on Long Island and in New York City, for one catches tantalizing glimpses of other daring spies who came and went very much as they pleased. One of Clinton's intelligence reports, for April 14, 1781, noted with some irritation a masterpiece of rebel impudence: "A Rebell Major by the name of Davis comes from Connecticut to East Hampton Regularly once a Week where he generally stays two nights, and is supposed to Return with Intelligence from this City." This bold spirit, clearly was the same "Major J. Daviss" who later almost secured advance information of the Arnold treason, and was probably Brewster's man, Joshua Davis. Whoever he may have been, the enemy never caught him, despite the nonchalant frequency of his visits behind their lines.

There was the mysterious "L.J.," who casually offered to get General Washington any information he wanted from Manhattan: "Right five lines to le me now what it is you wish to now from the Brithes [British]." There was the unidentified Smith, of Smithtown, Long Island, who, three hours before Tallmadge's raid on a Long Island Tory fort, crossed the Sound to Connecticut with full information of its weak points. The enemy found out what he had done, but too late. There was the less successful Francis Van Dyke, of whom nothing is known save that he attempted espionage in New York, collected three guineas, and vanished from the records. There was Mrs. Elizabeth Burgin, patriotic New York matron, who operated an escape line for American prisoners of war until 1779, when, finding herself suspected, she fled to safety.

The secret service records show Tallmadge, late in the war, receiving reports from half a dozen new spies, known only by initials then and now far beyond identification. He himself had at first no idea of the identity of "S.G.," one of the best of these agents, who was assuredly not "S.C.," or Samuel Culper, Sr. By May, 1781, however, he had met the spy.

A former Tory officer, known only as "J.B.," began to submit intelligence in 1782, probably because he saw that independence would soon be won and wished to curry favor with the victors. He is probably the "refugee"—a frequent term for Tories who had joined the British—who, being on friendly terms with Sir Guy Carleton's aide, pumped him for information, then passed it on to Washington.

Equally mysterious are several American spies, whose very code names are unknown, but of whose adventures, in or near New York one finds fascinating traces. Some of these may have been reporting, not to Washington, but to one of several American generals who were running separate intelligence services of their own, among them Robert Howe, Forman, Wayne, Stirling, Gates, Greene and Lafayette. General Alexander Mc-Dougall had a system covering the area around Morristown, New Jersey, in the latter part of 1776; and, as he was still active in military intelligence in 1779, he had time enough to extend it to Manhattan.

Since many of these unknown agents were permanently stationed in New York, they may have been employed directly by General Washington, who preferred spies "who live with the other side; whose local circumstances, without subjecting them to suspicions, give them an opportunity of making observations." He had on Manhattan Island a number of such secret agents, who knew nothing of the Culpers and of whom the Culpers knew nothing.

From one of these agents, close to Sir Henry Clinton's staff, came the warning, far in advance, of a scheme by the notorious Tory, Dr. John Connolly, to collect "Loyalist" refugees and attack Fort Pitt (Pittsburgh, Pennsylvania), where he expected aid from "disaffected people in Western Pennsylvania." General Washington, who knew all about the proposed attempt by April, 1781, warned General George Rogers Clark, in Kentucky, and Colonel Daniel Brodhead, at Fort Pitt, and the plan came to nothing. General Washington said only that the news reached him "thro' a good Channel."

In May, 1781, when General Washington was worried about British preparations for an expedition by sea, two daring whaleboatmen made a secret crossing to Long Island to meet a "Person." The spy had not risked being caught with a written report; and, as there was a Hessian post within two hundred yards of the house where the three met, no one dared strike a light and write out his intelligence there. But the mariners were able to bring it back to Pound Ridge in their heads and write out a report, when they reached safety there.

One resident agent in New York whom General Washington valued highly, was the oddly named Hercules Mulligan. Alexander Hamilton, when he first came to New York a few years before the Revolution, had lived with the Mulligan family. As the need for information became pressing after the British occupation, Hamilton suggested Hercules as a secret agent. Mulligan stayed in New York, undetected and untroubled, throughout the war, as "confidential correspondent to the Commander-in-chief," and is credited with "most important military information," though there are no traces of it in the Washington papers as they now exist. It is significant that General Washington's first breakfast in New York, after the British evacuation, was with Mulligan, whose son later remarked that his father had been in touch with an American agent on Long Island, perhaps Culper, Sr., perhaps Brewster, perhaps someone else. As late as 1780, Tallmadge himself was not sure what

Mulligan was doing and was asking Washington to give him at least "a hint of it."

In spite of his preference for such resident agents, living where they spied, General Washington sometimes had to make use of spies who lived outside New York City and made their way in and out as occasion required. One of the most successful of these was Captain Elijah Hunter, of the 2nd New York Militia, assistant commissary of forage in Bedford, New York, who "retired" from the army December 7, 1776—probably to undertake espionage for General Robert Howe. During the winter of 1778-1779 he is supposed to have been spying for John Jay and had, by the early months of 1779, wormed his way into the complete confidence of Sir Henry Clinton and Governor William Tryon.

A man who can only be Hunter, though he is mysteriously referred to as "the link to Sir Harry," emerged from New York in late March, 1779, with a budget of useful military information. He had been "closeted" with Clinton and Tryon, who, thinking him a trustworthy Tory, encouraged him to leave the city, pose as a patriot, and spy on the Americans. Tryon asked him to engage in illicit trading, work into a position of trust, then visit both Philadelphia and Washington's headquarters as a spy, and at the same time "to act apparently zealous for America—not to shake the Confidence of his Countrymen." All this Hunter dutifully reported to General Alexander McDougall, who sent him on to visit both Philadelphia and Washington's headquarters.

Though Hunter arrived at headquarters with a recommendation from that veteran spy catcher, John Jay, General Washington did not at first trust him. Admitting that Hunter looked like "a sensible man capable of rendering important services, if he is sincerely disposed to do it," he nevertheless felt it was always "necessary to be very circumspect with double spies." Besides, although Hunter had turned over for examination a letter addressed to General Sir Frederick Haldimand, commanding in Canada, that did not prove his good faith in the eyes of the American commander, who thought the letter looked as if "intended to fall into our Hands" and suspected Hunter might be "as much in the interest of the enemy as in ours."

Though Washington remained skeptical until August, Hunter soon turned in enough information to prove his good faith, and by early September the commander-in-chief "had not the smallest doubt of his attachment and integrity." Hunter managed to steal a letter of the veteran British cavalry raider, Colonel Banastré Tarleton, which he sent to Washington to read and return—evidently intending to replace it before its loss was discovered. He also supplied information about enemy troop dispositions and intended movements, with the assistance of a group of subagents, described by Washington as "Characters."

When, in May, 1779, Hunter asked for information of the American Army to be supplied to the British, Washington evidently gave him some and in August provided a correct report of the real American strength. He was careful to emphasize that he could assemble boats for five thousand men in two hours—news that would be certain to worry Clinton, as it indicated a prospective attack on New York.

This time, except perhaps about the boats, General Washington was telling the unvarnished truth, though only because he had "not the least objection to our real strength being known." But, however truthful the hero of the cherry tree was now being, he was also, on one point, thinking up deception for his spy to impose on the enemy's intelligence officers. Question of the authenticity of the strength report was certain to arise. In that case, General Washington advised Hunter, "it will be well for you to inform [them] that you came by the knowledge of it from inquiry and from observations of the troops when under arms." He recommended one more little falsehood: "To give your account, the greater air of probability you may observe that the Officers are very incautious in speaking of the strength of their regiments."

He also took the trouble to explain, in a personal interview with Hunter, just why the Continental Army now had more troops than when he had shown his spy earlier strength reports; and he obligingly provided the enemy with a correct list of his four main supply dumps—which he well knew were beyond their reach.

Hunter, of course, could not very well tell the British that the meticulously accurate strength report he brought in was a free gift from the American command; and General Washington seems to have felt that if any lying on that point was to be done, he was far better at it than anybody else.

Compared with the Culpers and other resident agents, Hunter never supplied a great deal of information, since he had to avoid rousing suspicion by too frequent visits to New York. As Washington put it: "the business was of too delicate a nature for him to transact it frequently himself," and the "Characters" who assisted him were rarely able to "gain anything satisfactory or material."

Though never a really important secret agent, Hunter continued to pull the wool over Sir Henry Clinton's eyes for two more years. In an undated note among British secret service papers for 1781, he coolly asks Sir Henry to provide an escort of redcoats for a little trip into Westchester County—where he could report to Washington! In 1783, Washington gave him a certificate testifying to what he had done.

Two spies named Moses and Abel Hatfield were believed by the Americans to be double spies whose real loyalty was to the British. Three times in January, 1780, Washington warned American officers against Moses Hatfield: "He is very capable of gaining intelligence if he pleases, but I fancy he carries as much as he brings." John Vanderhovan, the American agent working with the Hendricks brothers, flatly accused Abel Hatfield of deliberately planting false information and of betraying Colonel Matthias Ogden, active in American intelligence, to the enemy. One patriot spy had seen the Tory Brigadier Cortlandt Skinner instructing Abel Hatfield what to tell the Americans.

Two American secret agents, John Cork and a man named Jackson, had the entire confidence of their superiors; but they were so shrouded in mystery that it is impossible to learn very much about them. Both worked for Tallmadge. Equally mysterious is Swain Parcel, an American "deserter," who, though "captured" with British arms in his hands, suffered no penalty and received a post-war pension.

Into this web of deceit, the Americans, late in 1779 or in the very first weeks of 1780, wove a new strand of double-dyed imposture. This was the handiwork of Captain David Gray, a Massachusetts Yankee, one of the most successful double agents in history, who first persuaded the enemy to take him into their secret service; and who then, for nearly two years, went in and out of New York whenever he wished, casually betraying Tories along the way and obligingly pausing in his errands for Sir Henry Clinton to keep General Washington informed of what Sir Henry was doing—meantime giving the confiding British staff no American information whatever that could possibly be of any use.

When the Revolution began, Gray had been a youth of nineteen, living in Lenox, Massachusetts. As a volunteer under Ethan Allen, he was at the taking of Ticonderoga. Returning to Lenox and enlisting for five months more, he was in the expedition against Canada, participating in the siege of St. John's, until discharged because of illness. In January of 1776, he was back in Lenox again, enlisting for another year, after which he was discharged at Saratoga and again enlisted.

Transferred to the quartermasters, he was sent on supply missions to Lake George and into New Hampshire, where he discovered "a chain off tories that Reeacht from Canada to Rope ferry neear new lonon Corneticut." This discovery stirred his first interest in secret service. Ordered back from New Hampshire with dispatches, he visited Continental headquarters, whence he was sent to Lieutenant Colonel William Ledyard, at New London. Overtaken by darkness, Gray "put up at an in five milds from New Lonnon," and here "fell into Cumpany with one Capt Beckit who was a Carrying on all inteligence and strength that he could a Cumolate to newyork."

Extraordinary as it seems to find another member of the British staff running André's risks by traveling about in American territory, this may have been Captain William Beckwith, the British intelligence officer who had handled part of the treason negotiations with Arnold and was later much concerned with the attack by Arnold on New London. Gray may have gained the British officer's confidence by talking as if he were a member of the Tory network operating between Canada and New London. At any rate, the British captain—whoever he was—accepted the American captain as a genuine turncoat. Gray himself says: "i agreead with him to Carry me to long iland the next night in the morning i went to newlonnon and Delivared my mesage to Colo Ledgard [Ledyard] and the nex evaning went with sd Beckit to the iland and from there to newyork."

The supposed deserter went at once to the Tory intelligence officer, Colonel Beverly Robinson, on whose lands Gray's father had once been a tenant, and then to a Tory named John Cane, in Brooklyn. Next day he met Cane and Robinson together. Gray says: "Cane went with me to Colo Robinson and informed him that i had had a Comishon in washingtons army and that i could Bee usefull in Conveying news to any part off a miracan [America] for the loyalists or goverment on sd Canes Recommending me to Colo Robinson he gave me five guinies and offered me a Commishon in the new livies But mr Cane and myself Allowed that i could Bee off more use to goverment in going through the states with inteligence."

A few days later, the supposed turncoat received secret letters for Vermont Tories, delivered them promptly, and dutifully returned with answers. Presently, he was sent, with more letters, to Vermont and New Hampshire. As soon as he was safely off the island, he opened a few of these official missives and, seeing that they would be useful to General Washington, "went amediately and gave them to him."

According to Gray, "aftor he had Red them he Called me and asked Me how i Came By them i told him i had Been to new york and had got protexshon undor the British goverment and was likely to get inteligence to go to Calton [Carleton] inada [in Canada] he gave me the lettors And told me to delivar them to those they were dyreckted to i was furnished with an eligant hors and money By the ordar of his excelency and pass signed By his own hand to pass throug the states unmolested and to cross the Sound into the British loines when i saw cause." After that, Gray remained in the British secret service until 1782, in continual touch with American headquarters.

All this went on with General Washington's full knowledge. It was characteristic of his methods that he had Gray publicly and officially reported as a deserter on January 2, 1780, just about the time the British first sent him to Vermont. He had him again denounced—this time on a special list of deserters—July 13, 1780. It is perfectly clear that Gray was never a genuine deserter, but the astute Washington wanted to give any possible British spies good reason to think he was.

That Gray was still making similar secret journeys in 1781 is shown by two references to him as a trusted British secret agent, in Sir Henry Clinton's intelligence papers. A document of May 25, 1781, shows that he had returned to New York on May 24, after leaving Vermont more than a fortnight earlier. He told British intelligence that a party of rebels had seized most of the documents he was carrying—which may have been merely a convenient way of getting them into General Washington's hands; but the British, swallowing his story, sent him immediately on a similar errand. On June 28, 1781, the British intelligence report notes again: "David Gray is Just come in from the State of Vermont." This time, he had traveled very slowly, taking two weeks for the journey and five days to get from Hartford, Connecticut, to New York. Part of this delay was due to espionage for the British along the way—or so the British were allowed to think. Secret visits to General Washington himself, were probably the real reason.

Gray brought Sir Henry Clinton news that Ethan Allen was trying to "agree upon Terms" with the authorities in Canada; supplied information on American artillery and recruiting in Hartford; and also reported that General Washington "wanted men Enough to attack New York, to prevent the British sending men to the Southward."

Most of this was probably pure deception. Ethan Allen did not join the British, though he sometimes was in illicit communication with Canada. As for the news about Washington's proposed attack on New York, though it seemed important and was, at the moment, true, American headquarters probably allowed Gray to report it because Clinton was almost certain to have the same information from other sources.

Delighted with the achievements of this apparently reliable agent, the Brooklyn Tory, Cane, now took Gray to Major Oliver DeLancey, who offered him seventy guineas to carry a message to Sir Guy Carleton, in Canada, paying sixteen guineas down and promising the rest on his return. This message was put "in a lump like a bullet so if i was taken i could swallow it"—the same foolish device that had cost the British secret courier, Taylor, his life in 1777.

En route for Canada, Gray went down Long Island "to the Coverd place," where he met a Tory captain named Robinson, "who had been on the Corneticut Shore A plundaring." When Robinson offered him transportation across Long Island Sound next day, the ungrateful American spy hunted up an American officer, "Capt jones who was Concealed on the iland." From mysterious sources of his own, Jones mobilized twenty-three whaleboats and raided Robinson's camp at three o'clock in the morning, killing or wounding thirteen men and capturing forty-five.

Gray seems to have gone on to the Continental Army; for Sergeant Jeremiah Hull, who had been in the same regiment with him, remembered his entering the lines on a night in July, 1781, when Hull happened to be sergeant of the guard. The officer of the guard at first refused to let the spy through, whereupon Gray produced a pass from General Washington and his American captain's commission. Sergeant Hull does not say where this incident took place, but it was probably somewhere in Connecticut and not far from New London.

By this time Gray was understandably "forteaged and wanted Rest;" but, instead of taking his messages on to Canada, he stopped at New London sometime in the first few days of September, 1781, and turned all the enemy's papers over to Lieutenant Colonel William Ledyard, who sent the documents on to Washington. Knowing that Benedict Arnold's force was already assembled at Huntington, Long Island, to raid New London, Gray warned Ledyard that "arnol lay in huntington harbor with a numbar off men and no dout if the wind Should Bee fair he would visit newlonnon Before morning the next morning." Sure enough, "gust as the Sun Rose the British was landing on Both Sides off the harbor."

The American captain now—temporarily forgetting that he was also Sir Henry Clinton's secret courier—took command of some American militia, stripped to his shirt, since the day was hot, and fought through the first part of the action at Fort Groton. So fierce was the combat that Arnold was on the point of withdrawing his men, when the Americans broke at last. Gray escaped without time to get his coat, which probably contained his pass from Washington. He notes that when he "Rode out off the fort gate in good speead the front off the British was within twelve or fifteen Rods off me and the front Devishon fired at me But Overshot Me." He would have been in real trouble had the British captured their highly paid courier in action against them; or if they had found that coat and the papers in it.

Gray was again weary. "Beein allmost exsted i Retired for Refreshment. . . ." and there his manuscript breaks off. Presumably he got his dispatches back from Washington, and delivered them to Carleton. Major DeLancey had promised him seventy guineas and so far he had collected only sixteen.

Nothing further, however, is really known of his exploits as a spy. He returned to the Continental Army, March 5, 1782, when he was again officially listed as having "joined." Probably none of the British officers who employed him ever guessed how shamelessly they had been deceived. Gray must have seemed just one more spy who had disappeared—as spies do.

David Gray was not the only American captain who was lending a helping hand to the British intelligence service, with the delighted approval of General Washington. Captain Caleb Bruen, of Newark, had been an eager patriot from the beginning, serving as a second lieutenant of New Jersey minutemen in February, 1776, and rising to the captaincy of an "artificer" (ordnance) company by August. He had found it particularly annoying when, during an interval in this service, he was "shot at by the British while taking the cows to pasture."

After 1776, he disappears for a long time from American records and reappears eventually in Sir Henry Clinton's confidential papers as courier and spy, operating from his native New Jersey as far east as Rhode Island, bringing in the results of his own and other spies' observations in the field. He does not reappear in American records until 1783, when he is arrested for illicit trading with the enemy; on which occasion, it is significant, the officer arrested with him went before a court-martial, while Bruen silently disappears from the records. His service was to prove, if possible, more important than Gray's, during one of the crises of the Revolution, the mutiny of Pennsylvania troops.

Though Sir Henry Clinton's exasperated intelligence officers were well aware of what was going on, they could not identify Gray, Bruen or any of the other well-hidden American agents. They discovered the Culper line of communication across Long Island Sound almost as soon as it began to operate; for a British officer prisoner, returning through Connecticut in August, 1778, had reported "a number of Whail Bts lying at Norwalk, which passes over almost every night to Long Island." But the discovery did little good, since there was no way of keeping the boats from slipping across the Sound. Not until more than a year had passed did two British agents, working independently of each other, discover that Caleb Brewster commanded the whaleboats carrying the spies' reports. Laying hands on Caleb was another matter. They never caught him.

Brewster's opposite number in the British intelligence service was Nehemiah Marks—son of a prominent merchant in Derby, Connecticut—who had gone to New York almost as soon as the Revolution opened, to act as "despatch agent" for the British. From Long Island, he made regular secret crossings to Stamford and other Connecticut towns to spy and carry secret messages. He avoided his native Derby, where he was likely to be recognized, and where, until 1957, it was known only that he had "left town."

In the latter part of 1780, Marks reported several times that a certain "Bruster" was running dispatches. On November 26, 1780, the official British "State of Intelligence" report also noted: "There is one Brewster who has the direction of three Whale Boats that constantly come over from the Connecticut Shore once a Week for the purpose of obtaining Intelligence They land at Draun Meadow Bay"—just east of Setauket, in modern Port Jefferson.

Presently, "Hiram the Spy" (William Heron, of Redding, Connecticut) was reporting on Brewster, independently of Marks. On February 4, 1781, he wrote Clinton's headquarters: "Private dispatches are frequently sent from your city to the Chieftain here by some traitors. They come by way of Setalket, where a certain Brewster receives them, at, or near a certain woman's."

By December, 1780, Marks was exultant: "I have found ought wair Bruster holds a Correspondence of intiligince & how [who] Surplies him with Goods J Got my information from one that has a Commisson in the Rebels Servis for hee tels Mee that hee will due every thing to assist Mee to find ought thee peticler men that Send the intelegence from York & hee has told mee how wee might take him if you think itt Best But J am a mind to find ought more of the Persons Conse[r]nd with him."

Marks, in other words, wanted to play the old game of letting a partly exposed spy ring continue to operate, so as to learn more about it. He had already wormed his way so deeply into American secrets (perhaps through the treacherous American officer he describes) that he was soon able to give advance warning of an impending American attack and to list three American spies, otherwise unknown: "Nathanel Roe for intelegence & Philip Roe at Round Medo for [black market] Goods Jeams Smith att a place Called old mans these are the villin that assist Brewster and J gave thee person 3 Ginues & promised if hee wood find ought the holl & inform Mee J wood Reward him well for itt hee promised hee wood this Must Be Cept a secret." As Austin Roe is known to have been in the Culper organization, Nathaniel and Philip Roe were probably his relatives, also in the Culper network, though nothing hitherto has been known about them. Round Meadow and Old Man's are now within the village of Mount Sinai, about two miles from Port Jefferson, Long Island.

In May, 1781, another returning British prisoner told interrogating British officers that the patriots had two gunboats and sixteen whaleboats, and that they visited Long Island almost every night.

The British learned at last how dispatches, brought from these boats, were carried through Connecticut; and on September 4, 1781, Nehemiah Marks offered to land with British agents in Connecticut, lay an ambush along the road, capture the dragoon serving as courier, and seize the papers. He and John Marks, probably a relative, and two men named Smith and Lockwood, would "Gow & lie in the Cuntry & due thair Best indevore to inter Sept him or thair mails."

Perhaps someone at headquarters decided the plan was too risky and forbade it. Perhaps Marks tried and failed. At any rate, he never intercepted the dispatches.

A few weeks after this, in October, 1781, the British came still closer to the Culpers' secret, when one of their spies, named Patrick Walker, took supper with Caleb Brewster in Fairfield, chatted with him, and heard plans for the American attack on Floyd's Neck.

But there, in ignominious failure, the story of the British effort to detect the most dangerous of all patriot spy rings, ends. Walker had found the man who knew the facts. He had gotten him—perhaps a little drunk—to talking. He had learned a few patriot secrets. But on the essential facts on which the safety of the ring depended, Brewster—drunk or sober—was silent. The Culpers always knew their danger; but they never guessed how close the hangman's noose had dangled above their devoted heads that night.

XVIII

★ ★ ★

★

The Exploits of Ann Bates

SOON AFTER CLINTON returned to New York, his espionage service was strengthened by the addition of a woman agent —unknown then and unknown ever since—who may justly be described as the most successful female spy in history. Adroit, well-trained, intrepid, she penetrated the American lines again and again, made precise and accurate military observations, walked calmly into General Washington's headquarters, listened casually to official conversation there, marched with the general's own column, was captured twice, talked her way out of her difficulties, and then went cheerfully ahead with her espionage. Recognized at last by a British deserter, she escaped American pursuit and again went back to espionage —though in a safer area.

This was Mrs. Ann Bates, or Beats, who had been a Philadelphia schoolteacher, earning £30 a year and eking out that scanty income by keeping bees, running a little store, and raising a few sheep. There is nothing to indicate that she ever did any espionage for the British in Philadelphia; but in some way John Cregge, or Craigie, a civilian active in British intelligence, recognized her quality. Since she had married Joseph Bates, an "armourer" (i.e., ordnance repair-

man) in the British artillery train, she wanted to leave Philadelphia when the British evacuated it. In May, 1778, just
before Clinton began his march across New Jersey, Cregge
asked her to come to see him when she reached New York.

Though married to a British soldier, Ann Bates coaxed
Benedict Arnold—American commander in Philadelphia, not
yet a traitor—to give her a pass to General Washington's camp,
with which she calmly set out overland through New Jersey.
Meeting a party of British prisoners—paroled or released—she
went with them to New York, where Colonel Nesbit Balfour,
commanding the 23rd Regiment of Foot, sent her on to Major
Drummond, Sir Henry Clinton's aide, in Wall Street.

By the time she arrived, about the end of June, 1778, Sir
Henry badly needed information of General Washington's
movements, and Ann Bates was off on her first recorded secret
mission. Drummond gave her a token which would identify
her as a British agent to a disloyal American officer—unknown
to this day—who was himself a British secret agent in the 8th
Pennsylvania Continental Line. Devices of this sort are still
in use. The "atom spy," Julius Rosenberg, gave half of a Jello
box top to his courier, Harry Gold, who used it as identification
at his rendezvous with Ruth and Harry Greenglass, in Albuquerque, New Mexico. He might have made a better choice.
Gold was asked on the witness stand which Jello flavor his box
top represented. There was laughter in the court at his reply:
"Raspberry."

The British tokens, however, were used more successfully.
Nothing indicates that the Americans ever discovered them.
In fact, no one has ever learned just what they were.

Ann was also given five guineas for expenses. Buying medicinal rhubarb, thread, needles, combs and knives, she prepared to pose as a peddler, a scheme approved by Sir Henry
himself. The peddler's pack had by this time become a common cover for secret agents, since genuine peddlers were familiar figures, who could go anywhere. British spies, posing as
peddlers with forged certificates and licenses, were carrying a
good many secret military messages across New Jersey at this
very time.

On June 29, using the name Barnes instead of Bates, Ann was smuggled into a camp of Tory troops beyond Kingsbridge, to spend the night. Thence she had to make the rest of her way on foot, as was natural for a peddler, perhaps with occasional lifts from passing wagons. Once she had to wade the Crosswicks River in water up to her armpits, because the bridge had broken down.

Her mention of this stream, near Trenton, shows that the shrewd woman took a roundabout way to White Plains, passing through New Jersey to conceal the fact that, though carrying a pass from the American commandant in Philadelphia, she was really coming from New York. Benedict Arnold's pass would get her into Washington's camp, unsuspected, but only if she came from the right direction. She reached White Plains on July 2, 1778, only to find that the officer traitor from whom she had expected to learn all about American strength and positions had resigned from the army.

No whit discouraged, Ann Bates set to work to get the same intelligence herself. By dividing her little stock of merchandise (so that no one brigade could buy it all, thus leaving her without an excuse to move about), she was able to peddle her wares all through the Continental camp—"by which means," she said later, "I had the Opportunity of going through their whole Army Remarking at the same time the strength & Situation of each Brigade, & the Number of Cannon with their Situation and Weight of Ball each Cannon was Charged with." Since her husband had long been repairing Sir Henry Clinton's field guns, Ann Bates knew more about artillery than most women spies, and always reported on it in great detail.

Accidentally encountering an American acquaintance whom she could trust, the resourceful woman gave him money to attend a lodge of Freemasons and try to get information there—especially from a commissary's clerk whom she knew (Heaven knows how!) to be a Freemason, too. In a short time, the man gave her intelligence regarding American troop movements and the American organization of special troops to intercept British patrols.

Satisfied with what she had learned, this enterprising lady

started casually back to New York, only to be arrested on suspicion, four miles from White Plains. She was turned over to a woman, who, after stripping her stark naked and examining her clothing, found nothing suspicious, but—to Ann's indignation—kept her silver shoe buckles, a silver thimble, a silk handkerchief and three dollars. The secret token of British intelligence, whatever it was, escaped attention. After a day and a night in confinement, Ann went on to New York and reported to Major Drummond.

Her information was confirmed, at just the right time, by John Mason (probably identical with the British spy caught and hanged early in 1781) and John Romers, otherwise unknown, who had started on a daring trip from New York to Albany County, June 24, 1778, to distribute British propaganda. Spending a month in American territory for this purpose, they observed American forces at Paramus, New Jersey, July 12 and 13, while General Washington had his headquarters there. They reported his strength as sixteen thousand men, with thirty field guns, two eight-inch mortars, and a train of seven hundred wagons, all loaded with provisions. The spies probably exaggerated the quantity of rations, for a deserter reported, the day after Mason and Romers returned, that the Continental Army was living "from hand to Mouth on fresh provisions—No Rum allowed but when send on Command."

Like Ann Bates, Mason and Romers reported camp gossip that Washington would attack New York, while the French fleet attacked the harbor. They also secured a full report on American magazines and forage, and confirmed reports of the Wyoming Massacre, picked up among the Americans. Then, passing through the American forces undetected, the two spies returned safely to Paulus Hook (Jersey City), July 30, 1778.

Delighted with the intelligence Ann Bates had brought, Sir Henry Clinton gave her only one day's rest before ordering her out again. Once more she spent five guineas on peddler's goods, and by July 29, 1778, was again in the American camp, where she spent a busy week. Ann was now looking for another disloyal American soldier—a man named Chambers—but "unfortunately found that the Reg.ᵗ Chambers belonged to, had been detached from Belly Forge against the Indians under the Com.ᵈ of Col! Butler, & was positively assured that only the 17ᵗʰ returned, & that he fell amongst the rest." The Tory partisan leader, Colonel John Butler, with a detachment of "Royal Greens" and Seneca Indians had perpetrated the Wyoming Massacre about three weeks earlier. Apparently Chambers—British spy or not—had perished in pursuit of the raiders.

For three or four days, the fearless woman wandered undisturbed about the American camp, counting "119 Peices of Cannon," and estimating the American Army's strength at twenty-three thousand. She located General Washington's quarters "at Mᵣ.ˢ Purdies house to the left of the Lines," counted twenty cannon on a hill, located the brigades of Sullivan, Smallwood and Wayne, as well as the Virginia troops and Gates's command, about three miles to the rear, "upon a Hill that looks like a hat." She could see no indication that any troops had been sent to Rhode Island, but does not seem to have realized that General John Sullivan had actually been there since April. Being a soldier's wife, she knew the importance of rations and reported carefully: "Shad Fish delivered out twice a Week and other days fresh Provisions—Plenty of Bread & flour heard of no Magazines." American uniforms, she found, seemed better than before. During this trip the British agent was at Washington's headquarters and saw the general, though she learned nothing of any importance there. She left White Plains on August 2, and evidently returned to New York by a roundabout route, for her report in Clinton's intelligence record is dated August 6.

Again she was given practically no time to rest—a serious matter for a secret agent, since the nervous strain that builds up during such a mission makes itself terribly felt when the danger is over. On August 8, Ann Bates was off again, was held up on the lines for two days, then reached White Plains by way of East Chester. American security had tightened up by this time and she found that "it is with the greatest difficulty—any person can get within their camp." All the same, she was in Washington's headquarters on Wednesday, August 12, eagerly listening to the talk of a careless aide-de-camp and a general officer, who had just arrived and was asking for information. He got it—and so, thanks to Ann Bates's quick ears, did Henry Clinton. Boats were being prepared for a landing on Long Island. Two hundred were already finished. Four hundred would be ready in another two weeks.

At this point the chatty young officer came to his senses. "When he look'd Round & saw me a Stranger he turn'd the Discourse for me to hear," without in the least deceiving the shrewd woman, who had been eagerly memorizing all he said. When two French officers approached, this instructive conversation ended.

Peddling her wares about the American camp for several days, with her eyes wide open, Ann Bates found that Gates and Morgan had 3,800 picked light infantry near Dobbs Ferry. Lafayette, with three thousand Continentals and two thousand militia, had gone to Rhode Island—important information, since Clinton was getting ready to go there himself. Lafayette's move was confirmed by the fact that "their Camp was not near so numerous as when she was first there, nor their Parades half so full," and there were now only 16,000 or 17,000 men.

On August 15 she went through the artillery park, quite undisturbed, counting fifty-one guns and five mortars and carefully noting that nine more guns came in the next day. The Americans had plenty of bread and flour, but no fish, and "the Fresh Provisions very thin & poor." She was back in New York with her budget of news, August 19, 1778, just as Clinton was preparing his expedition to relieve the British in Rhode Island. She herself said a few years later: "My timly information was the blessed means of saving rowd island Garison with all the troops and stores who must otherwise [have] falen a pray to their Enemies." When this was shown to Drummond he said: "She asserts nothing but what is strictly true." She had also found time to visit Horseneck (a district in Greenwich), reporting American losses of fifteen hundred, though the rebels still expected to win Rhode Island, and warning that another British woman spy ought to be more discreet, "as she discovered her Errand to a man." The other woman must have taken the hint and maintained secrecy after that, for she is still unknown.

In Clinton's absence in Rhode Island, Ann had three weeks to rest; but when the Continental Army began to move, she was sent out to see what it was really doing. Two dates tell the story. On September 15, 1778, General Washington issued orders: "The whole Army will march tomorrow at seven o'Clock." On September 21, Ann was off again. Leaving New York, she found Putnam had been ordered up the Hudson. General Washington had set up new headquarters "within five miles of Danbury," and had eighty guns. In fact, he was at Fredericksburgh, September 21-30, not far from Danbury.

Finding the Continental Army in motion, she cannily attached herself to the column led by Washington himself, "being the likeliest to gain the best Intelligence." Deciding—when she had dogged the American commander as far as North Castle, near the Connecticut border—that she had enough information, she turned around and headed back for New Jersey. She knew exactly where to go. When she reached Crosswicks, at "a friends House," Cregge met her. Though New Jersey was in rebel hands, the British spy master had had no trouble getting there.

After reporting, Ann was told to rejoin General Washington's column at once and locate the new stations of all American divisions. Hurrying back, she overtook General Washington eight miles from "Morrisons Stores." She had hardly arrived, however, when she was recognized by "one Smith a deserter from the 27th [British] Reg.ᵗ" and fled "for fear of being taken up as a Spie."

Ann Bates, however, was a determined lady, who believed in thorough investigation. Though she had been exposed for what she was, the rebels hadn't caught her yet; and when, a little later, she fell in by chance with the New York Brigade, she paused to count their artillery—"Eighteen Field pieces Long sixes's & long ten's"—then decided she had better march along with them till she was sure where they were going. Somewhere behind her, the hunt was up; but, with characteristic courage, Ann Bates took time for one last bit of intelligence. This was on September 25, 1778.

There was no time now for the long, roundabout journey

through New Jersey. That had been safe enough before she had been recognized; but now the Americans would be looking for her everywhere; and her only hope was a plunge straight for the British lines.

What she unexpectedly plunged into, instead, was another American column—five thousand troops under General Charles Scott. They halted her, of course, and brought her to Scott, who had for some time been in charge of intelligence near New York, the last man in the world a British agent wanted to meet. Some women might have been a little frightened by this time; but, to the quick-thinking lady spy, her capture was just another golden opportunity. She had gotten a pass from one American general. Why not another?

Persuasively she explained to the credulous Scott that she "was a Soldier's Wife in the Centre Division & had forgot something about five or six Miles below the Plains." If Scott asked a few searching questions about the Centre Division, he got convincing answers. By that time Ann Bates knew more about the Centre Division than he did. Obligingly, the officer who had been directing American intelligence for some time wrote out a pass for the most dangerous secret agent in the enemy's service. No one can doubt that Ann Bates was sweetly and charmingly grateful to the kind general.

Again, her courage saved her. British troops under General James Grant were out on a reconnoissance in force that morning; and Major Oliver DeLancey, a New York-born British regular, was with the advanced guard. One can imagine the hunted creature's relief as the red uniforms appeared.

DeLancey, himself an intelligence officer, sent her to the rear, with an N.C.O. for escort. Presently they met the general with one aide-de-camp. A staff officer guessed Ann's identity. Was this lady "the Person sent out by Major Drummond?" She was. She could show her token.

Hastily getting rid of the N.C.O.—the less the ranks knew about this kind of thing the better—the aide sat down on a stump to write down "the Several Informations I had been able to Obtain." This was on September 28. Whether a report was sent back to New York or not, Grant's staff kept her with them two days—she had just the information they might need about the rebel troops ahead.

Again, a second source proved the accuracy of her information. James, a Negro slave belonging to Gilbert Ogden, at North Castle, had come over to the British in late September. He confirmed part of her news, reporting that Washington had marched to the vicinity of Fredericksburgh and had his troops distributed all the way from there to Danbury. After Ann reached New York on September 30, James was sent home to spy some more, with a reward of two guineas.

When Ann arrived in the city at last, she had to break the news to Drummond that she "durst not any more attemp't to prosecute discoveries in General Washingtons Army." Despairingly, the officer remarked "he did not know what they should do." Ann modestly took this as "a plain demonstration that I had been Serviceable to the English Army."

Though sending her back to Washington meant sending her to certain death, Drummond was quick to see that Ann could still continue her deadly work if he could get her far enough away from Smith, the English deserter. There was an American officer on Long Island at the moment—evidently another secret traitor, or posing as one, for Drummond knew all about him and, in fact, already had an appointment with him. Taking Ann by boat, Drummond hurried out to "a Certain Gentlemans House." (Even in 1785, when the war was over, Ann Bates was too close-mouthed to mention names—the unknown gentleman was probably still living on Long Island and now posing as a stanch patriot.) They were too late. The double agent, whoever he was, had left a few hours before; and Drummond had to give up his scheme of co-operation of some kind between the pair.

When next he met Ann Bates, after this disappointment, Drummond asked her to go to a place "about Forty Seven miles from Philadelphia"—perhaps Easton, Allentown or Bethlehem. Here she was to meet a "Friend that was in Connection with General Arnold." The friend turned out to be a woman secret agent, of whom nothing else is known. The incident seems to indicate that Arnold was already in touch with the British in 1778, six months earlier than is usually supposed.

Ann was given a list of safe houses, "where I might be accommodated through the Jerseys," then dropped on the Jersey shore. Through Middletown and Bordentown, she reached Philadelphia, and went on to her destination, the British spy nest, next day. Here she met with suspicion, because she had brought no token. Glibly she explained that the only officer who knew about the tokens was in London. When she had quieted the other woman spy's suspicions, Ann gave her directions for "the proper Houses of Reception she was to call at," and herself went back alone as far as Middletown. When the mysterious woman joined her—it was safer to travel separately as long as possible—they went on to "the Horse Shoe," where a boat took them to New York. Presently the other woman went back to Pennsylvania, doubtless to see what could be done with Arnold.

After that, there was, for a time, no more espionage for Ann, since her friend Drummond had returned to England after a quarrel with Sir Henry Clinton. In August, 1779, André, now deep in the Arnold treason scheme, sent for her to "go the same Journey again. and bring the same person to New York." Though she had to be given an armed guard part way into New Jersey, "the Rebel Scouts being at that time very Numerous," she had no difficulty in traveling the rest of the way alone. It seems clear she was still using the secret chain of "safe" Tory houses the British had established across the Middle Atlantic states. This was so effective that British prisoners, escaping in Virginia, could secretly return cross-country—not with one guide, but with two—going undetected straight through the American forces.

Ann Bates had no trouble bringing the other lady spy back, until they reached the New Jersey shore of the Hudson. Here, however, the two anxious women had to wait three days for a boat, "exposed to the Enemys Scouting parties as well as the Inclemency of the Elements." Ann found it uncomfortable to sleep with "nothing but a Stone Pillow to Rest my Head"— which means that some Tory, not daring to take them into his house, hid them in a barn or cellar. Their boat had been held up two days by a storm. But Ann reached André finally and, in addition to the spy she had been told to bring back, blandly produced a report on "Shipping at Philadelphia with their force whether equipt for sea or on the Stocks, also an Account of the Stock of Flour. The Rebels had at the Different Mills on Westahicking [Wissahickon] Creek." André thought it was worth ten guineas.

When Clinton captured Charleston, South Carolina, May 12, 1780, Ann Bates went with her husband, in the artillery train. During the British occupation, while her friend Colonel Balfour was commandant, she was twice alerted for a secret journey to Cornwallis's forces farther north, but each time the scheme fell through. On March 6, 1781, she and her husband received permission to sail for England. Occasional references in British headquarters documents after that date, to "the Fair one" and "a woman" who "went out from our lines," refer to some other female agent.

By this time, Ann Bates might not have found secret journeys through Pennsylvania quite so safe; for in 1781 Clinton's chain of safe houses was partly broken by the daring exploit of Captain Andrew Lee, of Paxtang, Pennsylvania, serving temporarily as an American counterintelligence agent. General Washington had been annoyed by the constant escape of prisoners from Lancaster. After getting out of their prison, the men utterly vanished, though the nearest British post was a hundred miles distant, and they were clad in the brilliant British uniform. It was evident that they were traveling by night and hiding by day in the houses of royalist sympathizers, who might also be concealing British spies.

General Washington turned the problem over to General Moses Hazen, who sent for Captain Lee. Lee suddenly disappeared, while his brother officers were allowed to understand that he was either on leave or "on command," about which it was better not to ask questions. Actually, he had been thrust into prison, so completely disguised in British uniform that the American "intendant" in charge, though an acquaintance, did not recognize him.

The new "prisoner" soon had his eye on an old woman, deaf and half-witted—or supposed to be so—who sold fruit to the genuine prisoners. Lee rather thought he saw "signs" exchanged between the crone and the captives. He knew that her son had been thrown out of the American Army in disgrace, after punishment of some kind.

One rainy, windy night when a careless or bribed sentry had taken refuge from the rain, a mysterious figure slipped into the prisoners' barracks and began waking some of them. Casually the disguised American joined the group.

"Not the man—but come," said the stranger.

The door of the prison barracks was unbarred. Outside, where a section of the stockade had been taken down, the old woman who had been selling fruit joined them; and presently, from a neighboring thicket, a male companion emerged.

The two guided the escaping prisoners to the woman's house, a mile away, where they were given food and took an oath not to try to move farther, except with the group. Lee was disturbed to find that among the escaping prisoners was one he had himself punished; but, to his relief, the man gave no sign of recognition. Just as an alarm gun sounded from the American camp, the fugitives started out through the night and were soon hidden in one of the large stone barns common in southeastern Pennsylvania. Night after night the group trudged along, making only a few miles from one haven to another, finding shelter in barns, cellars and caves when daylight came. Once they were hidden in a "tomb."

Although he had shrewdly given no sign, the British prisoner, whom Lee had earlier punished, had, in reality, long since recognized him as an American officer and guessed what he was doing. On the twelfth night, perhaps by this man's secret connivance, Lee was hidden alone with him in a barn, while the others were lodged in a cellar which had been secretly dug underneath a stone church. Now, for the first time, the Tory guide learned Lee's identity, a discovery which he insisted on keeping secret for the time being. If Lee really was a spy trying to slip into the British lines with the escaping prisoners, the safest thing was to keep him with the party till he had been lured to a place where the British themselves could seize him.

When at length the escaping prisoners reached the bank of the Delaware, no one could find a boat. Handing his pistol to the man who had identified the American captain, the guide went off with the others, to look for some means of crossing the river.

The American had by this time accomplished his mission; he knew how the escapes were being managed; knew the route; knew the Tories who were helping. It was time to break away. Once beyond the Delaware, he would soon be in British-held territory, illegally in British uniform and subject to execution by all the rules of land warfare.

Captain Lee may, by this time, have guessed that he had been detected. If not, he soon found out; for, when he tried to leave, the man hiding with him fired—harmlessly, since, strange to say, the guide's pistol had been loaded with powder only. There was a knife fight—vigorous enough, since Lee, though small, was agile—which lasted until an American patrol arrived, attracted by the noise, and arrested Lee, his assailant, and most (if not all) of the others.

The Americans took their catch before a magistrate, who merely laughed at Lee's claim to be an American officer, and had the whole group marched off to Philadelphia in irons. Lee was released only after he had managed to send a note to General Benjamin Lincoln, whose aide promptly arrived to take him to the general. Lincoln burst into roars of laughter when he beheld the forlorn figure of his brother officer, who had not shaved for a week and whose British uniform was by this time in tatters.

Returning to Lancaster, Lee retraced the route of the prisoners, exposing the Tories who had sheltered them. Fifteen arrests closed the escape line. In January, a Philadelphia grand jury found true bills against the guilty Tories.

It was perhaps for this reason that Ann Bates was allowed to leave the secret service. She had been identified in General Washington's command. The line of safe houses in Pennsylvania had been broken. She had not succeeded in the south.

Approve or not, as you will, of the things she did, Ann Bates was such a good secret agent that no one has ever heard of her. Only once before has her name been mentioned—and never her adventures.

XIX

★　★　★

★

General Clinton's Spies—and Some Others

THE BRITISH INTELLIGENCE service greatly improved after Sir
Henry Clinton took command, partly because of the enthusiasm of Major John André, who had begun to do intelligence
work long before Clinton made him acting adjutant general in
October, 1779. Benedict Arnold's first positively known offers
of treason, in May, 1779, were made to André; and there may
have been earlier offers of which the record now is lost.

As André organized it, the British spy net covered Vermont
and New Hampshire (both of which the British long hoped to
win over to the king), Rhode Island, Connecticut, New York,
New Jersey, Pennsylvania, Maryland and Delaware. Espionage
in Massachusetts was largely neglected during the latter part of
the war, since so few Tories were left and no campaign there
was planned.

As Clinton's espionage expanded, various assistants were
drawn into his headquarters to deal with the reports of innumerable spies. The Tory, Colonel Beverly Robinson, guided
espionage in and around West Point, near which his estate lay,
so that he had many friends, tenants and acquaintances in an
area of great military importance. John Cane, a Brooklyn Tory,
at times assisted him. The Reverend Jonathan Odell, a fugitive

New Jersey parson, took a hand, especially in the Arnold treason. Christopher Saur, the younger, one of the famous dynasty of Pennsylvania printers, dealt with secret couriers from the Tory plotters who planned to seize a large part of Delaware, Maryland and Pennsylvania for the king. Joseph Chew, a New London Tory, helped direct the agents in New York. Cortlandt Skinner continued the New Jersey espionage net he had begun for Howe.

A group of skilled and daring semiprofessional spies stood ready, in and around New York, for any secret mission that might be required. Among them were Mrs. Ann Bates, one of history's most remarkable female agents; the daring Moody brothers, James and John; Manuel Elderbeck, Sylvanus Hughson and William Jacobs, operating along the Hudson in 1778; Ezekiel Yeomans and the same William Jacobs along the Hudson, in 1781; Solomon Bradbury, observing American troops near Amawalk, New York, in 1779; Thomas Ward, operating in New Jersey and up the Hudson to Albany, with two assistants from 1779 to 1781; William Nelson, who made a secret tour November 1-12, 1781, to examine American positions in the Highlands, at West Point, Stony Point, Verplanck's Point, Continental Village and Pike's Hill; Joseph Clark, watching French movements in Rhode Island and along the Hudson in the first half of 1781; Samuel Shoemaker, the Philadelphia Quaker to whom Sir Henry Clinton paid £100 "for procuring Intelligence," and to whom Sir Guy Carleton, the last British commander, paid £200 more; Metcalf Bowler, chief justice of Rhode Island; Thomas Hazard, who "procured Intelligence for the British at very great risque," at Kingston, Rhode Island; Captain Sir James Wallace, R.N., commanding H.M.S. *Rose,* who received intelligence from Robert Ferguson and Dr. John Haliburton, of Newport, Rhode Island; Caleb Bruen, of Newark, New Jersey, who besides spying in New Jersey served as a secret courier, carrying Doctor Haliburton's intelligence to Clinton; David Gray, another secret courier and spy, operating in New York, Connecticut, Vermont, and northward to Canada. It would have grieved Sir Henry Clinton had he known that Bruen and Gray were both captains in the American Army, patriotically serving the British on orders from General Washington.

Clinton soon had so many well-trained secret agents in New York that he could hurry spies out to investigate, the moment a query came in. André, for example, at one time became suspicious that Arnold did not really mean to turn traitor, but was only leading the British on. The major's assistant, Joseph Chew, was able to "put two persons out in order to obtain an account of Mr. Arnold's movements," within two and a half hours!

In New Jersey a similar network of spies, who were never detected—probably Skinner's men—reported regularly to British headquarters. That this was a network and not a single agent is shown by one message: "All friends are Well." Among these men were Joseph Gould, operating in Newark as early as 1780 and probably to the end of the war; John Rattoon, active in the Arnold treason; Tunis Blauvelt, who boldly entered and observed an American blockhouse in 1781; and "Usual" (Uzal) Woodruff, who was spying on Washington at Morristown in 1781.

Another British agent in New Jersey was Benjamin Whitcuff, a free Negro from Long Island, who joined the British in 1776 or 1777, under Howe, and spied for nearly two years. Americans caught and hanged him "at Cranbury in the Jerseys," but British troops, arriving three minutes later, cut him down in time to save his life. The British spy's father was serving in the American Army.

Not quite in the same category was Edward Fox, a clerk in the Continental Treasury in Philadelphia, whom the British captured about August, 1779. He plotted (or pretended to plot) with André to place a man in the office of the secretary of Congress to secure intelligence, and to work directly with a mysterious "C——," who appears to have been in Congress, and who may have been Samuel Chase, a signer of the Declaration of Independence. André promised to send a secret courier to Philadelphia for such intelligence as Fox could gather, whenever Fox sent the code message: "The Compliments of Clapham." It was agreed: "The Messenger is to make a Cross in chalk on the pit door of the play house at night, & on the next day is to find an hour and address marked over it when to call for a parcell." (A worse method of secret communication it would be hard to imagine.)

André did, however, arrange a fairly adequate recognition system for his secret courier, who was to make contact with Fox. His instruction reads: "*Monmouth* is the first word in case of an interview *Penobscot* the Second." But all this plotting led to nothing whatever except Fox's freedom. His promise of future treason seems to have been wholly false—a mere trick to persuade the British to release him.

André worked out a system of code names for towns, rivers and patriot leaders, finding malicious amusement in giving two rebel strongholds the names of the worst places in the Bible: "Sodom" (Fort Wyoming) and "Gomorrha" (Fort Pitt). Indians were "Pharisees." Other code names were "Synagogue" (Congress), "Alexandria" (Detroit), "Rome" (Carlisle, Pennsylvania), "Jordan" (Susquehanna), "James" (General Washington), "Matthew" (General John Sullivan), "Luke" (General Edward Hand). Among British frontier leaders, Colonel John Butler was "Lazarus"; the educated Mohawk chief, Joseph Brant, "Zebedee." Let the rebels break the British cipher if they could! The deciphered message would still mean very little if these code names were used.

The identity of agents was protected by the use of false names, sometimes several for the same spy. Arnold called himself both "Gustavus" and "John Moore." One message to the Mohawk chief, Joseph Brant, was not signed at all. Instead, the last paragraph said only: "That you may not be at a loss to know who sends you this, it is the person at whose quarters you were when you had a particular conversation with General Tryon."

While Clinton was still under Howe's command, he had begun using a "dumbbell" paper mask. He also used another mask, with oblong holes cut in it. By 1778 and perhaps earlier, the British were also using a numerical code, beginning with the number 50, with a word for each number. Like Tallmadge, who devised a similar code for Washington, André made the mistake of numbering the words in their alphabetical order, so that each number gave some clue to the word it represented. In the Arnold treason, André used two secret inks, one developed by heat, the other by acid, and a dictionary code, in which numbers gave page, column and word in selected editions of Bailey's *Dictionary* or Blackstone's *Commentaries*.

Clinton's new ciphers were much better than the crude system General Gage and Doctor Church had used in 1775. One was a substitution cipher, in which the alphabet was reversed, "z" becoming "a" and "a" becoming "z." To destroy frequency clues, the cipher changed in each line of the message, using "y" for "a" in the second line, "x" for "a" in the third, and so on. When the cipher clerk reached "o," in the middle of the alphabet, he started over again. A spy using this cipher did not have to carry incriminating papers, since the system was so easy to remember.

Clinton also used another substitution cipher, with different alphabets for the first, second and third paragraphs. Even if an American cryptanalyst should break the cipher in one paragraph, he would have to start all over in the next. As late as 1781, however, Sir Henry was using one extremely clumsy substitution cipher, in which "a" was 51, "d" was 54, "e" 55. Finding that "a" was 51 and "d" 54, anyone could guess (correctly) that "b" was 52, "c" 53. Somewhat more complex was his "pigpen" cipher, in which twenty-five letters of the alphabet were placed in squares. Then an angle alone would represent a letter, the same angle with a dot another letter, the angle with two dots still another. In some cases, cryptography was used only for a few crucial words in an otherwise "clear" message, a method also favored by certain American officials.

Important information was brought in by the perpetual stream of Tory refugees, escaping British prisoners and deserting American soldiers. Reports of spies and interrogations of deserters or other informants were written down in four intelligence books, two of which are now in the New York Public Library, one in the Library of Congress, and one in the Clements Library, where there are also many manuscripts of the same sort.

From the spy system, military intelligence came pouring in.

The effect of Pulaski's death; American strength reports and order of battle; the garrison at Fort Wyoming, on the wild Susquehanna; artillery at Easton, Pennsylvania; settlement of dissatisfied Americans in "a place called Canetuck"; disposition, strength, sentries and alarm signals of General Washington's bodyguard; records of the Maryland Dragoons "taken from the Rebel Clothier General Books"; difficulties with provisions, clothing and currency—all swiftly reached Sir Henry Clinton. Once, New Jersey spies reported new official currency exchange rates before Congress had time to publish them. A report from Bergen, New Jersey, in August, 1779, locates American headquarters in "Moore's House" in the Highlands of the Hudson, which—as General Washington's orders show—is exactly where they were. After that, the British often knew what houses the Continental commander and other generals were living in. Once they knew where General Washington would sleep —twenty-four hours before his arrival! This was in accord with special orders to report Washington's whereabouts at all times.

Clinton's espionage was not confined to the theater of operations. The Americans captured Lieutenant Henry Hare—a Tory refugee from Florida, New York, who had joined the British armed forces—near Canajoharie, New York, with two companions, in June, 1779, and hanged him as a spy June 21, "to the general Satisfaction of every Person who knew him, except his own intimate Connextions." Hare's wife and children pleaded for his life in vain, but his companions may have saved their lives by giving information.

British spies continued to visit Connecticut. One of them, Andrew Patchen, of Redding, though twice captured, survived the war. Edward Jones, of Ridgefield, was less fortunate. Israel Putnam's outposts caught him in February, 1779; and a court-martial sentenced him to death on charge of guiding enemy troops and espionage. Jones may have been doing nothing worse than buying beef for the British Army; but as he was acting secretly, out of uniform, and within the American lines, he was technically a spy.

Jones's execution was an unusually ghastly business. He was brought to a twenty-foot gallows just in time to see the bleeding body of a deserter, whose uniform had taken fire from the muskets of the firing squad. Then, as poor Jones stood on the ladder with the noose around his neck, it was discovered that the executioner had lost his nerve and disappeared. From the ground, Israel Putnam shouted to the condemned man to jump—an order with which the spy excusably declined to comply; and eventually the ladder had to be turned over under him, throwing him into the air.

James Moody, the New Jersey Tory, who had been active under Howe, remained equally active under Clinton. He was out on a guerrilla raid through New Jersey in June, 1779, and in October went out to spy directly on Washington's army. In November he crossed New Jersey into Pennsylvania to observe General John Sullivan's army, after its raid on Iroquois New York. Having ascertained its strength, he started back, pausing in Morris County, New Jersey, for a secret examination of the ration books of the Continental Army, which gave him a good idea of American strength. He paused again in Pompton, New Jersey, to spy on Gates's forces, collecting "the exactest information, not only of the amount of the force then with him, but of the numbers that were expected to join him." During the trip he also managed to raid an American jail, releasing a British prisoner under sentence of death.

Moody was not always successful. He failed to blow up the American magazine at Suckasanna, about eighteen miles from Morristown, and his attempt to kidnap Governor William Livingston, of New Jersey, discovered almost at once, led to some tart correspondence between the intended victim and the British commander and to a proclamation by Governor Livingston, offering a reward for Moody's capture.

This was too much for Moody's sense of humor. He replied with a private proclamation of his own, offering two hundred guineas for "a certain William Livingston, late an Attorney at Law, and now *a lawless usurper* and *incorrigible rebel.*" Further: "If his whole person cannot be brought in, half the sum above specified will be paid for his EARS and NOSE, which are too well known, and too remarkable to be mistaken." The British spy's reference to the governor's nose was extremely unkind. A surviving silhouette, confirmed by a painted portrait, shows that it was of almost elephantine proportions. To make the unkind cut unkinder still, everyone knew that bounties for "vermin"—wolves, foxes and other troublesome animals —were often paid for the ears or nose.

In the end, Moody's daring led to his capture by Anthony Wayne's troops. He was sent to prison at West Point, where General Robert Howe was in command, was transferred to other prisons, was then sent back to West Point, where he remained a prisoner after Arnold had taken command.

The commandant of the West Point garrison, Colonel John C. Lamb, did not want so resourceful a prisoner, being apprehensive that, even in prison, Moody had learned far too much about the garrison. Benedict Arnold, only a few weeks before his own flight to the enemy, nevertheless ordered the spy's irons taken off, though he remarked virtuously, "I believe Moody is a bad man"! The irons went back on, however, when Lamb pointed out that Moody would escape within forty-eight hours unless fettered, and warned the traitor Arnold, with unconscious irony, "Every method ought to be taken to prevent the enemy from knowing the real strength of this post"—which Arnold had long ago betrayed.

Eventually, Moody was returned to General Washington's own provost guard, characteristically seizing a good chance to count American artillery on the way. One night the captive managed to break the bolt of his handcuffs, knock down a careless sentry, and escape with the man's musket. Other guards rushed past the quick-thinking spy, who had stayed in the open, musket on shoulder, posing in the darkness as one of his own pursuers. Knowing exactly where Tories lived, he passed from one friendly house to another and, at the end of September, 1780, arrived safely at Paulus Hook, about the time his late jailer, Benedict Arnold, also arrived in New York.

On March 6, 1781, Moody sallied into New Jersey again, in an unsuccessful attempt to intercept General Washington's dispatches. By March 10, he was lurking near Haverstraw Mountain, only to learn that the Continental Army's mails had already passed. But the indefatigable Moody continued to lurk until, in the middle of March, he at last captured the secret military pouches and brought them in triumph back to New York. On the following day, he was asking Clinton for two lightly armed men and some money for another "enterprise against the rebel mails."

In mid-May, 1781, headquarters sent him out once more, but the expedition was a failure. Moody was nearly captured several times and had to fight his way back to New York; but the very next night, May 18, the intrepid Tory tried his luck again, feeling sure no patriots would expect him so soon after his defeat. After a fight near Saddle River (probably between Passaic and Hackensack), he pushed on to Pompton, only to find that the official mails were now sent by a different route.

The word spread: "Moody is out." That undaunted individual quietly lay in wait along the dispatch rider's new route, which he had quickly discovered, noting with amusement that the local American militia was brought down "from the part where he really was, to pursue him where he was not." This time the spy got a rich haul—General Washington's agreements with Rochambeau, following their conference in Connecticut to plan the attack on New York. Two other mails were later seized by Moody's men.

The Americans had long since learned to fear the doughty guerrilla. On May 4, 1781, the American commissary, Charles Stewart, was panic-stricken on learning he was in the field again and hastily demanded protection for his quartermaster stores at Sussex Court House, New Jersey, which were in danger "from Moody—who is again in the country." The presence of Indian raiders at the same time did not worry him; but he wrote: "Moody is a fellow of enterprize and knows the Contry well he has traveled it through and through and will doubtless effect the Destruction of the Stores." Colonel Elias Dayton, however, was able to save them.

Eventually, the pitcher went too often to the well. Lieutenant General Baron Wilhelm von Knyphausen had captured Thomas Edison, or Addison, who had been assisting Charles Thomson, secretary to the Continental Congress. Edison talked his captors into believing that he had access to congressional papers (which was true) and that he would betray them (which was not). He was released and told when and where to meet the spies, near Philadelphia. On November 7, 1781, John Moody, the spy's brother, and Laurence Marr found Edison waiting for them on the Jersey bank of the Delaware, opposite the city, while James Moody himself lurked within hearing but out of sight.

Edison assured his dupes that next evening he could let them into "the most private recesses of the State-house," where secret papers of the Continental Congress were filed.

When the time came, John Moody and Marr crossed to Philadelphia, while James Moody waited openly in the ferryhouse on the New Jersey shore, telling a woman there that he belonged to the Jersey Brigade. He was entirely truthful. There was an American, as well as a British, Jersey Brigade. Moody did not feel called upon to state which one he belonged to, and no one troubled to ask him.

Returning to his room for the night—though not to sleep—Moody heard a new arrival from the Pennsylvania side remark, about eleven o'clock, that "there was the devil to pay in Philadelphia; that there had been a plot to break into the State-house, but that one of the party had betrayed the others; that two were already taken; and that a party of soldiers had just crossed the river with him, to seize their leader, who was said to be thereabouts."

Snatching his pistols, the British agent fled for a neighboring woods, saw cavalry ahead, and flung himself flat in a ditch. Searching troopers passed within ten feet, and he could see the men running their bayonets into shocks of corn in a field near by. When the searchers had passed, he hid for two days in one of the corn shocks he had already seen being searched. Later he found a refuge which he always refused to name; stole a boat, in which he rowed openly up the Delaware, conversing in a friendly way with other boatmen as he passed; and, working his way from one Tory house to another, across New Jersey, reached New York. John Moody was hanged November 13, 1781. Marr probably gave enough information to save his life. Congress paid Edison a cash reward of $266 2/3.

General Clinto 's least useful spy, Metcalf Bowler, of Rhode Island, joined the patriots just long enough to be made chief justice of the new state; then, on December 12, 1776, secretly wrote British headquarters in Rhode Island that he wanted to take advantage of the proclamation of amnesty—at the same time asking the British to let him retain his office and salary in the rebel government! When Clinton was in Newport in 1778, the chief justice agreed to send military intelligence, on condition that Clinton himself should be the only one to see the letters. Bowler proposed to get himself elected, as a patriot, to the Rhode Island General Assembly—if the enemy would provide money for his election expenses! He also wanted orders given to the British command in Newport to protect his person and property, and demanded compensation for the use of his house as a British hospital, and of his farm as a British encampment. Clinton's consent to these proposals put Bowler in the agreeable position of receiving his salary as chief justice from the rebellious state of Rhode Island, while receiving cash, or gratitude, or both, from the British crown.

Though Bowler sent a little military intelligence from time to time, none of it was of much importance. He gave some dubious information on naval movements and predicted (apparently in error) the movement of Huntington's regiment from New London to Rhode Island in 1779. He reported on American troops in Rhode Island and Connecticut, on American difficulties in recruiting, and on the defenseless state of Boston—which was of no use, as the British were no longer interested in Boston. There is nothing to indicate he sent any intelligence at all after October, 1779, and a large part of his correspondence is devoted to expatiating on his own danger. Bowler is chiefly of interest today not because he was a second-rate spy, but because one room of his house was so beautiful that the Metropolitan Museum of Art has preserved it.

A more successful British spy in Rhode Island was the Tory, Robert Ferguson, who supplied "material Intelligence" to Captain Sir James Wallace, of H.M.S. *Rose*. In 1777, he sent Sir Henry Clinton a detailed terrain study, describing the country around Providence and in other parts of New England, with a view to possible future military operations there, which never took place.

However successful Bowler and Ferguson may have been in evading detection, a far cleverer American spy, working under their very noses, was evading detection with equal success, and supplying a great deal more intelligence. For fourteen months, Isaac Barker, of Middletown, Rhode Island, and his assistants spied upon Clinton's forces in Rhode Island, supplying a continuous flow of news to Lieutenant Seth Chapin, the American contact officer detailed for this purpose, until the British abandoned Rhode Island forever. Barker employed a secret signal system and the same kind of "letter drop," or "post office," that the Mersereaus were using in New Jersey. Under this system, spies and couriers never met. The agent dropped his report at the place agreed upon; when he had gone, the courier picked it up.

Barker—a patriotic farmer, aged about twenty-six, living at Middletown, a few miles from Newport—later said he began espionage for the Americans when Clinton drove General John Sullivan out of Newport in August, 1778; but it is very likely he was the secret agent, signing only as "Anonymous," who was supplying information to General Sullivan from Little Compton in July. Again the Continental Army had realized the value of planting spies ahead of time, in areas it would be forced to evacuate. Isaac Barker was ready to commence intelligence work as soon as the Americans left, with the assistance of Samuel, Hezekiah and Gideon Barker, probably his brothers. Either then or very soon afterward, Lieutenant Seth Chapin was stationed at Little Compton, across the Sakonnet River, some miles east of Newport—"apparently without business or object." The lieutenant's real business would have surprised his brother officers in the Continental Army—for it consisted mainly of watching a stone wall.

Isaac Barker explained, after the war, how he had communicated with Lieutenant Chapin by "telegraphic signals," made with a "Stake & a Crutch & a stone Wall." Precisely how these familiar objects made a telegraphic code is by no means clear even now, in spite of an elaborate diagram that Barker himself drew. His sketch shows the wall, with numbers along it. The position of two barways (the old name for openings in a stone fence closed by bars) and a single tree are also indicated in the sketch, to which Barker has added a written explanation. "The signals were a *Stake* and a *crutch*," he says, for which the wall provided a basis. Apparently the place on the wall where these appeared could be made to indicate a number; and with a series of numbers a code is possible. The "crutch" was probably the crotch of a tree. Though Barker does not say so, it is very likely that the positions of rails, i.e., "bars," in the barways were also used.

The scheming lieutenant could see all this from the other shore, though he needed field glasses, for the fence was a mile from the western bank of the Sakonnet River, and he himself was observing from the eastern bank. Since Isaac Barker later asserted that he could receive instructions, another fence on the American side may have been used in the same way.

To transmit complicated intelligence, such signals were inadequate, though Barker later proudly told a friend that he could transmit about a dozen different messages with this crude equipment. To supplement his system, Barker maintained a post office under a flat stone on North Point, about a mile away. The lieutenant had a whaleboat, also known as a "lookout boat," with a crew including men whose names show that they were related to the secret agents on shore. The "pilot" was Hezekiah Barker. In the crew was William Taggart, probably the son of Judge William Taggart, who was busily collecting intelligence near Newport. In fact, the whole espionage scheme seems to have been a family affair.

With a crew of local men like these, who knew the river, Chapin had no trouble slipping over after dark and collecting the reports. In the later months of Isaac Barker's service, a window in Peleg Peckham's barn was left open to signal that papers were waiting under the stone.

William Wilkinson, of Providence, secretary to General Ezekiel Cornell, a Rhode Island brigadier commanding at Tiverton, speaks of handling Chapin's reports "during the Summer of 1779." Because Lieutenant Chapin "wrote badly and spelled worse," General Cornell left the task of deciphering to his secretary. As Barker wrote a good, clear hand, his written reports probably went straight to the general, who sent some of them directly to General Gates, Sullivan's successor in the Rhode Island command.

Barker's stake, "crutch," rails and stone wall sufficed to transmit full data on "all ships whether armed or not which arrived or sailed." The written reports probably dealt with British troops. General Gates declared Barker's information of great value.

The utmost secrecy was maintained. Even Wilkinson was not allowed to know Barker's identity till the war was over; and, though Cornell discussed Chapin with Wilkinson, he never spoke of him to anyone else and ordered Wilkinson never to mention the subject of intelligence in conversation.

These precautions were so successful that, despite some narrow escapes, Barker was never caught, though he was once stopped on the road and questioned by two British cavalrymen. He had, however, been wise enough to "talk Tory" loudly and constantly to a colonel of the invading army quartered in his home, and he usually carried a pass from this officer. Though he had failed to carry his pass the night the troopers caught him, he was able to persuade them to take him to the colonel, who at once released him. To Barker's amusement, his guest often discussed the "traitor and spy among us," whom the British well knew to exist, but whose identity they never learned.

Metcalf Bowler, unconsciously playing into Barker's hands, was accidentally responsible for providing the Americans with better information than he ever sent to Clinton. The privateer *Diana,* of which Bowler was part owner, captured the sloop *Kipple,* commanded by a German named Carl Hegel. Frau Hegel and her daughter Gertrude found work as servants at the Marquis of Granby Inn, at Newport, much frequented by Hessian officers, some of whom were billeted at the farm of Judge William Taggart, who had made friends with the little German girl.

The judge picked up what intelligence he could from the

officers in his farmhouse. How could they guess that another and younger William Taggart, probably the judge's son, was in Lieutenant Seth Chapin's whaleboat crew which carried Isaac Barker's reports? Meantime the Hessians at the Marquis of Granby, not realizing that the maid in the coffeeroom understood German perfectly, discussed military affairs freely in her hearing. Judge Taggart's Negro man, Cudjo, made a point of chatting regularly with little Gertrude, who guilelessly repeated what she had heard the officers say. From Cudjo, the information passed to Judge Taggart, whose son forwarded it to the American camp. It is said that Gertrude Hegel never knew what she had been unconsciously doing.

XX

Treason

AFTER SIR HENRY CLINTON had assumed command and Major John André had taken over intelligence, the British began a new and vigorous effort to corrupt American leaders. It is probable that Washington could have had a dukedom for changing sides, the difficulty being that he was unswervingly loyal—and, besides, no Tory dared so much as approach the granite leader with a treasonable offer.

André's notes, surviving in Sir Henry Clinton's papers, show that he had listed and carefully considered all American generals whom he thought corruptible. They also show the ironical fact that Benedict Arnold's reputation as a soldier stood so high that André wholly omitted him from the list! At one time André was sure that he could bring over Major General Samuel H. Parsons to the British side; but he never did; and it is doubtful that Parsons—unconsciously dealing with a British double agent who posed as an American spy—ever guessed that the man was trying to corrupt him. Major General Charles Lee—an eccentric of whom almost anything could be expected—did, as a prisoner of war, obligingly draw up a plan of campaign for the British; but it told them nothing they could not see for themselves; and the British staff themselves thought Lee's plan of so little value it was merely filed.

Within the lower ranks, there were a few traitors, as Ann Bates's story shows. Lieutenant Colonel Herman Zedwitz, of the 1st New York Continental Line, was caught offering intelligence to the enemy in 1776. William Demont, adjutant of the 5th Pennsylvania, slipped away to the British with the plans of Fort Washington a few weeks later. Major Daniel Hammill, an American officer captured in 1777, returned secretly in April, 1778, accompanied by a soldier who had also turned traitor, in an effort—vain, of course—to corrupt Brigadier General George Clinton, governor of New York, and his brother, Brigadier General James Clinton. They were caught because an American prisoner of war, in some miraculous way, smuggled information from Long Island to General Parsons, in Connecticut, that Hammill was a spy who had been seen in conference with Sir Henry Clinton.

Occasional veiled references in the British intelligence papers show that a few other American junior officers served the enemy as spies for indefinite periods, without ever being detected, ending their iniquitous careers at last, in complete safety, with the honors due to veterans and in an anonymity that still continues.

Benedict Arnold's story is painfully familiar. Arnold was resentful over belated promotions, trouble with his military accounts, and a court-martial on charges of improper commercial dealings while American commander in Philadelphia—an affair in which he was far guiltier than the court-martial ever guessed. His characteristic greed for money and personal extravagance were enhanced after his marriage to the beautiful, hysterical young madcap, Peggy Shippen, who was as fond of money as her husband, quite as unscrupulous, and conveniently well acquainted with Major John André, whom she had met during the British occupation of Philadelphia.

In May, 1779, or perhaps some months earlier, Arnold, without revealing his identity, secretly approached the British with an offer of treason. Lengthy negotiations with André followed. While still bargaining for the highest price he could get,

Arnold tried to prove his value by sending the enemy American secret military information, the most important intelligence thus betrayed being advance news of the French landing at Newport, which the traitor had learned in strictest confidence while dining with General Washington. So long as Arnold—temporarily incapacitated for the field by his twice-wounded leg—commanded in Philadelphia, messages in code and invisible ink were carried to New York by two Philadelphia merchants, Joseph Stansbury and Samuel Wallis, and by a British secret courier in New Jersey, John Rattoon.

Arnold concealed his identity so carefully that, although the British knew an American general was ready to turn traitor, they did not know for a long time which general it was. Clinton's staff had, however, made studies of the various American leaders and soon began to suspect with whom they were dealing. Eventually the traitor himself revealed his identity, though his real name was always concealed in correspondence. Once André accidentally wrote "Arn gen" in drafting a letter, but he crossed it out, substituted a pseudonym, and kept the draft—which would have revealed everything—in the secret headquarters file.

After intriguing to secure the command of West Point, solely to betray it, Arnold was horrified to have Washington smilingly give him command of the "light" troops, the left wing of the whole Continental Army, the post of honor. At the news, Peggy Arnold had a public fit of hysterics, which she passed off as anxiety for her husband's safety. When Arnold protested he was still physically unfit to take the field, General Washington, much puzzled, but suspecting nothing, granted him the West Point command he needed for his treason. Meantime the traitor was, so far as possible, converting his American property to cash, even transferring property to London, while Clinton held the wages of treason on account for him in New York, promising more money if the betrayal of West Point succeeded. After assuming command at West Point, Arnold continued his letters to André, whom he addressed as "Mr. John Anderson," a merchant, disguising all information as mere commercial correspondence.

This ruse was so effective that, although one message was

intercepted, it was ignored as a mere business letter. Shortly before the crisis, the British spy, William Heron, asked Arnold for a pass to enter the British lines on "business," as genuine merchants were sometimes allowed to do. Unaware that he was dealing with a fellow traitor and supposing that Heron was an American merchant, trying to turn an honest penny—or, at any rate, a penny—Arnold issued the requested pass, at the same time asking Heron to take a letter of his own into New York for him. Read in the light of after events, what Arnold was saying is perfectly clear. He was bargaining for cash, referring to André-Anderson's "commercial plan," and his own "first proposal," which was "not unreasonable," in view of "risks and profits." He also refers to the "quantity of goods at market" (men and stores at West Point) and "the number of speculators below" (the Continental Army), advising against "an immediate purchase" (attack on West Point).

For some extraordinary reason, though Heron carried the letter to New York, he did not deliver it, but brought it back to General Samuel H. Parsons in Connecticut, as a suspicious document. Parsons opened it, read it, mistook it for an ordinary business letter, and simply filed it, instead of sending it to headquarters. Under Tallmadge's or McLane's suspicious eyes, that "business" letter would have told the whole story in time to catch the traitor.

Preparations for the betrayal of West Point were by this time far advanced, and Arnold had done his best to render the fortifications nearly defenseless, by scattering the troops. Clinton had his troops ready to move, as American spies noticed, but no one, British or American, knew where—though André had given an indiscreet hint to his friend, the cavalryman, Lieutenant Colonel John Graves Simcoe, commanding the Queen's Rangers.

André's capture, the only thing that prevented a complete British victory, was due to his own blunder. He carried a perfectly authentic pass from Arnold, American commander of that military area. Deceived by a captured British or Hessian uniform coat one of his captors was wearing, he announced himself as a British officer. After that, Arnold's pass merely deepened suspicion. Even though André at first thought his captors were British, he ought to have presented Arnold's pass at once. If they had really been British, he would simply have been taken to his own army as a prisoner—to be released by the first officer who recognized him. Since his captors were in the American service, they would have honored Arnold's pass, if their suspicions had not already been aroused before André displayed it.

The tragic spy might still have escaped but for Major Benjamin Tallmadge. Lieutenant Colonel John Jameson, the Virginia cavalry officer on duty at the outposts that night, may have been a good combat soldier, but his wits were less than brilliant; the complexities of secret service were far beyond him; and he had the disposition of an army mule. His honest blunders almost enabled Arnold to complete the treason, in spite of André's capture.

Colonel Elisha Sheldon, of the 2nd Connecticut Light Dragoons, who would normally have been in command at the North Castle advanced post the day André was brought in (September 23, 1780), was absent, facing a court-martial on minor disciplinary charges. That left Lieutenant Colonel Jameson— far out of his depth—as acting commander. Like most officers temporarily in an important command, Jameson was nervous and obstinate. The facts that he was a Virginian with Yankee troops and that Tallmadge was another Yankee were no help at all.

It was obvious, however, even to Lieutenant Colonel Jameson, when André was brought in, that something was radically wrong. The mysterious prisoner looked like a British officer and had told his captors he was British; but he was out of uniform. He was carrying papers relating to the West Point garrison and defenses. He had tried to conceal them. Yet he had a genuine pass, signed by the American commanding general.

Jameson did what any outpost officer would do in an ordinary case. (The trouble was, this case was not ordinary.) He sent André, under guard, to the commanding general. But he also did one sensible thing—the only sensible thing he did that night: he sent André's suspicious documents directly to General Washington, though even in doing that, he blundered. The general, he knew, had gone to Connecticut to confer with General Rochambeau about the employment of French troops; but, forgetting that General Washington habitually returned to headquarters by a route different from the one he had followed on his outward journey, he sent his courier along the same roads the commander-in-chief had taken on his trip to Hartford. After making this useless ride, the man had to find which way the general was returning, then ride back around a circle.

Late that night Major Tallmadge, returning from a prolonged mounted reconnoissance along the front lines, learned that, during the "forenoon," a man "who called himself John Anderson" had been caught with suspicious papers.

Anderson? Tallmadge knew that name! He had himself received orders from Arnold to assist a man named Anderson who was expected to bring military intelligence from Manhattan. Hurrying to headquarters, the quick-witted Tallmadge at once noted several suspicious circumstances. Anderson had been arrested as a British spy. Arnold had arranged for Anderson's visit. Anderson was carrying full details of West Point and its garrison in Arnold's handwriting. He was carrying them in the wrong direction. Why had Arnold only ten days before written Tallmadge about a man with the same surname, coming from New York?

The American intelligence service had heard rumors that a traitor was preparing to sell out; but no one had identified him. If the American intelligence service knew this, Tallmadge almost certainly knew it. The incredible truth leaped to his mind. (To be fair to the slower wits of Jameson, it should be noted that he had not, like Tallmadge, so much information and so many reasons for suspicion.)

"Very much surprised," Tallmadge pointed out to his superior the "glaring inconsistency" of what he had done. If Jameson had been consistent, he would have sent the spy, his own report of the capture, and the documents, together, either to Washington or to Arnold. If he had sent them to Washington, the traitor would have been caught. If he had sent them to Arnold, the American traitor and the British spy could have escaped together, in time for Clinton to attack.

After listening to Tallmadge, Jameson was "greatly agitated." He was still more agitated when he heard what Major Tallmadge wanted to do. Since André, with the story of his capture, was already on the way to Arnold, Tallmadge, always resolute, suggested to Jameson, "a measure which I wished to adopt, offering to take the whole responsibility upon myself, and which he deemed too perilous to permit."

What this scheme was, Tallmadge refused to state when he wrote his Memoir and throughout his long life. But, though the major never explained what he wanted the irresolute Jameson to do, it is plain enough that he proposed to seize Benedict Arnold, even if he was commanding general, and hold him prisoner till General Washington arrived. Had Jameson let Tallmadge carry out this mutinous act of rank insubordination (which was exactly what the situation called for), General Washington, arriving next morning and receiving the treasonable military correspondence, in Arnold's own handwriting, would have applauded both officers.

Though he could not persuade Jameson to seize the traitor, Tallmadge did persuade him to have André—already riding under guard on his way to Arnold's headquarters—brought back. But no amount of expostulation could persuade the lieutenant colonel to delay the report on André's capture he had sent to Arnold—without which Arnold could not have escaped.

It is a strange thing to think of, that night of September 23/24, 1780. Arnold lay by the side of his beautiful Peggy, in "the treason house" across the Hudson from West Point. The die was cast. The papers had been sent on to Sir Henry Clinton, secure—they thought—in André's hands. British transports would soon be coming up the Hudson to surprise West Point. Success and wealth for Benedict Arnold lay only a week or two ahead. Beyond that lay—but who could tell how far royal gratitude might go?

André, riding as a captive through the night with mounted guards around him, knew his danger, but knew, too, there was still hope—if he could reach Arnold in time, as it seemed for a little while he would. General Washington and his staff, as yet placidly unaware of what was happening, had halted at Fishkill for a quiet night's rest. Far behind the general, somewhere along the winding Connecticut roads, through the darkness, pounded a horseman, with the evidence of treason. Tallmadge fumed. Jameson, one may feel sure, lay wondering uneasily whether he had done the right thing—and what on earth he should have done. He had, in fact, almost lost the American Revolution. Few officers in any army or in any war have ever made so many wrong decisions in so short a time.

It is astonishing how often the Americans came close to discovering Arnold's treason without ever quite doing so. Though General Washington had been deceived by Arnold's fiery courage and brilliance as a combat leader, two Continental officers had long since taken a more accurate measure of the man. Lieutenant Colonel John Brown, taking the precaution of first resigning from the army, had published an attack on him, April 12, 1777. "Money is this man's god," he wrote, "and to get enough of it he would sacrifice his country."

Major Allan McLane had become suspicious almost as soon as the Americans occupied Philadelphia. At that time he can hardly have found evidence of treason; but he detected enough of Arnold's dubious business enterprises to make him warn General Washington, in so many words, that Arnold was not to be trusted. Nevertheless, in spite of all warnings, the commander-in-chief did trust the traitor implicitly, up to the horrifying moment when Jameson's courier, catching up with him at last, laid the proofs of treason in his hands.

A few days after Arnold's flight, Washington sent for McLane, who "reminded him of his Suspecting Arnold in 1778." Far from resenting his junior's bluntness, the general remarked ruefully that if McLane had been in Jameson's place, "Arnold would have been secured."

From Manhattan, Culper, Jr., reported a few days after Arnold's arrival, "I was not much surprised at his conduct, for it was no more than I expected of him." It is a pity the Manhattan spy did not report his suspicions a little earlier.

According to Enoch Crosby, who had himself done enough

espionage to know what he was talking about, General Nathanael Greene, through his own secret service in New York, had already learned "that some secret expedition was on foot, at the city of New-York; but of its nature and direction, he could not obtain the smallest hint." Three secret agents, sent into the city "from three different quarters," had neither returned nor reported. This, General Greene wrote General Washington on September 21, 1780, two days before André was captured, made him "suspect some secret expedition is in contemplation, the success of which depends altogether on its being kept a secret." He wrote in the same vein to the president of Congress. André's capture, September 23, provided startling confirmation. What Greene's spies had detected, without realizing it, was Clinton's preparation for swift capture of West Point, as soon as André and Arnold had made final arrangements for the betrayal.

Another hint of treason, apparently Arnold's, is supposed to have come through a Negro, familiarly known as Black Sam, sometimes said to have been a tavern keeper on the Jersey shore, probably on Bergen Neck. Listening to the British officers who frequented his resort, Black Sam—whoever he was—heard enough to guess that there was a conspiracy of some kind under way in the Continental Army. He passed the word to Janetje Van Ripen (Mrs. Nicholas Tuers), who had come on a marketing trip and whom Sam knew for a stanch patriot. Janetje informed her brother, who took the information to a local American headquarters, refusing a proffered cash reward because he "did not serve his country for money." Important as it was, the intelligence does not seem to have been passed on to General Washington or Major Tallmadge, who might have used it.

The story is obscure. Samuel Fraunces, a West Indian mulatto, was also called Black Sam, and the whole incident may have taken place at Fraunces's Tavern, on Manhattan, especially as Congress after the war made the tavern keeper special grants for services to American prisoners of war and "other acts," carefully unspecified. The treason exposed may not have been Arnold's; but the incident appears to have been one more narrow escape for that unusually lucky scoundrel.

André had dangerously exposed himself before starting, though knowledge of his indiscretion—if it reached the Americans at all—came too late to expose Arnold. If such a warning ever arrived, it was given by the Culpers and passed through Major Tallmadge's hands. There is, therefore, a remote chance that these bits of espionage, mostly due to eavesdropping by patriotic private individuals, provided some of the facts Tallmadge always refused to talk about.

Culper, Jr., had a strong personal liking for Major André, whom he had known while André was busy directing British espionage from the adjutant general's office and Culper, Jr., was just as busy spying for the Americans. It is plain from what Culper, Jr., says, that they had met in a very casual, social way, perhaps at Townsend's father's home, Raynham Hall, at Oyster Bay—where André was for a time quartered—or at Rivington's coffeehouse on Manhattan.

It was mere bad luck that led André to the home of the father of the principal American spy operating against André's own intelligence service. Sally Townsend, the sister of Culper, Jr., was an attractive girl and Major John André delighted in feminine society. Then, too, André's friend, Lieutenant Colonel Simcoe, had lodgings in the Townsend house. Though it is hardly possible to prove that Culper, Jr., took advantage of this incredibly favorable situation for American espionage, it is utterly impossible to imagine that he didn't.

On Valentine's Day, 1779, Simcoe sent Sally Townsend a rhymed valentine with the lines (ironic, in view of what happened a little later):

> Thou knowest what powerful magic lies
> Within the round of Sarah's eyes.

Sarah Townsend's eyes were wide open all the time, but Simcoe never guessed what kind of magic there was in them.

Sally is said to have become curious when she saw a supposed Whig patriot slip into the Townsend kitchen and drop a letter into a little-used cupboard. Saying nothing whatever, Sally kept both beautiful eyes on that cupboard. Presently André, a guest of the Townsends that evening, came into the kitchen—not so odd a thing in eighteenth-century American social life as it would be today—took the letter without reading it, then suddenly feigned interest in a plate of hot doughnuts.

Shamelessly patriotic as Lydia Darragh, Sally eavesdropped outside Simcoe's room after André had entered it. She was always sure she heard the words "West Point," repeated more than once. She is said to have persuaded Captain Daniel Youngs, of the British Army, to carry a letter to her brother in New York, ostensibly asking for tea. It is said to have been in Tallmadge's hands next morning. If this tale is true—it is badly documented—it is no wonder Major Tallmadge blazed with suspicion when he heard "John Anderson" had been captured.

One other American unquestionably did hear André discuss his mission before he started, but so obscurely that the snatch of overheard chat meant nothing until the whole story came out. In 1780, only a little while after Andre's execution, a pamphlet appeared, with the proceedings of the board of general officers who sentenced him to death. A copy, owned by the Reverend Dr. Samuel Buell, minister at East Hampton during the Revolution, was inherited by his grandson, John Lyon Gardiner, who had often seen André at the home of Colonel Abraham Gardiner. On a blank page of the proceedings, the grandson told his story:

Toward the end of August, 1780, a month before the climax, Sir Henry Clinton, attended by André, came to Gardiner's. A woman who lived there, passing through a room, caught a few words. She heard "Major André say that if he must go he would, but he did not expect ever to return." This cannot be very accurate, since André would have been in no special danger on his fatal journey if he had obeyed Clinton's orders not to take off his uniform and not to enter the American lines. Some reference to the mission was audible; that is about all one can accept as fact.

The Gardiner family had more definite information, however. Presently a woman, "perhaps mistress to Col: Simcoe," remarked to Mrs. Gardiner, "One of your forts is to be delivered up to us soon by one of your Generals." She added that it was not New London. This vital information was never reported, though Mrs. Gardiner had one perfect chance to warn General Washington. Soon after she received the information she learned that "Major J: Davi∫s of the American Army was privately in town at M. Huntings." "Major J: Davi∫s" was probably not a major at all, but Joshua Davis, one of Caleb Brewster's whaleboat men, who had been visiting Long Island secretly since 1776. His trips into enemy territory were very private indeed; but Mrs. Gardiner managed to have a talk with him, to inquire about her son, a Continental Army surgeon. In her maternal solicitude, she quite forgot about the imperiled fort. "She was on the point of mentioning to Major Davi∫s what the woman told her but by some means or other did not— She thought it might be only the woman's foolish talk." If Tallmadge had had any information as definite as that, he could have convinced even Jameson. Instead, the tale lingered as an unknown note in an obscure pamphlet in a private library, till recent years.

Two other curious human touches have remained unnoticed. Sergeant Enoch Crosby, who had spied for John Jay and Nathaniel Sackett in Westchester, could not go to see André's execution because he was sergeant of the guard that day. Others in his company went to behold the ghastly spectacle.

Both the Culpers, whom André might have hanged if he had caught them, sent messages to General Washington, deploring André's death. Culper, Jr., wrote: "I never felt more sensibly for the death of a person whom I knew only by sight and had heard converse, than I did for Major André. He was a most amiable character." Culper, Sr., wrote: "I am sorry for the death of Major André, but better so than to lose the post."

The complex plots and counterplots of General Samuel H. Parsons and William Heron, both of Redding, Connecticut, are a dreadful example of the tangled web that military intelligence agents weave when several of them practise to deceive each other, on both sides, in several ways, and all at the same time. This episode, too, remained a complete secret for a hundred years—until 1882, when Dr. Thomas Emmett brought to America two manuscript volumes of Private Intelligence of Sir Henry

Clinton, now in the New York Public Library. These revealed a tale of treason nearly as bad as Arnold's. The documents show, beyond peradventure, that Heron—also known as Hiram the Spy—was regularly supplying secret official information to Major Oliver DeLancey, who, after André's capture, dealt with intelligence for Sir Henry Clinton. They also show that much of this information came through General Parsons.

British secret papers contain a long series of intelligence reports from Heron, who, as a member of the Connecticut State Assembly, was able to reveal secret information sent to that body by the Continental Congress, besides strictly military information given him—probably through mistaken confidence —by General Parsons, and other intelligence he could pick up for himself. Heron reported to Clinton's headquarters in person, when he could—often openly, under a flag of truce. If his reports had to be sent by courier, he protected himself, not by the usual single letter-drop, but by two. He himself left reports with one intermediary. From this point a courier took them to another. From the second intermediary they were picked up by a British courier.

General Parsons may have been deceived because Heron was, at the same time, undoubtedly spying for the Americans. On his rather frequent personal visits to New York, he had no trouble gathering intelligence of the British forces, which he promptly turned over to General Parsons, who relayed it to General Washington.

It is not hard to classify Heron. The crafty fellow was plainly a traitor to both sides, the usual self-interested double agent. If either side had discovered what he was really doing, either side would cheerfully have hanged him; but neither British nor Americans ever so much as suspected this shrewd and careful rascal. When the Americans won at last, he was able to continue his rôle as a prominent Connecticut citizen, a worthy and patriotic legislator, ever laboring for the public good—an illusory image of the man which remained wholly undisturbed until Clinton's intelligence papers appeared in 1882.

"Hiram's" reports at first sight seem to implicate General Parsons, whose war record is, in all other respects, that of an ardent and able patriot. There is no doubt that Sir Henry Clinton in 1781 had high hopes of finding in Parsons a second Arnold, and of finding as many additional Arnolds as he could. Neither is there any doubt that Parsons did let slip to Heron (who triumphantly sent it straight on to Sir Henry) information about the Continental Army and its commander's plans, which *seemed* important at the time. On the other hand, there are several weighty arguments for Parsons's loyalty. The weightiest is the plain fact that the only evidence against him is in Heron's reports to the British. No man can be condemned on the statements of that double-barreled rogue, who had every reason to lie to his British employers about his personal influence with a senior American general officer. It is also possible that Parsons was deliberately planting false or deceptive information; and it is clear that he kept much important intelligence inviolably secret. He thought Heron a valuable American agent and, in a letter to Washington, in 1782 listed the information Heron had supplied, praising his character and ability. Everything in Parsons's own record—except the secret, boastful and dubious reports of the double-dealing spy—points to stalwart and unswerving loyalty to the United States.

About another successful American traitor, there is no such doubt. Samuel Wallis, a wealthy and respectable Philadelphia merchant—whose summer home at Muncy, Pennsylvania, on the West Branch of the Susquehanna, became an important British intelligence center—concealed his treason quite as successfully as Heron and quite as long. André's ironic code name for Wallis's house was "Peter"—Peter, too, denied his allegiance. Like Heron, Wallis was never suspected until the Clinton papers became available.

In some way Arnold discovered that Wallis was a British agent. Perhaps the two rogues were brought together by the British secret agent, Joseph Stansbury, a Philadelphia dealer in glassware, china and crockery, and also a secret courier for André. A surviving document shows that Wallis had known Stansbury for years, since he had been buying bottles, china and stone quart jugs from him as early as March 19, 1776. (There was, however, nothing suspicious in that. General Washington bought cut-glass vinegar cruets and salt cellars from Stansbury only a few days later.)

Arnold—though quite without justification—soon became suspicious. How could he be sure the courier was really delivering the messages Arnold gave him? The British were not responding as Arnold had expected. Stansbury brought back only oral messages. Was he just making them up?

To find out, Arnold sent Wallis as a second secret emissary. To André he wrote, deploring the possible treachery of Stansbury and some other courier, who cannot be identified. He feared "the persons we have employed have been deceiving us." By this time Arnold was involved in such a tangle of deceit that he could not trust Wallis, either—the man he had sent to check up on another man he did not trust! He urged André to have Sir Henry Clinton personally threaten Wallis with British "resentment in case he abuses the confidence placed in him."

Samuel Wallis had been a rather desultory British secret agent long before this. Early in the war, he had been, in some unknown way, "extremely useful to General Howe"; and he returned eagerly to British espionage when he learned of General John Sullivan's projected march into the New York wilderness, against the Iroquois.

General Washington had decided to send Sullivan out to ravage the Iroquois towns because the Indian and Tory massacres at Wyoming and Cherry Valley, in July and November, 1778, had left no choice but retaliation. To keep the Pennsylvania frontier secure in his rear, the commander-in-chief had to knock the Senecas and other hostile Iroquois out of the war entirely, without injuring friendly Iroquois, like the Oneidas. By the early part of 1779, General Sullivan was deep in preparations for an advance up the North Branch of the Susquehanna and thence westward across New York state.

While these preparations were under way, Wallis, at Muncy, on the river's West Branch, was in a perfect position to spy on Sullivan. For years, he had spent his summers in the Susquehanna frontier country, where he was active in land deals; and he was well acquainted with Iroquois New York, especially

the western New York territory of the hostile Senecas. He was
—as Arnold's friend, Joseph Stansbury, correctly told Sir Henry
—"better acquainted with the Indian country than almost any
other person." Wallis had begun trading up the West Branch
of the Susquehanna and speculating in lands there very early.
By 1769 he had built his summer home, a superb example of
the early Pennsylvania stone house, which still stands near
Muncy. As early as 1774, he had made a surveying trip to the
Pennsylvania-New York border and was busy bringing in surveyors and dealing in lands all through the war.

Fortunately for the American cause, however, Wallis was not
so well acquainted with the Indian country into which Sullivan
would march as was another and more loyal Pennsylvanian—
who, by March, 1779, had completed a secret visit to the Indian
country, on orders from General Washington, himself. This
was Gershom Hicks, the son of pioneer parents living at Water
Street, a village in Blair County, Pennsylvania. Captured with
his family in boyhood, he had lived six or seven years among
the Indians, had learned the Delaware language, and had gained
some knowledge of the closely related Shawnee. Returning to
the settlements and becoming "servant" to an Indian trader,
he had again been captured, this time by Shawnees, in Ohio.
Escaping, he reached Fort Pitt in April, 1764, only to find that
British officers there thought he was spying for the Indians.
General Gage said in so many words he would like to see him
hanged; but Hicks managed to clear himself and went back
into land dealing, buying three hundred acres in Bedford
County, Pennsylvania, from Samuel Wallis, in 1773.

When the Revolution broke out, Gershom Hicks served in
the Pennsylvania Militia and, in view of his special qualifications, was assigned to special duty as scout and interpreter.
Early in 1779, he was absent from his unit "on command," by
order of General Washington himself, and he went into the
Iroquois country about March 1, or earlier.

Sometime in that same month, he appears as a mysterious
figure coming down the North Branch of the Susquehanna
from the Iroquois country. A letter from Northumberland,
Pennsylvania, in March, 1779, but without any indication of

the exact date, contains orders from Colonel William Patterson, commanding at Fort Augusta (Sunbury, Pennsylvania), to Colonel Zebulon Butler, commanding at Fort Wyoming (Wilkes-Barre, Pennsylvania).

> Mr. Lemmon goes to your post, to wait the return, and take into his care Gershom Hicks, who is not to be examined or searched until he goes before his Excellency Gen. Washington. I inclose you his Excellency's letter. Be careful that your people, who are out on duty, or fatigue, receive Hicks, who may appear painted, and in a canoe. His regimentals [i.e., uniform] I have sent by Mr. Lemmon.

Arrangements to send him straight to Washington were evidently made about the last week in March, for on March 25, 1779, a pass was issued: "This will serve as a passport for Gershom Hicks who may appear in Indian Dress, and the officer commanding will receive him. W. Patterson."

General Edward Hand, on March 29, reported that Hicks had journeyed "from Wyalusing to Niagara & Back"—that is, he had crossed New York from east to west. Hand's complaint that he "affects total Ignorance of the country" may mean only that Hicks was a discreet secret agent, who meant to report directly to the commander-in-chief. He did, however, talk more freely to Colonel William Patterson, in Cumberland County, Pennsylvania, about Indians and British troops at Chemung, just over the New York border, since Patterson was in charge of his secret mission. Hicks had been able to penetrate into Indian country, entirely undiscovered, until he was within half a mile of Chemung; and thereafter he had no trouble in talking openly with the enemy. His most important discovery was that the British had no supplies or munitions at Chemung and that a small fort, near it, was unoccupied. In other words, the enemy had no advanced base from which to attack Sullivan early in his march.

Colonel Patterson paid Hicks $300 and expenses, meantime placing Mrs. Hicks and the children with his own family, so as "to have him under my Eye ready for the same services." But General Washington objected to expenses "as large as in

Hicks's case"—and that seems to have ended Gershom Hicks's career in espionage.

His exploit is of interest because it shows General Washington extending his intelligence net into Indian country; because it was carried out, undetected, beneath the very nose of the British spy, Samuel Wallis, operating at that very time along the other branch of the Susquehanna; and because, when the war was over, the American spy, Hicks, went to work for the British spy, Wallis!

Gershom Hicks was only one of several American spies expected to emerge from the Iroquois country by way of the North Branch of the Susquehanna. On March 1, General Washington had given Colonel Zebulon Butler, at Wyoming, orders: "Persons presenting themselves at your post with passports signed by Colonel William Patterson, are to be suffered to pass and repass without interruption, and without search of their Canoes or baggage; they are farther to be supplied with five days provision on their applying for it; and you will afford them any other assistance their circumstances may require."

The same orders were sent to Fort Augusta (Sunbury, Pennsylvania) and to Fort Willis (location now unknown). General Philip Schuyler received constant intelligence from a few friendly Indian and French spies in Central New York, through a Negro courier. Obviously the Americans had sent several additional spies into the Iroquois country; but there is nothing to indicate that any of them, except Gershom Hicks, lived to tell the tale.

Just as this bold fellow was emerging from the wilderness, a ring of British spies within the American armed forces discovered General Washington's plans for Sullivan's expedition —discovered them, indeed, before the general had had a chance to complete them. From their home in Pennsylvania, Colonel William Rankin, of the Northumberland County Militia; one of his captains; and one other militia colonel had for some time been secretly in touch with Sir Henry Clinton, through the Germantown (Pennsylvania) Tory printer, Christopher Saur, now a refugee in New York. Rankin's brother-in-law, Andrew Fürstner, who had been a British secret agent for two years or more, carried the conspirators' reports to New York, where Saur turned them over to Clinton. In March, 1779, this spy ring sent the British word: "It is in Contemplation to send some Continental troops against Col. [John] Butler"—the chief leader of Indian guerrillas in New York state. The plotters hoped to put one of their Tory group in command of the militia that was to accompany Sullivan!

Under such circumstances, the British needed Wallis's knowledge of northern Pennsylvania and New York badly; and in May, 1779, he offered to resume his services as a secret agent. He would now be specially valuable to the enemy, because his countrymen, by this time, trusted him completely. In 1777, he had "taken & submitted the affirmation of Allegiance and Fidelity" to the patriot cause; and the official pass issued to this British spy describes him as "Friendly to the Liberty of America." People told him everything. A friend in Sunbury wrote him about the Sullivan expedition June 13, 1779. By July, Joseph Stansbury was promising, on Wallis's behalf, that if Clinton wanted "a perfect knowledge of everything relating to Sullivan's army," Wallis would send "exact accounts thereof every week or fortnight."

Wallis proposed to have an unnamed friend of his own volunteer in Sullivan's army, so that, from within Sullivan's own ranks, this secret informant could send back intelligence to Wallis, who, through Stansbury, would pass it on to André. This immediately interested intelligence officers at Clinton's headquarters, who were so deeply concerned over Sullivan's doings that, even after he had returned to the Susquehanna, they sent one of their star secret agents, the redoubtable James Moody himself, to ferret out fuller information—perhaps as a check on the double-dealing Wallis.

Wallis's most impudent accomplishment was supplying the Americans with a map of the Indian country, deliberately made incorrect, at the same time promising Sir Henry Clinton "a corrected copy of this drawing."

"Intelligence concerning Sullivan will be acceptable and the drawing we are anxious to receive," replied Major André, eagerly.

So far as this falsified map was concerned, the Americans had unconsciously played directly into Wallis's hands. In February, 1779, General Washington had asked Joseph Reed, president of Pennsylvania, formerly one of his own staff officers, to get maps for Sullivan's use. Reed, aware of Wallis's knowledge of the country but quite unaware of what the man was really doing, turned naturally to this respected Philadelphia merchant and asked the British spy to make the Americans "a drawing of the country and to assist them in their plan of an Indian expedition."

Before long, the secret courier, Joseph Stansbury, was reporting at British headquarters that Wallis had already drawn the map (incorrectly) and sent it to General Washington. Sullivan's expedition, Stansbury told the British, would be "formed on it." Fortunately, Sullivan's war plans were really formed on a great deal of other information, which General Washington had himself helped assemble by sending an extremely searching questionnaire to the three generals best acquainted with the area and probably to various others who might know the country. Wallis, with the very worst intentions, never did the damage he had hoped.

He must have carried out his scheme, though there is no proof of it in surviving documents. His correct map is not among Sir Henry Clinton's voluminous papers; his false map is not among General Washington's or General Sullivan's papers; but there are reports in the Clinton papers from a spy, who may have been the "volunteer" Wallis hoped to infiltrate among Sullivan's troops. There are only two of these, both obviously sent by a British agent accompanying the expedition. Wallis can hardly have been responsible for other information about Sullivan's march, which the British secured through a Brunswick dragoon, who had deserted from the German to the American forces and then deserted again—this time to the British.

There was one spy scare during the expedition; and Sullivan ordered an investigation into the suspected presence of a British agent named John Brown; but nothing further is known of this episode.

The British used Wallis in another scheme, which, fortunately for America, was never carried out. The enemy contemplated for some time another Indian raid into Pennsylvania—like that at Wyoming, but on a larger scale—which was to be supported by a formidable rising of armed Tories in Pennsylvania and adjoining states. Wallis's summer home at Muncy was to be an intelligence center for communication with Joseph Brant, the Mohawk chief, and his Indians. This was meant as a counter to Sullivan's expedition, for a friend wrote Wallis in June, 1779, that Sullivan's troops could not succeed, as Indians were "coming down to cut off the supplys before they reach Wyoming."

Though Brant's raid never took place, plans for it went so far that André had an unknown Tory leader standing by, ready to act, as soon as a prearranged password was sent to Wallis's house. Then, said André, the Tories must get in touch with Brant, or whoever else commanded the Indians at the moment. The Tories were to "give him information and when he meditates a blow second him by a sudden meeting of loyalists at a particular place which you may concert, to join and strike with him, or by intercepting convoys, burning magazines, spiking cannon, breaking down bridges, or otherwise as you shall see expedient."

André's cheerful little scheme may have been related to still another British plot, which likewise failed. This was to be a Tory rising in Pennsylvania, Delaware and Maryland, which would destroy the American arsenal at Carlisle, Pennsylvania, and then seize control of large areas in the three states, with the help of Colonel John Butler, Tory commander at the Wyoming Massacre. This scheme was being planned by Colonel William Rankin, supposedly a patriot officer. In the end, it came to nothing; and Wallis's own later espionage, though it went on for several years more, led to no striking results. He did, however, continue to do business for Benedict Arnold long after the treason was discovered. The only document among his own personal papers that connects him with the treason is Peggy Arnold's receipt for money collected within the American lines. It might have hanged him; but it was a business record; and, for Samuel Wallis, business was always business.

XXI

★ ★ ★

★

The Mysterious Adventure of Sergeant Major Champe

THE PERSONAL BITTERNESS of General Washington toward the traitor Arnold was without parallel in the life of that magnanimous man. Though the commander-in-chief had to approve many death sentences, Arnold was the only man he ever really *wanted* to hang. So savage was his resentment that Lafayette, marching south against Arnold's Tories, carried positive orders: the traitor, if captured, would go instantly to the gallows.

Though General Washington could not formally demand that the British return Arnold—who, in their view, as a rebel returning to his allegiance, was entitled to protection—at least three unofficial hints were given Clinton that André, his warm personal friend, would be spared, if Arnold was handed over. It is impossible to tell whether Washington, who pitied André, secretly instigated these offers or whether they were made on the initiative of tactful subordinates who guessed the private wishes of their chief. When the enemy sent representatives to confer under a flag of truce, General Nathanael Greene hinted to General James Robertson how André might be saved. But the British officer answered only "with a look." Later, the

British found, slipped in among the papers given them, the same proposal, written in a hand that may be Alexander Hamilton's and signed with initials that may be either "AB" or possibly "AH."

At about the same time, a third unofficial suggestion was quietly passed on by Captain Aaron Ogden, a New Jersey officer. Ogden received orders, not from Washington, but from Lafayette, to enter the British post at Paulus Hook (Jersey City) under flag of truce, arranging the time of his arrival so that he could spend the night with the British. He was instructed not to try to take the enemy's commander aside (that might be noticeable), but to seize any chance for private conversation that might naturally arise.

Should such an opportunity come, the captain was to promise André's release if Sir Henry Clinton would allow Washington to lay hands on Arnold. The story, as Ogden set it down long afterward, implies that Clinton was not being asked to surrender the traitor—merely to connive at his capture.

The American was hospitably received at the British post, where he dined and was offered a bed for the night. Sitting next to the post commander, as guest of the British mess, he found it easy to give him the message. The redcoat rose at once, left the table, and set out for New York City. Within two hours he was back, with word from Sir Henry himself: "A deserter was never given up." Captain Ogden was told that a horse would be ready to take him back to his own lines in the morning. He spent a quiet night with the enemy and, when morning came, departed.

Whoever may have been responsible for Ogden's mission, General Washington, if he knew of it, can have had but slight hope of its success. Another effort would have to be made.

When the general, after the appalling revelation at West Point, returned to headquarters at Tappan, he sent for Light Horse Harry Lee, father of the great Confederate. Though this was only a few days after André's arrest, probably about September 26, 1780, Washington may already have received the written plan for recapturing Arnold, which Lee drew up without dating it, and which is now among the Washington papers.

Lee found the commander-in-chief deep in paper work, was offered a seat, handed a bundle of documents, and told to read them. They showed that another American major general, "whose name was not concealed," was certainly as guilty as Arnold himself. The suspected general—though Lee does not say so—was Arthur St. Clair. The charge against him is now known to be false, though the enemy had been able to place a treacherous junior officer as a spy on his staff. This is known because, on May 13, 1780, a British spy in Philadelphia wrote Clinton that he had "settled matters" with an American officer who would soon be joining St. Clair's staff. Just about the time of Lee's interview with Washington, or perhaps a little later, came an alarming report from the spy, John Vanderhoven, in New York, which seemed to confirm suspicion of the general himself. Vanderhoven had learned that there was another "cut-throat general" in the American Army.

Lee protested. St. Clair was a man of unblemished record, who had always seemed flawlessly loyal.

Washington pointed out, bitterly, that "the same suggestion applied to no officer more forcibly than a few days ago it would have done to General Arnold." Then he explained his dual plan: he wanted St. Clair either cleared or arrested. He wanted to save André and he wanted to hang Arnold. To do either, he would have to kidnap Arnold first; and to kidnap Arnold would require some delicate plotting.

"While my emissary is engaged in preparing means for the seizure of Arnold, the guilt of others can be traced; and the timely delivery of Arnold to me, will possibly put it into my power to restore the amiable and unfortunate André to his friends."

Then a few specific instructions:

Arnold was "not to be hurt," above all, not killed. General Washington felt so strongly about this that he gave Lee definite orders "that he be permitted to escape if to be prevented only by killing him, as his public punishment is the sole object in view."

With due respect, the young major—he was only twenty-four —pointed out to his general certain difficulties. Such a task "required a combination of qualities not easily to be found unless in a commissioned officer"; yet to ask an officer to desert was quite impossible. His legion had, however, a sergeant major "in all respects qualified for the delicate and adventurous project." He was a good man (else he would never have become a sergeant major under Light Horse Harry), "yet it was very probable that the same difficulty would occur in his breast, to remove which would not be easy."

Who was the man?

Sergeant Major John Champe, a Virginian from Loudon County, about twenty-three or twenty-four.

What was he like?

"Rather above the common size—" said Lee, "full of bone and muscle; with a saturnine countenance, grave, thoughtful and taciturn—of tried courage and inflexible perseverance."

"The very man for the business!" said the general. If Champe showed scruples, tell him that "going to the enemy by the instigation and at the request of his officer, was not desertion, although it appeared to be so." Tell this to the sergeant major "as coming from him," said the general, dismissing his major with written instructions, two letters for Champe to deliver to secret agents in New York, and cash for expenses.

Back with his cavalry, Light Horse Harry sent for his sergeant major.

"What could not but be highly pleasing," his commanding officer told Champe, "he would be the instrument of saving the life of Major André"—who, from the first, had won the hearts of the men who soon would hang him. Otherwise, André would shortly be brought before a court, "the decision of which could not be doubted."

No doubt, in the first stages of the plot, one motive was to save André; but the British intelligence records show that Champe did not reach Manhattan until three weeks after the execution, which Washington felt had to be carried out promptly.

Champe, Major Lee went on, must also consider the suspicion now resting on an American general. "He would bring to light new guilt, or he would relieve innocence (as was most probable) from distrust; quieting the torturing suspicions which now harrowed the mind of Washington." Would John Champe undertake it? "Champe listened with deep attention, and with a highly-excited countenance; the perturbations of his breast not being hid even by his dark visage."

Champe was "charmed with the plan." Besides, "no soldier exceeded him in respect and affection for the commander-in-chief." But, as his commander had expected, the idea of posing as a deserter was too much. He demurred at "the ignominy of desertion, to be followed by the hypocrisy of enlisting with the enemy." Skillfully, Lee argued these doubts away. There was no reason to feel such scruples. The major "considered himself and corps highly honored by the general's call upon him for a soldier capable and willing to execute a project so tempting to the brave." In the end, Champe consented.

When he did, Major Lee gave him General Washington's written instructions. Since it would not be safe to carry such papers into the enemy's country, Champe "took notes so disguised as to be understood only by himself." Lee then gave him the two letters he had received from Washington, both with false addresses, so that, in case Champe was caught, the secret agents to whom they were addressed would still be safe. He reiterated one other point emphasized by the commander-in-chief: "forbearing to kill Arnold in any condition of things."

The next step was to arrange the desertion, and in this Major Lee spent a good deal of time. As he had long been in touch with the secret service, he knew a man in Newark—perhaps Caleb Bruen—who, though a loyal American, had "connexions with the enemy" that would help Champe. Lee promised him one hundred guineas, five hundred acres of land and three Negroes, if he would open a line of communication between Manhattan and Newark and would be ready in Bergen Woods when the sergeant brought the kidnaped traitor across the Hudson. Champe had orders to stay at his post, "however unfavorable the prospects may appear at first." To make sure everything was arranged, Lee himself made a trip to Newark the day before the "deserter" was to flee.

Now the actual flight had to be planned. It would be difficult for Champe to get away unless Lee took several officers into his confidence, and he was determined "that no third person be admitted into the virtuous conspiracy, as two appear to me to be adequate to the execution of it." The cavalry camp had the usual interior guards and outguards. Beyond his lines, American infantry and cavalry patrols were always alert. Guerrillas swarmed through the country, almost to Paulus Hook, where Champe expected to cross to Staten Island. He would have to stage-manage his own escape. Lee could give no help, lest he appear to be "privy to the desertion, which opinion getting to the enemy would involve the life of Sergeant Champe." The thing had to appear completely genuine. Champe would have to take the same chances as a real deserter.

Pocketing three guineas—it would not do to have too much money, if the British searched him—Champe asked his commander to hold back pursuit as long as possible. To get a fair start, he would need time, since he would have to "zigzag in order to avoid the patrols."

Champe went off to get his horse, cloak, "valise" (probably a saddlebag), and the legion's orderly book—the manuscript record of orders then kept in every headquarters. It would look well for a deserting sergeant major to bring along official papers. "He drew his horse from the picket, and mounting him put himself upon fortune."

Lee tried to get some sleep. "Useless attempt!" he notes.

Within half an hour, an agitated officer of the day was at his commander's quarters. By sheer misfortune, Champe, almost at the start, had encountered one of those far too eager beavers, loyal, alert and zealous, who make so much trouble for their own intelligence services. One of the men in a patrol had met a suspicious-looking American dragoon, "who, being challenged, put spur to his horse and escaped, though instantly pursued."

Light Horse Harry could have wished his command a little less efficient, for one night at least. But the only thing he could do was to assume the role of the bumbling, fussy, obstructive kind of commander, for the more he entangled the pursuit in red tape, the better for Champe. Major Lee began by pretending to resent the interruption. He was "extremely fatigued." Besides, he did not quite understand what it was all about. When he could not pretend to misunderstand any longer, Major Lee began to pretend doubt of the whole story. How could the man in the patrol be sure he had really seen a dragoon?

"Who can the fellow that was pursued be?" yawned the major. "A countryman, probably."

Captain Carnes must have stared in astonishment at his superior. This was not the usually keen and decisive Light Horse Harry Lee. Still, the major might be only half awake.

"No," replied Carnes. "The patrol sufficiently distinguished him to know that he was a dragoon." In fact, he looked like one of Lee's own men. The major must have groaned inwardly at that. Captain Carnes was another far too eager beaver. And Champe was out there somewhere, in the night, desperately trying to keep his own army from ruining his mission.

Since all he could do now was to keep up his original pose, Light Horse Harry ridiculed the mere idea. One of his men desert? Impossible! His legion was a corps d'élite—only one desertion in the whole war. But none of this convinced the embarrassingly efficient officer of the day. An American dragoon really had been seen on his way to the enemy, Captain Carnes insisted. He was sure of his facts. Indeed, the alert Captain Carnes already had a squadron falling in. That was standard operating procedure—or, as they called it in the Revolution, "established usage on similar occasions."

The captain dashed off to see about that squadron. Briskly, he returned to report.

"The scoundrel was known, and was no less a person than the sergeant major, who had gone off with his horse, baggage, arms and orderly book." The orderly book might or might not convince the enemy—if Champe ever reached them—but it had already convinced Captain Carnes. His pursuit party was ready.

Still playing for time, Lee pooh-poohed the whole idea. Champe a deserter? Impossible! The sergeant major had an "excellent character." So fine a soldier could not possibly be a deserter. Perhaps he had "taken the liberty to leave camp with a view to personal pleasure." Very reprehensible, said the commanding officer. But after all, Captain, such an example was "too often set by the officers themselves."

While Carnes fumed in respectful silence, and Champe rode for his life, Major Henry Lee took a great deal of time delivering a long-winded and excessively dull lecture on discipline and morale. He deplored the laxness that had grown up in his command, "destructive as it was of discipline, opposed as it was to orders, and disastrous as it might prove to the corps in the course of service."

In the end, Lee had to order the pursuit; but not before he had put on another magnificent display of sheer incompetence. Who would command the chase? The duty lieutenant? Nonsense, fellow wouldn't do at all. The major wanted Cornet Middleton. Go get Cornet Middleton. Major Lee wanted Cornet Middleton in command.

It was far on in the night. Cornet Middleton would be sound asleep. He would have to get into uniform, get his arms, and have his horse brought from the picket line. A gratifying waste of time, when every moment counted. Not only might this waste of time be made to reach nearly half an hour; there was a further advantage in selecting Middleton. Lee was counting on "the tenderness of Middleton's disposition, which he hoped would lead to the protection of Champe."

Cornet Middleton, alas! to his commanding officer's intense disgust, was a third eager beaver. Within ten minutes, he was reporting at the commanding officer's quarters. Written orders took up a little more time. There was no need of them, but anything to delay that zealous young subaltern, Cornet Middleton.

Champe must not be harmed: "Bring him alive, that he may suffer in the presence of the army; but kill him if he resists." (Champe would surrender, if overtaken. He would hardly fight his own comrades, merely for stage effect.)

But, of course, it would take a few minutes to give the cornet oral, in addition to his written, orders. Lee fussed with endless trivial details. He told Middleton, at great length, in which direction he ought to pursue. He must "take care of the horse and accoutrements if recovered." The cornet must look out for the enemy—a fact of which any cavalry officer, operating between the lines is well enough aware! Finally the major dismissed him, hypocritically wishing him success—that took up a little more time.

Lee had fussed about so long that Champe now had an hour's start. Would it be enough? The major, "very unhappy," spent a sleepless night.

Rain, which had by this time begun to fall, made the situation worse. The hoofprints of Champe's horse showed plainly in the moist earth. Worse still, the prints were unmistakable, for the legion's horses, shod by its own farriers, had foreshoes with a special mark. This was meant to help Lee's troopers recognize one another's trails and was often very helpful—but not that night!

To enhance this comedy of well-intentioned errors, no other horseman happened to be traveling the road that Sergeant Major Champe had taken. His pursuers were delayed only a little during the night by dismounting to look for tracks, "the impression of which was an unerring guide." When dawn came, the pursuit quickened. There was still only one trail in the soft earth of the road.

As Cornet Middleton's detachment came over the crest of a hill at Three Pigeons, some miles north of Bergen, they saw their quarry, half a mile ahead. Champe saw his pursuers at the same instant.

Middleton decided to do something clever. Beyond Three Pigeons, a short cut ran through the woods to a bridge just below Bergen. The legion, whose troopers reconnoitered this part of New Jersey continually, knew the ground perfectly. The cornet detached a sergeant, via the short cut to the bridge. The sergeant would block the bridge. The cornet would chase Champe down the road. He would thus be "closed" between the two parties.

Sergeant Major Champe, however, knew all about the short cut, too, and guessed what Middleton would do. Instead of now trying to reach Paulus Hook, he rode through Bergen, straight for the Hudson, hoping for "rescue" by two armed

British galleys, lying in the river. By choosing "beaten streets" through the village, he broke his trail at last.

The cornet, seeing his error, deployed his men in the muddy roads beyond the village, picked up the trail, and again gave chase. Knowing now he would have to swim for it, Champe paused long enough to lash his "valise" to his shoulders, which brought the pursuit within two or three hundred yards.

The final scene of the desertion was most impressive. As he neared the river, Champe saw the galleys. Dismounting, he plunged through the marshes along the bank, and swam toward the little ships.

On the British craft there was a stir. A fugitive? Pursued by the greencoats of the rebel legion? Opening fire to drive off the rebels, the galleys sent off a boat to rescue the swimmer, who came aboard, dripping but triumphant, still with his "valise" and orderly book. He was soon on his way to New York with a letter from the naval commander, "stating the circumstances he had seen." No "escape" could have been more convincing. Captain Carnes and Cornet Middleton had helped more than they knew. Sergeant Major Champe received a warm welcome. There was no suspicion. A British naval officer had seen Champe all but killed in his praiseworthy effort to return to his allegiance and to serve his king.

At three that afternoon—the Virginian Lee says "in the evening"—Middleton rode back into the American camp. The troops, seeing Champe's horse, set up a shout: "The scoundrel was killed." Major Lee, shocked and grieved, emerged from his tent, reproaching himself "with the blood of the high-prized, faithful, and intrepid Champe." Then he saw the "looks of disappointment" of the crestfallen cornet and his troopers, and his heart leaped up. "Lee's joy was now as full as, the moment before, his torture had been excruciating."

"Everything had gone perfectly. However unconsciously, Cornet Middleton had been a big help. His spectacular pursuit under naval gunfire had accidentally added artistic verisimilitude to Champe's narrative, which the British might otherwise have found bald and unconvincing. Lee sent the good news on to General Washington, who was "sensibly affected." The

plot moved ahead like clockwork. Almost at once came a report,
written in a "disguised hand," from the imperturbable sergeant
major. He had made contact with one of the American intelligence men on Manhattan Island.

Immediately on entering New York, the sergeant major had
properly reported himself to a British officer, at the same time
presenting the letter describing his "rescue," which the captain
of the galley had given him. The moment the British discovered
that this unique deserter was sergeant major of the Partisan
Legion—"heretofore remarkable for their fidelity"—he was hurried to the acting adjutant general, who had replaced André,
who had by this time been hanged.

Under interrogation, Champe told a harrowing tale of dis-
affection among the Americans, "in consequence of Arnold's
example"—a nicely chosen word! Champe dwelt on the "dis-
contents which agitated the corps to which he had belonged."
Yes, indeed, sir, he was sure that "if the temper was properly
cherished, Washington's ranks would not only be greatly
thinned, but that some of his best corps would leave him."
The British interrogator must have beamed. Champe was
shrewdly telling him just what he wanted to hear.

Intelligence sent its prize straight to Sir Henry Clinton, who
was affability itself. Sir Henry had an eager, hour-long chat
with General Washington's newest spy. Champe is unique
among secret agents. Within twenty-four hours of his arrival,
he was at the enemy's headquarters glibly lying directly to the
enemy's commander-in-chief.

Sir Henry had a great many questions. How far did disaf-
fection go in the Continental Army? Could it be increased?
How? Did General Washington suspect any other generals,
"as concerned in Arnold's conspiracy." (Champe must have
pricked up his ears at the question. He had come to investigate
that little matter himself, though he could hardly tell Sir Henry
so.) What other officers were suspected?

Champe answered "warily." Some of the questions he found
"perplexing." But he was always very gloomy as to American
prospects. He could hardly suggest "proper measures to encourage desertion." But yes, General, it would certainly be

possible to increase it. All Sir Henry need do was commence "proper measures." These, General, "would certainly bring off hundreds of the American soldiers, including some of the best troops, horse as well as foot"—the same story Champe had told the staff interrogator.

Much gratified, Clinton presented Washington's spy with two guineas, an unconscious and very acceptable contribution to the limited American secret service funds. A spy who can deceive the enemy commander within twenty-four hours is good. A spy who can get the enemy commander to pay the bills is even better. Sir Henry ordered an aide to write a letter recommending Champe to the man he had come to kidnap. Sir Henry was doing all he could to help General Washington.

Somebody on the British staff made a careful note of Champe's "information." The paper is now in the Clements Library: "Jno. Champ Serj. Major in Major Lee's Corps formerly of London [Loudon] County, Virginia, deserted last thursday night [Oct. 19, 1780], from Pisaick falls New Jersey— Says Major Lee's Corps consists of 90 Horse fit for duty & about one hundred infantry—that the Marquis La Fayette's Light infantry were there also—that provision was very irregularly given out. some days there was none—that the ration of provision consisted of one pd. flour & Do. fresh Beef—says that the soldiery in Genl. declare they would much rather join & beat the French out of America than fight against British Soldiers."

Such is Light Horse Harry Lee's account of his sergeant major's "desertion," an account which must be accepted as in the main correct, since Lee, as Champe's commanding officer, had every opportunity to know the facts. It is quite clear, however, both from the Clinton papers and from Lee's own correspondence with Washington at the time, that Champe did not reach New York till the latter part of October, 1780, long after André had been hanged.

Saving André was, no doubt, a motive when the Arnold kidnaping was first plotted; but André himself spoiled everything by his hasty and needless confession of the truth, after which the Americans had no chance to drag out the trial, thus giving

Champe time to act. Washington, "deeming it improper to interpose any delay," ordered the sentence executed.

Champe had no difficulty finding Arnold, whom he met by chance in a New York street. Since the pretended deserter brought Sir Henry Clinton's letter with him, the genuine traitor felt no suspicion, but plunged into "numerous inquiries." Champe had to invent some dexterous falsehoods in talking with Arnold, who had been a senior officer of the Continental Army only a month before and was not easy to deceive. Champe, however, handled the turncoat so cleverly that he was at once offered his own rank of sergeant major in Arnold's new legion. Since it would not do to be too eager, Champe at first pretended a "wish to retire from war." He dared not risk capture, he explained. The rebels would certainly hang him. In real fact, Champe's main problem was to keep the British from detecting and hanging him, while he himself was making suitable preparations to hang the man to whom he was talking.

"Assuring the general, that should he change his mind, he would certainly accept his offer," Champe left Arnold and began arrangements to kidnap his new friend. Of the two American secret agents with whom he was to make contact, one was to investigate the supposed treason of a second American general; the other would mobilize enough additional American agents (by this time, New York was swarming with them) for the kidnaping.

Champe found "one of the two incogniti," at once—the man who had sent the information about treason among American officers. Told that General Washington wanted immediate verification, the spy promised to set to work at once. He also agreed to forward Champe's first reports to Major Lee. These reached the legion's camp through swift and secret channels.

However, it took Champe five days to find the other "confidant to whom only the attempts against Arnold was to be intrusted." This agent at once promised to secure "a proper associate." In the end, Champe had two assistant kidnapers.

The next step was to get as close to Arnold as possible. The prospective kidnaper needed "uninterrupted ingress and egress to the house which the general occupied." Champe went back to General Arnold. He had decided to join the legion after all. A report from the newly made British sergeant went to General Washington, through Major Lee. The secret agent whom Champe had first interviewed must have had access to the most closely guarded intelligence records of the British Army. He now reported that the rumor of "additional treason" by another major general seemed "groundless," that the "report took its rise in the enemy's camp, and that he hoped soon to clear up that matter satisfactorily." A few days later, Champe sent documents showing the accused general's innocence. Orders went to Champe. He would "prosecute with unrelaxed vigor the remaining objects of his instructions."

Champe continued, in modern criminal parlance, to "case the joint." As a member of the "American Legion" (Arnold's new troop unit), he now had "every opportunity he could wish, to attend to the habits of the general." He noted that his prospective victim habitually came home about midnight "and that previous to going to bed he always visited the garden." The motive for the visit—though eighteenth-century documents do not mention such things—was purely physiological. Arnold was not communing with his soul in the darkness; nor was he searching a guilty conscience. There was no indoor plumbing in those days.

Champe quietly knocked several palings off the fence around the garden, enough to let Arnold and his captors through. He stuck them back carefully, loose enough to be pulled off without noise, tight enough not to be noticeable.

He and the resident secret agent would seize Arnold in the dark garden at midnight, gagging him instantly. They would then drag him through unlighted streets, with Champe at one shoulder, his accomplice at the other, following "most unfrequented alleys and streets." If questioned, they would simply explain they had "a drunken soldier, whom they were conveying to the guardhouse." A second "associate," whom Champe's secret service friend had provided, would be waiting "with a boat prepared, at one of the wharves on the Hudson River." Once in the boat, Arnold could be carried, still gagged and bound, across the river, "there being no danger nor obstacle in passing to the Jersey shore." The Royal Navy's guard boats could be avoided in the darkness.

When Champe reported his preliminary arrangements, Washington approved them at once, again emphasizing that he wanted Arnold "brought to me alive." A week or more passed before Champe could report all was ready. He would seize the traitor on "the third subsequent night." Cavalry were to wait at Hoboken, where "he hoped to deliver Arnold."

The eager Lee himself led the cavalry detachment, "late in the evening." With them went three led horses, "one for Arnold, one for the sergeant, and the third for his associate"—who is still a man of mystery. Reaching Hoboken about midnight, Lee put his party under cover in a neighboring woods, while he and three men watched by the river. "Hour after hour passed, no boat approached." At dawn, Lee withdrew, "to inform the general of the disappointment, as mortifying as inexplicable." No word came through the secret communication line from Champe, indeed no direct messages came from him for months.

Anxiety as to the faithful fellow's personal safety was set at rest and the failure explained, when a few days later a message arrived—carefully unsigned but from a source easily recognized. A resident secret agent in New York reported that, on the date set for the kidnaping, Arnold had moved to new quarters, to be nearer the embarkation point of troops for his Virginia expedition. By January 2, 1781, the general received a spy's detailed report on the expedition.

Champe himself, ordered to embark with the rest of the American Legion, had spent the night set for his great exploit aboard a transport, which he was never able to leave till Arnold landed in Virginia. Once he was back in his native Virginia, he escaped as soon as he could—in a day or two, according to the Tory officer who was his company commander in the legion; not until Cornwallis reached Petersburg, according to Lee.

Making his way "high up into Virginia" and through "friendly districts" of North Carolina, he joined General Nathanael Greene's forces in pursuit of Lord Rawdon, on the Congaree River. Giving him a horse and money, Greene sent him on to General Washington. There was much surprise in the Partisan Legion when the troopers beheld the warm welcome Lee, now a lieutenant colonel, gave his erstwhile deserter.

Washington, fearing the enemy's vengeance if Champe should be captured, discharged him from the service entirely. A spy who has returned to his own lines cannot thereafter lawfully be executed. But the British had a perfect right to hang him for deserting Arnold!

Having failed to capture Arnold, the Americans tried three other kidnapings, all of which failed. Daring raiders under Washington's aide, Colonel David Humphreys, landed on Manhattan after dark on Christmas Day, 1780, hoping to kidnap both Sir Henry Clinton and General von Knyphausen, but the attempt could be carried no further. British secret agents, scandalized at the mere thought of such a thing, found out about it a month later.

In March, 1781, Major Allan McLane also attempted to kidnap Arnold—being especially eager to succeed where Lee, whom he hated, had failed. From an advanced American signal station on the James River, McLane had noticed that Arnold rode out to the shore of Chesapeake Bay every morning. He laid a plot to intercept him; but the untimely arrival of British warships, which anchored in the wrong place, saved Arnold, for the second time.

XXII

★ ★ ★

★

Mutiny

THE ENEMY's last opportunity to stir up treason in the American forces was the mutiny of the Pennsylvania line, on New Year's Day, 1781, and of the New Jersey line, three weeks later. After watching for signs of incipient mutiny for a long time, the British had been encouraged when a revolt in General Jedediah Huntington's Brigade, in Danbury, had appeared imminent, two years earlier. Their intelligence system was quick to note the first indications. The spy, Elihu Hall, who had left New London, January 5, 1779, had evidently paused in Danbury long enough to investigate discontent among the troops. Though the difficulties of secret travel in wartime had forced him to take a very roundabout route, he was able to give Clinton's staff full information of the approaching mutiny on January 13, together with data on American strength, troop dispositions and supply shortages. The mutiny broke out, just as the spy had predicted, a few days later; but General Putnam quelled it before the enemy could take any advantage of it.

The mutiny of the Pennsylvania line, almost exactly two years after this, was far more serious, for the men were both resolute and embittered. While there is no possible defense for mutiny, these troops, after long and loyal service, had good reason for discontent. First, they had been paid in worthless money. After that, for months, they had not been paid at all. Besides this, they were badly clothed and equipped; bedding was in such short supply that, in the bitterest winter weather, several men at once had to shiver under a single blanket. Finally, though the soldiers believed their enlistments—for three years or the duration—had expired, they were not allowed to go home. They knew they had served three years; they refused to believe that they were, nevertheless, bound to serve till peace was made. They were infuriated by seeing short-service men re-enlisting every few months and drawing a generous bounty each time they did so, while the three-year men went on serving—without bounty, pay or hope of discharge.

In the end, the irate Pennsylvanians took matters into their own hands. At eleven o'clock on the night of January 1, 1781, they started from their camp at Morristown, for Philadelphia, determined to appeal to the Continental Congress and the Pennsylvania Council, first "scouring" the parade ground with a blast of round shot and grape shot, then advancing with fixed bayonets, firing as they went. Their commander, Wayne, and his officers tried to stop them with swords and espontoons, killing one man and wounding others; but the column, commanded by sergeants only, moved sullenly ahead, leaving a dangerous gap in the American defenses, which might widen if other troops joined the mutiny.

So efficient was British espionage in New Jersey that Clinton received the news at the same moment as Washington himself —at noon, January 3, 1781, thirty-six hours after the mutiny began. One question was uppermost in each general's mind: Would the mutineers join the British? Neither commander realized that the men had no thought of disloyalty. All they wanted was to get their pay and go home.

The first British spy to bring the news to Clinton was Joseph Gould, a Jerseyman who happened to be traveling to New York on one of his regular secret journeys, when he saw the smoke of beacons rising and heard artillery firing. Though wondering what it meant, he nevertheless went on, since he had an intelligence report to deliver. On his way, he met a man—apparently not an agent, possibly an American deserter—who gave him the first news of a mutiny or "drunken frolic" in Wayne's camp; but he was delayed on Staten Island and could not reach Manhattan till next morning. Otherwise, Clinton would have had the news before Washington.

Clinton sent Gould straight back to New Jersey, to consult a resident secret agent, Andrew Gaultier, at Paulus Hook. Next day Gaultier supplied enough news to encourage Clinton, who at once prepared a force sufficient to protect the mutineers—if, as he hoped, they meant to desert to the British en masse. Six British regiments were given warning orders, and boats were made ready to move them. More news came pouring into New York from casual travelers through New Jersey, as well as from spies. British reports throughout January, 1781, are filled with the details.

Meantime, however, all that Clinton and his staff were doing was being closely observed by the jaundiced eye of an American secret agent, still unidentified, who just happened to be in New York City at the right moment. As soon as he had had time to see everything, this spy went back across the Hudson to report. Long before dawn, he was at Elizabeth, New Jersey, telling Lieutenant Colonel Jacob Crane all about British action on receiving the news: "Nothing could possibly have given them so much pleasure. Every preparation is making among them to come out and make a descent on New Jersey. I think South Amboy is their object. They expect those in mutiny will immediately join them. . . . If they come out it will be with considerable force, and may be expected within twenty-four hours from this time." Whoever this man was, he was a quick-thinking and intrepid agent and an accurate reporter, who was wrong only in his twenty-four-hour time limit—and he qualified that with an "if."

By five o'clock Lieutenant Colonel Crane was relaying the information, with admirable promptness and with an evaluation: "I have had the above person present and examined him." Lieutenant Colonel Crane knew the value of personal interrogation: "Therefore you may rely on the above intelligence." As confirmation, he added that it looked as if small British naval vessels were getting into position to "cover the embarkation of the rioters in case they should take a turn towards the [British] line."

By six o'clock in the evening of January 5, another officer, Colonel Moses Jacques, was reporting, also from Elizabeth, that the British troops had orders for Staten Island, a jump-off line for New Jersey. Colonel Jacques even had details. Each man was "to have 2 pairs of stockings, 2 shirts and blanket, with three days provisions." That meant Clinton was ready for a prolonged advance.

An American spy in close touch with the enemy's headquarters now reported that Clinton had secured more information from "a man who went over from Woodbridge." This second British agent had reported "that the new commandant of the Pennsylvania Line" (this meant the sergeant heading the mutinous troops) was willing to join the British—a completely erroneous piece of information.

All this early intelligence of British preparations was soon supplemented by the report of another American secret agent, who left Elizabeth for New York about eleven o'clock on the morning of January 5, and had no difficulty in entering the city about five o'clock that afternoon. This man was able to observe British troop movements in Manhattan personally.

"I never saw the British exert themselves so much in my life," he reported. Through torrents of rain, four or five thousand troops were embarking for Amboy. "I think they will be there tonight," said this secret observer, "with 20 field guns, 18 of the heavy and 54 engineers." Wearily the faithful fellow ended his report: "I am almost tired to death, or I would set out again immediately—been two nights without sleep, and last night so wet that I had not a dry thread on me."

While the spies of both sides buzzed about, Sir Henry slowly awoke to the disconcerting fact that the mutinous Pennsylvanians were not making the overtures to treason he had expected. A traitor in the American camp, spying for the British, known only as "Captain G," reported the mutiny, but he could find no signs at all that the mutineers meant to join the redcoats.

Since the Pennsylvanians had not approached the enemy, it was high time for the enemy to approach them. On January 4, Sir Henry prepared his offer. He would pardon the Pennsylvanians' rebellious offenses and himself provide the back pay due from Congress, in hard British gold, not paper—all this without "expectation of military service." Any mutineers who then wished to put on the king's red coat might do so. The others might do what all soldiers want to do—go home, with money in their pockets.

By evening, copies of the proclamation were rolled up in the thin lead sheets then used for packing tea. If the British emissaries were captured and searched, apparently harmless packages of this kind might be ignored—or so British intelligence hoped.

Six or seven agents were sent out with these papers. Two copies were given Gould to pass to Andrew Gaultier, who would send on from Paulus Hook a still-unknown secret courier of his own. A third copy was given to John Mason, Tory spy and guerrilla, whose raids had begun to approach plain robbery so closely that he had gone to jail in consequence. To get out, he volunteered "to serve his Excellency in the character of a spy." Just the man! If caught and hanged, he would be no great loss. Robert Macfarlan, perhaps an American double agent; Caleb Bruen, certainly an American double agent, though the enemy as yet had no suspicion of him; and probably one other, unnamed agent, went out independently.

Gould and Mason were put separately aboard H.M.S. *Neptune,* in Raritan Bay. Gould landed at Elizabeth Point next day, covered the short distance to Gaultier's rendezvous, and got rid of his dangerous papers at once. Mason's task was not so easy. He would have at least a two-day ride to Princeton, through country that he did not know at all well; and, since there would be American guards or patrols on all main roads, he would need guides who knew back roads and paths.

He did not reach *Neptune* till eight in the morning of January 5, and then waited aboardship, because it was unwise to go ashore till dusk was approaching. It was the kind of long, inactive wait in safety, just before the plunge into danger, that saps a secret agent's courage.

Unwilling to lose time, the captain of *Neptune* found two horses somewhere and had Mason and the nags put aboard the armed galley, *Philadelphia*, which rowed up the Raritan River in broad daylight. Its commander was to put the agent ashore, wherever he wished, that afternoon. The January dusk would be falling by the time he reached the American forces. John Rattoon, British resident at South Amboy, who had carried messages for Arnold, took him as far as the Delaware, where he handed him over to James Ogden of South River (Willettstown). Little is known of Ogden, save that he had just been married to a bride who was going to be a widow in a few days more, and that he was part of the group of agents organized by Rattoon.

The pair had an easy journey, reaching Princeton late Saturday night (January 6, 1781) or early Sunday morning (January 7). With no idea that the mutinous Pennsylvania line were still entirely loyal to the American cause, Mason walked boldly up to the first sentry he saw, asked for the commanding officer, and was sent to Nassau Hall where the "President of the Board of Sergeants" had set up his command post.

The colloquy between the mutineer and the spy was brief. What did the visitor want? He was an "express." Express from where? Elizabethtown. Were the British coming? No. The sergeant then asked again, "Where do you come from?" Boldly naming Sir Henry Clinton, the spy produced his message in its lead wrapping. The sergeant read it; instantly arrested Mason; found Ogden; arrested him, too; took them both before the board of Sergeants; then—at four o'clock in the morning—sent them to Wayne, as prisoners. Mason must be the only secret agent in all the sordid history of his trade, who ever marched into the enemy's headquarters and announced his errand.

Wayne returned the painfully astonished spies to the mutineers, urging the rebellious sergeants to send them to Joseph Reed, president of Pennsylvania.

Two more of Clinton's other emissaries reached Princeton

undetected, but—warned by the arrest of the first pair—were cautious. On Sunday night, January 7, a copy of Clinton's offer was found "among the sergeant's" (Wayne's version), or "before the door where the sergeants met" (Reed's version).

The men who dropped these papers were probably Robert Macfarlan and Caleb Bruen, who had met at Princeton, discovered they were on the same errand, and pushed on to Trenton together. Learning that Mason and Ogden had been captured, they hastily rid themselves of their messages, which Bruen, as an American spy in British service, wanted the Americans to find. In some way, he got secretly in touch with them, probably through Colonel Elias Dayton, who later informed Washington that Bruen "first gave notice of Sir Harry's correspondence with the Pennsylvania revolters."

Next day, Bruen had the misfortune to encounter an American officer who knew that the Newark spy lived near the British lines and was suspicious at finding him so near the mutinous Pennsylvanians. Nevertheless, though interrogated, he was able to escape across the Delaware, into Pennsylvania, knowing that Colonel Dayton could protect him so long as he was near the Americans. Bruen may have been the agent who simply went to Morristown and handed over Clinton's proposals to Major General Arthur St. Clair.

Meantime, British spies were scrambling out of New York in all directions, to see whether the mutiny was spreading and what the rest of the Continental Army was doing. Joseph Clark set out for Morristown, to ascertain what troop movements the American command was ordering. Lieutenant Thomas Okerson went within four miles of Trenton and brought back a full report of the mutiny. Isaac Siscoe and Ezekiel Yeomans went —though probably not together—to West Point. Yeomans returned with a harrowing tale of a barely suppressed mutiny there; of troops at Pompton, New Jersey, huzzahing for the mutineers; of "Washington much cast down" and afraid to move his troops lest there be more mutiny. On January 15, he was off again.

In early January, Uzal Woodruff went up the Hudson as far as Kingston. Listening while Colonel Elias Dayton read orders to the New Jersey Brigade, he noted their sullen mood—which soon led to a second mutiny—chatted with some Pennsylvania troops, and returned safely by a back road through Chatham —the only route the Americans had not yet blocked. Woodruff, too, was probably a double agent.

Without waiting to hear from all these spies, Sir Henry Clinton himself crossed to Staten Island about noon on Friday, January 5, to be with the troops detailed there. Major Oliver De Lancey, now adjutant general (and therefore chief intelligence officer), went with his commander, leaving two assistant intelligence officers, Major Frederick Mackenzie and Captain John Stapleton, to deal with the spies' reports, as they began to come in.

On the American side, Joseph Reed rode into New Jersey to deal with the Pennsylvania mutineers and met the captured spies, Mason and Ogden, under guard, on the road between Trenton and Maidenhead (Lawrenceville). Reed went with the prisoners to Lawrenceville, where he delivered them to guards from the Philadelphia Light Horse (the famous City Troop). After a mild dispute with the sergeants as to whose prisoners the spies really were, he was allowed to turn them over to a committee of Congress, on the Pennsylvania side of the Delaware.

As soon as the mutinous troops handed Mason and Ogden over for trial, a court-martial met at Summer Seat, the home of Thomas Barclay, at Morrisville, Pennsylvania, just opposite Trenton. The trial was brief, since Mason had foolishly admitted to Sergeant Williams that he was a British agent; and Ogden had been caught with him. Mason tried to save himself by "revealing" yet another plot to kidnap General Washington. The British spy, Thomas Ward, with "thirty more desperadoes," he said, meant to waylay the Continental commander, while riding with his usual small escort. The court, unimpressed, sentenced both defendants to hang next morning, January 10, 1781.

David H. Conyngham, of the Philadelphia Light Horse, had the unpleasant duty of sitting up all night with the condemned men, who begged for some ray of hope. Conyngham went to

Wayne, who replied that "nothing could save them." Since it was the only thing he could do, Conyngham borrowed a Bible and spent the night reading it to the prisoners—Mason devout, Ogden in paroxysms of terror. Toward morning, Mason got a little sleep.

When the hour came, the two were taken to Patrick Colvin's ferry house, on the Pennsylvania side of the Trenton Ferry, where stood a handy tree. Colvin lent a wagon and a Negro slave as executioner. When, at the last moment, it was discovered there was no rope, Lieutenant James Budden, of the Light Horse, saw a "rope collar" on a horse Conyngham's servant had just ridden out from Philadelphia. Someone unwound the rope, while the spies watched. Mason died with a warning to Washington: "The intelligence he mentioned the previous evening was literally true"—but Ward never kidnaped General Washington.

Unknown to the spectators—and, apparently, to the victims—two other spies, Macfarlan and Bruen, stood in the group that watched the hanging. When they passed the gallows again, a day later, the bodies still swung on their ropes, where they were left dangling for several days more, as object lessons to any other British agents who might be lingering about.

This espionage during the American mutinies was the end of Caleb Bruen's career as a double spy—and very nearly the end of Caleb Bruen. After the Pennsylvania mutiny had collapsed, another broke out among New Jersey troops, and a new mutiny among the Pennsylvanians at York, Pennsylvania; but these were quickly crushed. Clinton, still unsuspicious, sent Bruen out once more, to see what the New Jersey mutineers were doing, on February 8, 1781, and on the tenth the spy was back in New York, reporting that the mutiny was over. On one or both of his missions, Bruen had been given papers for delivery to the mutinous troops. What he really did with them is not hard to guess; and headquarters in New York was worried. British intelligence officers had some questions to ask. All dealings with the mutinous troops had gone awry. Where were the messages that had been given Bruen? He had not delivered them to the mutineers.

Unmasked at last, the American officer tried to persuade the enemy's interrogators that he had been forced to destroy the papers to keep the Americans from arresting him; but the suspicious Britons sent him to the "Sugar House" prison in New York. They might have hanged him; but Sir Henry Clinton was a humane man who did not like to hang anybody, even spies; and Colonel Elias Dayton managed to get the secret agent back to Newark as an exchanged prisoner the following year—very much the worse for wear, but, anyhow, still alive.

The enemy had every right to be indignant, for the loyalty of the mutineers—plus whatever it was that Captain Caleb Bruen really did with those papers!—had ended their last chance of promoting successful treason. Terror reigned among Clinton's agents, some of whom almost fled from their posts.

XXIII

Spies Before Yorktown

As THE SPRING of 1781 wore on into summer, a desperate battle of wits between British and American intelligence services began. The first half of the struggle was a distinct success for the British. Sir Henry Clinton's spies supplied a steady flow of intelligence that enabled his staff officers to analyze General Washington's intentions nearly as well as if they had themselves been in American headquarters. They knew, far in advance, that he meant to unite the French and American armies and attack New York. But, forgetting that a general may change his intentions, they overlooked entirely a second American capability: General Washington might also attack Cornwallis, in Virginia.

When Sir Henry Clinton had divided his army to keep forces both in New York City and in the southern states the year before (1780), he had hoped for early victories there. After the South had been won, he meant to close in on the Middle Atlantic states, aided by six thousand Tories, secretly armed and ready to rise, in Pennsylvania, Delaware and Maryland. After these victories, the stubbornly rebellious New Englanders could be isolated and easily crushed, especially if Arnold's betrayal of West Point gave the British control of the Hudson River line—as it very nearly did.

Throughout the spring and early summer of 1781, Washington's war plan was exactly what the British thought it was. He proposed to bring the French Army from Rhode Island to the Hudson, unite it with his own, call out militia reinforcements, collect boats, and assault Manhattan and Long Island, while a large part of the British forces were far away in the South. In June, 1781, instructions went out to American secret agents in New York to "inquire minutely" into British strength in New York, reinforcements, troop dispositions in case of alarm, artillery, fortifications and shipping.

Then, suddenly, in mid-August, the whole American war plan changed. Washington and Rochambeau agreed to leave enough troops to pen Clinton on his islands, while they themselves swept south; concentrated the American northern and southern armies, together with the French, against Cornwallis; and won the war.

It is fascinating to follow the spies reports that poured into British headquarters, up to the time when Washington changed his plan. This earlier intelligence was complete and correct, reporting every Franco-American move as soon as it was made —and occasionally before it was made. The French move from Rhode Island to the Hudson was predicted accurately, far in advance. When the actual march began, British spies supplied Clinton with full details—routes, location of divisions, halting places, supplies, order of battle, and the daring movement of French artillery and stores along Connecticut coastal roads—though the British Navy failed to land marines and seize them. The mobilization and marches of American militia in New Jersey, New York and Connecticut were swiftly and exactly noted, sometimes by agents moving with the American troops, sometimes by agents ensconced in fields and woods along the route or by agents moving in disguise, past the American columns. Comparison proved to the British staff the accuracy of these reports, which confirmed one another.

The trouble was that, for two or three weeks after the French and Americans had decided to attack Cornwallis, most British spies' reports continued to indicate they would attack New York; for General Washington, up to the very last minute, had been careful to move his troops in such a way as to make the idea seem plausible. Besides, he himself—certainly once or twice, probably three times, perhaps oftener—had supplied the enemy with exactly the information he wanted them to have about his now-abandoned plan.

More than a year before the march to Yorktown, on July 7, 1780, a British spy in Connecticut had sent word: "The General Report is, that an attack upon New York & Long Island is designed as soon as the French Troops arrive, in conjunction with the Continental Troops—Mr. Washington is to have the Chief Command over the whole."

Early in 1781, faithful British spies (and one who was not in the least faithful) began to report the probability of a French move to join Washington, against New York. On February 10, 1781, Caleb Bruen came into New York—having apparently made a roundabout trip through New Jersey—with a message from Dr. John Haliburton, British agent in Newport, Rhode Island. Three French brigades were going aboard transports; Washington and Rochambeau would soon hold a conference at Newport.

In fact, the French troops were moving against Arnold in Virginia. There would be no conference at Newport, indeed no conference at all for some time. In other words, the intelligence was just true enough to seem plausible, yet completely misleading—and no wonder! For, no matter what message Haliburton may originally have sent, Bruen, as a double agent working for the Americans, had had every opportunity to tamper with it; and—although this cannot quite be proved—it is plain enough that he made his long detour through New York and New Jersey to see just what General Washington (then at New Windsor) wanted the enemy to believe.

The first indication that the French would move by land to join Washington reached Clinton on February 16, 1781, through a man named Robinson, living in New London, probably a Tory acting as a volunteer spy. On February 28, the supposed double agent, Macfarlan, had a chat with Colonel

Elias Dayton, in charge of American intelligence in New Jersey. Dayton offered Macfarlan three hundred acres of land and two hundred guineas if he would send a supposed Tory into New York to get information on troops and shipping there. He also wanted Macfarlan to arrange a courier service for American spies on Manhattan, shortening the long route through Connecticut, with which General Washington had always been dissatisfied. If Macfarlan's wits had been a little quicker, he might, by agreeing to the new courier scheme, have exposed the Culper group at last. Instead, he simply reported the whole conversation to the British. Dayton had, however, let slip one bit of nearly correct information, for Macfarlan reported: "The French are said to be moving." They were not, as a matter of fact, moving yet; but preparations were far enough advanced to make it appear so.

On March 8, 1781, a British spy named Joseph Clarke returned to New York from "the Country." He had penetrated as far as Warwick, Rhode Island, south of Providence, bringing back word that the French planned to move to the Hudson and that certain state militia units were on eight days' warning.

On April 24, Colonel Beverly Robinson, who had been active in the Arnold-André affair, started to Rhode Island to investigate in person. He saw no signs of an overland march, but did report that French troops were going aboard transports. At about the same time, another agent reported that the French fleet was taking on water, artillery and ammunition, while transports were standing ready. These were the ships which later carried troops from Baltimore and Annapolis into Virginia. Still another British agent reported, toward the end of April, probably about the twenty-eighth, that the French were actually "on their march for the North, i.e. Hudson, River, and it is said were to take part with some Continental troops at White Plains."

On April 30, the news was definite: "the French troops had marched to Providence, in order to join Gen¹ Washington's army." Six days later, Captain Marquard, of the British staff, reported hostile troops, not otherwise identified, marching from Providence for the Highlands of the Hudson, above Peekskill, where ground had been marked out for their camp. On May 31, "our friend in Rhode Island" reported to the British command that he was sure the French meant to leave their base there, though he could set no date.

To verify all this, a spy from New York, Wynot Williamson, made two trips up the Hudson during May. He reported General Washington's return (May 25, 1781) from his conference with Rochambeau at Wethersfield, Connecticut; the expected movement of the French 2nd Division; and collection of wagons for the French Army's baggage. Joseph Clarke again visited Warwick in the latter part of May, returning June 1 and then at once going into the field again. He returned June 5 with word that General Washington had brought his own troops across the Hudson and had laid out a camp for five thousand French troops at Crompond. Between June 14 and June 29, five other intelligence sources confirmed the report of the proposed French march. Presently spies observed French officers preparing a campsite.

William Heron, of Redding, Connecticut, sent word June 17 that he had already reported "the intended route of the French troops." He had learned the French plan from General Samuel H. Parsons, who had foolishly gossiped about it, after talking with French officers sent ahead of Rochambeau's column, to lay out the camp. Heron also reported General Washington's conference with the French at Wethersfield, though this was no news to Clinton, since the spy, James Moody, had captured Washington's dispatches of May 27-29, reporting the plans agreed on. These stated definitely that there would be a joint French and American operation against New York, with "a tolerable prospect of expelling the enemy or obliging them to withdraw part of their force from the southward." Though the dispatches were genuine, Sir Henry Clinton had been fooled so often by Washington's plants of false information that he at first thought these papers, too, had been deliberately sent out to be captured. Eventually, as he himself admitted, the captured document convinced him that New York City was the sole Franco-American objective.

Heron also reported that the American commander-in-chief

had officially notified the Connecticut legislature of the French march and had asked to have shelter provided for them en route. He expected the French to arrive at Crompond, about June 27, 1781.

An independent report from Doctor Haliburton, at Newport, confirmed intelligence of French movements, on June 19. Haliburton boasted he had had the news two hours after the French council of war broke up. A day later, Captain Marquard saw three thousand French troops between Danbury and Peekskill, together with American cavalry (Moylan's and Sheldon's dragoons).

On June 28, David Gray reported three hundred French at East Hartford and warned that General Washington meant to attack New York. As Gray was really an American secret agent, who had tricked the British into using him as their own secret courier, he was probably trying to give Clinton intelligence that would tell him nothing he did not already know, but would prove accurate, if tested. Since his most recent mission as a courier for British intelligence had taken Gray across the French line of march, he had to report something or he would have been suspected. General Washington could have had no hesitation in letting the British have Gray's information, since his own spies in New York had reported on May 8 that the enemy knew of the proposed French march.

While he was fooling Clinton, Gray went a little further and fooled Clinton's spy and courier, Nehemiah Marks. A little later (July 19), Marks was innocently sending information given him "By Mʳ Gray a person how [who] I Can Rely on." This report shows that Gray had visited Washington's camp before going on to the British—though the British had no idea why. Marks says that "a few days a Gow he whos [was] through the french & Washingtons in Campment & by the Best accompts that hee Can learn their is abought 6000 french troops and equal Number of Rebels and that thae expseted an Reinforcement of Boston Militia & then thae ment to force Newyork."

It looks as if Gray, after receiving General Washington's instructions what to tell the enemy, was "stuffing" Marks to the best of his ability.

About this time, the German General Baron von Riedesel sent two secret agents across Long Island Sound to make inquiries among Connecticut Tories. They, too, brought back details of the French march. The French 1st Division had reached Danbury on June 29; the 2nd and 3rd had reached Hartford on the twenty-eighth; the 4th was on its way "but its particular route or progress is not known."

On July 1, another report from Marks came in, dated June 29, at Lloyd's Neck, Long Island. A flag of truce had returned from Stamford. The British officer who had carried it reported "that their are four thousand French troops on their march from Rhode Island & that the first division has arrived at Danbury."

Confirmatory news continued to arrive throughout July. A certain Colonel Hunt, "as he lay concealed on the ground," had seen four hundred cavalry pass toward Williamsbridge. Remaining in observation, "about a q^r of an hour after sunrise he saw some French troops, about five hundred, marching the same road; a few Rebel troops were with them. He knew them to be French by their white Clothes, and language."

Though the British intelligence digest after July 19, 1781, is lost, many of the original reports on which it was based survive in the Clinton papers. They show that Sir Henry continued to be fully informed of all American plans and movements throughout August.

There were not, at first, many strictly American troop movements for the British spies to report. They did, however, note that the Americans were again collecting boats, which suggested they would attack Manhattan. Wynot Williamson who had gone again into Dutchess County, New York, came back March 19, 1781, with a report on American troop locations, alerting of militia, Washington's personal movements, ordnance and quartermaster supplies, and the number of boats available. He made another trip in April, spending a whole day with Colonel Beverly Robinson's "particular friend who lives very near West Point"—a man alarmingly well-informed about everything the Americans were doing.

Williamson learned all about American security measures,

troop dispositions, stores and artillery. He also learned exactly where General Washington was living—"at Elises House, New Windsor." Thereafter, for some time, British spies continued to note day by day, the houses in which the commander of the Continental Army had his headquarters, perhaps because they still dreamed of kidnaping him, perhaps because the location of the general showed where the main American forces were. On June 27, 1781, General Washington was reported moving to Peekskill. On July 6, he was at the house of Joseph Appleby, on Sawmill River (near the modern parkway). On July 8, the British spies reported he had moved to the house of Thomas Tompkins, "2 1/2 miles this side of Young's house, on the direct road." It was useless to attempt kidnaping at the moment, for the report also said: "Sheldon's Dragoons are with Washington." On July 13, British intelligence was able to report Washington's headquarters before the general himself reached them: The next day, said an advance report, he would be "at Edward Brown's, two miles above Phillips's, on the North River road." General Rochambeau's headquarters were located with the same meticulous precision, though not so frequently. By July 8, Captain Marquard was sending Clinton a complete and essentially accurate order of battle of both the French and the American armies, broken down by regiments, with full details on artillery.

In addition to his services as courier, Nehemiah Marks brought in news of the French, gained through various informants of his own—some unnamed Tories in Stamford, a "Mr. Lewis" in Newfield (either in Stamford or Stratford), and "a Capt of a Rebel whale Bote how [whom] J have hold a Correspondence with." This American traitor was bold enough to cross with his crew to Lloyd's Neck, Long Island, probably in April, 1781, to give information to the enemy in person: a large French fleet had sailed from Rhode Island; a quantity of entrenching tools had been sent to Middletown, Connecticut, in carts; two companies of artillery had been told to hold themselves "in Rediness att a moments whorning." Meantime, two of Marks's assistants, after a ten-day cruise, brought word that other American militiamen had been ordered to hold themselves in readiness with seven days' rations. Some militia were being drafted for nine months' duty. Taken together, all these facts confirmed the intelligence Clinton was getting from other sources.

There was further confirmation late in July, when Thomas Ward, head of a British spy ring operating in New Jersey, sent two agents from Bergen toward King's Ferry, to watch for any signs that more French or American troops were crossing the Hudson. Before the men could return, Ward himself had learned that "Report strongly prevails in the Country of Raising Militia and laying Seige to New York." On July 24, 1781, an unknown British spy, signing only as "F," reported: "If there is any Atempt Made you may depend on it will be made on the Island that will be first place of the Atackt." Many similar reports came in from American deserters and escaping British prisoners. Boats were repeatedly mentioned.

All this information was correct and the British believed it, since still more confirmation kept coming in. Colonel Elias Dayton—perhaps not unintentionally—let slip, where a British spy could pick up the information, plans to have a brigade of Continentals, reinforced by militia, "lay at" Fort Lee, on the Hudson above New York. British agents reported that General Washington had reconnoitered this very ground—in disguise. American artillery was moving south from West Point. At four o'clock the same day (July 31, 1781), the active British reconnoissance officer, Captain Marquard, also reported on American artillery. One of his agents had reached Washington's headquarters and observed the artillery parked near it. On August 2, Thomas Ward reported five hundred French and American troops, after crossing the Hudson, had reached Tappan, while New York militia were mobilizing.

British intelligence continued to keep a close eye on French and American movements. On August 10, a secret agent rode boldly through the Franco-American forces, meeting their first guard somewhere near White Plains or Kingsbridge, and going on through French cavalry and infantry to French headquarters, then on to General Washington's headquarters about two miles west, then past a force of about five brigades. Everything looked as if an attack on New York was still contemplated. It was. The Franco-American plan would not change till four or five days later.

With all this intelligence indicating an attack against New York, the British staff could not go wrong—or so they thought. But, after a preliminary letter on August 5, 1781, Rochambeau, on August 14, received a letter from Admiral de Grasse, announcing he would leave the West Indies for Chesapeake Bay with twenty-nine ships and three new French regiments. The moment General Washington had this news, he decided to attack Yorktown. On the seventeenth, a French general officer personally carried a letter to Admiral de Grasse, saying that the combined French and American armies would meet his fleet on Chesapeake Bay. On the nineteenth, General William Heath was told he would be left behind with a skeleton force to keep Clinton's army in New York. Meantime, on August 15, orders went off to Lafayette to keep Cornwallis, now at Yorktown, from getting away, an effort in which one courageous spy greatly assisted.

American espionage had been active in Cornwallis's force, even before he was shut up in Yorktown. While he was at Williamsburg, on his way into the trap of Yorktown, Colonel James Innis, a Virginian familiar with the local people, had established a "line of Intelligence" north and south of the York River, buying provisions for his spies, so that they could approach the enemy as illicit tradesmen. Lafayette was offering ten guineas to any agent who could prove he had been in a British camp—more to anyone who brought "material Information." Colonel Innis says that "very material service" was rendered by his agents on the north (Gloster) bank of York River; but that is all he says; and no other record of these spies remains.

There is record enough, however, of Private Charles Morgan, the boldest and most sensationally successful of Lafayette's spies. It was by this time essential to plant false information that would keep Cornwallis from trying to escape northward, across the James. To hold him where he was till the French and Continental armies could arrive, the British general had to be tricked into believing that Lafayette had boats enough to cross any river and follow instantly, no matter where his opponent went.

The marquis asked Colonel Francis Barber, commanding a New Jersey battalion of light infantry, to suggest a man who could do it. Barber suggested Morgan, one of his own men. Like Sergeant Major Champe, Morgan demurred—not at the risk he would have to run, but at the disgrace of desertion. Only when Lafayette promised to clear Morgan's good name, by publishing the facts in New Jersey, if his spy was hanged, did the "deserter" consent.

Besides being one of the most successful missions any spy ever carried out, this turned out to be one of the easiest. With special instructions to exaggerate the number of boats the Americans possessed, Lafayette's agent was soon in the British camp, chatting with Cornwallis himself, while Banastré Tarleton, the guerrilla leader, stood listening. Exactly as Lafayette had hoped, the question came. Had Lafayette boats enough for his entire force? Oh, yes, said Morgan, well rehearsed. Cornwallis turned to Tarleton.

"There!" he said. "I told you this would not do."

A few days later, Lafayette, returning from reconnoissance, was startled to find six British soldiers and a Hessian awaiting him. Private Morgan, still in the enemy's scarlet, stepped forth to report.

"Well, Morgan, whom have you here?" asked Lafayette.

Not content with deceiving Cornwallis, the American spy had persuaded five British soldiers to desert with him. On their way through the outposts, they had encountered a Hessian and, since the man might give an alarm, had brought him along as a prisoner.

Delighted, Lafayete offered Morgan a sergeant's warrant, but Morgan declined. He had tried to be a good private; he wasn't sure he would be a good sergeant. Well, what did he want? Private Morgan wanted his own musket, which had been given to another soldier. The cherished weapon was restored, and that is the only reward he ever did receive.

While Lafayette decoyed Cornwallis, Sir Henry Clinton, in

New York, was given no chance to observe troop movements closely enough to guess where Washington and Rochambeau were really going. When, on August 21, 1781, the French and American armies started southward, Heath sent covering forces to conceal their march by keeping the enemy away from King's Ferry, while the troops crossed the Hudson. The march through New Jersey was far enough west to escape observation by hostile patrols. One column moved through Paramus—New Brunswick—Princeton. The other took the route Suffern—Pompton—Morristown—Chatham—Middlebrook—Princeton.

So large a troop movement could not wholly escape British espionage; but, for a long time, it could be made to look like an attack on New York, by way of Staten Island. To encourage the enemy in this delusion, the whole force halted in New Jersey and began laying out an elaborate and apparently permanent camp, which included a large bakery at Chatham. The French set up four ovens, and Christopher Ludwick, the American "Baker-General," may have set up another. Let the British spies report that! They did. Clinton had news on August 22 that a big new oven was being constructed. The conclusion was obvious (it was meant to be). If Washington was setting up such a big bakery in New Jersey, he meant to base his troops there. The French helped matters along by making sure their unmistakable white uniforms could be seen on the New Jersey side of the Hudson, by watchful redcoats on the other bank.

General Washington assisted his opponents to further errors with a little more of the deception he loved to practice. An express with directions for a large camp—"it seems conformable with his instructions"—passed so near the enemy that he was captured. Colonel Elias Boudinot tells gleefully how General Washington managed to have a talk with an "old inhabitant of New York," well known to be spying for the British. Eagerly, the apparently naïve commander-in-chief asked questions about the water supply and landing beaches on Long Island, the terrain around Middletown, New Jersey, just west of Sandy Hook, and conditions on Sandy Hook itself. Blandly (and quite untruthfully) the general explained that there was no special reason for his questions—no, indeed, no special reason at all. He was just "fond of knowing the Situation of different parts of the Country, as in the Course of the war he might unexpectedly be called into that part of the Country." Nevertheless, he urged "the most profound Secrecy" upon the Tory. He was "by no means to lisp a Word of what had passed between them." To make it all seem more convincing, American troops began to move, an hour later, along a road which *could* take them to Sandy Hook—if they went far enough.

A child could have seen George Washington was lying. So could the British spy; but he wholly misjudged the motives of this elaborate prevarication. Later that day, Colonel Elias Boudinot was at pains to have an accidental conversation with the enemy agent, who repeated everything Washington had said and was positive New York would be attacked by way of New Jersey and Long Island. "I doubt not but that, the british Gen! had it also the same Night," said Boudinot cynically.

Within a few days, the first hints that American plans had changed were reaching the enemy's headquarters, but nothing whatever was done about them. By August 18, a German Jäger officer, Lieutenant Colonel Ludwig Johann Adolph von Wurmb, learned through spies of his own that the Americans had established depots of food and forage all the way across New Jersey. He also learned that a French officer had sent his American mistress to Trenton. From these two facts, he concluded at once that Washington would march south, but he could not convince Clinton. On August 22 a New Jersey agent, signing only as "Squib," sent word: "It is said they will go against New York, but some Circumstances, induce me to believe they will go to the Cheasepeak. Yet for Gods sake be prepared at All Points."

The destination of the American forces in New Jersey remained a mystery for some time, in spite of all the British secret agents who swarmed about it. On August 28, George Hamilton and Barnabash McMahon, of Goshen, Orange County, New York, came into New York. They had seen French troops at Pompton the preceding Sunday (the twenty-sixth); had estimated their strength as three thousand; had chatted with an

English servant of the Duc de Lauzun, who confirmed their figure. (Only an eighteenth-century army would have kept a British servant at headquarters, while fighting the British!) The two had watched American troops passing through their home in Goshen, had counted artillery and ammunition wagons, and had even noted their positions in the column. They could locate General Benjamin Lincoln with seventeen hundred men at Aquacanunk Bridge and could tentatively locate General Washington and his bodyguard at Pompton. The Americans were reported to be bringing boats to attack Staten Island.

On August 30, two more agents arrived, reporting that the French 1st Division had moved from Pompton to Old Whippany, ten miles from Morristown, where the 2nd Division had joined them. After a halt of two days they would move to Chatham, New Jersey; General Lincoln had marched toward Springfield, New Jersey; the militia toward Hackensack. These agents named the house where Washington had dined, reported his journey to Chatham, described artillery, noted that both French and Americans had boats with them, and gave a fairly accurate order of battle of both sides.

They had also picked up gossip from a careless American "forage master" and others about supplies of forage at Princeton and Trenton. This should have warned Clinton that the French and Americans might cross the Delaware at Trenton— as they actually did—and might use their boats in doing so. But the boats might also indicate an attack on Manhattan and Staten Island, from the Jersey shore.

The final plunge southward to attack Cornwallis at Yorktown was the best-kept secret of the Revolution. It is significant that the apparently loquacious General Parsons, who had babbled so freely to the spy, Heron, of previous American plans, was suddenly mute, though an officer of his rank could not fail to know the secret. Though British spies in New Jersey might watch the moving columns, they could form no definite idea of their destination. It was no use chatting with the troops. They themselves did not know where they were going, since the real plan had been kept from the enlisted personnel and most of the officers. The surgeon, James Thacher, had his suspicions, for he notes in his diary that New York was "ostensibly" the goal. Others shared his suspicions and there was "much speculation," but the Continental Army knew by this time that their wily commander matured "his great plans and designs under an impenetrable secrecy."

Not until September 1 were the British really sure that "some rebels" were moving on southward. General Washington's own arrival in Trenton might have given them a hint; but he had been careful to leave troops to threaten Staten Island as long as possible; and Clinton knew it was always possible that his sly opponent might only be making a long detour, after which he might double back to strike Sandy Hook and there co-operate with the French fleet against New York.

On September 2, the British commander at last had a clear idea what was happening, but even then he was not quite sure his idea was correct. He himself wrote: "By intelligence which I have this day received, it would seem that Mr. Washington is moving an army to the southward, with an appearance of haste and gives out that he expects the co-operation of a considerable French armament." A report of September 4 warned that De Grasse's fleet was landing troops to reinforce Lafayette on the south side of the James, and that Washington's army was approaching the Elk River, in Maryland. On September 6 an escaped British prisoner reported no American troops between West Point and Hackensack.

The first definite prediction of an attack on Cornwallis came in September 8 and was followed September 15 by a report from one "Isaac R——": "the rebels are in the highest spirits & expect to destroy Lord Cornwallis." Meantime, to make sure what Clinton himself was doing, a courageous but unknown American spy, I. Jagger, had made three risky trips into New York City during September.

More confirmation came to Clinton on September 18. A certain John Sturges, reaching New York on the sixteenth, was dilatory in reporting. It took him two days to visit headquarters with the news that Washington had passed Christiania Bridge, in Delaware, "on his march to Virginia"—news which came far too late, for the Americans had passed through Philadelphia

September 2, and the French September 4. Sturges also reported that the Americans were collecting "Oyster boats and every kind of Vessel capable of containing men" at Head of Elk. These were the boats that took troops down Chesapeake Bay to Williamsburg, while French frigates brought the rest from Baltimore and Annapolis, a movement duly reported by British agents in Philadelphia—again too late.

Two more British agents, specially sent into Pennsylvania, picked up full details of the movement down Chesapeake Bay, correctly reporting the movement of French and New York troops to Baltimore and of French troops to Annapolis, for embarkation. These spies thought it would take General Washington several days to "form a Junction with the Army in Virginia." They added that the French had brought thirteen field guns and had drawn sixteen days' rations; and they gave a fairly correct strength report—five thousand French, three thousand rebels—based on the ration issue at Head of Elk. One of the British spies even got a peep at an American "Commissary's Estimate of Rations," a document which should have been top secret. Since, however, this shows the French forces at a figure twenty-five per cent too high, it is just possible General Washington was playing another of his little tricks. Whether this information was true or false, Clinton did not receive it till the end of September, when the siege of Yorktown began.

These agents gave the usual report on the general's personal whereabouts: "Genl. Washington went immediately by land to Virginia," as, in fact, he did; but there was no military reason for this. Like any other GI, the commander-in-chief was simply homesick. It was his first glimpse of Mount Vernon in six long years, a detail the spies forgot to mention.

After assembling its full strength at Williamsburg, the international army, on September 28, 1781, converged on Yorktown, where Lafayette had pinned down Cornwallis. Though competent British spies had trailed the Franco-American Army all the way, it was too late now to save the redcoats trapped on the Yorktown Peninsula. French men-of-war blocked off the Royal Navy. Sir Henry Clinton could not quite make up his mind to march overland and assail Washington's rear. Sir

Henry just stayed on Manhattan, with the Culpers, Hercules Mulligan, Daniel Bissell, and David Gray watching him—though Sir Henry didn't know that.

At three o'clock in the morning of October 22, 1781, the clatter of hasty hoofs broke the morning stillness of Philadelphia. Lieutenant Colonel Tench Tilghman, of General Washington's staff, rode up to the house where Thomas Mc-Kean, president of the Continental Congress, lay sleeping. Colonel Tilghman had news that could not wait. He must have shouted it to the city watch as he rode in. Before the next hour struck, wakeful citizens could hear the hourly cry of the Pennsylvania German watchman on his rounds:

"Basht dree o'glock, und Cornwallis isht da-ken."

British intelligence had failed. Cornwallis's army was gone. The British Empire had lost the war, and soon knew it.

XXIV

Duping Sir Henry Clinton

As THE FINAL crisis of the Revolution approached, in the late summer of 1781, General Washington found himself in immediate need of more intelligence from New York City and Long Island than Tallmadge, the Culpers, Dayton, the Mersereaus, Mulligan, and the various secret agents assisting them could supply. Even after he had decided to attack Yorktown rather than New York, it remained necessary to keep a close eye on the powerful enemy force he was leaving behind. Washington and Rochambeau had to know what Sir Henry Clinton was capable of doing when they turned south, and several essential elements of information had thus far escaped the American intelligence service. How strong was Clinton's army? Ships loaded with redcoats had come in. Were they reinforcements from England? Or were Cornwallis's troops being moved north by sea?

The men were, in fact, paroled prisoners, released after the Spaniards captured Pensacola, who would fight no more. Oliver Pollock, American agent in New Orleans, knew all about this British defeat, but had not been able to send the news fast enough.

An entirely new spy would have to go into New York for a few days, secure last-minute enemy intelligence from personal observation, and return at once. By August 12, 1781, General Washington had begun looking for the right man. By reveille, August 13, he had found Sergeant Daniel Bissell, of the 2nd Connecticut Line. By nightfall that same day, the sergeant was on his secret way to the British lines. Then suddenly, on the fourteenth, came word from Admiral de Grasse that the French fleet would soon arrive; and the decision was made at once to attack Cornwallis, in Yorktown, rather than Clinton, in New York.

In that brief twenty-four hours, Sergeant Bissell had already won the confidence of the British and was moving freely through New York streets, secretly collecting the information General Washington wanted. It was too late to call the sergeant back, but that did not matter very much. Even though Washington's and Rochambeau's men would soon be foot-slogging southward, General Heath would have to stay behind to hold Clinton in place. Any information Sergeant Bissell could bring back would be useful to Heath—though, as affairs turned out, Sergeant Bissell did not return nearly so soon as expected.

At the close of a headquarters conference, August 12, 1781, the commander-in-chief had asked a small group of trusted officers to remain, among them Colonel Heman Swift, commanding the 2nd Connecticut Line, at Peekskill. Someone, General Washington told them, would have to enter the British lines. He "enquired of those present who there was that could be hit upon to go upon an enterprize so arduous, and attended with such a measure of danger." Colonel Swift spoke up at once: "If his paymaster sergeant Daniel Bissell would undertake it, he would be the best man who could go." Sergeant Daniel Bissell was a Connecticut Yankee, from Windsor; had served at White Plains, Trenton and Monmouth; had been wounded; and was an N.C.O. much respected in his regiment.

Accepting Swift's proposal at once, General Washington told him to arrange matters. British spies were still about. If any word reached the British, it must report Bissell as a genuine deserter. Just to make certain, General Washington would officially list him as such. Everyone was so completely deceived that the official records of his home town carried the sergeant as a deserter for a century and a half.

Swift knew better than to attract attention by ordering the sergeant to Continental Army headquarters. An accidental meeting was the thing. The colonel—one of those ideal regimental commanders who know all about their men as individuals—knew that his serious-minded quartermaster sergeant "usually rose the earliest of any," even before the drums beat reveille; and the cold gray dawn found him loitering near Bissell's tent.

Ere long, Sergeant Bissell emerged and, seeing his colonel, approached at once, learned what was needed, and—after some natural hesitation—agreed to go. Colonel Swift told him to walk in a specified direction and lie under an apple tree "till some one called him." After which, there can be no possible doubt, both colonel and sergeant went their separate ways as fast as possible.

Reveille sounded, soldiers cursed as they rolled from their pleasantly warm blankets, arms rattled, lines formed, the 2nd Connecticut began its garrison day. But Sergeant Bissell was not at his usual post. Sergeant Bissell was lying under that apple tree.

Within half an hour "a club was thrown into the tree." Just why this unusual method of attracting the sergeant's attention was used, is not at all clear. Clubbing a chestnut tree was a traditional American way to bring down the burs; but clubbing an apple tree injures the fruit, and there are not many apples in New York in mid-August anyway.

The officer whom Bissell saw, as the club crashed into the branches, was a country gentleman from Chusetown (now Seymour), Connecticut—Colonel David Humphreys, a staff officer then serving as private secretary to General Washington.

"Soldier, why are you here?" he asked.

"I was ordered here," replied Bissell.

The inconsequential conversation—not quite usual and yet natural enough to attract no attention, if overheard—bears all the earmarks of the usual arranged exchange of recognition signals.

Humphreys at once handed Bissell a paper "written on 3 sides," telling him to "go to some bye-place," memorize it, then destroy it. (The extraordinary triangularity of this remarkable paper probably means only that it was written on both sides, the writing on one side being then "crossed" in another direction.) It summarized the questions likely to be asked by the British guards and outposts, whom Bissell would have to pass on his way to New York. That the sergeant was able to reproduce these instructions in his pension application, nearly forty years later, does not mean he disobeyed orders to destroy the paper. One of Bissell's special qualifications as a secret agent was his remarkable memory, which later enabled him to carry complex figures of British strength in his head, after destroying his notes, and to reproduce his Purple Heart citation years after it had been burned.

The instructions Humphreys gave him are worth quoting:

> As Gen. Arnold is now in Virginia, with all the new raised corps, there will be no recruiting parties in New York; and as the fleet is not at the Hook, consequently there will be no press [gang] in the city; and with the money you carry in, you can get a protection from the Mayor or Police of the city, to go to Lloyd's Neck, thirty miles on Long Island, to cut wood for the Crown. After this, you will return to King's Bridge or Laurel Hill, and view the works there, obtain the number of each regiment, the number of men each contains, by whom commanded, their several alarm posts, the number of cannon mounted in each work. You will view the works on York Island [Manhattan] in the same manner; get the whole number of regular forces, distinguishing the British from foreigners; the number of the new raised corps, and also the number of militia enrolled for the defence of the city. Get what information you can of their works and force at Powler's Hook [Paulus Hook, or Jersey City], also that of Staten Island. Obtain the number of Shipping in the Harbour, and that at the [Sandy] Hook; and when you have completed your business here, you will pass over to Brooklyn, view the works there, ascertain their force on Long Island.

Colonel Humphreys further told the sergeant to "fix off as near as he could, as if he was going to desert." He was to take his silver shoe buckles and his watch, articles no deserter would leave behind, but which a spy would hardly carry (Nathan Hale had been careful to discard his silver shoe buckles, but he was not posing as a deserter), and put on two or three suits of clothing, one over the other. A real deserter, not daring to advertise his intentions by carrying baggage about the American camp, might naturally take extra clothing with him by this device, which, odd as it sounds, was not unusual.

Benedict Arnold is specifically referred to in the instructions, because the first task the British had given him was to organize a new force, composed mainly of American deserters. Such deserters as escaped Arnold's clutches were likely to be pressed into the Royal Navy; but, with Arnold in Virginia and the British fleet out of New York harbor, Washington hoped his new spy might have a chance of getting back before he was compelled to join the enemy.

When the sergeant had "got the business completed," he was to make his way to Whitestone, Long Island, where a boat would be waiting to take him off. He was expected to return "the seventh or ninth" night and the boat would lie offshore for these nights only. The time limit, as it turned out, was far too short. No agent, operating within the enemy lines, can keep to so strict a schedule. The boat should have waited a good deal longer and, in case Bissell failed to appear, one of the other networks should have investigated his fate.

The amount of information the sergeant was expected to collect in a single week was enormous. However, the area to be covered was fairly small; armies then were less complex than they have since become; and Washington can hardly have expected to get all the information he had asked for. Any secret service will ask for all it can get, then be content with a great deal less.

As the spy set out, Colonel Swift handed him a letter, addressed to the commander of the outpost at Croton Bridge, "whither he was directed to steer." In his account of this incident, as given in his later affidavit, Sergeant Bissell says that he was ordered to wait till "the time the army was on the parade for evening roll-call." That would keep most American soldiers out of the way. He was then to "quit the Regiment, go to a bridge between the army and Col. Schammel's Light Infantry, where I should meet Col. Swift, who would give me further instructions. Col. Swift directed me to call on Col. Schammel at his marquee at nine o'clock in the evening." By nine o'clock in a New York August, it would be growing dark. The "deserter" would get a fairly early start into the city, yet it would be impossible for anyone to recognize him.

Though Bissell does not mention the incident in his affidavit, the rare printed account of his adventures describes how he handed the letter Swift had given him to an officer at the outpost, who plainly must have been Colonel Schammel. The spy caught a glimpse of the letter, as the colonel opened it. "There was not a scratch of a pen inside." It seems clear that Schammel had orders to send forward through the lines any sergeant who handed him a blank letter.

Colonel Schammel personally took the spy past all his guards and, as they passed the last post, remarked "that he had ordered off all guards and patrols from the North River road (until after midnight) down as far as Croton Bridge, that being the extent of our lines." There would be no trouble from Americans. Sooner or later a British sentry would challenge. The sergeant was to reply: "Friend to Britain."

Since the British had by this time learned to be cautious in dealing with ostensible deserters, various officers questioned Bissell carefully, "a great number of ways," before allowing him to enter the city. Then he was turned over to a certain Captain Neff, who at once urged him to enlist.

Too late, Sergeant Bissell discovered that Colonel Humphreys had been wrong about Benedict Arnold. The New York spies had failed to inform Washington that, just before the sergeant's arrival, the traitor had returned to New York and established his recruiting parties, wherever deserters could come in. To make matters worse, the British fleet had also returned, and its press gangs were conducting what the sergeant later described as a "hot press"—that is, an unusually vigorous employment of the Royal Navy's legal right to seize men in the streets and force them into service.

Worst of all, Sir Henry Clinton had ordered no more protection given to deserters. Until shortly before Bissell's arrival, any American entering the British lines in New York could secure "a piece of stamped coin"—presumably some kind of metal token—which entitled him to wander New York streets unmolested. (No wonder Sir Henry was "somewhat troubled with spies.") The new orders required deserters to give bail, pay £70 cash—or enlist. As a practical matter, this meant they had to enlist, since no one in New York was likely to go bail for a total stranger, and no deserter ever had £70.

Thinking with commendable speed, Sergeant Bissell enlarged his family circle with an entirely imaginary Tory uncle, somewhere in New York. His uncle, he explained to the too-credulous Captain Neff, would provide bail as soon as Bissell could find him. If the captain had been just a little bit brighter, he would have demanded identification of the uncle. Instead, he gave the deserter a single guard and let him start looking for his nonexistent relative. In so small a town as New York City, this search could not be dragged out forever; but Bissell made it last all day and even persuaded the guard to let him stray from his assigned quarters to spend the night at a tavern.

When the wandering pair returned, a day late, Captain Neff exhibited irritation, which turned out to be mostly pretense. After the spy had explained volubly that, even if he could not find his uncle, he was sure he could get bail, the captain became conciliatory, sent out for wine, drank with him—and then put up the bail himself! Next day Bissell resumed his quest, getting a still better idea of the British forces as he moved about.

All would have gone well had he not, at this critical moment, been "violently seized with a bilious cholic." The only way to get medical attention was to enlist in the British Army at once and have the benefits of an army hospital. According to one account, Bissell was ill for six weeks, but this must refer only to the most violent part of his illness, for he did not get out of the military hospital in Flushing till December and was then sent to his regimental hospital—a barn on Harlem Heights. The barn was near the American lines, but Bissell was too ill to seize the chance this gave him.

A military hospital in the Revolution was not, in either army, in the least like the model institutions in which the U. S. Army Medical Corps takes care of modern GI's. Here, said Bissell in his later affidavit, "my suffering was truly great; without fire the greatest part of the time, only wood allowed for the purpose of cooking our pork and beans; without attendance; but one additional blanket to two men; without shifting my clothes for three months; covered with head and body lice; unable to walk."

Worst of all, he could not be sure what he had said in the delirium of his fever. The medical officer in charge gave him some queer looks and seemed to have very definite suspicions; but the doctor was either a secret American sympathizer or one of those medical officers who see little sense in restoring a man to health from fever, only to send him to a gallows, which will be even worse for his health. Later, the doctor gave him a quiet hint; and Bissell ruefully remarked long afterward that he always had talked in his sleep.

Since a good supply sergeant is always in demand, Captain Robert Rowley, Brigadier General Benedict Arnold's quartermaster, took over the American deserter as soon as he was able to leave hospital. Rowley was a decent fellow, of whom Bissell remarked later that "to his kind attention to my health, I owe my escape." Just to be on the safe side, the new quartermaster sergeant saw to it that "his best exertions were given to all the duties assigned him."

Humphreys's failure to arrange a line of communication led to disaster almost at once. Just as Bissell entered the city, Benedict Arnold was planning his New London raid and made the attack September 6, 1781, three weeks after the new spy had begun observation. Bissell knew all about it before going to hospital, but had no way whatever of getting the news to the Americans. Captain David Gray, another American spy operating within the British intelligence system—of whose presence Bissell did not know—learned Arnold's plans so late that he reached New London with warning only a few hours before the attack.

When Sergeant Bissell realized that there was no immediate chance of escape, he settled down to his duties, issued supplies, and won the esteem of the unsuspecting Captain Rowley, keeping the quartermaster records straight and his eyes open. Information of the most valuable kind passed through his hands, month after month. He knew the strength and location of British units, because he sent them their supplies. He could judge the number of men at a given post by the fuel and rations sent them. He was continually "enquiring of the Serg^{ts} & others," and once he heard a senior officer discussing the strength of the garrison and giving the figures. After assembling all this information, he "compared the several Reports together." Wholly unsuspected, he "exerted his utmost care & ability in obtaining information of the strength & state of the Enemy Force."

Even at this distance in time, it is maddening to think of all this information in the American spy's hands; of the Culper and Dayton networks, constantly forwarding much less valuable intelligence; of the American double agent, Gray, going back and forth between the innocent Clinton and the guileful Washington—and of the total waste of all Bissell learned, at the very time when the American staff needed it worst.

When on May 5, 1782, Sir Guy Carleton arrived to replace Sir Henry Clinton, Bissell's danger increased. The humane Clinton did not like to hang spies. Carleton ordered ruthlessly "that any Persons being discovered to have written Information would be treated as Spies."

Though Bissell made haste to destroy his notes, he had worked them over and corrected them so often that he retained the most essential information in his capacious memory. The oral report he gave Continental headquarters later includes the exact strength of regiments, troop movements, the condition of naval vessels, movement of naval vessels—all stated with careful distinction between information he had been able to base on personal observation and other information, obtained from secondary sources.

One account says that Bissell was with the British until May, 1782, when Sir Guy Carleton took command in Manhattan. Bissell himself is quoted as saying that festivities celebrating the king's birthday drew all officers away from Staten Island and enabled him to escape. But neither of these statements can be accepted. The only early printed account says that Bissell reached Washington's headquarters on September 29, 1782; and this is confirmed by the American intelligence report, which gives September 27, 1782, as the date of his escape from Staten Island. George III was born June 4. The British celebration on "York Island" was really in honor of the anniversary of his coronation.

Whatever the occasion, every officer who could leave his post went to New York to help celebrate. Armies being what they are, that meant that only a few very junior subalterns remained on duty. Bissell and a Virginian named Headwater saw their chance to get away. (Who Headwater was, and why he was serving with the British, has never been explained.)

As an excuse for wandering out into the country, the pair asked for a pass to go out to buy a pig and some butter. A lieutenant flatly refused it. At that moment, the officer's wife decided that she, too, would like some butter, and the pass was issued.

To disarm suspicion, the pair took along a ten-year-old boy, explaining that he was "to carry the rope and lead the pig." They wandered off into rural Staten Island, were caught beyond the limits of their pass, turned dutifully back, but—as soon as they were at a safe distance—took cover in the nearest woods.

For some reason never explained, they now told the child with them that they meant to desert. When he burst into a flood of tears, crying that deserters were always caught, they had to quiet him, and then took time to pray before trying to cross into New Jersey, an effort which went on all night, without success. When dawn came, they heard alarm guns, after which search parties with dogs appeared; and the fugitives had to stand the better part of a day, nearly submerged, on a rock in a swamp or stream.

When darkness fell, they waded ashore and again began seeking means of escape. Sometime after midnight, Bissell saw a boat approaching an old mill, its occupant probably being somebody smuggling fresh meat from the New Jersey shore, for the benefit of British troops—a popular and profitable activity among local farmers. As the man came within pistol shot, Bissell raised an object of some kind, about the size of a horse pistol, and ordered him ashore. One account says he leveled a stick at the man. Another account says it was a knife. Whatever it was, it looked dangerous.

"Come ashore or I will put this ball to your heart!" snarled Bissell, in his best gangster style.

Coming out of pitch darkness in a menacing tone, the threat had its effect. All the terrified Tory could see was a soldier with a long object pointing straight at him. There was a somewhat acrimonious interchange when he reached land and found how he had been tricked; but as the fellow was all alone in the night with two determined men, he had to take them on board and start for the Jersey shore. Somewhere en route, the ten-year-old disappears from the narrative. Probably he was simply sent home.

Bissell was well aware that the British command kept a guard boat rowing along shore at half-hour intervals. Now, it is a fatal mistake to keep any patrol moving on a fixed schedule, either afloat or ashore, since, if fugitives or intruders know the schedule, it is easy to avoid discovery. So it was in this case. As the guard boat splashed toward them, Bissell made the two others lie down with him. In a few minutes the British craft was out of sight, its occupants quite unaware of what they had passed.

At last Sergeant Bissell's troubles were over. The row across the Hudson was no great matter. The darkness gave shelter. Their oarsman was well aware that he was rowing for his life— there was no metaphor about that. Without difficulty, and probably before dawn, they reached New Jersey, where the magnanimous Bissell presented their involuntary Charon with a half guinea, after which he and Headwater left the bank of the Hudson as speedily as possible. By noon, they were in Newark, greatly embarrassed by their British uniforms.

The astonishing thing is that no one there did anything about it when two men in the enemy's uniform appeared openly in the streets. In Revolutionary Jersey, flags of truce were always coming in from the enemy's side of the river. Raids were just as possible as flags of truce. A whole column of redcoats might have been close behind that mysterious pair of British soldiers. Prudent civilians looked the other way.

Bissell and his companion did not strain their luck too far. Sooner or later they would encounter American troops, who might shoot first and inquire later. One of the two was acquainted with a local judge. Straight to his courtroom they went, the entry of their scarlet uniforms creating a mild sensation. His Honor recognized his friend (whichever one it was) instantly. Rounding up an American guard to protect them, he explained the situation to the puzzled Newark authorities. Bissell reached headquarters on September 29, 1782, with a great deal of valuable intelligence. By this time, however, intelligence was plentiful. An officer of the French forces at Morristown at this time notes: "Not a day has passed since we have drawn near the enemy that we have not had some news of them from our spies in New York and in several other towns in the neighborhood, or from some deserters."

Bissell's was the last secret service adventure of the war. Already flags of truce had begun to pass constantly to and fro. The war was not formally over, nor would it be until the provisional agreement of November 30, 1782, was confirmed by a definitive treaty. Nevertheless, Congress proclaimed the end of hostilities April 19, 1783, exactly eight years after Lexington and Concord, though the final treaty of peace was not signed until September 3.

Meantime, the late enemy became amusingly affable. Sir Henry Clinton announced to General Washington that his future intentions were entirely peaceful, after which Sir Henry himself gave up and went home, politely notifying his late adversary that Sir Guy Carleton would assume command. Sir Guy, equally polite, reported his arrival in New York to General Washington and eventually went up the Hudson to Tappan to confer with him.

"Partial though our suspension of hostilities may be called," said Carleton, he himself was "no longer able to discern the object we contend for." He even sent money to pay for wine which British prisoners had stolen from a French officer.

General Washington, not much impressed, remained suspicious. Was this a trick? If the British wanted peace so much, why didn't they stop the Indian raids on the frontier? Besides, there were rumors of a planned attack from Canada on Albany, and another attack on Boston.

Tallmadge and his spies still watched and waited. Nevertheless, as military operations were reduced almost to the vanishing point, espionage became less active, though General Washington, taking no chances, always knew what the redcoats were doing. In May, 1782, he still had a suspicious eye on what the enemy were about in Halifax, and General David Forman was ordered to maintain his watch upon the British fleet in New York harbor. Tallmadge crossed secretly to Long Island to consult Culper, Sr., though he failed to see John Cork, busily spying in Manhattan, with a special eye on the fleet. Other American secret agents, remaining at their posts, continued to report, and Tallmadge sent in new agents to supplement intelligence from the resident agents.

All the intelligence the spies could gather, however, indicated that the enemy was acting in good faith. It was interesting to learn that General Carleton expected to leave New York City before long, since he had leased his quarters only until May, 1783. Six spies at once, with new and hitherto unknown initials, reported on British troop dispositions in and near New York. Another spy sent a map, showing posts and fortifications on Manhattan; but they all seemed merely defensive. "Anonymous," from Charleston, reported that the British would leave the city soon and meant thereafter to evacuate New York. Culper, Jr., and General Forman both reported the fleet had sailed for Charleston to take them off. In January, 1783, there was more confirmation. Tallmadge's spies said the Charleston garrison was arriving in New York. Tories were leaving the city as fast as they could.

When the Americans were at last convinced the British were

sincere, the intelligence service became rather desultory. Spies' reports grew steadily less frequent during the first six months of 1783, until, on July 3, came the last message from Samuel Culper, Sr.—"account of expenses incurred in obtaining secret intelligence," prosaic conclusion to a romantic tale.

Finally—a strange irony—Sir Guy Carleton began to submit British secret service reports to General Washington! There seemed to be a plot to plunder New York and assault any remaining Tories. There ought to be no interval between the withdrawal of the red uniforms and the entry of the blue and buff, if public order was to be maintained.

Thus warned by the enemy's accommodating spies, General Washington took proper measures. There was no disorder, for the British were still in sight in the harbor as the Americans marched into the city. Tallmadge, at his own request, entered the city first, so that he might protect his agents. General Washington himself went to take his first breakfast in Manhattan with the spy, Hercules Mulligan; and one officer always said, in after years, that he had been with his chief and heard the clinking of the coin, when the general went to see the supposed Tory, James Rivington, with a great big bag of gold.

Epilogue

★ ★ ★

★

The Spies Go Safely Out of Business

WHEN THE WAR was over, the spies of both sides went thankfully back to everyday affairs as unobtrusively as possible, a little surprised to be alive at all after long service in their perilous trade. Only one, John Howe, ever did secret service work again.

Samuel Wallis, after innumerable acts of treason against his country, settled back into a rôle of utter Philadelphian Quaker respectability. He was loyal to his king, of course; but now the rebels were victorious; and there was no one to whom Samuel Wallis was quite so loyal as to Samuel Wallis. He had insured his own safety, in case the Americans won, by preserving an outwardly patriotic attitude. He had at the same time insured his safety, if the British won, by numerous and valuable—but secret —services to Sir William Howe and Sir Henry Clinton. When the independence of the United States was recognized, he remained one of its prominent, wealthy and respected citizens. His standing as a Quaker pacifist was unimpaired. He had never engaged in acts of war, which would have sinfully violated the principles of the Society of Friends.

Even after Arnold had fled and his Peggy had joined him, Wallis was still able to do business for the traitor, secretly. Peggy Arnold's receipt, dated New York, January 6, 1781, still

exists—"in full of all Accounts, of M: Samuel Wallace of Pennsylvania, the Sum of Two Hundred Guineas, ordered to be paid
by M: Wallace to General Arnold." Wallis was still doing business behind the enemy lines as late as October, 1781, and his
friend, Joseph Stansbury, as late as July.

Stansbury returned to Philadelphia in 1783; but, when a note
flung in at his door warned him he might easily die, he fled to
safe obscurity in New York. He was threatened only because
he was a known Tory; the real extent of his treason remained
undiscovered until modern times; and, when he settled in Nova
Scotia, a royal commission refused him compensation for his
losses.

By a crowning irony, Gershom Hicks—whose daring reconnoissance, alone in the Iroquois wilderness, had helped to
thwart Wallis's plots against the Sullivan expedition—went to
work as Wallis's employee. Both men died, never guessing they
had been on opposite sides in the secret service. Hicks appears
in Wallis's land records as owner of four hundred acres, April
5, 1793. A letter of Wallis's from the frontier in 1794 notes:
"Gershom Hicks and Samuel Oaks are sent down in order to
bring up a canoe load of stores to Chestnut falls."

Four other British secret agents ended their days in America,
unsuspected. John Rattoon, who had piloted so many spies and
carried so many messages for Benedict Arnold, remained quietly
in New Jersey. Though Metcalf Bowler, Clinton's Rhode Island spy, was impoverished by the war, he later made a name as
a horticulturalist and his daughter (who probably never
dreamed of her papa's doings) married a French officer—a marquis, no less! "Hiram the Spy" continued to dwell peacefully
in Redding, Connecticut. There may have been a few suspicious whispers, and people thought him a little haughty and
conservative; but they elected him to the Connecticut Assembly
again and again, until 1796. He died in the utmost respectability in 1819, and not till ninety-nine years after the Revolution was his treason proved.

John Howe, who had spied so successfully for General Gage,
settled in Canada. When the War of 1812 appeared on the
horizon, the British government, remembering his earlier serv-

ices, sent the old spy back to the United States, to make a secret report on American military preparations and the mood of the people. He traveled through the country, wholly unsuspected, went back to Canada, and turned in a model of what a secret intelligence report should be. It came to light only when the archives were opened, long, long after.

Known British agents rarely tried to see their homes again. Peggy Arnold paid one visit to her family, but had a very frosty reception in Philadelphia. Her husband met with some contempt in England and once fought a duel with the Earl of Lauderdale, who had alluded scornfully to his treason. But Clinton saw to getting pensions for Peggy and the children.

The British Army, understandably, did not want such a man on active duty. Arnold drew a colonel's half pay for life, engaged in business, visited New Brunswick, begat a bastard by an unknown woman there, was involved in an insurance scandal (being, for once, innocent). The story that he called for his American uniform on his death bed is pure fiction.

James Moody settled in Nova Scotia, became colonel of a militia regiment, died at sixty-five, on half pay. William Rankin and Cortlandt Skinner lived the rest of their lives in England, receiving compensation for their lost estates.

Ann Bates, deserted by her husband, sick and in direst poverty, is last heard from, desperately imploring the British government to pay the £10 pension promised in the days when her services were beyond price. She was a little bitter: "Haid I Doon half as much for the Scruff of Mankind I mean the Rabls I Should not be thus Left to Parish.—Was I in Amarica Now to share the same fate of my Noble Unfortunate frind Major Andrew [André]—it would be much better for me then to Drawg out a life Which all Laws humain and Divine forbids me to Putt a Period too."

Her old friend, Colonel Drummond, came gallantly to her rescue. In Ann's claim for pension, he wrote, she asserted "nothing but what is strictly true," and, during the war, "her information as to Matter and fact, was far superior to every other intelligence."

The widow of Moses Dunbar, the Tory spy of Bristol, Connecticut, was not molested, and later remarried. Passing through Hartford in after years, she glanced over toward Gallows Hill with the remark: "That is the tree on which my poor first husband was hung."

Some of the American spies let slip their secrets. Captain David Gray and Captain Caleb Bruen admitted having been the enemy's secret agents; but everybody knew it had been only on behalf of the Americans. After his return to the Continental Army, Gray continued to serve as quartermaster, until he was discharged in October, 1783, at Fort Wyoming (Wilkes-Barre, Pennsylvania). He seems to have been sent into the Susquehanna wilderness to make sure the British would never capture him. (Champe had been discharged for the same reason.)

Settling in Vermont, where he had done so much espionage, Gray published a pamphlet on his adventures. The last copy was burned in a fire at the State Library in Albany, in 1911. He told his story again in a petition to the Massachusetts Legislature, but that vanished, too. Fortunately, he told it a third time in his pension claim of 1823, which still survives in the National Archives. Discovery of this unknown manuscript in the course of the present study, makes it possible to tell his true story at last.

Bruen, suspected and imprisoned by the enemy near the end of the war, returned to Newark in shattered health, but recovered and lived on for years, a well-known businessman.

Enoch Crosby went back to farming, served as a justice of the peace in Southeast, New York, deputy sheriff, and deacon in the Presbyterian Church, receiving in the end $250 for his secret services. It was often said that he inspired confidence in all who talked with him. Many a rueful Tory could have testified to that! A book about his adventures, *The Spy Unmasked*, appeared in 1828, and Lafayette's grandson was interested enough to secure a copy. When a play based on James Fenimore Cooper's novel, *The Spy*, was produced in New York, the old man, appearing in a box, was much applauded. Cooper insisted he had never heard the name of Enoch Crosby, but the correspondence between some of his novel's episodes and the real spy's adventures is hardly accidental, though Cooper was sincere in what he said. He had heard the tale from John Jay, who, with a lawyer's caution, named no names.

Major Clark ended his days as a successful lawyer in York, Pennsylvania, returning to service to help defend Baltimore in the War of 1812. Each Fourth of July, he donned his uniform again—and sat on the front porch.

Isaac Barker lived on into his eighties, still farming, at Middletown, serving a term or two in the legislature. His exploits were no secret, now. The old man rather liked to talk about them, but never, for some strange reason, with his friend William Wilkinson, who had handled his reports for General Cornell.

The Quaker heroine, Lydia Darragh, remained in Philadelphia, telling her story, sometimes, to a daughter who was wise enough to write it down.

Sergeant Major Champe married and settled in Virginia, where, after the war, he received a visit from the Tory officer who had commanded his company in Arnold's legion. Amicably enough, the two old soldiers discussed what Champe had really been doing. Later, he moved to Kentucky, then to Ohio. When a French war loomed, as the century closed, General Washington remembered him and wanted to commission him— too late, for Champe had died in 1796. Light Horse Harry Lee had promised him a commission as a reward for his secret service; but, as Champe was released from the army for his own safety, as soon as he returned, the promise was never fulfilled. To become an officer had been the sergeant major's greatest ambition—another irony.

Sergeant Daniel Bissell was rewarded with the "badge of merit," being one of the first men to receive the bit of purple silk that is today the Purple Heart. It has been said he was, like Champe, discharged as soon as he returned, lest the British capture and execute him; but the military records tell a different story. Bissell was still on his company's muster roll till 1783, though there is an eloquent gap from August, 1781, to September, 1782, while he was with the British. He left Connecticut for Richmond, New York, lured by land at $2.12 an acre. When his house burned, he lost his military papers and the silken

Purple Heart, which he kept in the family Bible. When, in his old age, pensions were offered Revolutionary veterans, his remarkable memory, which had retained his secret instructions and the results of a year's espionage, served him again. He could write out the citation Washington had given him some forty years after the award. Two old army friends, David Humphreys and David Cobb, both generals now, made formal statements of his service, and the old spy received his pension.

The people of Windsor, Connecticut, though shocked when a local antiquarian found Bissell's name upon the town records as a deserter, built a monument to him when they learned the truth. Hale, André, and Bissell must be the only spies in history thus honored.

All three of the Mersereaus, Joshua, John and John La-Grange, lived on to ripe old ages. Joshua became surrogate, first of Tioga County, New York, then of Chenango County. John became a little boastful in his old age: "There was none in our army that run so many risks and underwent so many hardships and fatigues as I did." It was claiming too much, no doubt; but if we had the whole story, it might not be very far from the truth.

Samuel Woodhull and Robert Townsend allowed their identity as "the Culpers" to die, silently, though Robert Townsend was dreadfully embarrassed when his family discovered his British uniform among some old clothes. Major Tallmadge, as a prominent citizen of Litchfield, Connecticut, told part of the Culpers' story—not, alas! all he could have told—but never let slip the least hint of their identity. So far as known, neither of "the Culpers" ever said a word of their really brilliant services. Hercules Mulligan was nearly as silent. It is probable that neither the Culpers nor Mulligan ever guessed how many other spy rings had been at work.

Caleb Brewster and Joshua Davis, who had manned the Culper whaleboats, were less reticent. Everyone knew of their service and Davis told many a thrilling tale.

When, years after the war, President Washington visited Long Island, he let it be known he would be glad to see the men who had helped him so much. Austin Roe, riding to meet the President, took a fall, broke his leg, and could not go on. It is by no means certain that the Culpers even tried to go. It is possible they were a little ashamed of their great services to the nation. For them the spy's reward: danger, imminent disgrace, poor pay or none at all.

So, as the years went on, the spies died and the earth took them. Sergeant Bissell alone was decorated; but then, the Continental Army had only one ribbon to give, and few men received it. It was a century or more before the stigma of desertion was removed from Bissell's name, though Champe was publicly cleared as soon as he returned. Intelligence officers who doubled as spies received their ordinary promotions—nothing more. Elijah Hunter asked General Washington for a certificate of service and received it. Few, if any, others received even that. They had done their duty silently. Only an inner circle of specially trusted officers were allowed to know what that duty had been. After the war, silence still seemed wise; and even now the records will not give up the whole story. But the one man who knew most of that story—though even he was far from knowing all—was grateful. Perhaps the gratitude of the man at Mount Vernon was enough.

★ ★ ★

★

Acknowledgments

Inevitably, in a study extending over a period of many years, one accumulates more obligations for friendly and disinterested aid than one can possibly acknowledge; and I have been able to set down here only the greatest of my obligations. In this book, as in others, my chief debt is to the Yale University Library—where privileges were granted me by James T. Babb, Librarian—and to its incomparable staff, especially Harry P. Harrison, head of the Circulation Department, and Dr. Archibald Hanna, of the Coe Collection. Dr. Howard H. Peckham, Director, and Dr. William S. Ewing, Curator of Manuscripts in the Clements Library, University of Michigan, together with their staff, have replied swiftly, competently, and patiently to a continual stream of inquiries. Stephen T. Riley, Librarian of the Massachusetts Historical Society; Robert W. Hill, Keeper of Manuscripts and F. Ivor D. Avellino, of the New York Public Library; David C. Mearns, chief of the Manuscripts Division, and Mrs. Vincent L. Eaton, of the Manuscript Room, Library of Congress; Dr. R. W. G. Vail, Director, and James J. Heslin, of the New-York Historical Society; W. Neill Franklin, Frank E. Bridgers, McLeod Phanelson, of the National Archives; Dr. Francis S. Ronalds, Superintendent, and Dr. Walter Hugins, until recently Park Historian, at the Mor-

ristown National Historical Park, N. J., have all labored end-
lessly to assist me. Dr. Ronalds personally guided me to numerous sources that, without him, I should have missed entirely.
Edward O. Mills, New York City, performed a similar service.

Miss Mary McNerney, of the Seymour Public Library, and
Miss Marjorie Woodruff, of the Ansonia Public Library, have
aided in securing microfilms and interlibrary loans; and Miss
Woodruff guided me to records of Nehemiah Marks's family
in Derby. With the help of Major Kenneth C. Miller, Washington's Headquarters and Museum, Newburgh, N. Y., I was
able to locate Nathaniel Sackett's retained personal copy of a
report to Washington (the signature being torn from the original), which for the first time identifies Sackett as the head
of a spy ring working in New York early in 1777. Dr. Jo-
sephine L. Harper, Manuscript Librarian of the State Historical Society of Wisconsin, has helped locate obscure materials
in the Draper Manuscripts, which, though originally collected
as materials for western frontier history, sometimes provide
surprising information on events in the eastern theatre of
operations. Colonel Fairfax Downey has advised on the theft
and sabotage of artillery, and Walter Pforzheimer, of Washington, has allowed me to use his unique private manuscript
collection. Mrs. Marjorie G. Bouquet, Deputy Supervisor of
Reference and Research Services, Boston Public Library, solved
the problem presented by George R. T. Hewes.

In special problems, I have had special aid as follows:

The Barker spy ring and Geoffrey Wenwood: Herbert O.
Brigham, of the Newport Historical Society; Clarence S.
Brigham, American Antiquarian Society; Clarkson Collins, III,
Rhode Island Historical Society; Dr. C. P. Whittemore, South
Kent School; Miss Mary T. Quinn, Assistant for Archives,
Rhode Island Department of State.

Ann Bates: Professor Willard M. Wallace, Wesleyan University, who generously lent me his notes while I was waiting
for microfilm from London and who allowed me the privilege
of consulting about later discoveries.

Sergeant Daniel Bissell: Miss E. Marie Becker, Reference

Librarian of the New-York Historical Society, who called my attention to entirely unknown printed source material; A. R. Thompson, of West Hartford, who sent me his photostats; Miss Adeline H. Mix, Windsor Public Library; Miss Christine Stokes and Harold W. Ryan, of the National Archives. D. W. King, Librarian of the War Office, London, finally provided an explanation of Sergeant Daniel Bissell's escape from the British forces on which he was spying—a remarkable instance of international co-operation!

Daniel Bliss: Miss Elizabeth R. Pickard, Concord Free Public Library, and Clifford K. Shipton, Custodian of the Harvard University Archives.

Elias Boudinot: H. Kels Swan, South Bound Brook, N.J., owner of a collection of Boudinot manuscripts, and Miss Jeannette D. Black, assistant in the John Carter Brown Library.

Caleb Bruen: Miss Miriam V. Studley, Principal Librarian, New Jersey Division, Newark Public Library; Edwin A. Baldwin, of the Genealogical Society of New Jersey; Donald Lines Jacobus, of the *American Genealogist;* and Richard Lum, of Lum, Fairlie, & Foster, Newark.

Codes and ciphers: Colonel William F. Friedman, formerly of the Signal Intelligence Service, and former Director of the Army Security Agency; Dr. Julian Boyd, editor of the Jefferson Papers, who is familiar with Mr. Jefferson's secret communications; Robert E. Stocking, University of Virginia Library; William J. Van Schreeven, Virginia State Archivist.

Connecticut spies: Miss Hazel A. Johnson and Dean Gertrude E. Noyes, Connecticut College; Miss Ada M. Stoflet, Reference Librarian, University of Iowa; Kenneth B. Homes, Newspaper Librarian, State Historical Society of Missouri; Charles Van Ravenswaay, Missouri Historical Society; Mrs. Marjorie C. Hartman, formerly of the Connecticut State Library; Edward C. Booth, of Lennox Industries, Inc., Marshalltown, Iowa.

Espionage in Westchester, Long Island, and adjoining territory: Mrs. Amy O. Bassford, Eastchester Public Library; Miss Edna Huntington, Long Island Historical Society; Miss Charlotte M. Wiggin, Litchfield Historical Society; Mrs. Amos Struble, Corresponding Secretary of the Westchester County

(N.Y.) Historical Society; W. T. Horton and Carlton B. Scofield, both at various times city historians of Peekskill, N.Y., and Mrs. Kathleen M. Moynahan, assistant; Kenneth A. Lohf, of the Columbia University Libraries; Louis H. Bolander, former Librarian, U.S. Naval Academy; Miss Juliet Wolohan, Assistant Librarian, Manuscript and History Section, New York State Library; Kenneth E. Hasbrouck, New Paltz, N.Y.; Mrs. Addison Reed Hopkins, Brewster, N.Y.; Harry Hansen, editor of *The World Almanac;* Miss Jean L. Ross, Reference Librarian, New Rochelle Public Library; Robertson T. Barrett, Town Historian of Bedford; Cornel Lengyel, of Georgetown, Calif.; William A. Oldridge, of Brooklyn, who searched his manuscript collection for spy materials; John Howland Gibbs Pell and Miss Eleanor Murray, of the Fort Ticonderoga Museum.

Forged documents: Professor Kenneth Coleman, University of Georgia; Professor John R. Alden, Duke University.

David Gray: Crawford E. L. Donohugh, Rare Books Librarian, New York State Library; George N. Harman, Rutland County (Vt.) County Clerk; Miss Clara E. Follette, Librarian and Museum Director, Vermont Historical Society; Mrs. Constance T. Rinden, Assistant Reference Librarian, New Hampshire State Library.

John Hall: Frank E. McKone, Dover, N.H.

John Honeyman: Mrs. Maude Greene, former Librarian of the New Jersey Historical Society; Mrs. M. K. Cones, Reference Librarian, Free Public Library, Jersey City, N.J.; and Leonard Falkner, of the New York *World-Telegram.*

John Howe: Miss Ellen P. Webster, Halifax Memorial Library, Halifax, Canada, and D. C. Harvey, Archivist of Nova Scotia.

Captain Andrew Lee: Miss Elizabeth Kieffer, Librarian of the Lancaster County (Pa.) Historical Society; Richmond D. Williams, Director, and Miss Ernestine M. Kaehlin, Librarian, of the Wyoming Historical and Geological Society, Wilkes Barre, Pa.

Christopher Ludwick: Miss Gertrude D. Hess, Assistant Librarian, American Philosophical Society; Mrs. Margaret D.

Roshong, Secretary of the Valley Forge Park Commission; John M. Fogg and Edward D. Taulane, Jr., of the Ludwick Institute, Philadelphia; William Wood Condit, Falls Village, Pa.; Mrs. Venia T. Phillips, Academy of Natural Science, Philadelphia; Frederick B. Tolles, Director, Friends Historical Library, Swarthmore, Pa.; Professor Matthew W. Black, University of Pennsylvania; Miss Katharine Shorey, Librarian, Martin Memorial Library, York, Pa.; George E. Nitzsche, and Horace Mather Lippincott, Philadelphia.

Medical men as Revolutionary spies: Sir Arthur McNalty, K.C.B.

James and John Moody: John D. F. Morgan, Executive Director, Camden County (N.J.) Historical Society; Miss Dorothy Hammond, Librarian, State Teachers College, Glassboro, N.J.; Charles S. Grossman, Acting Superintendent, Independence National Historical Park, Philadelphia.

Charles Morgan: William S. Dix, Princeton University Library; Harry F. Green, Historical Society of Gloucester City, N.J.; Samuel Smith, Librarian, Monmouth County Historical Association; Donald A. Sinclair, Curator of Special Collections, Rutgers University; Charles E. Hatch, Chief, Research and Interpretation Division, Colonial National Historical Park, Yorktown, Va.

New Jersey military records: Lieutenant Colonel Samuel F. Brink, AF, Adjutant General, Lieutenant Colonel F. Paul, AGC, and Captain J. F. Callahan, Arty, all of the New Jersey National Guard.

Valley Forge, Philadelphia, and adjacent New Jersey: Alfred Hoyt Bill, Princeton, N.J., Mrs. Howard M. Stuckert, Library Director, Free Public Library, Haddonfield, N.J.; Henry J. Young, Senior Archivist, Pennsylvania State Museum; John M. Nugent, Philadelphia Suburban Newspapers, Inc.; Edward W. Hocker, Germantown Historical Society; Miss Anna L. Cladek, Perth Amboy Public Library; John D. Kilbourne, Director, Historical Society of York County; Henry C. Shinn, Mount Holly, N.J.; Loring McMillen, Vice President of the Staten Island Historical Society; Miss Mary J. Messler, head of the Reference Department, Free Public Library, Trenton.

Notes

Reference numbers are to page and paragraph, an incomplete paragraph at the top of a page being reckoned as the first paragraph. Thus "25.1" indicates the first paragraph (or partial paragraph) on page 25. In the same way, "25.2" indicates the second paragraph, "25.3-4" the third and fourth. Where source references support the statements on several pages, they are indicated by pages only, thus: 244-49.

The following abbreviations are used:

AGO: Adjutant General's Office

Accounts: "George Washington's Accounts of Expenses" (ed. by John C. Fitzpatrick). MSS. in WP/LC.

Am. Arch.: American Archives, ed. Peter Force

Cal. NY Hist. MSS.: Calendar of New York Historical Manuscripts

CP: Clinton Papers, Clements Library, University of Michigan

DAB: Dictionary of American Biography

DAH: Dictionary of American History

Egerton: H. E. Egerton (ed.), *Notes of Royal Commission on Losses and Services of American Loyalists,* by D. P. Coke

Facsim: B. F. Stevens's *Facsimiles of Manuscripts*

Freeman: Douglas Southall Freeman, *George Washington: A Biography*
French: Allen French, *General Gage's Informers*
GP: Gage Papers, Clements Library, University of Michigan
GW: George Washington. Also J. C. Fitzpatrick (ed.): *Writings of George Washington*
HCL: Harvard College Library
HS: Historical Society
Journals Cont. Cong.: *Journals* of the Continental Congress
LC: Library of Congress
LWS: L. W. Smith Collection (MSS.), National Historical Park, Morristown, N. J.
MAH: Magazine of American History
Nat. Arch.: National Archives, Washington, D.C.
NJNG: New Jersey National Guard
NY: New York
NYPL: New York Public Library
NYHS: New-York Historical Society
Pa. Arch.: Pennsylvania Archives
Pa. Mag.: Pennsylvania Magazine of History and Biography
PRO: Public Records Office, London
Qy.: Quarterly
Transcripts: Audit Office Transcripts, MS. Room, NYPL
Van Doren: Carl Van Doren, *Secret History of the American Revolution*
WP/LC: Washington Papers, Library of Congress

10.3. William Farrand Livingstone: *Israel Putnam* (1901), pp. 258-59. There is a good account of the Church episode in Freeman: III, 474-75, 487-88, 547-54.
11.1. 4 GW 10. On Washington's payments to Church, see Warrant Book I, Aug. 26, Sept. 26, 1775, WP/LC.
12.1. The few books that mention Wenwood, spell his name Wainwood. The spelling here used is from his own advertisements in the *Newport Mercury*. Henry Ward's letter to Greene, Sept. 26, 1775 (WP/LC), says the girl approached Wenwood in July, 1775. Church wrote on Oct. 3, 1775, that Wenwood had had his letter two months. See also the Church ALS (so called but probably copies) in Sparks MSS., HCL. On butter biscuits, see George Richardson's Scrapbook, No. 971, p. 81, in Newport HS. The article, signed only "J. C. S.," is believed to be by James C. Swan.
12.3. GP, Aug. 25, 1775; Egerton, pp. 262-66; French, pp. 188-89; 4 GW 10. See also Church to GW, undated, and Ward to Greene, Sept. 26, 1775, WP/LC;

S. S. Purple: "Treason of Benjamin Church" (MS), unpublished collection of materials, including verse from Rivington's *New York Gazette*, Oct. 19, 1775, MS. Room, NYPL; Church's examination before House, in *Colls. Mass. HS*, pp. 84-94 (1792, published 1806); J. S. Loring: *Hundred Boston Orators* (1852), pp. 37-44.

13.4. Ward to Greene, Sept. 26, 1775, WP/LC.

14.2. *Ibid.;* Reed to Church (unsigned draft), Sept. 24, 1775, WP/LC.

14.4. The letter is in WP/LC.

15.2-4. 4 GW 9-13; *Am. Arch.*, 4th ser., 3:809; Freeman, III, 546; Ward to Greene, Sept. 26, 1775, WP/LC; *Warren-Adams Letters*, I, 121-22.

16.2. On resignation, see Reed to Church (unsigned draft), Sept. 24, 1775, WP/LC. On Church, see Gilbert Saltonstall to Nathan Hale, Oct. 9, 1775 (original in Conn. HS; Henry Phelps Johnston: *Nathan Hale*, p. 52. Cf. 4 GW 11.

17.5. Gerry to Reed, Oct. 5, 1775, WP/LC.

19.1. The second letter is in Mass. Archives, 138, 327; 4 GW 9-13. See also Paul Revere's letters in *Colls. Mass. HS* I, 1, iii (Jan. 1, 1798), also Sparks MSS., Norton autographs, HCL, and other documents in Sparks MSS., Church, HCL.

20.1. 4 GW 11-17; *Journals* Cont. Cong., IV, 401, 442, 616; V, 693; IX, 784-85; Council of War, Oct. 3/4, 1775, and Church to GW, Oct. [?], 1775, WP/LC; Minutes NY representatives, April 1, 1777, copy in LWS-762-1.

20.7. *Journals* Cont. Cong., III, 334. On confinement by Trumbull, see Johnston, *op. cit.*, p. 153. Original in Conn. HS.

22.1-3. *Warren-Adams Letters*, I, 254-55. On the cartel vessel, see *Independent Chronicle*, July 17, 1777. On Mrs. Church's troubles, PRO, A.O. 13: 73, quoted by French, pp. 199-200.

23.1. Thomas Brown to William Perry, Halifax, May 16, 1782, in PRO, A.O. 13:73, quoted by French, pp. 200-01. The will is in Suffolk County Probate Records, 1757: LXXX, 570-73, and is partly quoted by French, p. 201-n. See also Church (Sr.) to Hancock, June 16, 1779, LWS-1343-1.

25.3. Revere's own story is accessible in various texts. It is here quoted from French, p. 164.

27.1. Church's letters are in CP, where they may be traced by date. On very early British intelligence, see *Facsim*, XXIV, 2024, "Account of Money Issued for His Majesty's Secret and Special Service."

28.3. On John Hall, see GP, 1775, *passim*.

29.2. GP, March 16, 1775. The story of the unknown Concord agent is well told in French, *passim*. It has been verified from the original reports in CP, arranged by date. On other British agents, see Egerton, pp. 169-70; *Winslow Papers*, p. 364.

32.1-2. Ditson to Gage, March 9, 1775, GP. See also letter of March 21, April 23, May 12, 1775; Lorenzo Sabine: *Biographical Sketches of Loyalists of the American Revolution* (1864), II, 30; Egerton, p. 65; Marquis de Chastellux: *Travels in North America* (1787), pp. 218-19. Also letters of "Mr. Hoare," otherwise unknown, GP, Aug. and Sept., 1775, and an unsigned letter of Feb. 25, 1775, GP.

33.3. Thompson's reports are in GP, under dates. See also French, pp. 126-45; N. H. Adj. Gen. *Report* (1866), p. 262-n; Ellis: *Memoir*, p. 83; Richard Frothingham: *History of the Siege of Boston* (1873), p. 185; James Renwick: *Life of Benjamin Thompson* (in Jared Sparks, ed.: *Library of American Biography*,

2nd ser., V, 39-40). A last-minute report of the Concord spy, dated April 18, 1775, probably reached Gage too late to be of any use.

38.3. De Bernière's Narrative is in *Bostonian Society Publications*, 9: 72-98 (1912) and in *Colls. Mass. HS*, 2nd ser., 4. It is confirmed by the fact that the people he names in various towns can be identified by local documents and histories. This officer is not to be confused with John De Bernière, in CP. Captain Brown's full name does not appear in the narrative but is in the British Army list, 1774. Gage's request for a topographical officer is in Allen French (ed.): *A British Fusilier*, p. 27. See also GP, March 8, 1775.

42.2. The editor of De Bernière in *Bostonian Soc. Publs.*, 9:77 (1912) gives this man's name as "Isaac" Jones, evidently because the first Isaac Jones described him as a "namesake." He was evidently William Jones, whose inn stood near what is now the junction of Main and Southbridge streets, Worcester. See C. A. Wall: *Reminiscences of Worcester*, p. 36.

43.3. Justin Winsor (ed.): *Narrative and Critical History of America*, III, ii.

48.9-49.1. On Dr. Curtis, see *Bostonian Soc. Publs.*, 9:85 (1912).

52-53. George Tolman: *John Jack the slave and Daniel Bliss, the Tory* (copy in Concord Free Public Library); Lemuel Shattuck: *History of Concord*, p. 96; Allen French: *Day of Concord and Lexington*, p. 160-n; *Colls. Worcester HS*, XIII, 251ff.; obituary, *Columbian Centinel* (Boston), Mar. 8, 1806.

55.1. See *Journal kept by Mr. John Howe while he was employed as a British Spy*, Concord, N.H.: Luther Roby, Printer, 1927. Copies of this survive in the N.H. HS, NYPL, and American Antiquarian Society, Worcester. It is reproduced in Mass. HS Photostat Series, No. 82. Quotations here are from the reprint in *MAH*, Extra No. 132, vol. 33, No. 4, pp. 165-90 (1927). Like De Bernière, Howe is confirmed by the accuracy with which he reports local individuals and taverns, as confirmed by local histories and early tax lists. The snowstorm he reports is also reported in diaries or annotated almanacs by the Rev. Breck Parkman, Ebenezer Parkman, the Rev. Samuel West, and the Rev. Jeremy Belknap. Original documents by the first two are in the American Antiquarian Society, the last two in Mass. HS.

56.3. "Worcester" in the text is plainly a misprint for "Watertown," as it is described as being six miles from Boston.

58-59. Smith, Jones, and Wheaton, mentioned by Howe, all appear in Waltham tax lists and vital statistics of the period.

68.1. Revere's espionage system is described in his own story but is confirmed by other documents, especially the Gage Papers. (Where dates for documents in the Gage Papers are given in the text, they are not repeated in the notes, a rule usually followed with the Clinton Papers.)

70.3. Revere to John Lamb, Sept. 4, 1774; Esther Forbes: *Paul Revere and the Times He Lived In*, p. 225.

70.4. On the Portsmouth raid, see Charles L. Parsons: "Capture of Fort William and Mary," *Proc. N.H. HS*, 4:14-47 (1906), which has a good Bibliography; *Letters and Papers of Major General John Sullivan* (ed. Otis G. Hammond), III, 420; *N.H. State Papers*, VII, 420-21; Elwin H. Page: "King's Powder, 1774," *New England Qy.*, 18:83-92 (1845); John Alden: *General Gage in America*, p. 224; C. P. Whittemore: "New Hampshire's John Sullivan" (MS., Columbia Dissertation, 1957), pp. 40-48.

71.2. Thomas Newell's Diary, Sept. 15-20, 1774, printed in Frothingham, *op. cit.*, cf. pp. 15, 364; GP, May 12, 1775; Fairfax Downey: *Sound of the Guns*, pp. 23-24; "A Bostonian" (B. B. Thatcher, supposed author): *Traits of the Tea-Party* (1835), pp. 257-58.

75.5. Justin Winsor (ed.): *The Memorial History of Boston*, III, 68-n.

77.1-2. On Dawes, see *DAB*, V, 150. On the lanterns: John Lee Watson: "Paul Revere's Signal," *Mass. HS Proc.*, 17:164-177 (1876); *Boston Daily Advertiser*, July 20, 1876; Forbes, *op. cit.*, pp. 254-56; C. F. Gettemy: *True Story of Paul Revere*, pp. 93-97.

79.3. Devens's own statement is in Frothingham, *op. cit.*, p. 57; J. T. Austin: *Life of Elbridge Gerry*, I, 68.

81-84. GP especially May 25, June 2, 5, 22, July 16, Sept. 10, 1775; Proceedings of the Committee of Safety, April 24, 26, 30, May 3, 14, 23, 24, 1775; Allen French: *First Year of the American Revolution*, pp. 190-92.

85.2. GP, July 26, 1775.

85.3. *Ibid.*, *passim*.

86.1-2. On Galloway, see Egerton, pp. 88-99. On Kearsley and Brooks, Secret Service Accounts, CP; *Diary of Jacob Hiltzheimer* (ed. Jacob C. Parsons, 1893), pp. 17, 19, 20, 32; Egerton, pp. 106-09, 143, 355-56; Alexander Graydon: *Memoirs* (1811), pp. 111-12; *Book of the First City Troop, Philadelphia City Cavalry* (1915), p. 6; Minutes Philadelphia Committee of Safety, Oct. 24, 1775; Caesar to Thomas Rodney, Oct. 9, 1775, in *Extracts from the Letters of Caesar Rodney* (ed. George Herbert Rydan, 1933), p. 65; *Diary of Christopher Marshall* (1847), pp. 8, 149.

87.1-3. The forged documents are in GP. The stolen originals were for a long time in possession of John Drayton, of Georgia. See Drayton: *Memoirs of the American Revolution . . . as relating to South Carolina*, I, 347-48, 357; R. W. Gibbes: *Documentary History of the American Revolution*, I, 100; C. C. Jones: *History of Georgia*, II, 180; *Am. Arch.*, 4th ser., 1:1109-11; *Coll. Ga. HS*, III, 229-30 (1873); Kenneth Coleman: *American Revolution in Georgia*, p. 51.

88.1. Reed to Baldwin, July 28, 1775, WP/LC; Baldwin to GW, Aug. 15, 16, 1775, WP/LC; Winthrop Sargent: *Life . . . of . . . André*; p. 440; John Leach's Journal, Timothy Newell's Journal, July 20, 1775, *New England Historical and Genealogical Register*, 19:255-63; *Colls. Mass. HS*, 4th ser., 1:261-76 (1852); H. Commeger and R. Morris: *Spirit of 1776*, I, 147, 847.

88.3. *Diary of Anna Green Winslow* (ed. Alice Morse Earle, 1894), p. 110; Peter Edes Journal, *Mass. HS Colls.*, 4th ser., 1:264 (1852), also Leach and Newell, as above; Loring, *op. cit.*, pp. 29-37; *DAB*, XI, 438; *Publs. Colonial Soc. Mass.*, 17:149 (1929-1930); H. C. Burnett (ed.): *Letters of Members of the Continental Congress, passim*; 4 GW 174, 287, 295, 312; 5 GW 323-n, 324, 336-37, 365, 384; Historical Manuscripts Commission, *Stopford-Sackville MSS.*, p. 42; Egerton, p. 143; Arthur Lee Papers (MS.), (HCL), Vol. II, Nos. 68, 69; Vol. IV, No. 7 (MS. Am. 811 FX).

89.1-2. *Traits of the Tea-Party*, pp. 213, 217-18; interrogation of an unknown man, GP, May-June, 1775; James Hawkes (supposed author): *Retrospect of the Boston Tea-Party* (1834), pp. 59-61; Daniel T. V. Huntoon: "An Old Bostonian, Robert Twelves Hewes," *Weekly Transcript*, Jan. 26, 1886 (Boston Public Library).

89.3. *Accounts*, pp. 6-7.

90-92. Henri Doniol: *Histoire de la participation de la France à l'établissement des Etats-Unis d'Amérique*, I, 128, 138-39, 265-66, 287; *Facsim.*, XIII, 1301; G. O. Trevelyan: *George the Third and Charles Fox*, pp. 38-39; Charles H.

Sherrill: *French Memories of Eighteenth Century America,* p. 19; Cornelis de Witt: *Thomas Jefferson,* Appendix.

95.3. On Dawkin, see *DAB* and Bibliography there given. One of his advertisements appears in *Pennsylvania Journal,* July 19, 1758. Two of his scientific plates are in *Transactions of the American Philosophical Society,* 1771.

96-99. *Cal. NY Hist. MSS.,* I, 296, 308, 345-46, 491; Egerton, p. 168; *Am. Arch.,* 4th ser., 6:1054, 1159; 5 GW 194; Worthington C. Ford: *Correspondence and Journals of Samuel Blatchley Webb,* I, 148; Solomon Drowne to his sister, June 24, 1776, quoted in Freeman, IV, 121. The Drowne letter, formerly in the Tomlinson Collection, belonging to the Mercantile Library and in custody of NYPL, has been sold to an unknown purchaser.

100.2. *Cal. NY Hist. MSS.,* I, 357. On the conspiracy in general, see William Gordon: *History of the Rise, Progress and Establishment of the Independence of the United States* (1788), II, 276-77; John Marshall: *Life of George Washington* (1850), II, 392; Washington Irving: *Washington,* II, 242-46; *Proceedings of the Committee for the Hearing,* etc., June 22-26, 1776; Diary of Ezra Stiles, June 28, 1776; P. T. Curtenius to Richard Varick, June 22, 1776; Joseph to Sarah Hodgkin, July 17, 1776, all in H. Wade and R. Livingston: *This Glorious Cause,* pp. 29, 210; Henry Russell Drowne: *Sketch of Fraunces Tavern,* pp. 12-13; *Minutes of a Conspiracy Against the Liberties of America,* (Philadelphia: John Campbell, 1865); Benson J. Lossing: "Washington's Life Guard," *Historical Magazine,* 2:129-34 (1858).

101.4-5. *Cal. NY Hist. MSS.,* I, 325, 373, 375.

102.1-3. Ketcham swore at Hickey's court-martial that the defendant had been committed to jail "last Saturday week," or June 15, 1776. Caleb Clapp's Diary, *Hist. Mag.,* 3rd ser., 3:135 (1874), says Hickey was jailed June 21; but Ketcham was himself already in jail when Hickey arrived. See *Journal of the Provincial Congress,* I, 495. See also *Cal. NY Hist. MSS.,* 258, 343; *Am. Arch.,* 4th ser., 6:1411-12.

103.1. *Cal. NY Hist. MSS.,* I, 295, 342-44, 373, 425; Benson J. Lossing: *Washington* (1860), II, 175; Frank Moore (ed.): *Diary of the American Revolution* (1860), I, 254-56 (June 26, 1776). The arrests are in the service records given in Carlos E. Godfrey: *Commander-in-Chief's Guard.* Godfrey's statements must be treated with caution, as he depends on *Minutes of a Conspiracy Against the Liberties of America* which is based on *Minutes of the Trial and Examination of Certain Persons in the Province of New York* (London: J. Bewick), part of which is certainly fraudulent. See John C. Fitzpatrick: "George Washington Scandals," *Scribner's,* 81:389-95 (1927).

103.2. Lossing in his *Washington* (I, 176) states that he had the facts from one W. J. Davis, who had them from Peter Embury, of New York, who knew Phoebe Fraunces. The story is repeated in Drowne, *op. cit.,* pp. 12, 17. Freeman, IV, 121-n, believes the whole story a fabrication. The story was certainly widely accepted at the time. The alleged warning by a waiter named William Collier, or Corbie, rests on the doubtful evidence of *Minutes of a Conspiracy.*

103.3. 5 GW 193.

105.2. *Am. Arch.,* 4th ser., 6:1085.

106.3. *Cal. NY Hist. MSS.,* I, 375.

106.5. *Am. Arch.,* 4th ser., 6:1085-86.

107.2. *Ibid.,* 4th ser., 6:1084-86, 1109, 1119, 1148. MS. Orderly Book of Colonel Charles Webb, June 27, 1776, Conn. State Library; Diary of Ensign Caleb

Clapp, June 27, 1776, *Hist. Mag.*, 3rd ser., 3:136 (1874); *New England Hist. & Geneal. Register*, 23:206 (1869).

108.1-3. Eustis to Townsend, *New England Hist. & Geneal. Register* 23:208 (1869). See also Caleb Clapp's Diary, *loc. cit.*

108.2-3. Godfrey, *op. cit.*, p. 29ff.; Moore, *op. cit.*, I, 257, quoting a letter from a certain S. Gwyn to "Colonel Crafts"—presumably the Massachusetts artilleryman. Pension statement of Anthony Cherdovoyne, Nat. Arch.—R.1908.

108.5. *Am. Arch.*, 4th ser., 6:1148.

111.2-3. Livingston to GW, Aug. 21, 1776, WP/LC; Thomas Jones: *History of New York During the Revolutionary War*, I, 602; Sidney George Fisher: *True History of the American Revolution*, pp. 301, 311; George Bancroft: *History of the United States* (1886), V, 28; Robert Beatson: *Naval and Military Mem. of Great Britain*, VI, 44, 53; Maria Campbell: *Revolutionary Services and Civil Life of General William Hull*, p. 45. On Mascoll's mission, see *Accounts*, p. 43.

112.1-3. 6 GW 1-2, 18-19, 33; *Cal. NY Hist. MSS.*, p. 268; the original report is in Papers of the Continental Congress, LC. On Colonel Nicoll, see James A. Roberts: *New York in the Revolution*, I, 271; II, 244, 255; *DAR Lineage Book*, CXL, 24. See also *Public Papers of George Clinton*, I, 346-47, *Journal of the New York Provincial Congress*, Sept. 13, 1776.

112.4. George Dudley Seymour: *Captain Nathan Hale and Major John Palsgrave Wyllys*, p. 25.

113.3-4. William Henry Shelton: "What Was the Mission of Nathan Hale?" *Journ. Am. Hist.*, 9:269-89 (1915); Victor H. Paltsits: "Use of Invisible Ink During the American Revolution," *Bulletin*, NYPL, 35:361-64 (1935); Bezaleel Kerr to Aeneas Urquhart, May 22, 1779, WP/LC and documents immediately following; *Journals* Cont. Cong., III, 392; *Colls. NYHS,* (1886), pp. 178ff.; William Jay: *Life of John Jay* (1833), I, 64-66.

114.2. Maria Campbell, *op. cit.*, pp. 34-35. This was not published till 1847. General Hull had, however, told part of the Hale story to Hannah Adams, who used it in her *Summary History of New England* (1799). Sergeant Hempstead first published his account of Hale in the *Republican* (St. Louis, Mo.), Jan. 18, 1827 (files in Missouri HS and in State HS of Missouri). It was reprinted in the *Hartford Courant*, April 2, 1827, in the *Long Island Star*, April 5, 1827, and in George Dudley Seymour: *Documentary Life of Nathan Hale*, pp. 311-14. On Hannah Adams, see Johnston, *op. cit.*, p. 100-n.

115.2. "Testimony of Asher Wright," Stuart Papers, Conn. HS. This was taken by R. N. Wright, of Hanover, N.H., when Asher Wright was eighty-two. It was probably written, or rewritten, by Cyrus P. Bradley, who collected much Hale material for a never written biography. See Seymour, *Documentary Life of Nathan Hale*, pp. 315-18. Wright's military papers are in the Nat. Arch., S-36854, but they are of little value. See also Maria Campbell, *op. cit.*, p. 23.

115.4. Nathan to Enoch Hale, June 3, 1776; Seymour, *Documentary Life of Nathan Hale*, p. 312-n; *Republican* (St. Louis, Mo.), Jan. 18, 1827.

116.2. Johnston: *op. cit.*, p. 80; Benson J. Lossing: *The Pictorial Field-Book of the Revolution*, II, 609; Benson J. Lossing: *Two Spies*, pp. 16-17. See also a book by Morton J. Pennypacker, with the same title, p. 10.

118.3. *Despatches of Molyneux Shuldham*, July 6, 1776 (ed. Robert Wilden Neeser).

118.5. Johnston, *op. cit.*, pp. 111-12. This document was discovered, probably in the 1890's, by William Kelby, Librarian of the New-York Historical Society.

It has been described as "Howe's" orderly book. It is certainly an orderly book originating in Howe's army. There is another MS. copy in the Clements Library. For various accounts of the capture, see Johnston, *op. cit.*, pp. 115, 372.

119.3. Frederick Mackenzie's *Diary*, I, 61-62. Bellamy Partridge: *Sir Billy Howe*, p. 92. On Samuel Hale's denial that he betrayed his cousin, see Seymour, *Documentary Life of Nathan Hale*, pp. 303-06, reprinting *Essex Journal*, Feb. 13, 1776, and *Captain Nathan Hale and Major John Palsgrave Wyllys*, pp. 7, 22, 28, 32. There are casual references to Hale's death in the papers of David Canada (Nat. Arch., W. 25388; BL Wt.-26313-160-55) and John Molthrop (S-36081) both privates in Hale's company, and in *Diary of Samuel Richards* (Philadelphia: 1909), p. 71.

121.1. Joseph Addison: *Cato*, Act. IV, Scene 2.

121.4. On the "painted soldier," see *Kentish Gazette*, Nov. 9, 1776. (Files in Royal Museum and Public Library, Canterbury, Kent, and NYPL.) The passage is quoted in Shelton: "What Was the Mission of Nathan Hale?" *loc. cit.*

122.1-2. Enoch Hale's Diary (MS.), quoted in Seymour, *Documentary Life of Nathan Hale*, pp. 56-57; Maria Campbell, *op. cit.*, p. 38.

123.1. *Cal. NY Hist. MSS.*, I, 669-71. The British were still trying to recruit troops around Albany as late as Mar., 1778. See *Minutes Albany Committee of Correspondence* (ed. James Sullivan), I, 954.

123.2. 6 GW 280; 7 GW 24; 8 GW 50.

124.2. *Cal NY Hist. MSS.*, I, 669-73; Egerton, p. 190.

124.3. *Cal. NY Hist. MSS.*, I, 669-71, 674-75; Hoffman Nickerson: *Turning Point of the Revolution*, pp. 89-103.

125.3. 4 GW 487-88; 8 GW 131.

125.4. *Cal. NY Hist. MSS.*, I, 338; *Journal of the Provincial Congress*, May 22, 24, 1776, I, 476-78; Diary of Ensign Caleb Clapp, *loc. cit.*, 3:249; Victor H. Paltsits, *Minutes of the Commissioners for Conspiracies*, I, 413.

126.1. *Cal. NY Hist. MSS.*, II, 64.

126.2. *Ibid.*, II, 198-99.

126.4. *Ibid.*, II, 135.

127.1. Heath Papers, Mass. HS, 116-17, copy in WP/LC; 6 GW 497-98; Otto Hufeland: *Westchester County During the American Revolution*, III, 214-15.

127.2-3. *Cal. NY Hist. MSS.*, II, 83, 86, 587; *Transcripts*, XXII, 535, 537.

127.5. *Cal. NY Hist. MSS.*, II, 128-38; *Mass. HS Proc.*, 2nd ser., 12:139-42 (1898).

128.2. Paltsits, *Minutes*, I, 157-58; II, 658-59, 698, 701, 711, 724.

128.3. *Cal. NY Hist. MSS.*, II, 198-211. Davis may be identical with the man referred to in *Mass. HS Proc.*, 2nd ser., 12:142 (1898).

128.4-5. *Cal. NY Hist. MSS.*, II, 165-66, 179-80; *DAB*, XX, 422-23.

129.3. *Cal. NY Hist. MSS.*, II, 165ff.

132.3. Robert Bolton: *History of Westchester*, II, 672-73; Hufeland, *op. cit.*, III, 214-15; Heath to GW, Jan. 9, 1777, GW to Heath, Jan. 12, 1777, WP/LC; court-martial record of Daniel Strang, Jan. 4, 1777, Heath Papers, Mass. HS; Josephus C. Frost: *Strang Genealogy* (1915).

134.3. *Cal. NY Hist. MSS.*, II, 179-82. Accompanying documents show court-martial was in session in early June, 1776.

137.3-4. James Montgomery Bailey: *History of Danbury*, Chapters X and XX.

Only the pension statement gives Bunker's name. "Esquire" Young was probably Samuel Young.

138ff. The main sources for Enoch Crosby's story are: H. L. Barnum: *The Spy Unmasked* (1829); Crosby's pension statement and supporting affidavits (Nat. Arch., S/10/505); and *Minutes of the Committee and First Commission for Detecting Conspiracies (Colls. NYHS,* LVII-LVIII, 1924-1925). On Crosby's later life, see Charles H. Haswell: *Reminiscences of an Octogenarian,* pp. 129, 249. Barnum's book was reprinted by the Fishkill *Weekly Times* in 1886. On Crosby as an Associator, see *Cal. NY Hist. MSS.,* I, 76.

142.3-4. Jay to Sackett, Dec. 30, 1776. Original at Washington's Headquarters and Museum, Newburgh, N.Y. In the same collection, see also the order of Jan. 3, 1777, signed by John Jay, empowering Sackett to use the militia. Robert Harpur's letter of Oct. 7, 1777, also seems to refer to Sackett's counter-intelligence agents. On the spies' reports, see *Colls. NYHS,* LVII, 93, 94 (1924).

142.5. Original Sackett letter in *Colls. NYHS,* LVIII, 420 (1925).

143.6. *Ibid.,* LVIII, 32 (1925), records Morehouse's commission.

144.3. Louis S. Patrick: "Secret Service of the American Revolution," *Conn. Mag.,* 11:269 (1907). The officer was Colonel Henry Ludington, NY Militia. On Crosby's later services, see *Archives of the State of New York. The Revolution,* I, 214, Col. 1, and Assembly Papers, 24-350; Military Register, N.Y. State Library, Albany (MS.).

145ff. Main sources for the Palmer story are: Putnam's letter of Aug. 4, 1777, CP; Transcripts XVII, 145-51, XXIX, 19; Frost, *op. cit.,* pp. 38-39; Sergeant Daniel Ware's Orderly Book (Conn. HS), reprinted in W. C. Ford: *Putnam's General Orders,* p. 31; W. F. Livingston: *op. cit.,* pp. 350-51; David Humphreys: *Life of Putnam* (1818), p. 147; Oliver W. B. Peabody: *Life of Putnam* (ed. Jared Sparks), pp. 200-01; Benson J. Lossing: "Romance of the Hudson," *Harper's,* 311:647 (1876); Increase N. Tarbox: *Life of Israel Putnam,* pp. 313-14; Hufeland, *op. cit.,* III, 215-19; *Cal. NY Hist. MSS.,* I, 188; II, 88, 258-60; Diary of Sergeant Major Simon Giffin (Photostat, Yale), Aug. 8, 1777.

148.1. Jedidiah to Joseph Huntington, July 24, 1777, *Colls. Conn. HS,* XX, 355; Stirling to GW, July 24, 1777, WP/LC; Putnam to GW, July 26, 1777, WP/LC.

148.2. Fellows to GW, July 24, 1777, WP/LC.

148.3. *Colls. NYHS,* LVIII, 342-48, 354, 363, 443 (1925); Burgoyne to Clinton, July 9/21, 1777, Sept., 1777, CP; interrogation of Joseph Bettys, Oct., 1777, CP.

151.3. The text of Clinton's note follows that of the retained copy in CP. The text actually sent may have some minor verbal changes, but is now nearly illegible.

152ff. The warning with the description of Taylor is in Putnam to GW, July 24, 26, 1777 WP/LC; Fish to Putnam, July 24, 1777; 8 GW 468. The best account of the incident is in the *Public Papers of George Clinton,* II, 398-401, 403-29, 443. See also Lossing: *Pictorial Field-Book,* 389, 684; William B. Willcox: *American Rebellion,* p. 77-n; Willard M. Wallace: *Appeal to Arms,* p. 164. Publication No. 34 of the HS of Newburgh Bay and the Highlands contains a sketch of Dr. Bigby and gives a description of his house in Mildred Seese: *Old Orange Houses,* II, 14. The original letter, in rather bad condition, and the silver bullet are at Fort Ticonderoga. There are two other copies in CP. See also John M. Eager: "Daniel Taylor, the Spy," *Hist. Mag.,* 1st ser., 8:149-50 (1864); Edward J. Lowell: *Hessians and Other German*

Auxiliaries, pp. 154-55; *Pa. Arch.,* 1st ser., V, 639-40; Diary of Sergeant Major Simon Giffin (Photostat, Yale), Oct. 18, 1777.

154.2. Transcripts, XXXVIII, 49-51, 71; Egerton, pp. 113-14.

155.1-3. Transcripts, XXXVIII, 71; Egerton, pp. xliv, 113-14, 155-65, 173-n, 211-12; *Winslow Papers,* p. 321. On Skinner's general services, see Transcripts, XXXVIII, 49-51.

155.4. *Ibid.,* 58, 69; Egerton, pp. 114-15; 7 GW 117.

156.1-4. Egerton, pp. li, 4, 5, 33-34, 113, 156; William A. Whitehead: *Contributions to the Early History of Perth Amboy,* pp. 103-06; William S. Stryker: *New Jersey Volunteers; Am. Arch.,* 4th ser., 4:476.

157.2. Intelligence Papers, July 27, 1777, CP; 8 GW 503.

157.3-4. 17 GW 368-70; Stryker, *op. cit., passim.*

158ff. On Moody, see Egerton, xlvi, xlviii, 132, 134, 144; Sabine, *op. cit.,* II, 90ff.; Edwin Salter and George C. Beekman: *Old Times in Old Monmouth,* pp. 51, 58-60; Memorandum Book of Intelligence, CP, *passim;* Stryker, *op. cit.,* pp. 15, 17, 22; Moore, *op. cit.,* II, 307, 466; Transcripts, XXXVIII, 119-30; Moody's own story as told in his *Narrative of the Exertions and Sufferings of Lieutenant James Moody* (London, 1782, 1783), reprinted by Charles I. Bushnell, 1865, and in his *Crumbs for Antiquarians,* pp. 9-98; and by R. M. Dorson (ed.): *American Rebels,* pp. 134-46.

158.3. American Revolution Papers, Intelligence, LC. Anderson may be identical with Thomas Anderson, Tory blacksmith, of the Manor of Livingston, whom the Commissioners for Conspiracies did not release on recognizances until June 30, 1778. See Paltsits: *Minutes,* I, 142-43, 146, 152, 161.

158-59. Ambrose Serle to Earl of Dartmouth, April 25, 1777, Dartmouth MSS., in *Facsim.* XXIV, 2057.

159-60. *Ibid.,* 2055, 2057, 2059-85, 2087-98, 2100; McLane MSS. (NYHS) Vol. II, No. 40; *Despatches of Molyneux Shuldham,* pp. 237-38. The Parker map is in CP.

On Shanks, see Washington's Warrant Book, II, folio 101-v, LC; GW to Board of General Officers, Lee to GW, Shanks court-martial record, all June 2, 1778, WP/LC; Diary of Elijah Fisher, printed in Godfrey, *op. cit.,* and in *Hist. Mag.,* Extra No. 6 (1909); *Pa. Arch.,* 5th ser., III, 473, 480, 495; Edward W. Hocker: "Spies, Hangings and Other Crimes During the Winter at Valley Forge," *Picket Post* (1948), p. 48. Henry Woodman, early amateur historian of Valley Forge, talked with people who saw the hanging. Cf. 12 GW 11, 14 and, on Church's fate, Fisher's Diary, June 4, 1778.

160.3. On Galloway's value, see Egerton, pp. 85, 88-89. On Potts and Badge, *ibid.,* pp. 136-37; 172; Van Doren, p. 91; CP *passim.*

161.2-3. *Documents Relating to the Colonial History of New York,* VIII, 711. The guide already with the British was Ephraim Deforest, of Redding, who had joined the British in Nov., 1776. See Transcripts, XII, 277-79. On Zechariah Hawkins, see his confession, May 2, 1777, WP/LC; Samuel Orcutt and Ambrose Beardsley: *History of the Old Town of Derby* (1880), pp. 175, 202, 231, 238, mention a Zechariah Hawkins probably identical with the innkeeper.

161-62. On Dunbar, see records of Hartford Superior Court and Depositions in Revolutionary War Archives, VIII, 219-21; XXIX, 67-71, in Conn. State Library; N. Smith, G. B. Smith, and Allena J. Dates: *Bristol, Connecticut,* pp. 141-49, Epaphroditus Peck: *Loyalists of Connecticut,* pp. 12-13; Epaphroditus Peck: *History of Bristol,* Chapter VII; Joseph Anderson: *History of Waterbury,* II, 434-38, 442, 458; Carleton Beals: *Making of Bristol,* pp. 66-69; T. Jones:

History of New York, I, 175; Anon.: *Bristol, Connecticut* (1907), pp. 141-55; *Connecticut Courant,* Jan. 7, March 3, 17, 24, 1777 (file in Conn. State Library).

162.3. Transcripts, XII, 288.

163.3-4. Report of Corporal Tompkins, Aug. 22, 1877, CP; terrain report, Oct. [?], 1777, CP.

164.1. List of ships in Portsmouth, May 22, 1777; list of French officers; other documents, *passim,* April and May, 1777, all in CP.

165.1. Mifflin to Gerry, Nov. 21, 1776, Walter Pforzheimer Collection.

166.1. John Mersereau Papers, Nat. Arch. (W.17137); Gordon: *History of New Jersey,* II, 128, 150, 198; 2 GW 243.

166.2. 6 GW 369; *N.J. Archives,* 2nd ser., III, 316; *Pa. Mag.,* 8:392 (1884); the last for exploits of Joseph Reed, not strictly espionage.

166.4. 6 GW 370; Henry Knox to Mrs. Knox, Dec. 28, 1776; Stryker, *op. cit.,* pp. 371, 372; *Am. Arch.,* 5th ser., 3:1342-44; Freeman, IV, 304; Chambers to GW, Dec. 16, 1776, LWS-1342/1; 6 GW 350.

167ff. Honeyman's story is best told in John Van Dyke: "Unwritten Account of a Spy of Washington," *Our Home* (local magazine of Somerville, N.J., x.1.455-52 (1873), file in NYPL. Van Dyke deposited a MS. with the Adjutant General, NJNG, but it has been allowed to disappear. There is an excellent article, Leonard Faulker: "Spy for Washington," *American Heritage,* 8:58-64 (1957). See also Charlton Beck: *Roads of Home,* pp. 95-106; William S. Stryker: *Batles of Trenton and Princeton,* p. 89; *History Qy* (Somerset County, N.J.), 8:250, 270, 276 (1919); J. P. Snell: *History of Hunterdon and Somerset Counties, N.J.* (1881), p. 51. Certain Honeyman family documents are in the possession of Mrs. Maude Greene, formerly of the Library of the N.J. HS. See also G. O. Trevelyan: *The American Revolution,* II, 93-94. For Honeyman's imprisonment on treason charges and his subsequent release, see *Minutes of the Council of Safety . . . NJ,* Dec. 5, 1777 (p. 169) and Dec. 20, 1777 (p. 176).

170.2. Snell, *op. cit.,* p. 51; *Am. Arch.,* 5th ser., 3:1343-44; Trenten HS, *Trenton,* I, 120. Cf. W. B. Reed: *Life and Correspondence of Joseph Reed,* I, 272.

170.3-4. 6 GW 457. Cf. *Accounts.* Map reproduced in Freeman, IV, 430, and A. H. Bill: *Campaign of Princeton,* p. 100. Original in LC; 6 GW 457.

171-73. The best account of Sackett's network is in his own letter to Washington of April 7, 1777. This had never been identified as Sackett's because the signature and a few lines of text were torn from the original—probably by some cautious staff officer, eager to veil Sackett's identity. However, Sackett's own retained copy, hitherto unknown, is in the Sackett MSS. at Washington's Headquarters, Newburgh, N.Y. The text of the original in Freeman, IV, 638-39, tells most of the story. See also 7 GW 92, 101; *Accounts,* p. 43; Warrant Book II, LC.

174.1. Journal of the Honourable Hessian Grenadier Battalion at one time von Minnigerode later von Loewenstein, June 5, 1777, Hesse Hanau Jäger Corps: German Transcripts at Morristown (N.J.) National Historical Park.

174-77. Costigin's papers are in Nat. Arch., S/43/337, BL Wt. 403-200 (RG 15 A). See also "Z" to GW, Dec. 7, 16, 19, 1778, WP/LC; memorial to GW, April 4, 1782, WP/LC. On Pollock, see Draper MS., 49-J-4-8, 65. On the Costigin family, see *N.J. Archives,* XXIV, 110; Christ Church Parish Register, 1774 (typed copy in Rutgers University Library); for Washington's correspondence with his intelligence officers about Costigin, see Index of GW. See also GW to Maxwell, March 15, 19, 1779, WP/LC and 14 GW 240, 12 GW 346; Maxwell to GW, March 17, 1779; "Z" to Matthias Ogden, Dec. 28, 30, 1778;

Stirling to GW, Jan. 13, 1779, all in WP/LC; Francis B. Heitman, *Historical Register of Officers of the Continental Army* . . . (1914), p. 172. A spy's report signed "Z" or "T" to Ogden from New York, Nov. 16, 1778, is in the Houghton Library, Harvard (*53M-163) but is in a handwriting different from that of the "Z" reports.

177-79. Papers of John La Grange Mersereau (S-7217), John Mersereau (W-17137) and Joshua Mersereau, Jr. (S-7234) in Nat. Arch. See also HR. No. 737, 1st Sess., 36th Congress, Report No. 546. The elder Joshua Mersereau has no record in Nat. Arch. See also *New York Genealogical and Biographical Record*, 27:195, (1896); Emma Mersereau Newton: "Genealogical History of the Mersereaus." *Adams Mag. of General Literature*, 26-10 (1892). (File in NYPL.)

Lawrence Mersereau: "Mersereau Family Genealogy," *New York Geneal. and Biog. Record*, 28:17, 19-20, 71, 125 (1897), Gordon, *History of New Jersey*, II, 128, 150, 198.

Addison to Joshua Mersereau 4 or 14 (no month, paper torn) 1782, in Pforzheimer Collection; Warrant Book, No. 2, Dec. 20, 1776, WP/LC; Joshua Mersereau to Elias Boudinot, LWS-1481/1; GW to Smith, March 12, 1783, LWS-2130/1.

179-81. Washington to Stirling, July 26, 1777, 8 GW, 278, original in Pforzheimer Collection. Text here follows the MS. On Meeker, see S-2815 and S-5087, Nat. Arch. See also 6 GW 280; 8 GW 353, 480; 10 GW 329; 12 GW 178. Morgan to GW July 24, 1777, WP/LC. Washington authorizes black marketing in his letter of Sept. 29, 1777, HCL. Reports of the other spies named here are in WP/LC, chronologically arranged and alphabetically indexed. Maxwell to GW, Sept. 12, 1778, WP/LC, may refer to the Hendricks incident. See also *Accounts*, pp. 67-69. On the black marketing, see also LWS-603/1.

181.3-5. Asher Fitz Randolph's military record is in the archives of the Adjutant General, NJNG, but it is silent as to his intelligence activities which are in WP/LC. Documents relating to Forman's ring are in the Pforzheimer Collection and WP/LC.

182.2. Trevelyan, *American Revolution*, III, 223; 7 GW 361. The spy aboard H.M.S. *Centurion* is reported in Ogden to GW, July 24, 1777, WP/LC.

182.3-4. 3 GW 385; 7 GW 385; 7 GW 462. General Adams Stephen's letter, warning Washington, is in the Papers of the Continental Congress (LC). Colonel Sylvanus Seeley's Diary is in the Morristown (N.J.) Historical National Park, Nov. 2, 4, 1779. It is not clear why it took two years to catch and hang this man.

184-87. J. J. Boudinot, *Life of Elias Boudinot*, I, 72-74; Elias Boudinot, *Journal of Historical Recollections;* Elias Boudinot's original MS. in John Carter Brown Library. Quotations are usually from the MS., which differs slightly from the printed version. On Luce, see Egerton, pp. 269, 313-14, and Transcripts, XXXIX, 47-60. Boudinot places this incident in the years 1777-1778; but, as he also places it at Morristown, it must have taken place in 1777. Cf. 7 GW 168.

187.3. The falsehoods planned for the spy are in Washington to Boudinot, March 29, 1777, which was purchased by the NYHS in 1957. It was called to my attention by Mr. R. W. G. Vail.

188-89. Alexander Bryan died in 1825. In 1852, his son, Daniel Bryan, made an affidavit to the story his father had told him, with confirmation by his mother. The original MS. is in the Pforzheimer Collection. See also Nathaniel

Bartlett Sylvester: *History of Saratoga County*, p. 151; *DAR Lineage Book*, XLV, 284; *Minutes Albany Committee of Correspondence*, I, 419, 421.

190.4. 10 GW 1-4.

192.1-5. 10 GW 2-4, 8-9. Clark's original reports are in WP/LC but are more conveniently accessible in *HS Pa. Bull.*, 1:15-18 (1864). This is a separate section in the back of the volume, with its own paging.

194.2-4. 16 GW 87-88; 14 GW 291-92, 304; 15 GW 3-4-n; 18 GW 81-82; 19 GW 162 (Mersereau).

198ff. Major John Clark's military papers are in Nat. Arch. S/41482; BL Wt. 3-850, Special Act Feb. 20, 1819. See also E. W. Spangler: "Memoir of Major John Clark." *Pa. Mag.*, 20:77-87 (1896). William Grayson to Clark, Dec. 11, 1776 (LWS) and Freeman, 304-n, show Clark on duty in Dec., 1776. Boudinot, *Journal*, p. 50, and 10 GW 169, 183, mention hucksters. See also McKenny to [McLane], May 31, 1778, WP/LC.

200.2. 9 GW 417-19; *HS Pa. Bull.*, 1:3-4 (1864). Clark to GW from Goshen, Pa., Oct. 27, 1777, WP/LC.

200.4. Ellis and Harris to Bradford, Oct. 14, 1777, WP/LC; *Philadelphia History*, I: 170, printing a letter whose original is in WP/LC, Nov. 17, 1777; 10 GW 8-9; *HS Pa. Bull.*, 1:5 (1848).

201ff. Craig's reports, arranged by date are in WP/LC. Cf. 10 GW 73-77.

201.2-3. *Pa. Mag.*, 19: 361, 370 (1895). Cf. 10 GW 73, which fixes the date as "night before last," i.e., Nov. 15/16, 1777. The report of Nov. 17, 1777, may have come from Henry Hesmire, who on Oct. 23, 1777, was paid $160 for secret services. See *Accounts*, p. 53, and Warrant Book, WP/LC, this date.

202.2. *HS Pa. Bull.*, 5:13-14 (1848); *Pa. Mag.*, 19:483-84 (1895).

203.3. *Ibid.*, 483-85.

204-05. Diary of Robert Morton, *Pa. Mag.*, 1:31 (1877); Marshall's *Remembrancer* (Philadelphia), p. 162; Captain John Montresor's Diary, *Colls. NYHS*, 14:480 (1881); *HS Pa. Bull.*, 1:21-22 (1864); Spangler: "Memoir of Major John Clark." *loc. cit.*, 20:79. On Rankin, see CP and Index, and Van Doren, *passim*. On Morton's Diary and *Remembrancer*, as above.

206.1. GW to Chambers, 11 GW 151-52; *Phila. Hist.*, I: 17 (1917).

207.1. The best sources for Ludwick are William Ward Condit: "Christopher Ludwick, the Patriotic Gingerbread Baker," *Pa. Mag.*, 81:365-90 (1957); L. H. Butterfield: "Psychological Warfare in 1776," *Am. Philos. Soc. Bulletin*, 236-37 (1950); J. F. Watson: *Annals of Philadelphia*, II, 44; Edward A. Hocker: "Baker General of the American Revolution" (MS.)—original in Ludwick Institute, 1500 Morris Bldg., Philadelphia, and photostatic copy at Valley Forge Park; Benjamin Rush: *Life of Ludwick* (1801).

207.2. On Bankson, see 12 GW 1, 151; *Accounts*, p. 53; Warrant Book II, fols. 88-r, 91-r, April 11 and May 1, 1778; Livingston to GW, April 9, 1778; Hamilton to Moylan, April 3, 1778, WP/LC.

207.3. On the Green Boys and the Leverings, see *Phila. Hist.*, 1:9, 17 (1917); Horatio Gates Jones: *Levering Family*, p. 44; *Pa. Mag.*, 50:353, 358 (1926); 58:232, 252-53 (1934); John Levering: *Levering Family History and Genealogy*, pp. 13, 144, 885. Military records of all three Levering Brothers are in the Nat. Arch., but only John's record refers to espionage and even this gives no details.

208.2-4. T. A. Daly: *The Wissahickon*, p. 32; *Phila. Hist.*, I:15-17 (1917). Mrs. Rinker's exploits are largely based on legend, but there is no doubt that she existed and no reason to doubt the story.

209.1-3. W. S. Baker: *Itinerary of General Washington*, p. 107. Henry Darrach: "Lydia Darragh, One of the Heroines of the Revolution," *Phila. Hist.* I:377-403 (1917), based on what Friend Lydia Darragh told her daughter; *DAH*, II, 185; Alexander Garden: *Anecdotes of the American Revolution* (2nd ser., 1828), pp. 46-48; Harry Emerson Wildes: *Valley Forge*, pp. 142-44; Marshall, *op. cit.*, I, 183-84. Armstrong's report is in *Pa. Arch.*, 1st ser., 6:43. Cf. Darrach, *op. cit.*, p. 398. Lydia Darragh's story was first told anonymously in *Am. Qy. Rev.*, 1:32-33 (1827).

210.1-5. Craig to GW, Dec. 2, 3, 1777; Smith to GW, Dec. 3, 1777, WP/LC; 7 GW 368-69. On Captain Robert Smith, see *Pa. Arch.*, 6th ser., 1:498. Clark's report is in WP/LC and in *HS Pa. Bull.*, 1:22 (1848), separately paged in back of volume. On McLane, see Marshall, *op. cit.*, III, 317, and McLane Papers (NYHS), II, No. 57. W.D. to GW, Dec. 4, 1777, WP/LC.

211.1-3. Watson, *op. cit.*, I, 441; T. Westcott: *The Historic Mansions . . . of Philadelphia*, p. 190; J. T. Scharf and T. Westcott: *History of Philadelphia*, II, 869. See statement of Mrs. Thomas Newton, great-granddaughter of Lydia Darragh, in *Phila. Hist.*, I:386-88 (1917).

212.3. Darrach, *op. cit.*, pp. 386-87; *Pa. Mag.*, 23:86ff. (1899); Records Philadelphia Monthly Meeting, 4 month 27, 1781, 8 month 29, 1783.

214.1. *Am. Qy. Rev.*, 1:32-33 (1827).

214.2-3. On the use of Lydia Darragh's route by spies, see Diary of Robert Morton, Nov. 23, 1777, *Pa. Mag.*, 1:31 (1877), which discusses the Rising Sun Tavern, Dec. 8, 1777, p. 35.

216.2-4. Benjamin Tallmadge: *Memoirs* (1858), pp. 26-27.

219.4. Howard Swigget: *The Great Man*, p. 147.

222ff. *Accounts*, pp. 68-69. On Meeker, see S-2815 and S-5087 in Nat. Arch.; 10 GW, 329, 353, 398, 416. GW's letter authorizing black marketing, HCL.

223.3. Max von Elking: *German Allies in Revolution* (1893), p. 154; Moylan to GW, May 13, 1778; 11 GW 302; T. Jones, *op. cit.*, II, 210.

223-24. On British intentions, see 11 GW 398; 12 GW 2. Montresor's Diary, *Pa. Mag.*, 6:284 (1882); 11 GW 469, 471.

224.2-4. 11 GW 307-08, 398-402, 418-20; McLane Papers, II, No. 57 (NYHS); Freeman, V, 8-9.

225.3-4. 11 GW 399, 403-04, 413, 451, 455, 468-72; Moylan to GW, May 13, 1778, WP/LC.

226.2-3. Montresor's Diary, *Colls. NYHS*, 14 (1881) under dates. Reprinted *Pa. Mag.* 6 (1882). Alfred Hoyt Bill: *Valley Forge*, p. 185; 12 GW 482-83; *Pa. Mag.*, 25:21ff. There are scattered references in *Pa. Arch.*, 1st ser. George Roberts is not to be confused with John Roberts, a British spy. See Scharf and Westcott, *op. cit.*, I, 394-95; W. S. Stryker: *Battle of Monmouth*, pp. 65-66; *Pa. Mag.*, 13:304 (1889); *Colonial Records of Pennsylvania*, 13:304 (1889); 24:117 (1900).

226-27. Scott to GW, Sept. 12, 1778, WP/LC; Morton W. Pennypacker: *General Washington's Spies*, pp. 31-33; Tilghman to Scott, Sept. 21, 1777; Scott to GW, Sept. 20, Oct. 13, 1778; GW to CO Militia, Hackensack (not in Fitzpatrick) WP/LC, which also contain correspondence with Clough and Leaven' worth; 12 GW 355-58. Tallmadge to GW, Nov. 17, 1778, refers to Scott's transfer as if it had taken place some time earlier and as if Scott had been in touch with one or both Culpers.

228.1. Peters to McLane, April 26, 1804. This remarkable discovery and many others relating to Rivington were made by Dr. Catherine Snell Crary and reported in "The Tory and the Spy," *William and Mary Qy.*, 16:61-72 (1959), with full documentation.

228.4. On secret whaleboat traffic across the Sound, see Diary of Sergeant Major Simon Giffin, microfilm at Yale, Dec. 6, 14, 1777. On Brewster, see commission issued to him by Governor Clinton, March 12, 1783, retroactive to June 23, 1780, in Pforzheimer Collection; GW to Tallmadge, Dec. 26, 1782, commenting on Brewster's gallantry (Goodspeed Cat. No. 482, Item 400); Brewster to Tallmadge, Aug. 18, 1780, WP/LC; Heitman, *op. cit.*, p. 119; Nat. Arch., S-28367, on Brewster's pension claim; pension claim of Joshua Davis, Nat. Arch., W-17698; Pennypacker, *op. cit., passim;* Tallmadge to GW, Nov. 17, 1780, April 20, 1779; May 8, July 28, 1780; May 2, 1781, WP/LC.

229-31. Paltsits: "Use of Invisible Ink . . . ," *loc. cit.*, 35:361-64; *Journals Cont. Cong.* (1905), III, 392; Howard Swiggett, *op. cit.*, p. 232. The code books and Culper correspondence are in WP/LC. Washington's correspondence is filled with references to "stain," i.e., secret ink. Some of the documents used by Pennypacker are now in the Public Library, East Hampton, L.I., N.Y. The Deausonbury incident is described by Deausonbury himself under date of March 23, 1780, WP/LC.

236. On Colonel Floyd, see Tallmadge to GW, Nov. 1, 1779, Litchfield HS.

237-38. The only Major with the initial "J" in the army at this time was John Davis, local militia officer at Little Compton, R.I. His papers indicate he was engaged only in local militia service. See Nat. Arch., BL Wt. 544-500 (RGA-15-A), and BL File 26787/Wt.3/583-160-55 (RGA-15-A). Joshua Davis's papers make it perfectly clear he was engaged in espionage with Brewster. See Nat. Arch. S/28367 and W.17698; Heitman, *op. cit.*, p. 119. The Joshua Davis in Warrant Books I, II, 401, 403, WP/LC, may be a different man but he is in espionage and the first entry relates to whaleboats. See also Samuel Canfield to Humphreys, from Stamford, Sept. 19, 1782, WP/LC.

238ff. These minor agents are in WP/LC and may be traced by Index. Tallmadge to GW, May 2, 1781, shows he was then acquainted with "S.G." This MS. is at Litchfield. See also Tallmadge to GW, Sept. 2, Nov. 28, 1782; GW to Tallmadge, May 18, Sept. 3, Oct. 17, 1782; Anon to Tallmadge, Dec. 1, 5, 8, 1782; other letters of Aug. 31, Sept. 1, Dec. 8, 1782, all in WP/LC.

239.1. Burgin to GW, Nov. 19, 1779, formerly in WP/LC, now in Nat. Arch; 17 GW 319; *Journals* Cont. Cong., XV, 1424; Papers of the Continental Congress, No. 152, VIII, fols, 271, 312.

239.3-4. On the "refugee," see Tallmadge to GW, Aug. 12, 1781, Litchfield HS. Aaron Burr assisted some of the generals in sending out spies. See Matthew L. Davis: *Memoirs of Aaron Burr*, pp. 129-30, 149-50.

240-41. Dayton to GW, April 14, 1781; GW to Brodhead, April 25, 1781; GW to President of Congress, April 25, 1781, all in WP/LC; Clark to GW, May 21, 1781 (*Ill. HS Colls.*, VIII, 388-90); Louise Phelps Kellogg: *Frontier Retreat*, pp. 398, 400; Michael J. O'Brien: *Hercules Mulligan*, pp. 93-96 and *Hidden Phase of American History*, pp. 150-51; G. W. P. Custis: *Recollections and Private Memoirs of George Washington* (1933), pp. 19, 46; Narrative of Hercules Mulligan (MS.), Hamilton Papers, LC, photostat at Columbia and printed text in *William and Mary Qy.*, 3rd ser., 4:203-25 (1947).

241.1. Tallmadge to GW, May 8, 1780, at Litchfield HS.

242. 16 GW 87-88, 136-37, 146, 231, 246-49; 14 GW 304; 17 GW 291-92, 304, 338, 369, 438-39; Hunter to Clinton, dated only "Thursday 5 O'Clock P.M.," Intelligence Papers, 1781, CP. There was also in Hunter's native Bedford,

N.Y., a spy with the initials E.H., who is supposed to have been "Elisha Holmes," described as "one of Washington's most confidential spies." As no trace of Elisha Holmes can be found, this may have been a pseudonym of Hunter's. See Scharff: *History of Westchester County*, II, 338, 599-n. On Hunter's life, see *The Christian Course*, sermon pamphlet by the Rev. John Stanford, in NYPL. It was preached Dec. 22, 1815. He is mentioned in the will of Hugh Hunter, proved 1869 (William S. Pelletreau: *Early Wills of Westchester County*, No. 508, pp. 268-69); Lea Luquer: "Tarleton's Raid Through Bedford in 1779," MS. in Westchester County HS (1868); Charles Burtis Hunter: "Captain Elijah Hunter." *Museum Intelligencer* (Ossining, N.Y.), 3:3 (1942); Jay to GW, March 28, 1779; Hunter's report in McDougall to GW, May 23, 1779; Hunter to GW, May 21, 1779, all in WP/LC; Pennypacker, *op. cit.*, p. 134; Van Doren, p. 300-01.

243-44. 17 GW 221; Cork to Tallmadge, Oct. 13, 1783, WP/LC. On Swain Parcel, or Parsel, see Archives, AGO, NJNG, Trenton; Edwin F. Hatfield: *History of Elizabeth, N.J.*, p. 509. There is no trace in Nat. Arch., though N.J. records show he applied for pension, Invalid No. 34466.

243.5-6. On Hatfields: Vanderhovan to GW, Nov. 6, 1780, WP/LC; 17 GW 338, 369, 438-39; T. Jones, *op cit.*, I, 266; *Docs. Relating to the Colonial Hist. of N.Y.*, XV, 390; *DAR Lineage Book*, III, 98; XXII, 154; Frederick G. Mather: *Refugees of 1776 from Long Island to Connecticut* (1913), p. 997. This shows Moses Hatfield had served under General Scott—which may explain his intelligence work. See also Nat. Arch., LW/11-19-58.

244-49. Gray's story is best told in his pension statement, Nat. Arch. S/38/776 (RG15A). The Massachusetts legislative records Index shows a petition from Gray in 1823 and action granting and then revoking it; but the document itself has disappeared. See *Massachusetts Soldiers and Sailors of the Revolution*, VI, 766; *Colls. Hist. and Misc.* (Concord, N.H.), 2:80-81 (1823); *New England Galaxy*, Jan. 31, 1823; 17 Feb. 1823; Lossing: *Pictorial Field-Book*, I, 691-n; *MAH*, 11:434-35 (1884). The David Gray in CP is easily identifiable as the same man. The David Gray in Hemmenway's *Gazetteer*, living in Wells, Vt., may be some one else. See also Hiland Paul: *History of Wells, Vt.*; George S. Bryan: *The Spy in America*, pp. 92-93.

246-47. Secret Intelligence MSS., NYPL; *MAH*, 11: 434-35 (1885). There are also two MS. versions of this in CP.

247-48. Statement of Charles Chittenden, who actually saw Ledyard at New London at this time. See also Gray's own statement. Both in Gray pension file, S/38/776 (RG15A), Nat. Arch.

249-51. Marks is known by his reports in CP and two obscure references in Historical Manuscripts Commission, *American Manuscripts in the Royal Institution*, Vol. 40, No. 164, 2 pp. and Sabine: *op. cit.*, II, 47-48. The MSS. were presented to Queen Elizabeth II by President Eisenhower, but there are photostats in NYPL. See also Samuel Orcutt: *History of Stratford*, pp. 1243-44 and Eliza J. Lines: *Marks-Platt Ancestry*, pp. 33-34, for the Marks family.

250.1; 251.1. Location of Draun (Drowned) and Round Meadows and Old Man's by Mrs. K. Stryker Rodda, of the Long Island HS. See also Beers: *Atlas of Long Island History* (1873).

250.2. Secret Intelligence MSS., NYPL; *MAH*, 10:413 (1883).

252-65. Ann Bates is known by her pension application in the PRO, London, Treasury Documents, T1/611, Mar. 17, 1785, with supporting documents. It is confirmed by British Intelligence Book (III.20.11) in MS. Room, LC, where she is referred to only as "the Woman," but where dates and facts correspond to and, to some degree, are confirmed by Washington's Papers.

253.3-4. Oliver Pelat: *Atom Spies,* pp. 5, 214, 216, 275, 280.

253.6. On peddlers, Burnett, *op. cit.,* VI, 246.

255.2. Intelligence Book (III.20.11), LC. Cf. statement of the deserter, John McMullen, *ibid.,* July 31, 1778.

260.2. Memorandum Book, Sept. 30, 1778, CP.

260.5. On Ann Bates and Arnold, see Frances Vivian: "Capture and Death of Major André," *History Today,* 7:813-14 (1957).

261.3. Drummond was in Portsmoth, England, in April, 1779. See *Facsim.,* X, 992; Auckland MSS., King's College, Cambridge, April 16, 1779.

262.2. On "the Fair one," see Beckwith to Delancy, Sept. 3, 1781; report of Joseph Clark, June 1, 1781, CP.

262-65. On escaping prisoners, André's Intelligence Book, July 23, 1779, CP. The Lee story comes mainly from the "intendant" of the prison, who had every opportunity to learn the facts. An article based on his account appeared in *New England Mag.* This was reprinted by J. I. Mombert: *Authentic History of Lancaster County, Pa.,* pp. 298-306. See also Sherman Day: *Hist. Colls. Pa.,* s.v. Lancaster; "Captain Andrew Lee," *Notes and Queries Relating to Pennsylvania,* 1st ser., 1:167-76 (1894); W. H. Egle: *History of Dauphin and Lebanon Counties,* pp. 45-48 (Lebanon section); H. B. Plumb: *History of Hanover Township and Wyoming Valley* (1885), pp. 444-45; *Lancaster County HS Publs.,* 11:338-39 (1906-1907); *ibid.,* 9:203 (1904-1905); *Hist. Mag.,* 15:203 (Feb., 1872); *Pa. Mag.,* 3:167 (1879); 5:119 (1881); *Pa. Arch.,* 5th ser., 3:765; Parsons: *Diary of Jacob Hiltzheimer;* Ellis and Evans: *History of Lancaster County* (1869), pp. 298-303; Arthur D. Graeff: "The Legend of 'Major' Lee" in " 'S Pennsylfawnisch Deitsch Eck," Allentown (Pa.) *Morning Call,* Sept. 26, 1946. There is a report on Lancaster County prisons in *Lancaster Co. HS Publs.,* 10:157-61 (1906). For the legal action against Tory conspirators, see *Colonial Records of Pennsylvania,* 1st ser., 13:442, 495, 512, and Hiltzheimer, as above.

267.2. Most of these agents are in the CP. For further data, see notes below and Index of William S. Ewing: *Guide to the Manuscript Collections in the William L. Clements Library,* and Egerton, pp. 283-84 (Shoemaker), 181 (Hazard); T. Gilpin Smith: *Exiles in Virginia,* p. 72.

268.2. Chew to André, June 20, 1779; Van Doren, p. 271.

268.3-4. Ewing, *op. cit.,* lists most agents. See especially Intelligence Papers, CP, Aug. 31, 1779, Feb. 10, 25, 1781, March 2, 1781. On Whitcuff, Egerton, p. 132.

268.5. On Fox, see Fox to Stevenson (?) dated only "Thursday morning," but presumably Sept. 16, 1779; "State of Affairs with F—" both in CP; Van Doren, pp. 224-28.

269.4. Anon. to Brant, Haldimand Papers, *Vt. Hist. Colls.* 2:345 (1871).

269-71. Code and cipher keys in CP; Intelligence Papers, Nos. 1-7, Jan. 1, March 20, 1780, CP.

272-75. James Moody, *op. cit.,* pp. 18-20; Isaac Q. Leake: *Memoir of the Life . . . of General John Lamb* (1850), pp. 248-75; Wagenen to Malcolm, Aug. 7, 1780; Arnold to Lamb, Aug. 16, 1780; GW to Arnold, Aug. 19, 1780; Heath to GW, Sept. 27, 1780; Stewart to Dayton, May 4, 1781, Stewart Papers (bMX/ Am 1243, No. 389), HCL; GW to Lafayette, May 31, 1781; 22 GW 144, 155, 161, 168; Mackenzie, *op. cit.,* II, 536; James Thacher: *Military Journal of the American Revolution,* p. 263; Reed, *op. cit.,* II, 383; Duer to Malcom, Aug. 7, 1780,

Lamb Papers, NYHS. *New England Hist. & Geneal. Reg.*, 23:104 (1869); Sabine, *op. cit.*, II, 48, 90-98; Salter and Beckwith, *op. cit.*, pp. 51-60; Egerton, p. 144-n; Peters to Dunlap, Oct. [?], Nov. [?], 1781, in *Book of First City Troop*, pp. 43-44; Moore, *op. cit.*, II, 307-08; Parsons, *op. cit.*, p. 47, Nov. 13, 1781; *Pennsylvania Gazette*, Nov. 14, 1781; *Pa. Mag.*, 16: 160-61 (1892); *Journals Cont. Cong.*, (ed. Hunt), XXI, 1160 (Dec. 5, 1781); Edison's letter to Congress, VIII, 375, in Papers of the Continental Congress, LC; Freeman, V. 275a.; Moody to Clinton, *passim*, 1781, in CP. Sabine, *op. cit.*, II, 48, seems to be in error in stating Marr was also hanged. Occasional references to this man as "La Marr" seem to be due to the abbreviation of Laurence to "La." Moody appears as a first lieutenant in Gaines's *Register*, 1782, and in Rivington's *Army List*, 1783.

276. Bowler's correspondence with Clinton is published in Jane Clark: "Metcalf Bowler as a British Spy." *R. I. HS Colls.*, 23:101-17 (1930), originals in CP. See also Van Doren, pp. 127-29, 235, 429. On Ferguson see Egerton, pp. 259-60 and Ferguson to Clinton, Aug. 25, 1777, CP.

277-79. The Barker story is best told in Isaac Barker's pension statement, Nat. Arch., R/21772 (RGI5). See also statements of Hezekiah Barker and Seth Chapin (R/1861). Benjamin Cowell, the local official who handled Isaac Barker's pension application, tells the story in his *Spirit of '76 in Rhode Island* (1850), p. 182. See also Edward Peterson: *History of Rhode Island*, p. 220; Samuel G. Arnold: *Historical Sketches of Middletown, R.I.*, p. 31; *Representative Men and Old Families of Rhode Island*, p. 181; Eleanor Barker MSS., Newport HS. On General Cornell, see *DAB*, IV, 444. In the R. I. Dept. of State, Providence, see MS. "Council of War," IV, 30, Nov. 26, 1779; "Letters to the Governor," XV, 62. Edward Field: "Isaac Barker's Signal," *Newport Mercury*, Nov. 28, 1903, in Newport HS. The writer of Anon. to Sullivan, July 3, 23, 1779, WP/LC, may well be Barker. On Seth Chapin, see *Massachusetts Soldiers and Sailors of the Revolution*, III, 319. On the Taggart-Hegel story, see "Interesting Memoir," undated clipping from *Providence Literary Journal*, in a scrapbook in Newport HS. There is a similar article in *Newport Mercury*, Dec. 18, 1863. See also George Champlin Mason: *Reminiscences of Newport*, p. 183. There is some information on the Taggarts in Nat. Arch. papers.

281.1. On Washington's dukedom, see Draper MS. (State HS Wis.) 23 J 52; *Pennsylvania Packet*, Aug. 2, 1781; Sir John Dalrymple: "Thoughts on Instructions to the American Commissioners," Historical Manuscripts Commission, *Stopford-Sackville MSS.*, II, 103-04; Commager and Morris, *op. cit.*, II, 694; Clare College (Camb. 1928, I, 174); Van Doren, p. 80.

282.2. *Ibid.*, pp. 15-17; Graydon, *op. cit.*, p. 215; T. Jones, *op. cit.*, I, 630.

285.2. Benjamin Tallmadge: *Memoir* (1858), p. 35; Tallmadge to Sparks, in Pennypacker, *op. cit.*, p. 168; C. de W. Willcox: "Ethics of Major André's Mission." *Journ. Mil. Service Inst. of the U.S.*, 57:368-78 (1915).

288.2-5. Willard M. Wallace: *Traitorous Hero*, p. 130; William Teele Stone: *Life of Brant*, II, 116-19. The handbill is summarized in *Am. Arch.*, 5th ser., III, 1158-59. See also Papers of the Continental Congress, 162, I, fol. 86, LC; *Journals Cont. Cong.*, VII, 371, 373: McLane Papers (NYHS), Vol. I, Nos. 62, 75, 113; Vol. II, No. 57; Pennypacker, *op. cit.*, p. 186; McHenry to McLane, June 3, 1778, WP/LC.

289.1. H. L. Barnum, *op. cit.*, p. 153.

289.2. Black Sam is described in Daniel Van Winkle: *History of the Municipalities of Hudson County, N.J.*, I, 55.

291.2. Pennypacker, *op. cit.,* pp. 112-16, probably following local tradition. There is nothing implausible in this story, though it has been questioned by writers unfamiliar with military intelligence.

291.3-5. The MS. note is reproduced in Pennypacker, *op. cit.*

292.2-3. On Crosby, see his pension statement, Nat. Arch. S/10/505. Culper's comment is in his letter to Tallmadge, Oct. 20, 1780, WP/LC, and in Pennypacker, *op. cit.,* p. 186, 270.

294. The efforts to draw Parsons in are set forth in British Private Intelligence Papers, Emmett Collection (MSS.), NYPL, reprinted in *MAH:* 10, 11 (1883-1884), see also Charles S. Hall: *Life and Letters of Samuel Holden Parsons,* pp. 308-09; Jonathan Trumbull and Joseph Gurley Woodward: *Vindication of Patriots,* pp. 13-55; G. B. Loring: *Vindication of General Samuel Holden Parsons.* See also Parsons to GW, April 6, 1782, WP/LC.

294-95. Original MS. is among Wallis Papers, now in possession of Howard Wallis, Muncy, Pa. Microfilm copies in HS Pa. and Muncy HS. Receipt is in Reel 2. The individual documents are not numbered. On Wallis's background, see William Wade Hinshaw: *Encyclopaedia of American Quaker Genealogy* and MSS. records of Deer Creek, Exeter, and Philadelphia Meetings, now in possession of Department of Records, Philadelphia Yearly Meeting. There are further notes on Wallis's doing in Catawissa Meeting Records, now in Friends Historical Library, Swarthmore, Pa. On Washington's purchase, see *Accounts,* pp. 22, 23.

295.4. Stansbury to André, July 12, 1779 (CP); Van Doren, p. 217.

296.1. The Wallis Papers are filled with details of Wallis's business activity. See also Peletiah Webster to Silas Dean (*sic*), April 2, 1774, *Now and Then,* 9:19 (1927); T. Kenneth Wood: "History in the Making of the West Branch," *Northumberland Co. HS Proc.* 4:46-66 (1932); Field-Book of John Henderson (MS.) in Wallis Papers. Papers relative to Wallis's road are in the Court House, Sunbury, Pa. See Index to Vols. 5 and 6 of *Now and Then.*

296ff. Nat. Arch. have an envelope on Gershom Hicks, but it is empty. Carded records, however, list him as receiving Bounty Land Warrant No. 9570, April 20, 1796, for service in the Pennsylvania Line and he is mentioned in military records in *Pa. Arch., passim,* see Index. Hicks's espionage is recorded in 14 GW 168-69; Charles Miner, *Hist. of Wyoming,* p. 260 and 14 GW 170-n, the original MS. being (1959) in possession of Gilbert S. McLintock, Wilkes Barre, Pa.; Hand to GW, March 29, 1779; Patterson to GW, April 3, 1779, WP/LC. On early British suspicion of Hicks, see deposition of William Grant, April 14, 1764; Gage to Bouquet, May 14, 1764, Bouquet Papers, Public Archives, Canada (BM, Addit. MSS. 61366-61368). See also Uriah J. Jones: History of Juniata Valley (1855), pp. 234-35; Sylvester K. Stevens and Donald H. Kent: *Wilderness Chronicles of Northwestern Pennsylvania* (Harrisburg, Pa., 1941); Hicks's land purchases from Wallis, Nov. 1, 1790, April 23, 1793, Wallis Papers, Reels 1 and 2; Patterson to GW, April 3, 1779, WP/LC.

299. Details of Wallis's negotiations with the British are in CP *passim,* during 1779. But Wallis's pass and Stephen Chambers's letter from Sunbury, June 13, 1779, are in the Wallis Papers, Reel 4. See also Van Doren, pp. 218-19.

300.1. 14 GW 160; Van Doren, p. 219.

300.3-4. Charles Tornier's statement, June 9, 1779, and undated statement immediately following, CP. On the spy scare, see "Orderly Book of Lieutenant Colonel Francis Barber," in *Notes from the Craft Collection in the Tioga Point Museum on the Sullivan Expedition,* pp. 51-52.

301.1. Stephen Chambers to Wallis, June 13, 1779, Wallis Papers, Reel 4.

303.1. J. G. Simcoe: *Military Journal*, p. 294; H. C. Lodge: *Hamilton's Works*, VIII, 28; Van Doren, pp. 266-67; Freeman, V, 217-n; Wallace: *Traitorous Hero*, p. 257.

303.4. On Aaron Ogden, see *N.J. HS Proc.*, 2nd ser., 12:13-31 (1894); 51:172-73 (1933); *National Portrait Gallery* (1834 ed. only).

304.1. Letter of May 13, 1780, CP. See also "State of Affairs with F.—" [Andrew Furstner] CP, which gives a list of American generals with whose loyalty the British sought to tamper, and "Extract of a Letter received the 25th of April 1740," folio 4, CP.

304ff. The main source for the Champe story is Henry Lee: *Memoirs of the War in the Southern Department*. Writing in his old age, Lee makes it appear that Champe was sent out to save André, whereas the CP show he did not arrive till nearly a fortnight after André had been hanged. It is, however, entirely possible that Lee merely became confused and that saving André really was a motive at the beginning of the plot. The story as told by Lee is confirmed by Mrs. Phoebe Champe in her petition now in Nat. Arch., File W/4/153, Bl Wt., 948-100 of John Champe, Rev. War (RG 15A) and in HR 558, Feb. 17, 1838, 25th Cong., 2nd Sess. Report No. 568 (on the petition); 9 *US Statutes at Large* 697. Major Allan McLane, who hated Lee, is rather caustic in McLane Papers (NYHS), Vol. I, No. 113.

306-07. Lee's contemporary papers on the plot are Lee to GW, Sept. [?], 1780, Oct. 21, 25, 1780, WP/LC. Cf. 20 GW 223-24. Secondary accounts, not all trustworthy, are George Lippard: *Legends of the American Revolution* (1876), pp. 224-53; Ida MaBelle Judy: "John Champe the Soldier and the Man," in *Antiquities of Virginia*; Daniel Van Winkle: "Hudson County During the Revolution" *HS Hudson Co., Papers*, No. 4, pp. 28-32 (1908); *Pa. Mag.*, 15:82 (1891). Jared Sparks: *Life of George Washington* (1844), p. 318-n; *Life and Treason of Arnold*, p. 267; *William and Mary Qy.*, 2nd ser., 18:322-42 (1939); 19:548-54 (1940). An alleged interview between Champe and his former Tory commander, after the war, seems to be mainly based on Lee.

317.3-4. McLane Papers (NYHS), Vol. II, Nos. 27, 41, 42.

318.1. Elihu Hall is in *Facsim.*, I, No. 122.

319.3. S. Hazard (ed.): *Register of Pennsylvania*, II, 165 (1828); Henry Clinton: *American Rebellion* (ed. William B. Willcox, 1954), pp. 240-41. British intelligence reports not otherwise documented in this chapter are from CP, where they can be located by names and dates.

319-20. Van Doren, p. 66; Rochambeau: *Mémoires* (1809), I, 260-61.

320-21. Hazard, *op. cit.*, II, 165-66.

321.6. "Captain G." is mentioned in MSS., Secret Intelligence, NYPL; *MAH*, 10:332 (1883).

323.4. A clipping from an unidentified source in the Perth Amboy Public Library states that Rattoon himself betrayed the British agents. The American accounts here quoted show that Mason revealed his own identity; but it is possible that Rattoon, acting as a double agent, also provided information. A letter of May 22, 1779 (WP/LC), warning Washington of British movements, was credited to "Mr. Rattoon of So. Amboy," supposedly Robert Rattoon, innkeeper and later postmaster there, but possibly John Rattoon. See Van Doren, p. 202.

325-26. Conyngham's Diary, in *Book of the First City Troop*, pp. 38-40; Wayne to GW, Jan. 12, 1781, WP/LC; Robert MacFarlan, Isaac Myers, Jonathan Odell, John Rattoon, "Mr. Fotts," Uzal Woodruff, Jan. 15-25, 1785, CP. On Captain Caleb Bruen, see CP, Index, *passim.*, and *Newark Daily Advertiser,* Dec. 29, 1863, Aug. 5, 1864: AGO Archives, NJNG; William S. Stryker: *Jerseymen in the Revolutionary War,* p. 442; William H. Shaw: *History of Essex and Hudson Counties;* David L. Pierson: *Narratives of Newark* (1917), p. 213; *History of the City of Newark* (1913), I, 362-63; Joseph Atkinson: *History of Newark, N.J.,* p. 116; Carl Van Doren: *Mutiny in January,* pp. 170-73; Kenny to GW, Feb. 8, 1783; Hazen to GW, Feb. 12, 1783; GW to Hazen, Feb. 18, 1783; Hazen to GW, Feb. 28, 1783, all in WP/LC. On Bruen's later career see *N.J. Archives,* 1st ser., XII, 175; XLI, XLII, 313; Abstracts of Wills, XIII, File 10849-G; and will of Simeon Baldwin, of Bloomfield, Newark Township, Essex Co., Aug. 3, 1806, *N.J. Archives,* 1st ser., XI (Abstracts of Wills, XI), 20, File 10392-G. See also Index to CP.

329.2. Elias Boudinot: *Memoirs* and MS.

330.2. André's Intelligence Book, July 7, 1780, CP. Where names and dates are given in the text, documents from the CP are not usually noted here as they are easily located in the collection.

331.1. Private Intelligence (MSS.), NYPL. On MacFarlan's identity, see Carl Van Doren: *Mutiny in January,* pp. 141, 170-76, 184, 212, 248, 264-68, 269.

332.3. 22 GW 143; Mackenzie, *op. cit.,* II, 536; Thacher, *op. cit.,* p. 263; Leake, *op. cit.,* pp. 274-75; H. Clinton, *American Rebellion* (ed. William B. Willcox, 1954).

333.2. Egerton, p. 188. Haliburton states he had been in medical practice in Newport for seventeen years.

334.2. For some reason his July 1 report is the only one of the Marks reports that was copied into the Private Intelligence MSS., NYPL. See also *MAH,* 11:440 (1884). The text here follows the MS. in CP.

335. On Williamson's report, see Private Intelligence MSS., NYPL; *MAH,* 11:57, 61 (1884). "Elises House" was the home of William Ellison.

336.4. British Intelligence Book, LC, Aug. 11, 1781.

337.2. Freeman, V. 309. In his *Mémoires,* I, 295, Rochambeau says he had news from De Grasse, Aug. 5, but apparently this was an advance dispatch without details. See Doniol, *op. cit.,* V, 520-22.

337.3. Innis to Harrison, Feb. 11, 1782, Cal.VaSP, III, 58-59.

338. Morgan's story was told to Jared Sparks by Lafayette himself. It is interesting to note that Sparks mentions Colonel Barber as Morgan's commanding officer. This is correct, and Barber's battalion had gone south with Lafayette. See Sparks: *Writings of Washington,* VIII, 152-54-n; Lossing: *Pictorial Field-Book,* II, 511-n; Morgan's military papers, AGO, NJNG; Nat. Arch., BL. Wt. 8538-100 (Rgl5A).

339-40. On ·he ovens, see Elias Boudinot: *Memoirs* and MS; Rochambeau, *op. cit.,* I, 286; G. W. P. Custis: *Memoirs and Private Recollections of Washington* (1860), p. 230. On the captured dispatches, see Lossing: *Pictorial Field-Book,* I, 781-82 and Custis, *op. cit.,* pp. 231-32 and notes. While Custis is obviously quoting Lossing, in part at least, his close association with Washington makes this partially confirmatory.

342. Jagger appears only in *Accounts,* p. 89.

342.3. Clinton: *Narrative of the Campaign in 1781,* II, 193; CP, Sept. 4-6, 1781.

344.2. Moore, *op. cit.,* II, 518. The hour is fixed by a postscript Elias Boudinot added to a letter five hours later. See Burnett, *op. cit.*, VI, 246; *Pa. Gazetter*, Oct. 24, 1781.

346ff. The MSS. on Bissell are in his military records, Nat. Arch. and in the Library of Congress. In Nat. Arch. are a jacket showing his service in the 2nd Conn., eleven cards; Pension File W-23604; old army records, a jacket showing his service in the 2nd Conn. and his citation, Vol. 74, p. 92. Among published sources are unidentified clippings in the Ontario County (N.Y.) HS; pay rolls of 2nd Conn. Revolutionary War ser., Vol. III, documents, 35-37 (1781) in Conn. State Library; Henry R. Stiles: *History of Ancient Windsor;* Ichabod Jeremiah Perry: *Brief History of Life and Services of . . . to which is added the escape from the British of Bissell, the American spy* (Rochester, 1828; NYHS); *Report of the Centennial Celebration . . . at Windsor, Conn.* (1876), p. 17; Daniel Howard: *New History of Old Windsor.*

347. Bissell omits many details in his 1818 affidavit, but he says nothing that contradicts this account, which is based on Bissell's own statement to Perry. The dialogue is, of course, from Bissell's own account. Arthur R. Thompson: *Road to Glory* is an historical novel about Bissell. See also *Colls. Conn. HS,* 8:68 (1901); 12:85 (1909) and William Brown Meloney: "Secret of the Purple Heart," originally published in the *New York Herald-Tribune Magazine,* reprinted in pamphlet form by the Military Order of the Purple Heart, Chicago, n.d., pp. 9-10.

350-51. Captain Neff does not appear in the British Army List for 1782. He probably held an emergency commission. On Bissell's stay in hospital, see Perry, *op. cit.*

353.2-3. Document 370, fols. 1246-47.

356.2. Date of return is given by Perry, *op. cit.* It corresponds with the payrolls of the 2nd Conn.

357.3. On Halifax, see GW to Hancock, May 8, 1782, HCL.

360. Peggy Arnold's receipt is in Wallis Papers, Reel 4 of the microfilm. On Stansbury's business activities, 1781, *ibid.*, Reels 2 and 5. On his flight, *Now and Then,* 5:171 (1936), Wallis Papers, Wallis to Hollingsworth, July 12, 1794.

360-61. On Howe, see *Am. Hist. Rev.,* 17:70-102, 332-54 (1911-1912). See also *Colls. Nova Scotia HS,* 29:99-102 (1951).

361.3. On Moody, Transcripts, XXV, 250-56; XXXVIII, 119-30; *New England Hist. and Geneal. Reg.,* 23:104 (1869); Sabine, *op. cit., passim.*

361.5. Bates Petition, PRO, Treasury Document TI/611.

362.5. Barnum, *op. cit.,* II, 128.

363.6. County Clerk's Records, Ontario Co., N.Y.; clipping in Ontario Co. HS, Canandaigua, N.Y.; Bissell's statement, Nat. Arch., also in records of the Court of Common Pleas, Ontario Co., May 29, 1818; Washington's Orderly Book, Vol. 74, p. 92 (Newburgh, N.Y.).

364.4. The post-war story of the Culpers is in Pennypacker, *op. cit.,* pp. 60-61-n, *Supplement* (1948), pp. 1-7, 33-36.

395